ENGLISH LITERATURE AND THE WIDER WORLD

General Editor: Michael Cotsell

Volume 1

# 1660–1780

# All Before Them

ENGLISH LITERATURE AND THE WIDER WORLD

General Editor: Michael Cotsell

---

Volume 1

1660–1780

# All Before Them

edited by

JOHN McVEAGH

THE ASHFIELD PRESS
London – Atlantic Highlands, NJ

First published in 1990 by The Ashfield Press Ltd.,
3 Henrietta Street, London NC2E 8LU
171 First Avenue, Atlantic Highlands, NJ 07716



**Library of Congress Cataloging-in-Publication Data**
(Revised for vol. 1)

English literature and the wider world.

Includes bibliographies and indexes.
Contents: v. 1. All before them / edited by John McVeagh—v. 3. Creditable warriors, 1830–1877 / edited by Michael Cotsell.
1. English literature—Foreign influences. 2. Travel in literature. 3. Exoticism in literature. 3. Authors, English—Journeys. I. Cotsell, Michael. II. McVeagh, John. PR125.E54 1990 820'.9'008 88–7489
ISBN 0–948660–08–2 (v. 1)
ISBN 0–948660–10–4 (v. 3)

**British Library Cataloguing in Publication Data**

English literature and the wider world.
Vol. 1: All before them: attitudes to abroad in English literature 1660–1780.
1. English literature, 1660–1918 — Critical studies
I. McVeagh, John, *1940–*
820.9

ISBN 0–948660–08–2

Printed in the United States of America

# CONTENTS

CONTENTS

# LIST OF ILLUSTRATIONS

# GENERAL EDITOR'S PREFACE

The expansion of Europe is arguably the most momentous development of modern history. Britain has played a major role in that expansion. As tourists, travelers, and explorers; as traders and colonists; as warriors and imperialists, the British have been an expanding people. The idea has been familiar for three hundred years and is a recognized thematic for the historian. But in literary studies the overall significance of British expansion for the understanding of what is called English literature has not been fully addressed. Recent critics and scholars—Martin Green, Edward Said, Gayatri Spivak—have begun to point to this fact and to speculate about what is a surprising, even disturbing omission.

Literary history, it seems, has been developed to reinforce an ethos of homogeneous and high-minded nationhood. We may think that two things have been concealed in the traditional account: the relation of the imagination to power and the demand of the national imagination for something more than the national life has provided. Comparative literature has indeed studied analogous developments in cultures and traced influences of ideas and forms, but has not explored the manner in which English literature has been shaped by the undeniable experience of what we are here calling "expansion," and the extent to which it has sought to supplement the domestic experience.

The series *English Literature and the Wider World* seeks to rectify these omissions. The four volumes of the series, dealing with the period 1660–1918, demonstrate that the response to the geography and peoples of the non-English world has always been a major part of the story of the British literary imagination. They show that few literary genres or writers of significance can be properly understood without consideration of this perspective.

Each volume contains a substantial editor's introduction, which discusses the political events of the period, conditions of travel, the literary response to the wider world, and the response to the particular regions of the world. The introductions provide the context for a dozen or so essays by contributing scholars which read the important authors in each period whose work draws significantly on the non-English world; this turns out to be the majority of important English writers. A guide to authors' travels and to further reading completes each volume.

The essays represent a variety of critical approaches, and it is hoped that they will provide stimulus to further interpretations. Of necessity, the essays concentrate on major figures. The unwished-for effect is that minor writers and travel writers of great interest go relatively neglected outside of their treatment in the introductions. But the series will encourage further studies of relations between the canon and writers on its geographical and other margins.

The series looks at how the British have imagined the world. It is in a sense an account of both an experience and an illusion—that of British centrality—and it thus runs the risk of duplicating anglocentrism. We can only hope that we have proceeded with some awareness of this limitation. The term "English literature" has been retained, though it refers also to Scots and Welsh literature: we have tried to recognize that the British margins may well experience different relations with the world beyond Britain. Ireland has been treated as part of the wider world, although for the period covered by these volumes it was, in one way or another, politically attached to Britain. The reader who is unhappy with this choice might like to consider the alternative. British interrelations with Ireland have been and are complex: the inclusion of writers of Irish birth or residence in this volume is not an attempt to appropriate them for a British tradition.

The series has been supported by a generous subvention from the University of Delaware, and in this connexion I would like to thank Provost Leon Campbell, Dean Helen Gouldner, and Professor Jay Halio.

The series is gratefully dedicated to Mario Pazzaglini.

MICHAEL COTSELL
University of Delaware

# ACKNOWLEDGMENTS

I am grateful to Bob Owens, Nick Furbank, and Simon Gatrell for commenting on earlier drafts of the introduction to this book, and to my colleagues Dave Sturdy and Tony Bareham for discussions of some of its ideas. I thank Professor Claude Rawson for putting me in touch with some good contributors, and for being encouraging. Ken Wilson sorted out some computer problems. Patricia Ferguson gave valuable bibliographic help when it was needed. Jan O'Neill helped with some of the typing. Special thanks go to Michael Cotsell, ex-colleague, and friend, whose high standards of scholarship I have struggled to meet.

Thanks are due to the following institutions for granting permission to reproduce illustrations: the British Museum; the Tate Gallery; the National Museum of Wales; the National Maritime Museum; the National Gallery of Ireland; the Dixson Library, the Library of New South Wales, Sydney, Australia.

I am grateful to the University of Ulster and the British Academy for grants awarded in 1986 that enabled me to read some of the travel literature discussed here.

# INTRODUCTION

**John McVeagh, University of Ulster**

## Political Developments

This study of literature's response to the wider world begins in 1660, the date of the Restoration of the monarchy, and not earlier, because in seventeenth-century creative writing we can detect a new apprehension of the globe as an accessible unity. This is not to call 1660 the beginning of the story. Rather, to understand the Restoration mentality, we need to go further back in English history.

Elizabeth I termed herself "mere English", stressing the notion of a pure separate race. She intended a contrast with her stepsister Mary, Queen of Scots, unpopular because of her Spanish and Catholic connections, and perhaps because of her Scottish ones. The emphasis on a tightly knit English people holding the world at bay, further enforced by the cult of the Armada victory and of the great deeds of the Elizabethan voyagers, is developed in John of Gaunt's island speech in *Richard II:* he celebrates a virgin England guarding herself from undesired contact with the world that begins at Dover. This Elizabethan sense of apartness disappears from subsequent literature.

The first result of Elizabeth's death, in 1603, was that James VI of Scotland entered London as James I of England. The king, it seemed, brought among the disgruntled English a stream of Scottish followers and dependants whose strange accents and habits annoyed and offended them. The English were being given a lesson in race relations. They were having to widen their attitudes of mind and learn to assimilate foreigners and foreignness. It was to be the first of many such lessons.

Not only was James I non-English, he was Spanish-influenced—a contrast sharp indeed with the monarch imagined by Elizabeth and Shakespeare. Charles I, succeeding in 1625, deepened the foreign sense in English life by importing into it French cultural influence, the result of his marriage to the French king's daughter Henrietta Maria. As the century advanced, England grew more involved with other nations, not less, and the idea of intact England died with her intact queen. We may see in the alienation, preciosity, and withdrawal of Jacobean literature some reflection of the pain of these pressures on a nation fragmented and stretched. By the mid-seventeenth century England was awkwardly united with Scotland and distracted by the centuries-old problem she had created for herself and for the Irish in Ireland. These problems would never go away. Even the Acts of Union with Scotland in 1707 and with Ireland in 1800, by their aftermath of rebellions, accentuated the fact that English politics has always been a tug of war between races.

From Cromwell's time, which the present volume chooses as its moment of departure, England was to extend her contact with Continental Europe and with the wider world more systematically and successfully than before. Further, she assumed an international role and eventually a position of political and economic world dominance. Between 1650 and 1680 the English fought three strange wars with the Dutch—hated yet admired as trading rivals, but acknowledged as allies against the religious-imperial threat of the powers of Catholic southern Europe. Ambivalence, therefore, characterized English attitudes to the Low Countries; but the dominant feeling was rivalry. "Good night, Amsterdam" was the slogan coined for the times by Sir George Downing; it threatened the destruction of Dutch power. Cromwell's Navigation Act (reinforced and extended after the Restoration) initiated the achievement of this aim over the next century.

On the other side of the issue, later in the century, it was a Dutchman who, as King William III, "saved" Protestant England from the Catholic menace of the Stuarts, with their unpopular connections with Rome and France. Most English men and women agreed with expelling the Stuarts in 1688–89 as the price required for rebuffing the French king's design—as the English perceived it—for universal monarchy; most, but not all. A minority of Stuart sympathizers remained unconvinced, and Jacobite uprisings in 1715 and 1745 gave warning of these tensions persisting within the nation. After Culloden the extermination of Highland life in Scotland solved the problem brutally and simply by removing the main Jacobite power base from the face of the earth, an operational solution perhaps suggested by England's dealings with Ireland under Cromwell.

It is true that, even among the consenting English, King William and his nation remained objects of dislike. Defoe's admiration of him in the early 1700s (given expression in *The True-Born Englishman* [1701] and elsewhere) and Sir William Temple's praise of Dutch polity in the 1670s were minority sentiments. Marvell and Dryden had lambasted the clodhopping culture of the inhabitants of the Low Countries, and Swift in Queen Anne's reign showed in *The Conduct of the Allies* (1711) that anti-Dutch racial hatred had lost none of its force after the turn of the century. But, countering this overt hostility, a cultural interinfluence grew out of the merging of Dutch and

English political destinies. It shows, for instance, in Wren's simpler Dutch style in the rebuilt Saint Paul's Cathedral, and in other buildings of the period in which the Italianate character of earlier architecture is being displaced.

A more important neighbor than Holland was France; and whereas in time the influence of Holland faded, that of France rose. English attitudes to seventeenth-century France were a mixture of imperial rivalry and cultural admiration. Charles II brought over in 1660 French ideas about kingship that, as might have been predicted, provoked resistance among his subjects. But he also imitated Louis XIV in encouraging music, which meant importing to London French composers and dancers who affected the development of music and ballet in the English theater. In the political sphere, Charles II used French money secretly advanced to try to stay independent of Parliament and was suspected of aiming to become, like the French monarch, an arbitrary ruler. Perhaps, less ambitiously, his policy was to remember his father and stay alive.

England's uncertain international relations reduced her European influence in the late seventeenth century. Under Cromwell she had been a force in European affairs. In the two decades after his death the war against the Dutch, the alliance with the Dutch against the French, and the alliance with France against Holland confused and reduced her role. But after the 1670s the overwhelming issue of European politics in the coming age—foretold by Sir William Temple—began to define itself: France was on the move; could she be stopped? William III's accession in 1689 gave England a massive shove toward significant involvement in European politics, and when he died the impetus was kept up. Marlborough, for example, Captain-General of the allied forces in the War of the Spanish Succession (England, Holland, the German states, and Savoy), wrested the political initiative from France when he won the battle of Blenheim in 1704. His victory placed this initiative firmly in London. After a decade of war England emerged in 1713 with a dominating position in European politics and a world role. When Queen Anne died a year later as the last Stuart monarch, and the Hanoverian Elector, leaving behind his principality in the Continental heartland, traveled to London to become George I, isolationism—John of Gaunt's dream—seemed to have become a nonoption for Britain's policymakers.

And yet it was this same policy that Robert Walpole sought to implement during the second quarter of the eighteenth century, and for a while successfully—but only for a while. Despite the British navy's increasingly international role (for example, standing between Sweden and Russia in 1715–16), Walpole pursued noninterventionism from the 1720s and the 1730s against a background of rising fury from bellicose patriots—the young Samuel Johnson among them. At last he unwillingly declared war on Spain, but shortly afterward, in 1742, was forced out of office. It was in 1740 that James Thomson inserted "Rule, Britannia!"—a command to the nation—as a closing chorus in his friend David Mallet's masque *Alfred*. Two Scottish expatriates produced the British national anthem and the lyric of the age. As the song makes clear, and despite Walpole, Britain had lost her island sense. She now boasted of her world role.

The 1739–48 war broke out over French and Spanish threats to trade in the British New World colonies of the West Indies, Canada, and South America. There were some humiliations, such as the 1741 Carthagena expedition described by Smollett; and on land Marlborough's magic touch was not to be felt again throughout the rest of the century. The war's issues, too, became general ones: dynastic questions based on Austria, added to complicated European territorial problems and the intricacies of international political relationships. Austria, plus Sardinia backed by Britain, was to expel France and Spain from Italy—such was Carteret's plan, created at Worms in 1744, which brought France into the war. Once France had become involved, the issue of the century clarified itself into the struggle for world domination between France and Britain.

Eight years of nonconflict rather than peace followed the conclusion of this war in 1748, but war between the two powers again broke out in 1756 and lasted until 1763, spreading rapidly east and west across all the regions of the globe. J. R. Jones has termed this conflict, which operated across three continents and two oceans, a "world war."[1] Canada and India were the prime areas of action, from which Pitt aimed to expel the French, and Pitt also utilized the British navy to pick up French colonial possessions in the West Indies and on mainland Africa. The outcome was largely successful. By 1763 Britain controlled much of India and "owned" Canada. Further east, though, China and Japan remained unseduced by British trading initiatives, and as yet militarily inaccessible.

While Britain was gaining Canada, she was losing America. What explains this paradox? British politicians, it has been said, saw in American events only a reform issue, not a brimming revolution. Burke and Chatham, for instance, criticized the government but remained parliamentary in outlook; Dunning attacked patronage; Wyvill sought a remedy in extending representation. Such blindness did not afflict them with regard to France in 1789, and in the 1790s Ireland too found British statesmen capable of stamping her political initiatives instantly as revolutionary and summarily crushing them. A lesson was learned here, perhaps, from the American experience. One reason why the British undervalued the seriousness of American developments in the third quarter of the century may have been that, after 1650, the North American colonies remained politically less important (because economically less powerful) than the sugar islands of the

Caribbean. British policy after the Restoration had been strongly influenced by the West Indian interest in Parliament, for the reason that sugar was the largest single import into Britain. The sugar islands formed the most important connecting point in the triangular trading pattern between Britain, Africa, and the West Indian and North American plantations. This trade dealt in slaves: human merchandise at one end of the economic cycle and the luxury goods of sugar, coffee, and chocolate at the other. And this three-way trade provided a sizable part of Britain's overseas economic earnings. It was Britain's intimate relationship with the West Indian plutocracy, Angus Calder suggests, which depended for its power on the trade in men and women, that explains why the Caribbean islands took no part in the colonial revolt of the 1770s; they had come to see their advantage in union with Britain. It had not always been so. Barbados planters in the 1650s, agitating for membership in the London Parliament, were the first to coin the slogan "No taxation without representation", and they had done so a hundred and twenty years before the American revolutionaries transformed the phrase into the battle cry of a revolution. What happened was that after 1650 the West Indian sugar barons created a Westminster lobby, benefited from British markets, accepted protection from the British navy, and, as individuals, dreamed of returning to England to enjoy their fortunes. None of this applied to the North American colonists. Hence, the West Indians were not encouraged to form resolutions of independence.[2]

India, compared with North America, was cut off from European influence, but in its subcontinental territories and oceanic hinterland it reenacted the squabbles and jockeyings for power of the European political scene. Already by the late seventeenth century British and French trading companies formed a major presence in the region, but India's distance from Europe meant that it took ships a very long time to get there and back, and consequently the English-French wars of 1689–97 and 1702–13 were not fought out in India; trade competition prevailed, but not organized fighting. By the mid-eighteenth century this entente had disappeared; now sea power under La Bourdonnais and land armies under Dupleix were met by British military force in an all-out struggle for control of the subcontinent. After Clive's 1757 defeat of the French at Plassey, Britain assumed supreme power in India; as a consequence she became the main European influence throughout Asia.

By the close of the eighteenth century, Britain—compared with the England of Elizabeth—lived more assertively than before in the wider world and enjoyed or endured a deeper involvement in the struggles of international politics. She had also annexed more of the world's area than her European rivals. But by the 1780s Britain's lost American colonies and Indian crisis had begun to shake her imperial confidence. Burke and Sheridan fed the unease, and a further jolt came when Ireland in the 1790s staged her short, bloody challenge—the first on Irish soil for a hundred and fifty years—to the British colonial presence. Trading Britain, long used to ruling the waves, was sharply rebuffed in 1797 when Macartney's embassy to Peking was turned away empty-handed. During the same years West Indian and East Indian nabobs—adventurers of mushroom wealth and, it was felt, bad manners—were upsetting the establishment and the accepted power structure of Britain by buying themselves political influence on returning home. This may strike us, it is true, as a minor complaint compared with the loss of America. But as empire in three continents began to strike back and as the rivalry of France and other countries intensified, the sense among the cultured and privileged few in England of a threat to genteel values added a tremor to the anxiety regarding empire that ran through Britain during the final quarter of the eighteenth century.

Such a change makes it natural to terminate the present volume in the 1770s, when the familiar worldview of an expanding Britain and the cultural outlook of the Enlightenment were both beginning to crumble. In 1660 England's only foreign possession had been Ireland; by 1800 the British Isles, forming a political unit, controlled Canada, much of India and of the Caribbean area, extensive coastal territories in Africa, and several places among the islands dotted around the Pacific—including Australia. This expansion of England, or sense of a contracted world about her, was the major experience of English life between the Restoration and the loss of the American colonies. The world, it is true, would further contract after steam transport, and further still—would seem to shrink to the global village—when air transport brought all people into all lands. Such developments do not reduce the significance of Augustan expansionism. It was in eighteenth-century Europe that men and women first perceived this contraction of the world, and in Britain, because of her history and geography, the experience was felt at its sharpest and earliest.

## Travel and Travel Literature

In far travel and journeys of discovery, the seventeenth and eighteenth centuries before Cook represent for the English a slowing down period. Much exploration still took place; it produced travel literature of great interest. But the glamorous world journeys of the fifteenth and sixteenth centuries were not matched again in the seventeenth and eighteenth—perhaps were not to be matched again until the twentieth century set out to conquer space. Instead, in most of the period covered by the present volume we are dealing with assimilation and consolidation. That the deeds of the older voyagers still held their appeal is testified to by the continual reedition of accounts of their journeys. But the literature of far travel undertaken between 1660 and 1780 reflects a reduced sense of wonder consequent upon the more limited objectives then in vogue.

In near travel the seventeenth century saw the establishment of the European grand tour among the rich and noble. In the eighteenth century, the touring habit spread socially downward. It became the accepted way in which men and women of means acquired knowledge of the countries and cultures outside England and educated themselves in some of the realities of life in the wider world. Far voyaging and grand touring were highly publicized forms of travel; they fill the books and periodicals and private journals of the age.[3] But other, less-prominent journeying needs fitting into the picture. Travel was continuous, varied, and extensive, if difficult to compute. During Marlborough's wars, from 1702 to 1713, thousands of ordinary soldiers found themselves fighting in the Low Countries and the Rhineland or in Portugal and Spain. Not all remained there to be buried. British soldiers during the period fought also in India, the West Indies, and Canada. Sailors, both willing and pressed, private passengers, and condemned prisoners added to the number of British men and women gaining experience of life abroad by journeying to the plantations in the West Indies or America; or cruising and fighting in the Baltic and the Caribbean, the Indian Ocean or the Mediterranean Sea; or participating in the African commerce of ivory, slaves, and gold. Though hard to assess, the impact made by journeyings of this sort on the British world outlook of the time must not be overlooked. Augustan literature supplies examples of it in the struggling figures in Defoe and Smollett, at one extreme of seriousness, and, at the other, in Sterne's Uncle Toby, comically reliving his Flanders service against the French of fifty years before. Glancing ahead, we may add the deckhand who becomes the Ancient Mariner.

At the other end of the social scale were military leaders like Marlborough's generals, or rich adventurers like Pitt or Clive, who settled in England after their exertions abroad and created in country house and town mansion a cosmopolitanism drawing largely on their varied experience of other climates and manners, other cultures. James Brydges, Duke of Chandos, Handel's patron, is an example; he had served as paymaster-general of the British forces abroad from 1707 to 1712. These were star figures, but more numerous were the diplomats whose job was to travel, and who brought back to England their deep and detailed knowledge of the wider life of the globe. Such foreign experience fed quite naturally into literature, since writers often accompanied diplomats, or were diplomats themselves. Sir William Temple to the Low Countries, Marvell to Moscow and northern Europe, Matthew Prior to Paris as peacemaker at the end of the War of the

Spanish Succession are some examples. A more famous traveler is Lady Mary Wortley Montagu. Her letters from the Middle East, where she accompanied her diplomat husband, from 1716 to 1718, are full of appreciation of the exotic cultures she encountered. But Lady Mary's letters, if outstanding in their rich detail, are only typical in the way they testify to the interest British travelers took in the doings of the wider world. A further instance might be Launcelot Addison (father of the essayist), who in the 1670s served as chaplain to the English community in Tangier and wrote about it when he returned home. Such writing cannot be classed with creative literature, but the travel influence of the elder Addison on the outlook of the younger is not one to ignore, for Joseph Addison was to be an important poet of abroad. English writers between 1660 and 1780 did not all spend time abroad—consider Dryden and Pope—but, actual travelers or armchair travelers, their writings reflect a world in which travel was diverse, increasing, and taken for granted. By the middle of the eighteenth century, if you had not made the journey to Italy, you felt at a disadvantage in polite company, as Samuel Johnson confessed he did to Boswell.[4]

More should be said on the two travel patterns already mentioned: remote exploring travel, and near travel, or the tour of Europe. Exploration and voyaging, far from ceasing, increased between 1600 and 1800; but they underwent a change of purpose. Augustan geographers and writers rather consolidated and scrutinized what was known than discovered new worlds. Russian explorers during the same period penetrated eastern Asia to open up the largest landmass on earth, but, from Raleigh to Cook, British far travel was a modester and more pragmatic enterprise: scientific-imaginative rather than lacking imagination, and concerned above all with matters of practical life. National temperament might have played a part in this.

For example, take the New World. Before 1800 the English seaboard colonies of North America had penetrated hardly at all into the continent spread out to their west, and a reason for this might have been their limited idea of what America really was. H. Savage, Jr., notes that early settlers imagined they inhabited a narrow country with the Pacific lapping the other side of the Appalachian foothills.[5] North and south of them, by contrast, French explorers were making immense solitary journeys deep inland. Limited river systems in New England but extensive waterways in Canada and Louisiana must have contributed to the difference.

North America was a single case, but generally from the seventeenth century onward, English men and women became more pragmatic in their attitude toward the globe. New ventures and remote travel continued to be undertaken, but profit, which had always been important, now loomed larger as a consideration, and usually in the form of investment plans or calculations about trade returns deriving from settlement and colonization rather than, as before, windfall treasure plundered from the Spanish fleet; method gradually replaced one-off sea-dog coups. (Still, 1680–1720 were the heyday years of piracy in the Caribbean and the Indian Ocean.) Nevertheless, in seventeenth-century England the great colonizing and trading companies were built up: the East India Company (1600), the Levant Company (1581), the Royal African Company (monopoly renewed 1651). These systematic organizations developed under the free trade theory of the eighteenth century into open structures accessible to any trader on the payment of a fee. Thus, in a century and a half, uncoordinated forays into the wider world by adventurers relying on their strength and luck had yielded to a large-scale outward push. As well, settlement colonies multiplied. They sprang up in the New World, in the Caribbean, on the West African coast, in Ulster, in South America. Some, like Raleigh's Guiana project or the Darien settlement, failed conspicuously. Others petered out, or secured a foothold and slowly grew.

If the main constituent of the new purposeful attitude was profit hunger, there were other feelings present: among them, scientific curiosity. Men and women of the Enlightenment period were deeply interested in the makeup of the globe with its tides and climates, its plant and mineral life. They became even more interested in the living creatures it sustained, particularly (as might be expected) the multitude of peoples and races who were brought to light as the blank spaces on the map were filled in. Emanating from Bacon in the early seventeenth century, spreading widely if silently during the interregnum, a zealous yet skeptical inquiring spirit found its sense of purpose in the eventual foundation of the Royal Society in the 1660s. Bacon's championship of exact observation and plain style, popularized by Hooke, Sprat, Ray, and others, assumes a knowable, unmysterious world ready to yield up its secrets to the patiently inquiring mind. This is the assumption, typical of its times, that Thomas Sprat recommended in his *History of the Royal Society* (1667).

We may find Sprat's ideology crude, but it need not be so. Take the case of John Evelyn, a dedicated Continental traveler whose account of French life shows him a minute analyst and meditative thinker. He traces the strength of the French monarchy to its revenue collection and its policy, and derives its weakness from the sharp division between rich and poor. His history of navigation and his letters describing life in Italy, Switzerland, Holland, and the Spanish Netherlands are packed with close detail. Yet behind their concern with material progress, a sense of mutability conveys a strangely subtle vision. Reading Evelyn's diary, one encounters a stirring curiosity about facts highly suggestive of the Royal Society scientist, yet alongside it an artistic sensibility no less distinct. For example, in his Continental journey of 1646 Evelyn attended medical lectures and dissection classes at Padua University, explored the arsenal and the opera at Venice, recorded the scientific rarities and social entertainments of Naples: crocodile, salamander, mandrake roots of both sexes are among those described. In an earlier tour of the Low Countries, in 1641, he had taken notes on the buildings of Antwerp, Amsterdam, The Hague, and Rotterdam.

How intense and widespread was this intellectual zeal we may determine from the Royal Society's directions issued to far travelers not trained in observation who, nevertheless, wanted to help the cause of scientific knowledge. The society spelled out what information it wanted: compass bearings in all places; tidal movements; drawings of coastlines and of islands and ports; measurements of the declivity of the seabed; records of wind and weather changes and of meteors, comets, and other manifestations. Among other countries, Poland, Turkey, Arabia Felix, Cyprus, the Caucasus, Persia, Surat, Sumatra, Japan, Coromandel, Java, Borneo, parts of India, Saint Helena, Virginia, Greenland and its region, the Bermudas, Egypt, Guinea, Guiana, and Brazil are named in specific inquiries within a few years of the founding of the Royal Society.

After 1660 this optimism, global range, and practicality (character marks of the age) started to produce a new kind of zealously scientific travel literature. Robet Knox's book on Ceylon, for example, produced in 1781, carried a Royal Society appeal that some reader conversant with plantation life might undertake a similar account of the West Indies.[6] After the turn of the century, Hans Sloane filled this gap; and other writers in the period—such as John Ray on the Low Countries; Daniel Beeckman on Borneo; William Dampier and Henry Maundrell on the Far and Near East; and Josselyn, Lawson, Beverley and Catesby on America—helped to further the society's ideal of the accumulation of detailed knowledge about specific parts of the globe; all were piecemeal applications of the Baconian vision.[7] The confidence of these writers, their efforts to be exact, and their belief in number, weight, and measure characterize the English attitude to the wider world for more than a century after Bacon's death. R. W. Frantz discerns in the literature after 1740 a partial return to the discovery sense of an earlier age as writers react to the voyages of Anson, Wallis, Cook, and foreign explorers like Bougainville.[8] A qualification, though, is that negative revelations, not miracles, remain the typical product of eighteenth-century voyaging: the great southern continent not found, the Northwest and Northeast passages both disproved, the tiny civilizations of Tahiti and Hawaii transformed without loss of time into paradises lost. Augustan world wonder is tinged with disillusion.

While extending their knowledge of the wider world, wealthy English men and women also turned more toward European travel. In the years after 1600 the tour of Europe developed into an accepted practice among the

John Webber, *Snug Corner Cove, Prince William's Sound*

privileged class, and reached its height during the eighteenth century. Though the tour continued to exist after 1800 (just as European travel had been common before 1600), the grand tour of the Augustan age became a widespread habit with accepted, if not rigid, conventions.

In their appeal to English travelers, France and Italy headed other countries, followed by the Low Countries, then the Rhineland and Switzerland. These lands made up the tour's normal itinerary; but all the time the tour itself was changing, and attitudes to individual countries changed also. For example, the Low Countries, highly admired during the seventeenth century, fell in estimation during the eighteenth century, while, by contrast, Switzerland and the Alps grew more popular. Naturally, not all tourists visited all countries. Smollett toured only France and Italy, Sterne only France (though Tristram Shandy had adventures in Italy); Milton a century earlier had concentrated on the cities of Florence, Rome, Naples, and Venice during his visit to Italy in 1638 and 1639.

Varied though its itinerary was, the grand tour had an object: to reach Italy and Rome. This, if they wished, travelers could do by a direct sea voyage to Leghorn, taking between a couple of weeks and a couple of months and risking interference from the pirates who, up to and beyond Byron's time, added spice to Mediterranean travel. But more usual was the land journey from one of the French Channel ports to Marseilles and by felucca to Leghorn, which had the advantage as then considered of skirting the difficult Alps; Smollett chose this route. Most usual of all was the land journey complete, by way of Paris, Lyons, and the Mont Cenis pass to Turin and Italy. Gray and Walpole described the journey over these mountains, which Gray was unusual enough to like. Journey patterns and response patterns to abroad established themselves steadily through the period, as did ways of writing about the travel experience, as guide books and tour narratives amply show; but what the grand tour literature also reveals are the variety and idiosyncrasy of European travel in the Augustan age, not its conventionality. Perhaps writers usually travel on their own; at any rate, before the Victorians, organized group travel and reactions to it are not much in evidence. Cook's tours date from the 1850s, like Mrs. General in Dickens.

An early account establishing itself as a guide in the first half of the eighteenth century, but soon out of date, was Misson's *A New Voyage to Italy* (translated in 1695). Misson records a journey through the Low Countries to Cologne, then along the Rhine to Munich and the Tirol, and on to Rome by way of Verona, Venice, and Ravenna. He leaves out France, perhaps because he was French, perhaps because at the time England and France were at war. We may gauge the changes in eighteenth-century travel by contrasting with this Thomas Nugent's *The Grand Tour* of nearly a century later (it was published in the third edition in 1778), which in its turn became for a time the standard guide book of the tour. Nugent's is a bigger and more varied book than Misson's, expressing a freer concept of travel. Instead of a single linear progress, Nugent describes a number of journey options radiating outward from Hamburg, Venice, Rome, and Paris, which at the same time offer systematic coverage and a sense of the variety of the life of the road. He suggests three ways of getting from Paris to Lyons and four ways of getting from Lyons to Italy; twelve traveling companions equipped with his guide could separate outside their Paris inn and meet up again in Rome after taking twelve different routes. There was no single itinerary. The tour historian W. E. Mead describes two routes from northern Italy to Rome, then adds as a third option the route Goethe later chose, traveling on foot from Bologna; and going northward, he says, like Nugent emphasizing variety, travelers went from Turin and

> Susa, over Mont Cenis, often through Chambery, Anney to Geneva, and from there through Basel, Strasbourg and down the Rhine; or from Milan through Como, Lugano, Bellinzona, Airolo, St Gotthard, Altorf, Lucerne, and then northwards; but the most frequented route lay through Trent, Botzen, Brenner, Innsbruck and on to Munich and Augsburg.[9]

Mead draws here on Nugent, whose representation of flexible journeying again shows how eighteenth-century tourists made up their own tour and determined for themselves what kind of Europe they would be seeing.

Travel conditions can only have deepened this impression of adventurous variety, sometimes of ordeal, in journeying through Europe, and will have further highlighted the importance of passage over arrival before steam and telecommunications, the car and the airplane regularized transport between countries. Eighteenth-century Britons, of course, usually sailed between Channel ports, but they could go by water direct from London to within the Continent (to Amsterdam, for instance) or, like Fielding, aim for Lisbon and southern Europe, or go right round the Iberian peninsula into the Mediterranean itself. Every way had its share of risk. The boat Goldsmith failed to catch from Newcastle to Holland sank with all lives. When ships depended on wind power, schedules had to be unreliable: to cross the Channel might take forty-eight hours, commonly took ten (but more often five), and in ideal conditions could be over in three. Before anything else, the traveler would probably be sick, as Coryat declares he was, opening on the subject with a rather forbidding archness:

> after I had varnished the exterior parts of the ship with the excremental ebullitions of my tumultuous stomach, as desiring to satiate the gorman-

James Gillray, *Le Débarquement du Chevalier John Bull et de sa Famille à Boulogne sur Mer* (1792)

> dizing paunches of the hungry Haddocks (according as I have hieroglyphically expressed it in the front of my booke) with that wherewith I had superfluously stuffed my selfe at land, having made my rumbling belly their capacious aumbrie.[10]

When they got out of the boat, travelers were not through the worst of it. Arriving at Calais and Boulogne, passengers reached land by being carried on porters' backs from boat to beach at low tide; or they waded; or they disembarked into smaller boats to negotiate the last niggling stretch of water. Smollett is amusing on the irksome routine.

Once past the Channel, travelers found a wide choice of travel methods; variety is the notable feature. Tour guides comment approvingly on the Low Countries' extensive canal system and, in general, their authors seem to have liked that orderly region. In France water travel was extensive if less systematic; from Paris to Fontainebleau, Rouen, and Sevres, from Toulouse to the Mediterranean (via the Languedoc Canal, a hundred and fifty miles of it), from Lyons to the Mediterranean or to Avignon were all possible boat journeys. The coast-hugging felucca took travelers from southern France to northern Italy if, like Smollett, they wished to avoid the Alps, and they could coast from Rome to Naples, and from Ferrara or Padua to Venice; alternatively, in the latter case, they might choose to drift along a slow canal from Ferrara to Venice by way of Bologna, and very enjoyable it must have been stealing along those palace-lined waterways in the genial Italian air—travel sickness no problem, no pirates in sight, and the risk of drowning minimal. Tourists in Germany used the Rhine, Danube, and Elbe to move between regions but were subject to river tolls, and, furthermore, paying passengers or not, they had to take turns helping to row the boat. Such boats were adapted for sleeping and cooking in for travelers who had brought with them their own equipment but were otherwise primitive, and Boswell is entertaining on the unpredictable sleeping arrangements of his German tour. River travel was not normal in Spain, where in any case, it has been said, eighteenth-century travelers went rather as explorers than as tourists. E. S. Bates remarks that such an emphasis on water travel meant travelers could get to know out-of-the-way places like the eastern Mediterranean islands, and he quotes Lithgow's enthusiasm for Chios (like touching heaven with the fingers—perhaps a false note?), and musical Crete, dangerous Zante, Coos, Corfu, Lesbos, and volcanic Stromboli.[11]

Road travel varied even more. French main routes were praised, but not those of Britanny and La Vendée or between Auxerre and Dijon. Italy off the major routes possessed no roads, simply tracks, but even the best Italian roads were classed as poor; and in the hills around Genoa and Tuscany and between Bologna and Florence, where carriages could not go, litters or sedan chairs or walking furnished the only means of transport, with mules (as in Naples) being used as pack animals. In southern Italy conditions deteriorated; Sicilian roads were so hopeless that travelers wishing to get from one side of the island to the other commonly went by boat, pirates notwithstanding. German roads between Cologne and Mainz could not compete with the Rhine journey, upstream though it was, although coaches traveled with some difficulty from Augsburg to Munich and from Nuremburg to Ingoldstadt. The road to Hanover was similarly trying, although the route grew in use, of course, through the eighteenth century.

## The Literary Response

"Ask where's the North?" Pope wrote in the 1730s, challenging his reader to fix the locality of the geographic region. Nothing could be easier, it might seem; the north is up that way. But how far up that way?

> at York, 'tis on the Tweed;
> In Scotland, at the Orcades; and there,
> At Greenland, Zembla, or the Lord knows where.
> (*Essay on Man* 2.222–3)

Geography is really just an image here for Pope, helping him to liven up some moralistic lines on self-love, but in the present context the image may be more instructive than its subject. It shows for us a typical Augustan feeling of mastery over the globe. The lines cross an immense distance—a segment of the earth—yet remain casual. Pope is amused by the paradox that a geographic term remains unattached to place, that on a round globe north will be everywhere and nowhere depending on where you are standing; and so will south, east, and west. He is not a poet whom the globe appals or threatens; for him it has become domesticated. Pope's poetry abounds with evidence of this commanding attitude to the remote as well as the more familiar parts of the earth.

Such confidence, typical of the Augustans, arises from a sense in the writer that more or less the whole earth is now known, and man's relation to it understood; and if parts do remain obscure, they are probably not worth finding out about. Writing in the 1730s, Pope plays on his readers' acceptance that concepts like home and abroad, near and far, are relative; that because everywhere is joined, distant places are reachable; yet that somewhere is always going to remain out of reach. Whether it will be worth reaching might be another matter. Does anyone know what comes after Zembla—besides the Lord? Does anyone care?

Pope surely does not; but his reminder that horizons melt away as they are approached illustrates for us the important fact that the Augustans felt their London culture to be a center to the multitude of lives and histories inhabiting the globe, especially as the British empire grew in size. Doubtless this was arrogant. Yet they also recognized that by their nature the diverse tensions that subordinated some cultures to others, and most to theirs, qualified all claims to cultural superiority. Of the latter truth they became increasingly aware over the years; Enlightenment relativism eventually helped to undermine its own confidence. Pope's image suggests the world's places and spaces connecting up with each other as an accessible unity. Further on in the poem he urges the idea that "Nothing is foreign" and that all parts together form "one all extending, all preserving Soul". Geography is not exactly the subject he is writing about, but geography is on his mind.

I have begun with Pope as a writer centrally placed in the literary period we are considering. Also, his dismissal of boundaries speaks, in a sense, for his age. But to see the way in which his attitude emerged, we need to go back, and back about a century. The Augustans, perhaps for the first time in history, felt that traveling anywhere and everywhere was possible; but this sense of normality was a comparatively recent feeling—less than a century old. For example, it is not found in Elizabethan literature. Marlowe, who among early dramatists displays the sharpest sense of geography, makes his lines resonate with the wonder of far places, as if drunk with distance. In Shakespeare, Puck boasts of girdling the earth in forty minutes as a frankly magical feat. In the early seventeenth century, on a similar theme, John Donne writes of the round earth's imagined corners—an attractive paradox, perhaps expressing the bafflement of an age coping with the strange idea that flat and round are the same. But after a half-century, such imaginings were no paradox; they had become commonplace. In *Bermudas,* Marvell makes the voices of the hymn-singing English sailors rise from the ocean, bounce off the sky, and describe a curve through the atmosphere that takes them beyond the horizon, over the Bay of Mexico, and out of range. More significant than the idea is Marvell's nonchalant tone. The verse rhythms are unhurried. He is not surprised by the poem's conceit.

Oh! let our voice His praise exalt,
Till it arrive at Heaven's vault,
Which, then (perhaps) rebounding, may
Echo beyond the Mexique Bay.

(33–6)

In the decades from Donne to Dryden, poetry reflects how the sense of mankind struggling in a strange world gives way to an easier outlook.

Writers take on board the new perception of a reachable, intelligible, even familiar earth. Seeing the world in the round becomes commonplace. Cowley and other poets express the same attitude, and Evelyn and Sprat argue for it in prose. The new sense is of the wholeness and, despite its variety, the smallness of the globe. Marvell is sometimes distinguished for his ability as poet to apprehend large spaces on the globe's surface, but, though special, he is not unique in this; the outlook is typical of the literature of the later seventeenth century.

If we ask for a more thorough manifestation of it, no better example could be found than the poetry of Milton. *Paradise Lost* and *Paradise Regained* offer a profound, detailed example of that obsession with geography and astronomy that so marked the intellectual life of the seventeenth and eighteenth centuries. The subject cannot be fully treated here. But *Paradise Lost*'s opening alone will suggest Milton's cosmic range—his ease in the universe. Without ado in Book 1 he leads his readers from the Middle East to Greece, from Greece to the abyss of space, then back to the earth's axis connecting the icecaps, all within the first seventy-five lines of the poem. From the pole Milton travels down to the North Sea and Norway, south through Europe to Italy and Sicily, then further south to Egypt and Arabia until he comes to rest in the Red Sea region: the setting of his story. But instead of remaining there he executes another series of panoramic movements of the mind's eye, sweeping to northern Europe, then over the Mediterranean, Crete, and the eastern isles to North Africa, then westward to Europe's ultimate isles situated beyond the Celtic seas. From here he leads the reader into space, recalling the existence of other worlds, other suns, and other creatures inhabiting them, before coming down to earth again with speculations on mining and exploration. Rather modest excursions into Mesopotamia and India bring the first book of the poem to a close.

Some of these exotic depictions are incidental; others are more filled out. But they are all there. And in the rest of the poem (and in his other poems), Milton's inclusive, extensive eye covers the known and unknown world. In this aspect, Milton may be said to represent his period. Augustan literature exudes the confident outlook because, in Milton's and Dryden's lifetime, a breakthrough in geographic knowledge had changed the world from a bewildering to a homelier place in which men and women knew their way around—or felt they did. The sense of ease leads to a change of tone almost as important as the greater knowledge itself; thinkers and writers move from admiration to appraisal. R. R. Cawley has written of "the child-like wonder of the Renaissance" evident in creative literature and in the literature of far travel.[12] There was little that was childlike in 1651 about the wonder people felt concerning the wider world. In fact wonder was being replaced by an appreciation more worldly-wise in its bearings. The year 1651 was the year of the first Navigation Act, which declared England's assertion of her right to a share of the mastery of the seas. With time, as the pragmatic emphasis grew stronger, remote regions came to seem more practicable territories than they had done. They came to seem less remote.

As this happened, and also helping it to happen, the interest in travel increased. Boundaries were not denied but could be overleapt. For example, Johnson's hero in *Rasselas* (1759) learns that happiness is not to stay in the Happy Valley but to see the less-happy world; so he sets off on his travels, whose end is to be their beginning. Satirized here is the Augustan literary convention of traveling in order to learn about life, but Johnson in real life admitted to Boswell that for him, if responsibilities could be shelved, the idea of rapid travel somewhere or anywhere, and with an attractive, intelligent woman by his side, seemed the most desirable activity on earth.[13] Such an attitude to travel gives passage priority over arrival, and a new sense of the earth's roamability and accessibility is what lies behind the new perception. In other moods of course Johnson could be scathing, and was, on travel cant; he was no worshiper of abroad. Yet opening *The Vanity of Human Wishes,* written two decades after Pope's poem, we notice how coming to the poet is the image from geography, and how easily, like Pope before him, Johnson pans the earth when he embarks on his analysis of human life:

> Let Observation with extensive View
> Survey Mankind, from China to Peru;
> Remark each anxious toil, each eager strife,
> And watch the busy scenes of crowded life.
> (*The Vanity of Human Wishes* 1–4)

Comparing this with Johnson's model in the tenth satire of Juvenal underlines how typical of the eighteenth century, but not of an earlier time, is the idea of a whole globe suddenly open to view. Here, for example, is what Juvenal had written; the translation is Dryden's (1695):

> Look round the Habitable World, how few
> Know their own Good; or, knowing it, pursue.
> How void of Reason are our Hopes, etc.

For the Roman satirist "the Habitable World" seems a kind of small preserve, a reservation; and the whole of the rest of the world fails to figure in the discussion. Johnson feels no such contrast. He seems at ease, if not at home, everywhere on earth.

It is a sentiment common in literature after 1700. Purposeless on the

Bengal coast, Robinson Crusoe in Part 2 of Defoe's novel (1719) finds new energy on hearing a chance remark that "all the world is in motion, rolling round and round . . . why should we be idle?" Struck by this, Crusoe sets off for China and eastern Russia, then returns overland back to Europe, making light of the immensity of Asia. Although Crusoe claims a trading motive for what he is doing, shopkeeper profit hardly explains such prodigious wandering, and we might suppose pure travel—motion across the earth—is the real impulse behind it. Defoe was very interested in big distances, but then so was the poet James Thomson. Writing *The Seasons* (1726–30), he found it natural to combine a description of the English climate with a catalog of wider weather changes, which, in turn, more or less allows him to sketch in the geography and meteorology of the whole terraqueous conformation of the globe. Thomson's poetic eye ranges the planet. He dwells on the inferno of the tropics and the deserts, and moves on to the ice regions, water systems, and mountain structures of the world as if, somehow, they were natural extensions of English geography; and, of course, they are; only the fact had never struck earlier writers with quite the same force.

Growing empire, extending trade, and a preciser science and geography made it seem natural to Restoration and Augustan men and women, when they discussed England, to assimilate with the home scene the whole subject of the wider world beyond English shores. Pope depicts Belinda's dressing table in *The Rape of the Lock* (1714) as a miniemporium of the produce of every region under the sun:

> Unnumber'd Treasures ope at once, and here
> The various Off'rings of the World appear;
> From each she nicely culls with curious Toil,
> And decks the Goddess with the glitt'ring Spoil.
> This Casket India's glowing Gems unlocks,
> And all Arabia breathes from yonder Box.
> The Tortoise here and Elephant unite,
> Transform'd to Combs, the speckled and the white.
> (29–36)

The Far East, the Middle East, the New World, and Africa all meet as a sacrifice to vanity on the dressing table of the star of Europe. Besides rebuking upper-class triviality, the lines show how fascinated Pope was by geography, how easily for him strange things and familiar things were connected, how far cultures and London domesticity joined together to form one single world.

His poem *Windsor Forest* had said the same thing in its closing lines, added in 1713 to a 1704 text and meant to support Tory plans at the conclusion of the War of the Spanish Succession (1702–13). The appended lines show how in a decade, and because of the war, the British sense of the significance of their place in the world had deepened. All countries of the globe now bring to Britain their produce and allegiance. In the picture of the trees of Windsor rushing into the waters to become British ships so that they can scour the oceans, imperialism is first nicely clothed and then revered; the slave trade monopoly, won by Britain at the peace table, is the fact being glossed. But the lines are imaginative as well as boastful, for it was the age of Dryden and Pope that for the first time saw with excitement that its world was a unity all within reach. If Pope catches the last whiff of this optimism in his early poems, Dryden in flamboyant mood forty years before had celebrated a British diaspora first covering the unexplored earth, then eyeing the neighboring planets and star systems with an unsatisfied hunger:

> Instructed ships shall sail to quick Commerce,
> By which remotest Regions are alli'd;
> Which makes one City of the Universe,
> Where some may gain, and all may be suppli'd.
>
> Then we upon our Globes last verge shall go,
> And view the Ocean leaning on the Sky:
> From thence our rolling Neighbours we shall know
> And on the lunar world securely pry.
>
> (*Annus Mirabilis* stanzas 163, 164)

Looking at these lines after a century, Johnson criticized as ridiculous the image of the ocean leaning on the sky. Possibly he disliked Dryden's bounce. Johnson in the 1780s was surrounded by evidence of the troubles and problems of imperial expansion. Suggestive though is the detail that for Dryden the planets are neighbors; they are visitable, even if to be visited they had to wait till our own time.

Defoe it is, perhaps, of eighteenth-century writers, who best understands and expresses the new outlook. His pages are crammed with speculation about the uses of the wider world. Apart from his detailed knowledge of the globe and of the literature of travel (especially distant travel), he appreciated that new values ought to distinguish his period from its predecessor, and he asserts the difference with energy. Here, for instance, opening *A New Voyage round the World* (1725), he sharply contrasts routine modern travel—wrongly judged to be rare, and hence noteworthy, by writers behind the times—with the bold traveling ventures of their Elizabethan predecessors:

> It has for some ages been thought so wonderful a thing to sail the tour or circle of the globe, that when a man has done this mighty feat, he presently thinks it deserves to be recorded like Sir Francis Drake's. So soon as men have acted the sailor, they come ashore and write books of their voyage, not only to make a great noise of what they have done themselves, but pretending to show the way to others to come after them, they set up for teachers and chart makers to posterity. Though most of them have had this misfortune, that whatever success they have had in the voyage, they have had very little in the relation; except it be to tell us, that a seaman when he comes to the press, is pretty much out of his element, and a very good sailor may make but a very indifferent author.
>
> I do not in this, lessen the merit of those gentlemen who have made such a long voyage as that round the globe; but I must be allowed to say, as the way is now a common road, the reason of it thoroughly known, and the occasion of it more frequent than in former times, so the world has done wondering at it. (chapter 1)

Circumnavigating the earth has become ordinary. However, Defoe's superior tone need not mislead us into thinking him cynical. His makeup included a store of wonder. For all their sophistication, the Augustans generally still admired (because they still did not understand) the secret forces behind the variety of the earth's phenomena. James Thomson speculates in *The Seasons* (1726–30) about the geologic and climatological diversity of the earth around him, including the secret water systems linking oceans and seas, rivers and lakes and springs, the principles of wind movement, and the makeup of the world's inward parts. Not just Thomson and Defoe, but other poets and writers—Blackmore, for instance, in *The Creation* (1712)—share this mixture of know-how with speculation, the mixture issuing in a subtle Augustan zeal.

One reason why the novel emerges into prominence as a literary form during the eighteenth century is that it feeds off and feeds this heightened interest in travel and journeying, particularly overseas journeying. Unlike the traditional genres of drama, epic, lyric, and satiric poetry, bound by conventions that can shackle a writer keen to discuss exotic material—see, for example, the essays by George Parfitt, Tim Cook, and Tony Bareham in this volume —the eighteenth-century novel is a form free enough to address directly its readers' curiosity about other lands and civilizations and to articulate their growing sense of a relationship with the wider world. Hence the importance of journeying, episodes, stories within stories, adventures of passage and return, in the fiction of Defoe, Swift, Fielding, Smollett, and the other early novelists; they accept the structural patterning that the imagination demands, yet offer the novelists a way of including diverse material about the extensive wider world (as well as the home scene)—material that readers wanted to read about. They invite new material, yet offer a means of making it feel complete and coherent instead of random. The novel, one might say, had to be invented then; there was no better way of writing about abroad. Both Percy Adams, expanding on the complex affinities between travel literature and the rising novel, and Martin Green, on the connection between adventurous images and colonialism, have suggested that histories of the novel, domestic in orientation, need to take more account of the overseas settings and the push into the outer world that novels go in for.[14] There is the oriental tale, for instance, a whole subgenre of fiction exploring and exploiting ideas about the east that arises in the middle of the Augustan calm; somber or lurid, as in *Rasselas* (1759) or *Vathek* (1786), it creates the concept "orientalism", Edward Said has argued.[15] Such writings, relocating guilty wishes abroad (always a function of travel), transform them into fictions of fulfillment; the east is viewed as female, passive. Then develops the Gothic novel, cultivating ideas of Italy and of the north in a strange amalgam; here too deeper currents are tapped than in earlier works, and geography supplies an inner as well as an outer dimension.

If Thomson, Pope, and Defoe reflect the mid-Augustan outlook, hopeful about knowledge, confident about empire (Pope's confidence like shot silk, threaded with doubt, and fading), the later and more troubled Augustan sensibility might be represented by Goldsmith, Smollett, or Burke. They take us on a couple of generations from Defoe, as Defoe had taken us forward from Milton; and we note in their mid- and late-eighteenth-century writing a further change in register or mood. Goldsmith, for example, is more detached and critical than Defoe about England's relationship with the wider world. Being Irish, he is less impressed by empire. In addition, the polyculturalism of the 1750s and the 1760s enabled him to doubt British and European claims to world centrality. Smollett, like Defoe, is a writer who ranges the globe, but he laces his informative books with acid, no doubt because he knew more about the negative side of travel, especially remote travel, than Defoe. He had seen the shambles in Carthagena, and the grand tour had irritated him. Smollett's picture of Lismahago among the Indians (compare Crusoe with Friday) suggests the change in outlook. Burke in the 1770s and 1780s surveyed breakup in America and breakdown in India and mourned the passing away of a civilization. Of the three, Goldsmith is the most persistent. He sets alongside his portrayal of English life an awareness of other lands and civilizations deriving partly from his own experience and partly from reading, and stresses the fragile, tentative nature of England's relationship with abroad. He makes "the citizen of the world" his own concept; it carries an elegiac, not a pioneering, ring. For the exhilaration of space in Milton, the assurance of Dryden and the Royal Society writers, the energy of Defoe, Goldsmith offers a subdued reminder of the provisional imprint man places on an earth he never truly owns. This insight carries the flavor of a period more conscious than its predecessors of some of the disturbing aspects of expansion: slavery, loss in North America, the implications for Europeanism of the miniworlds newly discovered in the Pacific.

## The Literary Response Region by Region

English travel to France, though interrupted by wars, was always very great. Periods of closure or difficulty, like the years from 1756 to 1763, when Britain and France were at war, or part of the 1670s, when John Ray had to hurry home because of Louis XIV's sudden ban on the English, contrasted with more normal times when tourists flooded across the Channel. Forty thousand English travelers, it has been estimated, crossed to France in 1763 when the War of the Austrian Succession came to an end. Yet travel did not automatically cure national dislike; like international sport (in George Orwell's view), it could fuel it.

It is sometimes said (and some Restoration and eighteenth-century drama may give the notion credit) that the English admired French culture more than anything else for its stylish living. Certainly the diaries and letters of travelers are full of details concerning fashionable clothes, deportment, manners, and food. But English travelers were also interested in the palace art treasures in Paris and in Versailles, whose holdings Nugent lists in detail, and they found much to attract them in the colleges, academies, libraries, and theaters. Garrick drew ideas from French theater, and Burney researched in Paris for his history of music.

English attitudes to France were ambivalent during the Stuart period. On the one hand, and naturally, French influence was widely felt in art, literature, and ideas; sympathy could be expected between the king's circle and the country that had sheltered them during the bad times. But of foreign places themselves, Charles had had enough; he declared his intention never to go on his travels again. Meanwhile, national rivalry with France grew and was focused after William III's accession. Defoe in 1704 began his *Review* (originally called *A Review of the Affairs of France*), to alert the sleepy English to growing French power. Literature in general, while it plays with the idea of the frenchified English fop (like Sir Fopling Flutter—a stage more ridiculous than the Frenchman himself), in other ways recognizes French achievement. Even the fop stereotype, as in Johnson's *London* (1738) and elsewhere, has the serious propaganda function of cutting a menacing figure down to size. But in Evelyn's perceptive response to French greatness in the early part of the period, a deeper analysis is offered, as it is in the later part, in different moods, in the grand tour writings of Smollett and Sterne.

Italy was a country not admired politically or socially by the English, who judged it degenerate after ancient Rome and, as Protestants, feared its religious menace. In imaginative literature from Nashe onward the unscrupulous, lustful Italian matches the stereotyped French fop. Nevertheless, Italy, and in particular Rome, formed the chief destination for English travelers on the Continent. In the seventeenth and eighteenth centuries the peninsula consisted of independent states and cities, and tourists found the variety attractive. This is not the place to catalog the features of Italian tourist life; they are too numerous for the limited space available in this essay, and other books cover the subject.[16] But visitors would witness the pre-Lenten carnivals at Rome, Naples, or Venice, or the Holy Week or Ascension Day ceremonies, as well as rarer events, like the 1700 Pope's jubilee. (George Farquhar's *The Constant Couple* [1700] exploits the last.)

The Italian lakes were neglected in the period, but Vesuvius was visited, and Naples was much admired—a fashion, it has been said, not lasting into the next century. Evelyn had praised Genoa's harbor, and the catacombs at Rome and at Naples excited travelers' curiosity; Johnson introduces the catacombs into an African setting in *Rasselas*. Misson points out the variety of reasons that impelled travelers to Italy: some for antiquities, others to look at painting and architecture, others to consult libraries, others curious about churches and in search of religious ceremonies. Not included by Misson, but a high priority, were curiosity and pleasure seeking. No better example exists of this than Boswell's travel narratives.

Italy was seen as more complex and interesting than other European countries (though in appeal it yielded eventually to Greece), and British visitors busied themselves less with Italian politics than with the artistic and classical treasures housed there as in the repository of Europe's culture, and with pleasure. The artistic commitment was serious and intelligent. More generally, British travelers lamented the desolation and fragmentation of the great empire of the past whose relics they traveled through and witnessed around them, and whose heirs they felt themselves to be. They loved Italy's fertile landscapes and perfect climate, revered its art, and relished and were impressed by its capacity and genius for enjoyment.

Addison's *Letter from Italy* (1702) and *Remarks on Several Parts of Italy* (1705) reinforce the stereotype of a degenerate people, but even Addison's appreciation colors his description of Italy, modern but with a strong sense of its classical past. One senses, though, in Addison's elegance a detachment compared with Milton's passionate response. By Gibbon's time the detachment has deepened into alienation. His Roman experience—barefooted friars singing in the temple of Jupiter—rouses in the historical classicist only a profound antipathy. Italy was seen by Augustan writers as an analogy of

Richard Wilson, *A View from Tivoli over the Campagna* (1752)

Richard Wilson, *Landscape with Banditti round a Tent* (1752)

England, England as the modern Rome, and the perception informs much poetic moralizing on empire.

In addition the Italian scene influenced poets in its own right, sometimes unexpectedly. For example the Italian landscape feeds into Milton's poetry in recollected images like the Vallombrosan leaves and the Phlegraean fields, the latter shaping his description of hell's pavement (*Paradise Lost* 1.302–3, passim). Few poems might seem more essentially English than Gray's *Elegy in a Country Churchyard* (1750), but as Joseph Burke has shown, the melancholy imagery of the Italian landscape that Gray recollected from his travels, as well as his English eyes, confers on the poem its melancholic charm.[17] Gray, however, also responded with energy to lively Rome. He found its antique magnificence overpowering and watched with deep interest the modern Easter ceremonials. Richardson's imagined, not recollected, Italy figures as a seduction and a threat to the hero's English Protestantism in *Sir Charles Grandison* (1754), and, at the period's end, the somber atmosphere surrounding Anne Radcliffe's Italian settings—never seen; all imagined—emphasizes the menace surrounding her heroines. In the move from Richardson to Radcliffe, Catholic Italy gives way to classical-Gothic Italy as part of the general development of the Gothic taste in literature.

The Alps, Switzerland, and the upper Rhineland feature as one region in Augustan travel literature (for instance in Misson and Nugent), and a general overall impression is that people traveled through them to other places rather than saw them as destinations in their own right. This would change as the appreciation of mountainous scenery grew stronger with the age, but, of our period—though Coryat in 1611 had appreciated mountain travel—a typical attitude is John Ray's. Ray traveled through Switzerland in 1673 on his return journey from Italy and, though observing en route the political constitution of the Swiss and approving of neat Lucerne, clean houses, and polite, honest people, gave the area bare treatment compared with his copious response to the Italian and Dutch cities and the technological and commercial processes that had so interested him in the south of France.[18] Fifty years later John Breval responded somewhat more energetically to the "rude kind of Magnificence" (Breval 2.2) of rocks and precipices and waterfalls, but even with Breval it remains still a rather constrained reaction. The sight of the clouds below his feet, for example, moves him to the utterance of a Latin quotation. When he sees the view across the hills around Lausanne, he writes:

> One of the finest and most astonishing points of Sight, perhaps in the World, is from the Churchyard of Lausanne; for there the Eye ranges at liberty in a very spacious Horizon, diversify'd by the vast expanse of the lake, the rich plains of the Vaud, and the high Mountains of Chablais, so

> that the whole Scene wants nothing that it can borrow from nature to make it surprisingly perfect and beautiful. (2.35)

The phrasing here suggests Breval's response to majestic scenery but also—in the frigid "wants nothing that it can borrow from Nature"—his assumption that civil matters are what really require comment.[19] That towns and people are what count for Breval may be seen in his enthusiastic response to the vineyards, pasture lands, convents, and castles of the French landscape between Mascon and Lyons, leading, however, to the qualifying admission that "I remember no Town upon this Road, except Villefranche" (1.224).

Twenty years later, for instance, in Peter Martel's description of his travels among the mountains of Savoy, a change is discernible. Martel had struck in with the famous traveler Pococke, just back from Egypt and the Levant, and he relates how the two of them traveling to Bonneville and Chamouny are struck by the "Beauty and Variety of the Situations and Prospects that we observed in this unfrequented Part of the World".[20] Passing over the Arve, they acknowledge fine landscapes of singular appeal, and Martel describes how the distant glaciers hanging in the air like white rocks draw them on by their strange beauty. Disregarding advice, they set out for the ice hills, pick their way through fallen avalanches, and skirt vertiginous heights to arrive at the top, and here Martel declares himself at a loss for words to describe what he sees. But in spite of the disclaimer, his account is precise and striking, and may be said to point the way to a new aesthetic. Referring to "the Description which Travellers give of the Seas of Greenland", he adds in an image worthy of Coleridge: "you must imagine your Lake put in Agitation by a strong Wind, and frozen all at once, perhaps even that would not produce the same Appearance" (8). He adds that the mountains shooting upward are "something resembling old Gothic Buildings of Ruins" (8). But reminding us that he and his companions belong to a group of patriotic Englishmen of the eighteenth century, not a band of Faustian romantics, he describes them sliding four hundred feet down to the ice surface, stepping gingerly over the cracks in it, and collecting in the middle to drink Admiral Vernon's health and success to British arms.

Looking to future expeditions, Martel advises taking arms, scientific instruments, proper equipment, and provisions, and, in fact, stressing what still remains unknown, plays down the significance of his own achievement. But his short book is suggestive. George Keate's minor Thomsonian poem *The Alps* (1763) shows the way in which the new attitude to mountains was growing in its description of the Alps as "Nature's true sublime", which dwarf man's works:

> Rocks above Rocks appear,

Mix with th'incumbent Clouds, and laugh to scorn
All the proud Boasts of Art. (p. 3: lines unnumbered)

Mediocre enough, Keate claims notice as a writer who moves from Thomson's sweeping subject of Britain-in-the-world to a smaller excursion 'round the Alpine regions, and he conflates the traditional emphasis on Swiss civility with the new interest in mountainy landscapes. Eighteenth-century tourists remained impressed by the polity and civil achievement of the Swiss cantons. But there was no English guide book to Switzerland during the period covered in this volume.

Parts of Germany, like certain Swiss cantons, were admired by English travelers out of religious sympathy, but the fact most observed was the fragmentation of the empire; no one apprehended a united Germany in the modern sense. After 1700 and especially 1715, English knowledge of Germany increased. The first reason for this was Marlborough's 1704 victory over the French forces, when "Blenheim"—the Augustan Waterloo—entered the national vocabulary and focused European attention on the country's southern region. Then, after 1715, when the Hanoverian elector became George I of England, the politics of Germany and her northern neighbors became a prominent factor in British foreign attitudes. Travel between the two countries also increased; the royal retinue made numerous visits back to the electoral possessions during the eighteenth century. Assessing the impact of this high-level traveling on ordinary people and on writers is not easy. The evidence suggests that more Germans traveled to London than Britons to Germany, and that English attitudes were not improved by this. But even before the Hanoverians, London had attracted ambitious German musicians, like Handel and Pepusch, Finger and Babell, as well as Italian singers and French dancers. To such foreigners in general (like New York in the twentieth century) England offered scope and opportunity for talent, and their presence increased the cosmopolitan awareness of English society.

The travel literature suggests an increasing knowledge. On Germany, Misson (1695) offers little but anecdotes and folklore—for instance, giving details on fleas for sale at Augsburg, Nuremberg drinking feats, the Heidelberg tun. (Coryat had described this in identical terms; travel literature fed upon itself.) Although Misson devotes space to Munich, details are thin on Cologne, Bonn, Coblentz, and other Rhineland towns. A century later Nugent's guide reveals a changed outlook. Copious information is now offered on the geography and politics of Germany, and in addition Nugent tackles inaccurate stock attitudes by stressing her attractive buildings; these, he says, make Germany second only to Italy. This may be too Hanoverian of him. He admits that travelers usually sleep all together on straw and recommends that to prevent such rigors they take plenty of their own provisions. Despite the fashionable preference for warmer and culturally richer southern regions, English men and women did traverse the area. W. Carr remarked in 1688 that he had twice been round the grand tour circuit of Germany, Hungary, Italy, and France ("Hungary" here is thought-provoking), and then journeyed a third time "through Holland as far as Strasbourg, and so back by Franckfort to Denmark and Sweden".[21] Carr traveled at an interesting time. He found Cologne dispeopled because of the recent banishing of Protestants, but, traveling by water from Cologne to Heidelberg, judged the latter's countryside equivalent to "the paradise of Germany for its fruitfulness in wine, corn, and all sorts of fruit" (133). Noting the colonies of exiled English in Continental towns—Rome, Ratisbon, Wistzburg in Lorraine, Liège, Louvain, Brussels, Dunkirk, Ghent, and Paris—he contrasts with England's failure to accommodate people of different religious and political persuasions the tolerance of Holland and Germany, where these things are ordered better. Carr would not have found the English record much improved a century later when Jacobite exiles lingered out a fading political existence in Continental towns. John Ray in 1673, proceeding from Cologne to Vienna through Heidelberg and Munich, passes over the scenery of mid-Europe in silence. He offers little comment on accommodation and travel conditions in Germany, but if we want such details, they are recorded by Lady Mary Wortley Montagu early in the next century and then, fifty years after her, by Boswell. Both describe the primitive roads and inns (where inns exist) but also convey plenty of interest and excitement.

If during the eighteenth century Switzerland and the Alpine regions became more popular, the Low Countries lost in esteem; and they are linked developments. Flat civility began to appear tame, altitude thrilling, as travel increased and adventurous possibilities became less imaginable in the near regions of western Europe. Political and economic realignments also changed attitudes. The seventeenth-century Dutch republic had been a major European power, and to English eyes therefore the Dutch appeared greatly admirable and hateful. Observers praised the Dutch achievement; satirical writers and essayists like Marvell and Swift ridiculed their pragmatic, earthbound temperament. The firm but not blind admirer Sir William Temple describes their strength as an openness to all people and their weakness as a loss of political flexibility derived from too much success over a period of time. His rather unexpected image suggests Holland among the nations as a mistress rather than wife; she attracts visitors but not settlers.[22]

Unlike England, Temple remarks, where much natural beauty is on display, Holland shows in her great beautiful towns "whatever Art can bring to pass" (198). This is why early Augustan travelers admired the Low

Countries; they laid a higher value on art than on scenery. Burnet, Carr, and Ray fall in with Temple's judgment here.[23] Travel guides too approve of the good transport arrangements, neat towns, and reliable inns that mark the Dutch section of the Continental tour. Occasionally something deeper is suggested. Breval, conceding in 1724 that regular Holland at first pleases but eventually wearies the traveler's eye, offers the aesthetic judgment that flatness of line explains poor Dutch painting—so he judges it—whereas in Salvator Rosa and Poussin variety in the landscape produces a richer canvas. Possibly in Breval a changing taste is being registered; nevertheless, Augustan travelers in the Low Countries continued to enjoy the visual appeal of low horizons and a stretched landscape along with the material comforts of orderly travel by tree-lined canal followed by reassuring lodgings in good inns. The university connections between Britain and Holland affected London's cultural life. The poet Bernard Mandeville, Dutch-born, settled in England, and when he came to write *The Fable of the Bees* (1714) introduced into the poem's notes a sardonic exposure of English sexual hypocrisy illustrated by firsthand knowledge of the freer attitudes of Holland.

British involvement in the Mediterranean grew after the acquisition of Gibraltar and Minorca established British control of the western area, developing the importance the Levantine trade had had for the Elizabethans. Growing power meant that British ships were privileged in Mediterranean waters—freer from pirate attack than other ships (which sometimes sought British passes), but still the region was a dangerous battleground of trading and territorial interests, and of cultures. From Defoe to Byron writers respond to the region with fascination and fear, drawn to it as the frontier region in which Turkish and Christian religions, Asian and European civilizations mingle and jostle one another. Perhaps the obsession with Italy and France helps to explain the English Augustans' comparative neglect of Greece, but, as the period advanced, interest steadily grew until, by the close of the eighteenth century, Greece ousted Italy in its appeal to creative writers. But much travel still took place in the earlier period. Jacob Spon and George Wheler in the 1670s, it has been said, seeking to identify Greece's classical monuments, "took up from Pausanias, after a gap of 1500 years and with modern sentiments".[24] The two men were differently motivated—Spon a Greek enthusiast, Wheler a scientific traveler extending his grand tour. In the next century Robert Wood visited Greece, Syria, Egypt, and Greece once again; met Stuart and Revett in Athens, authors of the influential *The Ruins of Palmyra* (1753) and *The Ruins of Balbek* (1757); and was an influence behind Chandler's 1764 expedition to Greece, a journey undertaken to explore and describe ancient sites. David Constantine connects Wood's interest in Homeric composition with the growing cult of poetic origins in the ballad researches of Percy, the Ossian cult, and the work of the younger Romantic writers of the late eighteenth century in literature. Less highly pitched is the approach of Alexander Drummond, whose journal of travels from Germany and Italy to Greece, then to Cyprus, Crete, and Near Asia, combines a knowledge of other writers, like Pococke and Maundrell, and mildly takes issue with them, but in general goes no deeper than noting the conjuncture in the lands visited of modern ignorance and past greatness.

Over the period the British Levantine trade yielded place to the Indian and Far Eastern commerce, the latter no longer operating through Turkey, Persia, Afghanistan, and Pakistan (then part of the Mogul Empire) but by sea around the Cape of Good Hope. But interest in the Levant remained high, and contact could be real, not cursory, between the British traders around Aleppo and their Turkish and Arabic neighbors. Henry Maundrell published in 1703 a highly readable account of his journey from Aleppo to the Holy Land that includes much detail on the *kanes*, or road lodgements, and the burial structures of the region, and the superfine ceremonies of a Turkish visit.[25] Ruins and remains take Maundrell's eye, and he is intrigued by classical and other relics, like the smashed-up crusader court at Beirut. Being a clergyman and a scientist, he reacts interestingly to the Holy Land. For example, he describes no churches (a relief to the reader), but scans the Dead Sea for a sign of the ruined cities, and half skeptically tries walking on the water. Beneath the skepticism he is impressed by Christian Europe's meeting Muhammedan Asia, and by the modern's mixing with the past, and he registers the region's richness in history, legend and the modern exotic: the hajjis setting out to Mecca, the hundred wrecked churches around Tyre and Sidon, all of them—strange fact—displaying to the intrigued observer a completely undamaged eastern wall.

Maundrell describes swimming in the river Jordan while Arabs on the far bank shot at him; it reminds us that travel in the Mediterranean (especially the eastern Mediterranean) was always interestingly unsafe. In an earlier journey Sir Kenelm Digby had hauled up the skippers of passing ships to check their papers and cargoes; challenged, grappled, and fought with other vessels; required priority in the sea lanes from Venetian ships; and quelled a mutiny among his sailors. Between this hard work Digby writes of peaceful drifting between islands and between Egypt and Greece, and the leisurely contemplation of their time-softened statuary, an account strangely appealing in spite of Digby's connoisseurship. It is like a glimpse into the lost world that Byron was to discover for poetry. A similar recognition of the mixed danger and beauty and modern decay of Mediterranean travel informs the younger Dryden's account of his 1700 visit to Messina and Sicily. He notes rebels' property put up for sale but finding no buyers. He is impressed by the scenic wildness of rocky Capra, and sardonically observes the fountain of Arethusa filled with thumping laundresses. He visits the catacombs, the amphitheater in Syracuse, Dionysius's prison. On Malta Dryden appreciates the fine, inaccessible women and the grandeur of the African-speaking inhabitants.[26] Digby, Maundrell, and Dryden with their different sensibilities testify to the richness a Mediterranean experience could add to the awareness of visitors from the cold north.

Though less visited by Britons, Sweden, Norway, and Denmark were important because the Baltic provided naval supplies. Explorers were drawn to the far north, looking for the Northeast Passage; and the region appealed to the imaginations of Pope, Thomson, and others as a place of extremes. Literature in a sense swung northward during the eighteenth century; the poetry of Gray, the Ossian cult, and Percy's ballad collection are examples of the changing taste. Possibly this owed something to an interest felt in Peter the Great of Russia, Charles XII of Sweden, Gustavus Adolphus of Sweden, Christina of Sweden, and Frederick of Prussia, all hero figures for a time who appealed, perhaps, as warriors embodying their tough countries: the climate unyielding, the sense of danger ever present, strong leadership always needed. In such races the British could read images of a warrior culture matching that of Sparta and early Rome. Such ideas fed into the contemporary argument about luxury and cultural decline. Goldsmith and Smollett explore the idea in the 1770s, as Hume had done thirty years before, and though Gibbon discounted oversimple explanations for the fall of Rome, he too pressed the contrast between vigorous northerners preying on the passive inhabitants of the warm south. An adjustment was taking place within the literary imagination. Romantic writers came to appreciate cold regions more strongly—the Alps, polar oceans, icy wastes—whereas, by contrast, the Augustan imagination preferred the warmer climate: nearly all Defoe's adventures are set in tropical or subtropical regions.

Between 1600 and 1800 Britain's presence in India massively increased, but literature shows no deepening of interest in the region; it rather neglects India. To this paradox we may add a second: Chinese culture, although it could be disparaged by some, generally appealed to writers and artists after 1660, but with little basis in knowledge or firsthand contact. Britain possessed much of India by the mid-eighteenth century, but her writers were uninterested. She was fascinated by the idea of China, which did not reciprocate and, in fact, in Peking in 1797 administered to Macartney's embassy one of the finest snubs in history. Perhaps ignoring what is yours is human, as well as yearning for what is not. But lying behind the literary preference too may be the piecemeal acquisition of India, its instability after Aurangzeb, and its ethnic and religious diversity: all prevented observers from seeing it whole. China offered an impression of unity and homogeneity that could not fail to be striking.

The major experience of the British in India in the eighteenth century was one of rapid expansion. The India speeches of Burke, Sheridan, and others reveal a crisis of conscience about English doings in the subcontinent. So does the literary treatment of the returning Anglo-Indian or mushroom millionaire: the nabob.[27] There were serious orientalists like Bolts, Hastings, and Jones; but literature preferred to concentrate on the Englishman as exploiter and expropriator. Already at the beginning of the century Pope's summarizing lines had characterized Anglo-Indian relations as the plunder of the innocent by strong English adventurers—as organized piracy;

> Asleep and naked as an Indian lay,
> An honest factor stole a Gem away:
> He pledg'd it to the knight; the knight had wit,
> He kept the Di'mond, and the rogue was bit.
> ("To Bathurst" 361–64)

Thomas Pitt is suggested as the one here referred to: governor of Madras in 1700 and grandfather of the future Lord Chatham. City treachery is identified with Eastern robbery, and is seen as more devious. Sheridan and Burke near the century's close read in the Indian problem a question placed over the nature of empire, commercial culture, and British expansionism. If literature between Pope and Burke reflects little experience of India herself, at least writers deal with the returning English adventurers who, like the sugar barons coming home from the West Indies, inspired fear in insular English society. Smollett, Goldsmith, Churchill, and other writers handle the subject. Burke probes deeper. Speaking of British India, he queries the morality of commerce transformed into sovereignty, rejects the profit motive in government, fixes responsibility on the British nation for the crimes committed by individual Britons let loose in a far country. For Sheridan as well as for Burke, India may tie in with Ireland, when both protest against imperial commerce's exploiting the inhabitants of conquered lands.

Some real study of India took place. Encouraged by Warren Hastings (Burke's target), Charles Wilkins translated the *Bhagavad Gita* in 1785, and in 1776 Nathaniel Halhed produced his *Code of Gentoo Laws*.[28] At the close of the period here surveyed, in 1784, the Asiatic Society, founded in Calcutta, began to publish its *Asiatic Researches*. William Jones, the period's most famous student of India, was a company servant. The Hastings scandal provoked pamphlets by Hastings and Clive, Lord Pigot, Luke Scrafton, William Bolts, Harry Verelst, Philip Francis, and others, all of which conveyed information to the British reading public regarding the Indian scene, as did the Hastings trial and the parliamentary inquiries it provoked. The controversy comes together in the writings of Burke, who impressed all

William Hodges, *Tomb and Distant View of Rajmahal Hills* (1782)

observers by his factual command of British deeds in India and some by his assessment of their significance.

China's influence had pervaded English literature from the seventeenth century onward. However, it was a post-Jacobean phenomenon. Elizabethan drama contains no Chinese element, and W. W. Appleton remarks that such interest as Burton, Raleigh, and Bacon took in things Chinese is "essentially transient".[29] Curiosity deepened to a craze, but not always a blind craze, as is shown by Sir William Temple's essay "Of Heroick Virtue" (1692). This focuses a wealth of knowledge about China, Scythia, Peru, and Arabia in its discussion of the prejudice behind contemporary assumptions regarding Western superiority. Temple stresses hierarchy, antiquity, and respect for wisdom in praising China and endorses the Chinese maxims against innovation, individualism, indolence, and foreign contact; to him these form a prudent social policy and statecraft. Reading Temple in this vein, we think of Swift, who may not mention China but whose Brobdingnag chapters in *Gulliver's Travels* (1726) owe something to Temple's critique of English pride.

Other, more skeptical writers and travelers—Dampier, Defoe, Samuel Johnson—take the opposite view and challenge the idea of Chinese superiority. Defoe in the second part of *Robinson Crusoe* (1719) is openly contemptuous; Wotton and Bolingbroke add critical comments. The Chinese craze was itself satirized, as by Pope and Arbuthnot, who projected a third book of travels for Martin Scriblerus, "Upon Cunturs to China"—never written, more's the pity. (Cunturs are fabulous birds.) But generally such criticism went against the prevailing opinion. In dramatic writing Settle, Howard, Burnaby, Rowe, Hill, Clancy, Garrick, Woodward, Murphy, and others reflect a growing interest in things Chinese. They distort and satirize China, mock and admire the Chinese fashion, but testify to an obsession with the Chinese idea. Goldsmith in his midcentury essays assimilates cosmopolitanism from different sources—Cicero, Plutarch, Bacon, Addison, Montesquieu—to fashion the sage Lien Chi Altangi, citizen of the world, perhaps the most attractive of that succession of imaginary foreigners—from the Turkish visitor once ascribed to Defoe to Southey's traveling Spaniard—with whom writers highlighted the insularity and partiality of British manners. It is, of course, a cosmopolitan habit to satirize your own limitations.

Gradually the craze faded. W. W. Appleton's theory is that the English interest in China declined when discoveries in Herculaneum, Palmyra, and Balbek were generating interest in the nearer antiquity of classical Greece. Appleton points out too that orientalists became interested in Hindu culture and that the South Sea islander highlighted by Cook gradually replaced the Chinese sage as an exotic stereotype. Meanwhile, real Sino-British relations were also worsening. William Hickey records quarrels between mainland Chinese officials and British traders, the mandarins scornful of their visiting "apostles of Adam Smith" (Appleton 60) while the latter in turn disdained a traditionalist, static culture. Perhaps the admiration of China needed lack of contact with the Chinese to survive; closeness to the object proved fatal to the craze. Anson expressed hostility to the China he visited in the 1740s. A couple of decades later Cook reported similar tensions. Macartney's Peking embassy of 1797 summed up the souring of attitudes. He had hoped to clear trading restrictions between China and Britain but met with total failure. The next stage in Sino-British relations would be the opium trade leading to the Opium Wars.

There had been some increase in real knowledge as a result of the modest contact. Limited though it was, the China trade grew; from four company ships in 1720 to thirty by 1800, plus thirty to India. Literature and language study improved. James Flint learned Chinese in the 1730s, and further evidence of a serious interest in Chinese learning was shown by the publication of Thomas Percy's *Han Kiouu Choaan; or, the Pleasing History* (1761), a translated Chinese play, and by William Chambers's *Designs of Chinese Buildings* (1757). Other accounts include John Bell's 1763 memoir of a 1722 journey from Russia to Peking, the translated Jesuit letters that appeared in English in 1707–9, 1714, and 1743, and Du Halde's edition in its English version of 1736. These and other accounts in Churchill's and in Harris's collections of voyages contain some authentic knowledge of Chinese civilization, but the real cultural achievement of the Chinese remained beyond the ken of European observation.

Important journeying took place in other Far Eastern parts, and was written about, but not in Japan, which Britain learned about only from the Dutch—for instance, from Kaempfert's account, translated under Sloane's influence as *The History of Japan* in 1728. Daniel Beeckman's *A Voyage to and from the Island of Borneo* (1718) describes the island's weather, animal life, and native habits, including dancing and warfare, opium addiction, and devil worship. From Borneo, Beeckman made for Java and Table Bay, Saint Helena and Ascension Island, and describes the places in great detail. Roberty Drury's Madagascar journal, long thought to be Defoe's but (it now appears) at best touched up by him, presents another unusual insight into a little-known country and its people. Ceylon was explored by Robert Knox (for a time held captive on the island), who describes in detail both the country and the culture of its inhabitants.

Of the Eastern seas the best account remains Dampier's journal-narratives, describing a life's privateering, exploration, adventure, and scientific investigation. As a writer, Dampier is conscious of the Royal Society tradition. He offers his *New Voyage round the World* (1697) as a store of gleanings added to the magazine of foreign knowledge built up by others before him; but Dampier is more than a gleaner. His findings include closely observed descriptions of plants and creatures, and information on topics as diverse as catfish, cotton trees, and Indian hatchets. The descriptions relate to the Ladrones, the Philippines, Mindanao, Manila, the bay of Siam, the half-mapped waters around Formosa and Macao, and also Celebes, Timor, and New Holland, or Australia; here Dampier encountered aborigines whom he judged so brutal as to come lower on the human scale than the Hottentots. He sailed too around Sumatra, to the Nicobar islands and westward to the Cape of Good Hope. In his account of these wanderings Dampier conveys succinctly what Kipling was to term the east of Suez feeling—excitement and strangeness and that sharpening of the individuality induced by being far from home. Reading him, we understand how suggestive he was to Defoe, and recognize similarities in the writers' minds. But, as with Knox, the comparison underlines the genius of Defoe, who imagined the world Dampier saw and made works of art out of the materials that in the sailor-writer's hands issue as vivid documentary.

North America maintained closer relations with Britain than any other colony except Ireland, yet in the 1770s America successfully rebelled. The fact suggests a basic failure in Britain to recognize that despite the shared traditions, America was developing a foreign polity and culture. A good deal of seventeenth-century literature describes American settlement conditions, relations with the Indian peoples, and religious and other developments in social life; and there are ample accounts of the geography, produce, and wildlife of the East Coast territories. Richard Blome's collection *America* (1687) includes many such descriptions. Yet imaginative writing shies away from North America, preferring the subtropical regions to the south, and ignores the East Coast, on which the British actually settled, for remoter Peru, Mexico, the Caribbean area, and the northeast-facing coast of South America with its seawide river mouths and multitude of unknown islands. In Restoration New World drama—for instance, in the Peru and Mexico of Dryden and Davenant—a stylized culture clash is presented in which the barbaric splendor of ancient civilizations appears to be the appealing element. This presumably would not have seemed possible in a North American setting. Here the emphasis was on hard graft: not the stuff of opera.

The seventeenth century's obsession with paradise lost defines the way in which writers imagined the new worlds they wrote about. Dryden's prologue to *The Indian Queen* (1665) expresses the period's cynicism mixed with awe in its survey of exotic cultures freshly encountered on stage but, outside the theater, long wiped off the face of the earth. Purcell's incongruous, tender music deepens the impression: fragile barbarism is viewed with a yearning sophistication recognizable as the exact Restoration touch. Shakespeare, for instance, does not have it; *The Tempest* (the obvious parallel with Dryden's play) places sophistication rather lower on its scale of values and is simpler in its handling of the theme of cultural opposition. The same elegiac quality lingers on even in Defoe's handling of the encounter between civilizations, and in Gay's *Polly* (1729), the sequel to *The Beggar's Opera* (1728) set in the West Indies, and in other Augustan writings.

The three million square miles of North America, H. Savage, Jr., has written, was in 1600 "virtually terra incognita" (3) to Europeans.[30] Savage stresses the strange fact that the bountiful land proved so hostile, and in popular thought long remained unattractive. By 1700 British settlements extended only from Maine to South Carolina—a thin strip of coast; could the grim start and final domination be correlated? Such tentative efforts Savage calls "a far cry" (6) from the penetrations of the wilderness made by Britain's Spanish and French rivals. Ideas of North American life could be wide of the mark. Defoe's favorable plantation scenes in *Moll Flanders* (1722) and *Colonel Jacque* (1722) are connected with this fact. He tries to undo the misrepresentations of other writers. Robert Beverley, the historian of Virginia, is quoted by Savage as complaining about the common English mistake that "servants in Virginia are made to draw in cart and plow, as horses and oxen do in England, and that the country turns all people black who go to live there, with other such prodigious phantasma" (14). Beverley's own book affirms the potential of colonial life: meadows, forests, coal, and other resources are described. John Lawson offers a similar message in his book on Carolina. And a natural history circle including James Petiver, Sloane, Samuel Dale, and William Sherard sponsored investigative journeys like that of Mark Catesby, whose *Natural History of Carolina* appeared in 1731–43.

Creative writing on North America does not match this interest among the naturalists—if we except Defoe and Smollett. There was, however, more discussion of the North American Indian in the larger context of the primitive innocent or noble savage; here, received ideas concerning Indian savagery and Indian endurance both figured as themes. Marshall and Williams remark that Locke, Ferguson, and Haylyn saw the Indian as early-developmental man; later, Beverley and Lawson, turning pro-Indian, laid emphasis on European maltreatment. France and England were angling for Indian support in their North American struggle. The Iroquois kings' London visit of 1710, which created a stir among many writers, including Defoe, Pope, Addison, and Steele, fits in with the theory. The Indian also figured much in graphic art and, in later Augustan literature, in the writings of Shebbeare and Mackenzie. All helped to fuel discussion about the sociology of the New World and the relationship between civilizations, a discussion that the American war intensified. Burke and others stressed bloody Indians; Rogers, Adair, and Carver wrote more sympathetically.

England's attitude to America varied, but, it seems, she was unable to see the real country that was developing across the Atlantic. Defoe termed it inconceivable that America could exist outside the British connection and stressed her use as a safety valve or dumping ground for undesirables; this is to see America as existing for Britain, not in her own right. Opposition to the slave trade would take us beyond our period, but it grew vocal and more searching before 1780, and we may see the changing attitude epitomized in the movement from Sir Hans Sloane in the early years of the century, casually callous toward West Indian slaves, through the pragmatic Defoe and the sentimental James Thomson, to Samuel Johnson, robustly hostile to slavery in the later decades of the century.

Continental Africa remained mostly unknown in the period. But it provoked much speculation. Defoe in *Captain Singleton* (1720) invents a zigzagging trek across the continent from Monomotapa to the West African coast in which strange meetings (including one with the devil) are constantly taking place; and he wrote on Africa in numerous other tracts and books. By contrast, contact with coastal Africa and its offshore islands increased for the British: in North Africa because of the British Mediterranean presence, and in West Africa and the Cape hinterland because of the growing importance of the slave and East India trades. Launcelot Addison described West Barbary in 1671 with a mixture of intolerance and tolerance, terming Moorish savagery only a different civility yet holding the Koran to be a devilishly corrupting text.[31] The reactions derive from Addison's double role: amateur anthropologist, Anglican chaplain; it is his religious character that is the less-tolerant one.

In *The Golden Trade* (1623), an early account, Richard Jobson describes a journey inland up the river Gambia and makes the point that Moorish traders from across the Sahara could be upstaged by European entrepreneurs; he advised buying gold and slaves at source. Reaffirming this, a later anonymous writer emphasizes England's imperial destiny—keynote of the new era: Britons, he affirms, no longer cut off from the world as they once were, are negotiators bound by the limits of the world itself.[32] Like other travel-trade pieces of the time, the book is disorganized, but it conveys some sense of the English experience of Africa: intoxicating heat and danger, dust, the sense of fabulous wealth. Far Eastern voyagers like Daniel Beeckman offer some account of the landscape and inhabitants of southern Africa, and admire the land but despise the people. Robert Drury's journal of his Madagascar captivity describes the nonstop warfare of native life, though a gleam of irony suggests a narrative (like *Gulliver's Travels*) that aims at European analogies.

The African was despised. Marshall and Williams refer to numerous writers showing disdain, including Thomas Philips in 1693–94, Bosman in 1704, James Houston in 1722, Snelgrove, Atkins, Moore, and William Smith. But imaginative writers like Southerne and Defoe question the stereotype, and travelers too began to observe the African rather than condemn him out of hand. This led to Mungo Park's more dispassionate writings in the 1790s, which cannot be discussed here, but, along with Cook on Polynesia, illustrate an interest in other worlds that is in a sense beginning to depart from the Eurocentrism of the Enlightenment.

More significant were the Pacific civilizations discovered during the later eighteenth century. The Pacific Ocean was charted by Tasman, Dampier, Anson, Cook, Bougainville, and Vancouver, in a period spanning almost two centuries from Tasman's birth in 1603 to Vancouver's death in 1798; Australia was defined. As the British presence increased in the trans-American world, public interest in the region also grew, and literature reflects this—for example, in the modifications introduced by writers into the concept of the noble savage. Originally a South American racial type, as in Dryden's Montezuma, he turns Caribbean (for instance, Friday in *Robinson Crusoe*) or Negro-Caribbean (as in Oroonoko), then, following Anson and Cook, Polynesian, as in Omai, whose English visit caused a sensation in the 1770s.

Perhaps the literary impact of Pacific voyaging is stronger in Romantic than Augustan writing: Coleridge's *Ancient Mariner*, some of Keats, and Shelley's world-ranging *Alastor* assimilate eighteenth-century far travel. But Augustan literature renews its awareness. Primitivism and relativism, already widespread, were deepened by the discovery of Pacific civilizations dotted over the waters, unconnected, enigmatic in origin, but blowing to smithereens the accepted notion of the history of the world in which Mediterranean culture was original. Polynesian life with its different politics and strange morality, surrounded by the relics of earlier civilization mysterious to itself, baffled Europe. It provoked wonder rather than hostility. There were points of conflict like the one in which Cook died, but as Marshall and Williams point out, no Pizarros are found among eighteenth-century European commanders. In fact, in Cook emerged an efficient, scientific, and plain hero, a new voyaging type; he replaced the buccaneering adventurers of the past. The main Pacific voyages were collected and published by John Callender in 1766–68 in a work entitled *Terra Australis Cognita*.The title fits the era. Now, writers felt, the world was known.

Ireland and England were each other's oldest problem: one of England's making. Scotland offers a contrast. The unidealistic union of 1707 lasted, and also worked in the sense that it did not prevent—it might have aided—a cultural flowering in Scotland during the later Augustan years. The Irish experience was different. After 1660 Ireland produced wonderful writers

John Webber, *Tereoboo King of Owybee Bringing Presents to Captain Cook* (1776–80)

and artists who, to achieve anything, had to emigrate to London because their backward and subjected country offered them no opportunity for talent. Thomson, Mallett, Smollett, Boswell, and other Scottish writers, it is true, all left Scotland; but some stayed behind. Boswell returned. No Irish equivalent to the Scottish Enlightenment took place. The sea between the countries was too wide for union and too narrow for independence—or so England judged. The American rebellion succeeded in the 1770s; the Irish rebellion failed in the 1790s. Geographic distance played a part in the two different outcomes.

And yet, though a mere Atlantic creek separated Ireland from England, the creek could be dangerous; this made Ireland too far away for easy assimilation (on the Welsh model or the Scottish model) with the rest of Great Britain. Religious difference sharpened the sense of foreignness on both sides. Hence the specialness of Ireland among the countries that formed the English world context; nowhere else combined being so near physically with being so remote culturally. English literature was enriched, though Ireland was impoverished, by the one-way traffic between the countries, as writers from the Restoration onward traveled to London to make their mark in the world: Farquhar, Goldsmith, Sheridan, and Burke are among the major figures. Lesser ones include Tate, Macklin, Murphy, Bickerstaffe, Kelly, and O'Keeffe. These personalities channeled into English literature a varied experience drawn from another culture, and the impact of this sense of otherness (touched on here and there in literary history, never properly examined) was considerable. Farquhar's rendering of the tensions of fashion, Goldsmith's detached critique of the English ideology, Burke's historical sympathy with the colonized, Sheridan's critical trenchancy, and perhaps the wobble in the temperament of all four invite critical attention. The sensibilities differ, but all focus on the English scene with an awareness of life drawn from a fundamentally different background.

This, it is true, is not the same subject as the English reaction to Ireland; it is an aspect of the Irish reaction to England, seen in the writings of certain master spirits. But since these authors contribute to English literature, the effect of their Irish background must come into the discussion; though oblique, it is a connection. Swift's case may be the most unusual: Irish by birth, English by descent, in politics an Anglo-Irish patriot, hater of the English establishment, resenter of Ireland, student of old Irish culture—where can such an author be placed? *Gulliver's Travels,* which cannot be taken out of the English tradition, is informed by Irish perceptions of the world. But this is not unique. Similar ambiguities affect the work of Sheridan, Goldsmith, and some others. Interesting though minor is the case of Charles Macklin, who made his life in England but drew on Irish and Anglo-Irish traditions to write a half-dozen plays that bristle with the issue of nationality. Their titles show that Macklin meant this: *The Man of the World* (1770), *The True-Born Irishman* (1767) recast in London as *The Irish Fine Lady* (1762). The title looks back to 1701, when the English were bickering with the Dutch followers of William III and Defoe got a good laugh out of it. Macklin's plays are comedies; but theirs is a rather angry laughter.

As the century advanced, Ireland's economic condition improved because English constraints were relaxed, and as a result English travel to Ireland increased. Artists and musicians and its own creative energies made Dublin second to London as a cultural center; it was in Dublin in 1741 that Handel first conducted *Messiah*. Impresarios and entrepreneurs visited Dublin to try out new ideas or when at a loose end in England; further accounts of visitors will be found in Constantia Maxwell's book.[33] Yet Ireland was neglected by England, and stopover visits to her capital city by entertainers needing a break from London did not obliterate the fact. Defoe, who crisscrossed Britain as a traveler and developed deep connections with Edinburgh, never became familiar with Ireland. He did describe it. She figures in an insulting aside in *The Storm* (1704) as "the Piss-pot of the World, with its Loughs, Lakes, Fens, and boggy Places" (17–18). Swift was enraged at his Dublin appointment—for him, banishment. Dryden twisted the knife into Thomas Shadwell by giving him an Irish name: MacFlecknoe. There was no Irish blood in Shadwell's veins.

The racial slur is typical of English attitudes during the Augustan years, and since. But a similar disdain also found its way into literature produced by the Irish themselves, or by the Anglo-Irish—for example, the caricature Teague in Farquhar's *Love and a Bottle* (1699). But when Irish writers apparently accept the English stereotype, new depths can be revealed. Farquhar is sharper against silly English fashion than against anything else, in spite of his laughter at the common Irish. Sheridan's Sir Lucius O'Trigger seems to endorse the stereotype; looked at more closely, he undermines it. Macklin wrote sardonically about racism in half a dozen plays.

The surface peace of eighteenth-century Ireland issued in Grattan's Parliament, a settlement swept away by revolutionary pressures welling up from a frustrated nation. The spasm of rebellion takes us beyond our period, and was to fail of lasting results, but reflects more accurately Ireland's tortured historical condition than does the seeming equanimity of much of the literature and the travelers' accounts and the history books that came out after 1660. But to generalize about equanimity in Anglo-Irish literature would mean excepting Swift. His evocation of the despair of a subjected country shows in *A Modest Proposal* (1729) and *Gulliver's Travels* (1726)—a literature nightmarish but funny and peculiarly Irish. In Swift's writing Irish experience combines with the English literary tradition to produce a critique of Britain's extrovert energy and of the outward-bound imagination of the Enlightenment—the qualities this essay has discussed—on those who bore the brunt of them: the colonized. Swift inserts into Gulliver's mouth a summary of English imperialism that derives authority from the fact that its author knew about life on the receiving end of such energies; and the judgment may be allowed to end the present discussion.

> For instance, a crew of pirates are driven by a storm they know not whither; at length a boy discovers land from the topmast, they go on shore to rob and plunder; they see an harmless people, are entertained with kindness, they give the country a new name, they take formal possession of it for their king, they set up a rotten plank or a stone for a memorial, they murder two or three dozen of the natives, bring away a couple more by force for a sample, return home, and get their pardon. Here commences a new dominion acquired with a title by divine right. Ships are sent with the first opportunity; the natives driven out or destroyed, their princes tortured to discover their gold; a free licence given to all acts of inhumanity and lust, the earth reeking with the blood of its inhabitants: and this execrable crew of butchers employed in so pious an expedition, is a modern colony sent to convert and civilize an idolatrous and barbarous people.
>
> (4.12)

Swift—if Swift here speaks through Gulliver, which is by no means certain—sets his personality against the extrovert confidence of the day. And at the same time (to end on a literary note), he uses *Gulliver's Travels* to ridicule the novel form that Defoe had just shaped into a means of expressing that very spirit.

# NOTES

1. J. R. Jones, *Britain and the World 1649–1815* (London: 1980) 207.
2. Angus Calder, *Revolutionary Empire* (London: 1981) passim.
3. See Jeremy Black, *The British and the Grand Tour* (London: 1985).
4. *Life of Samuel Johnson*, ed. G. B. Hill, rev. L. F. Powell (Oxford: 1934, repr. 1979) 3.36.
5. H. Savage, Jr., *Discovering America 1700–1875* (New York: 1979) 8.
6. Robert Knox, *An Historical Relation of the Island of Ceylon* (London: 1681) preface.
7. Hans Sloane, *A Voyage to Jamaica* 2 vols. (London: 1971); John Ray, *Observations . . . Made in a Journey through Part of the Low-Countries,*

*Germany, Italy, and France* (London: 1673); Daniel Beeckman, *A Voyage to and from the Island of Borneo* (London: 1718); William Dampier, *A New Voyage round the World* (London: 1697); Henry Maundrell, *A Journey from Aleppo to Jerusalem* (Oxford: 1703); John Josselyn, *Account of Two Voyages to New-England* (London: 1674); John Lawson, *New Voyage to Carolina* (London: 1709); Robert Beverley, *History . . . of Virginia* (London: 1705); Mark Catesby, *Natural History of Carolina* (London: 1731–43).

8. R. W. Frantz, *The English Traveller and the Movement of Ideas 1660–1732,* U. of Nebraska University Studies vols. 32–33 (1932–33), introduction.
9. W. E. Mead, *The Grand Tour in the Eighteenth Century* (Boston: 1914, repr. New York: 1972) 336.
10. Thomas Coryat, *Crudities* (London: 1611) 1.
11. E. S. Bates, *Touring in 1600* (New York: 1911) ch. 3.
12. R. R. Cawley, *Unpathed Waters: Studies in the Influence of the Voyagers on Elizabethan Literature* (New York: 1967) 117.
13. Boswell 3.162.
14. Percy Adams, *Travel Literature and the Evolution of the Novel* (Lexington, KY: 1983); Martin Green, *Dreams of Adventure, Deeds of Empire* (New York: 1979).
15. Edward Said, *Orientalism* (London: 1978).
16. See references to Black and Mead in notes 3 and 9 above; also Paul F. Kirby, *The Grand Tour in Italy (1700–1800)* (New York: 1952) and Christopher Hibbert, *The Grand Tour* (London: 1969).
17. See Joseph Burke, "The Grand Tour and the Rule of Taste", *Studies in the Eighteenth Century,* ed. R. F. Brissenden (Canberra: 1968) 231–50.
18. John Ray, *Observations, etc.* (London: 1673) 414ff.
19. J. Breval, *Remarks on Several Parts of Europe* 2 vols. (London: 1726).
20. Peter Martel, *An Account of the Glaciers or Ice Alps in Savoy* (London: 1744) 1.
21. W. Carr, *Remarks of . . . the United Provinces etc.* (London: 1688) 117.
22. Sir William Temple, *Observations upon the United Provinces* (London: 1673) 197.
23. G. Burnet, *Some Letters Containing an Account of . . . Switzerland* (Amsterdam: 1686). For Carr and Ray see notes 21 and 18 above.
24. David Constantine, *Early Greek Travellers and the Hellenic Ideal* (Cambridge: 1984) 7.
25. Henry Maundrell, *A Journey from Aleppo to Jerusalem* (Oxford: 1703) 1–31.
26. John Dryden, *A Voyage to Sicily and Malta* (London: 1776) 40ff.
27. J. M. Holzman, *The Nabobs in England* (New York: 1926).
28. Some of the following Indian material is drawn from P. J. Marshall and Glyndwr Williams, *The Great Map of Mankind* (London: 1982).
29. W. W. Appleton, *A Cycle of Cathay* (New York: 1951) 18–19.
30. Savage 3.
31. L. Addison, *West Barbary* (London: 1671) preface, 144.
32. *The Golden Coast, or a Description of Ginney* (London: 1665), from the section "Situation of Ginney" following the address to the reader.
33. Constantia Maxwell, *The Stranger in Ireland from the Reign of Elizabeth to the Great Famine* (London: 1954).

# EDEN, ISRAEL, ENGLAND: MILTON'S SPIRITUAL GEOGRAPHY

## Jason P. Rosenblatt, Georgetown University

The volume in which this essay appears takes its title from a description near the very end of *Paradise Lost* of our fallen parents' long perspective: "The world was all before them, where to choose / Their place of rest" (12.646). In considering the idea of geography in the work of a poet and thinker as encyclopedic as John Milton, it is helpful to keep in mind the sense of vastness and the problem of choosing a single focal point that these lines convey. The biographical facts, emphasized variously, can support a multiplicity of Miltons, each of them representing only a partial truth: there is the young citizen of the world who toured the Continent in 1638–39, to improve his knowledge of Italian literature and culture, to visit the remains of antiquity, and to meet some of the last exemplars of Renaissance humanism;[1] and there is the young patriot who cut this tour short:

> Although I desired also to cross to Sicily and Greece, the sad tidings of civil war from England summoned me back. For I thought it base that I should travel abroad at my ease for the cultivation of my mind, while my fellow-citizens at home were fighting for liberty. (*A Second Defence of the English People, Prose Works* 4.618–19)

We can emphasize the nationalist who signed his name "John Milton, Englishman", or the disillusioned old man who wrote, perhaps from a spirit of ultimate internationalism but more likely from one of sheer weariness, "One's country is wherever it is well with one" (*Familiar Letters, Works* 12.115). Although his exercise in cultural geography, *A Brief History of*

*Moscovia,* begins, "*The study of Geography is both profitable and delightfull*" (*Prose Works* 8.474), the most recent editor of this Russian history characterizes it as "akin to a foreign-office briefing," a useful guide for a diplomat bound for Russia (*Prose Works* 8.463). We can only wonder whether the vast outside world that began at his own shores absorbed Milton's imagination, or whether his powerful centripetal consciousness distorted that world as it pulled it inside. No doubt, Milton's official position in Cromwell's government as Secretary for Foreign Tongues to the Council of State contributed to the growth of his consciousness of geography. As Robert R. Cawley has noted, the "correspondence over which he had either direct or indirect supervision immeasurably broadened his knowledge of foreign lands beyond the European horizon. Through it possessions in the far west as well as the far east became better known to him."[2] Cawley interprets this increased familiarity with the policy of distant nations as the sign of a growing conscience, though it is equally possible to see it as the sign of an imperialist stance, proprietary toward England, adversarial toward the rest of the world.

A letter written by Milton, dated November 8, 1656, more than four years after he had gone totally blind, furnishes equivocal evidence regarding the relationship between the poet's mind and the outside world. In it Milton thanks "the very accomplished youth, Peter Heimbach", for carrying out his request, to find out the lowest price of a reliable atlas:

> You write that they ask 130 florins: it must be the Mauritanian mountain *Atlas,* I think, and not a book, that you tell me is to be bought at so huge a price. Such now is the luxury of Typographers in printing books that the furnishing of a library seems to have become as costly as the furnishing of a villa. Since to me at least, on account of my blindness, painted maps can hardly be of use, vainly surveying as I do with blind eyes the actual globe of the earth, I am afraid that the bigger the price at which I should buy that book the greater would seem to be my grief over my deprivation. Be good enough, pray, to take so much farther trouble for me as to be able to inform me, when you return, how many volumes there are in the complete work, and which of the two issues, that of Blaeu or that of Jansen, is the larger and more correct. (*Familiar Letters, Works* 12.83)

Phrases in the letter take us from Milton's life to his poetry. The vain survey with blind eyes reminds us of the complaint in the great invocation to Light: "thou / Revisit'st not these eyes, that roll in vain / To find thy piercing ray, and find no dawn" (*Paradise Lost* 3.22–24). And a prosaic complaint that a beautiful book is a waste of money ("on account of my blindness, painted maps can hardly be of use") becomes, in the invocation, a tragic rejection of the world outside the mind:

> . . . Thus with the year
> Seasons return; but not to me returns
> Day, or the sweet approach of ev'n or morn,
> Or sight of vernal bloom, or summer's rose,
> Or flocks, or herds, or human face divine;
> But cloud instead, and ever-during dark
> Surrounds me, from the cheerful ways of men
> Cut off, and for the book of knowledge fair
> Presented with a universal blank
> Of Nature's works to me expunged and razed,
> And wisdom at one entrance quite shut out.
> (*Paradise Lost* 3.40–50)

These lines renounce the world, whose creation in six evenings and mornings the angel Raphael had described. Following the order of Genesis 1, he had sung the wonder of the third day's vernal bloom, the "flocks / Pasturing" (*Paradise Lost* 7.461–62) and "broad herds" upspringing (7.462) on the sixth day, and at last the creation of man in God's image. The blind postlapsarian narrator compresses the six days' creation into three lines (3.42–44)—from "ev'n or morn" to "human face divine"—complaining that all is lost to him. Here it is not merely painted maps that are useless but the secondary revelation of God in his works, Nature itself, the "book of knowledge fair". Later the poet, in a world dark and boundlessly wide, discovers a compensatory interiority with the "paradise within" (12.587) and with "Eden raised in the waste wilderness" (*Paradise Regained* 1.7) through the power of Christ's obedience. A less-orthodox but more powerful statement is Satan's

> The mind is its own place, and in itself
> Can make a heav'n of hell, a hell of heav'n.
> (*Paradise Lost* 1.254–55)

And yet, of course, returning to the letter, we read that Milton intends to buy an atlas and wants his correspondent to find out which of the two issues is the larger and more correct. In *Paradise Lost,* whether describing Eden, hymning the creation of a visible universe ("this world / Of heav'n and earth *conspicuous*" [7.62–63]), or speculating on astronomy, Milton celebrates the attractions of an external world. Two unusually lengthy passages are crammed with exotic place names: when Michael, in Book 11 of the great epic, leads Adam to the top of the mount of paradise to view the world outside and its history (11.385–411); and when Satan, in the brief epic, conducts Christ to a mountaintop and reveals all the kingdoms of this world and their glory (*Paradise Regained* 3.267–321).[3] Somehow, with the help of an amanuensis, Milton remembered the names that could have come from a number of sources he knew: perhaps from the atlas he mentions in the letter, or from the voluminous indexes of the 1625–26 edition of *Purchas His Pilgrimage*, or from the huge folded maps in the more or less contemporary travel books by Heylyn, Fuller, and Sandys. Both of these long epic passages reflect the poet's delight in enumerating detail, but they also imply that the fate of every one of these great cities and countries is decay. And we read them accordingly in a double sense, enjoying the beauty of the external world all the more for its instability.

Each of Milton's puns and comparisons in his letter to Heimbach plays on the relation between the world and the word: Mount Atlas and an atlas; the furniture in a villa and the books in a library; the actual globe and a painted one. If geography for all of us lies ultimately neither in the actual external world nor in the painted globe that represents it, but only in the sphere of our mind, then this is even truer for a blind man. Frances Yates, in her magisterial study of the development of the artificial memory, has described various mnemonic place systems, some of them global.[4] From Quintilian's architectural model to Peter Ramus's imageless dialectical method, works that Milton knew provide models for improving the memory. Turning from Yates's book to, say, Milton's lengthy, detailed catalog of pagan deities and the places in the Holy Land that they invaded (*Paradise Lost* 1.376–521), we are tempted to speculate that a detailed mental map of the Holy Land, with Jerusalem at its imagined center, an internal equivalent of the folded-map frontispiece adorning Thomas Fuller's *A Pisgah-sight of Palestine* (London, 1650), might have furnished the poet with *loci* (places) that could then have been stored with images (*imagines*). Like the epic catalogs of Homer and Virgil, Milton's catalog of demon-idols describes a procession. Yet because the spatial range of all these epic catalogs is so vast (Book 2 of *The Iliad* lists 175 towns or other locations, and Milton isn't too far behind), their patterns can be traced only by a study of the topography that is evoked. The parade is flattened into a map of intricate reticulations, where the way back to the larger world of the poem is not always clear.

Milton's cavalcade of pagan deities, flattened into a map of the Holy Land, where they were worshiped, affords us at last a resting place. The focal point of the remainder of this essay is Milton's spiritual geography—specifically, the conjunction in *Paradise Lost* of Eden and Israel, or, more specific still, of paradise and Jerusalem, with England (or London) as an implicit member of the triad. Geographic locations as well as spiritual states, paradise and Jerusalem furnish additional evidence regarding the poetic tension between Milton's interiority and his celebration of the external world.

This triad was something of a commonplace, and its uses varied. For John Lane, the death of Elizabeth brings ruin to an England conceived of as Eden and Israel:

> Let *Israel* weepe, the house of *Jacob* mourne,
> *Syon* is fallne, and *Judah* left forlorne,
> The Hill of *Hermon* drops no precious oyle,
> Nor fruitfull *Bashan*, from his fattest soile,
> But *Davids* throne has all his beautie lost,
> So farre admir'd through every forreigne coast,
> The Paradice and *Eden* of our Land,
> Planted and kept by GODs almightie Hand.[5]

Josiah Nichols, in *Abraham's Faith*, emphasizes continuity among the dispensations of Eden, Israel, and England in order to attack canon law as a conspicuous and aberrant disruption of that continuity. A virulently anti-Catholic tract, *Abraham's Faith* surveys various Christian doctrines, beginning with the Trinity, finding them progressively revealed, from Old Testament obscurity to New Testament clarity:

> as touching the manifestation of the spirit, marke with me, that the same promise, which to Adam was generall in the seede of the woman, was more speciall to Abraham to be in his seede, and in his posteritie more certaine in Juda. . . . Howbeit that grace of revelation, which was in the Apostles, excelled all the rest . . . and therefore in comparison of the clere manifestation of the gospel, now in these last times, to the more obscure revelation of former ages, it is called a mistery had since the world began and from all ages, but now is made manifest to his saints, and this most abundantly in all wisedome and understanding.
>
> (24)

For Nichols, such continuity is a witness against the "new broached" religion of Catholicism. Acknowledging differences in ceremonies and forms of government, Nichols insists that "from the beginning of the world" the true church remains the same "in one rule of faith & religion": "the religion and faith publikely professed in this Realme, and maintained by the righteous scepter and sword of our dread soveraign and gracious Queene Elizabeth, is of the onely truth, most auncient, catholicke, and unchangeable. . . ." (16, 19, sig. B2v).

Writing about the religion of Eden, Israel, and contemporary England, Milton acknowledges discontinuities, changes in the decorum governing a particular dispensation, and differences in God's relationship with humans, angels, and the Son. Yet in his strong commitment to what might be called the principle of transposition, he transfers terms from one dispensation to another when he wants to emphasize God's continuous ways with his creatures. Thus, for example, in *De Doctrina Christiana,* discussing "THE SPECIAL GOVERNMENT OF MAN BEFORE THE FALL," he mentions that Adam and Eve in Eden follow natural law by being good, holy, and just (*Prose Works* 6.352). When, in the same work (*Prose Works* 6.517 ff.), he writes of the Mosaic law that governed Israel, he differentiates among the moral, ceremonial, and judicial laws, each of them a precise counterpart to a precept of natural law (goodness, holiness, justice). And when Milton, whose radical views of theology made him a seventeenth-century English congregation of one, turns to the gospel, he devotes an entire chapter of the *De Doctrina* (1.xv; *Prose Works* 6.430–37) to the triple function of Christ's mediatorial office, "PROPHETIC, PRIESTLY and KINGLY," each of these in turn corresponding to a mode of behavior under natural law and to a division of the Mosaic law.

The aesthetic counterpart of this as yet unremarked theological principle of transposition is the well-known tripartite crescendo movement in Milton's poetry: the development of the idea of *katharos* in the successive quatrains of the twenty-third sonnet, which begin with Euripides' *Alcestis*, extend to the Levitical rites of purification after childbirth under "the old Law", and conclude with a vision of absolute purity in a Christian heaven;[6] and the continuous but developing sense of the pastoral in *Lycidas,* narrated by a shepherd whose consolation is measured at least in part by the literature he evokes, pagan, (Old Testament) prophetic, and Christian. Adam and Eve's Fall makes *Paradise Lost* disjunctive rather than continuous. But here too, the first four books derive primarily from pagan authors, who are governed by natural law; the middle books draw most heavily upon Hebraic revelation that is beyond nature's law, provided by the "Divine Interpreter" Raphael; and the last books, introducing typology as a fallen symbolic mode, replace both the natural and the Mosaic laws with the gospel.

In the Miltonic epic, generally speaking, the triad of Eden-Israel-England appears at three points: before the Fall, where it represents the enclosed holy place, besieged by forces intent on destruction; after the Fall, where the contrast between present ruin and past glory exemplifies the central contrast of the epic, delight eclipsed by woe; and, briefly, as a subsidiary agent of the doctrine of *felix culpa,* here expressed as the replacement of the external by the spiritual: the physical paradise celebrated in *Paradise Lost,* Books 4–9, superseded by the paradise within, available now to any believing Christian;

and the temple in Jerusalem, with its holy of holies, replaced by God's saints, "godlike men, / The Holiest of Holies" (*Paradise Regained* 4.348–49).

It is by now a commonplace that for Puritans the identification of England and New England with biblical Israel as holy nations entering into a covenantal relationship with God was a thoroughgoing and comprehensive procedure. And in prose tracts of the early 1640s, Milton makes this identification often, as in this passage from the *Areopagitica:*

> the favour and love of heav'n we have great argument to think in a peculiar manner propitious and propending towards us. Why else was this Nation chos'n before any other, that out of her as out of *Sion* should be proclaim'd and sounded forth the first tidings and trumpet of Reformation to all *Europ*. (*Prose Works* 2.552)

Here Milton alludes to Isaiah 2:3 ("out of Zion shall go forth the law, and the word of the Lord from Jerusalem"), comparing England as the first nation to hear the trumpet of Reformation with Israel, the first nation to hear the divine word. Elsewhere in the tract, he compares at some length the "spiritual architecture" of the Reformation with the construction of the Temple at Jerusalem (*Prose Works* 2.555).

In *Paradise Lost*, the Israel-England comparison figures often in the contrast between present ruin and past glory. Christopher Hill notes that when Milton's friends heard the title of his great epic, "they feared that it would be a lament for the loss of England's happiness with the downfall of the revolutionary regime."[7] Surely this fear is not unfounded, and such a lament can be heard, though it is not loud. Milton's fallen opinion of his countrymen may well have been a factor contributing to his choice of an epic subject.

In a less urgently political context, the sacred travel literature of the day dramatizes an unintentionally comic proprietary attitude toward the Holy Land. Under the heading "English resemblances" in the huge index of *A Pisgah-sight of Palestine,* biblical towns, cities, and rivers are correlated with their local namesakes: Tirzah ("sweet or delightful") with Beaufield, Kent; Ramah ("High or exalted") with "Upton, Upham Hamsh., Upburn Bucking.sh, Uphall Hartf.sh, Hie-gate Midlesex", etc. Thomas Fuller's near colonialist point of view appears in countless remarks, as in this casual inversion: "*Sion* . . . may be called the *Westminster* of *Jerusalem;* because the kings thereof resided there while living, and rested when dead" (*A Pisgah-sight* 335).

I should like to concentrate on the less immediately obvious conjunction of Eden and Jerusalem and on Jerusalem itself as the triadic center, the diplomatic mediator in *Paradise Lost* that allows Eden to become intimate with England. Shakespeare requires no such mediation. John of Gaunt's stirring paean in *Richard II* fuses England and Eden:

> This other Eden, demi-paradise,
> This fortress built by Nature for herself
> Against infection and the hand of war,
> This happy breed of men, this little world,
> This precious stone set in the silver sea . . . (2.i.42–46)

Milton, too, sees Eden as central, difficult of access, a sacred enclosure, but by association with Jerusalem, a city described in the travel literature that he knew as "a Diadem crowning the head of the mountaines":

> the chief Glory . . . of all the whole World . . . was the famous City of *Hierusalem;* seated upon a rocky Mountain, every way to be ascended with steep and difficult Ascents (except towards the North) environed on all other sides also with some neighbouring Mountains, as if placed in the midst of an *Amphitheatre.*[8]
>
> Concerning the generall situation of *Jerusalem*, three things herein are remarkable: first it was placed, as *Josephus* reports it, in the very middle of *Judea*. But herein critical exactness is not to be observed, (the heart itself is not so unpartially in the midst of the body, but that if not in position, yet in motion it propends to the left side) for *Jerusalem* inclines more to the south of the Countrey. As *Jerusalem* was the *navell* of *Judea*, so the Fathers make *Judea* the middest of the world, whereunto they bring . . . those places of Scripture, *Thou has wrought salvation in the midst of the earth. . . . Jerusalem* was the *Center* whence the *lines of salvation* went out into all lands. . . . Secondly, it had high mountains under it, and lower about it, which as dutifull servants at distance seemed to attend it. *Jerusalem* had a mountain for her footstool, and her floor was higher than the roof of other Cities. . . . Lastly, it was distanced from the sea. . . . For God intended not *Jerusalem* for a staple of trade, but for a **ROYALL EXCHANGE OF RELIGION,** chiefly holding correspondence with Heaven itself . . . . Besides, God would not have his virgin people the *Jews,* wooed with, much less wedded to outlandish fashions. (*A Pisgah-sight* 315)

Milton's descriptions of secure Eden's difficult ascent (*Paradise Lost* 4.135–49) and of the delights of paradise recall many famous *loci amoeni*, but the sacredness of Jerusalem would have held a special appeal. God's "righteous altar" stood in the Temple at Jerusalem (1.434), and "earth's great altar" in Eden sent up silent praise to heaven (9.195). The trees of paradise, cedar, pine, fir, and branching palm (4.139; 9.435), remind us of the trees used to build Solomon's Temple (1 Kings 5 and 6) and of those described by Isaiah in a vision of Zion's future glory (60:13). Indeed, when the angel Michael describes God's sanctuary "framed / Of cedar, overlaid with gold" (*Paradise Lost* 12.249–50), we may remember the "sylvan scene," the "loftiest shade, / Cedar" overlaid by the vital gold of the sun's rays: "goodliest trees . . . / . . . On which the sun more glad impressed his beams" (4.147, 150).

Michael Lieb, citing Mircea Eliade, identifies one of the essential characteristics of a sacred, mythic geography: "an enclosure that separates profane space from sacred space within which a divinity dwells and communicates with those who have been able to penetrate the consecrated area."[9] A sense of increased circumscription attaches to the description of holy place in the epic's last book:

> . . . their land,
> Their city, his temple, and his holy ark
> With all his sacred things . . . (*Paradise Lost* 12.339–41)

A few lines later the angelic narrator describes the sanctuary in terms of enclosure:

> . . . such delight hath God in men
> Obedient to his will, that he vouchsafes
> Among them to set up his tabernacle,
> The Holy One with mortal men to dwell:
> By his prescript a sanctuary is framed
> Of cedar, overlaid with gold, therein
> An ark, and in the ark his testimony,
> The records of his cov'nant; over these
> A mercy-seat of gold between the wings
> Of two bright Cherubim. (12.245–54)

In Eden before the Fall, our first parents delight their creator, who vouchsafes to dwell with them. Paradise is "hallowed ground" (11.106), whose "inmost bow'r" (4.738) is forbidden to all but Adam and Eve ("Other creature here / . . . durst enter none" [4.703–04]). From this bower, our first parents, priests in the Temple, immured by privilege, offer rites of "adoration pure" (4.736).

Yet the Temples in Jerusalem and Eden are invaded by evil: "and next to life / Our death" (4.220–21). The sack of the Temple interested Milton, and the "Taking of Jerusalem" is a projected topic for a tragedy in the Trinity Manuscript (*Works* 18.239). Certainly the catalog of pagan deities that invade God's holy places anticipates Satan's invasion of Eden. One can mark the operation of a sort of demonic typology by which the idols in the catalog dimly set forth the appearance, location, and strategy of Satan in Book 9.[10]

Like Comus's crew, the glittering golden idols of the catalog are in reality monsters. Moloch has the head of a calf;[11] Baal-Peor is identified with "the beastly God Priapus" (*Pisgah-sight* 13); Astoreth, with "crescent horns" (*Paradise Lost* 1.439), has the head of a bull; and Dagon is a "sea monster, upward man / And downward fish" (462–63). "The brutish gods of Nile" (*Nativity Ode,* 211) include Isis and Orus, to whom the cow and the hawk, respectively, are sacred, as well as Osiris, worshiped under the form of a bull, "Trampling the unshow'red grass with lowings loud" (*Nativity Ode,* 215). These monsters blazon forth their leader, who can only tempt his human victim in the transformed "Image of a Brute" (see *Paradise Lost* 1.371. 9.507–08). But even as a serpent, Satan outdoes his legions; he is transformed into a towering idol of living gold, more splendid by far than the golden forms of the catalog:

> . . . on his rear,
> Circular base of rising folds, that tow'red
> Fold above fold a surging maze; his head
> Crested aloft, and carbuncle his eyes;
> With burnished neck of verdant gold, erect
> Amidst his circling spires, that on the grass
> Floated redundant. (*Paradise Lost* 9.497–503)

The catalog insistently repeats the idols' invasions of Jerusalem, which anticipate Satan's invasion of Eden. In Book 9, Satan's vast global circuits, covered in the space of "seven continued nights" (63), end, finally, in Eden. Satan's legions follow this strategy, moving from "the Nations round" to the Holy City itself. Projected against a background of confusion (since the catalog appears to be a mélange of images and themes), the image of Jerusalem becomes that much more vivid. We are reminded after the description of virtually every idol that the Holy City has suffered the irruptions of Satan's legions. The narrator, describing the invasion of each pagan deity, alternates emphasis from the demonic to the holy. The design can be visualized as a wheel, with Jerusalem at the hub, and with many spokes radiating to the rim. Moloch holds Ammon in thrall:

> Nor content with such
> Audacious Neighborhood, the wisest heart

Of Solomon he led by fraud to build
His temple right against the Temple of God. . . .
(*Paradise Lost* 1.399–402)

Though Peor has already seduced the Israelites in Sittim, he enlarges his orgies "Even to that hill of scandal, by the grove / Of Moloch homicide" (1.416–17).

Baalim and Ashtaroth are less differentiated than the other idols. They give plural collectivity to the various manifestations of Baal and Astoreth, and the entire country lies within their bounds. Their general seduction of the Israelites from God's "righteous altar" is stressed. Astarte is already famous among the Phoenicians: "In Sion also not unsung, where stood / Her temple on th'offensive mountain, built / By that uxorious king" (1.442–44). The wound of Thammuz allures Sion's daughters, "Whose wanton passions in the sacred porch / Ezekiel saw" (1.454–55). Josephus recounts in detail the plagues of "sickness and mishappes" that oppress the worshipers of Dagon when they seize the Ark of the Lord.[12] Rimmon, too, "against the house of God was bold", drawing King Ahaz to disparage and displace God's altar (1.470–76). Last comes Belial, who does not need to storm God's Temple because he is its priest:

. . . who more oft than he
In temples and at altars, when the priest
Turns atheist, as did Eli's sons, who filled
With lust and violence the house of God?
(*Paradise Lost* 1.493–96)

With Belial the worst is reached: sin enters the Temple and contaminates the holy. Victims of the rape described in the passage dealing with Belial (1.503–05) include the city itself: Jerusalem must suffer the violent thrusts and withdrawals of her enemies. And with Belial, the violation of Eden and of the Temple at Jerusalem are joined by a third atrocity, the restoration of Charles II to the English throne. As Professor Rajan has noted, Belial represents "the cavalier type in Puritan eyes—suave, dilettante, dissolute and lacking in courage."[13] The narrator effects the transition from ruined holy places of the past to Restoration London invaded by rioters and muggers simply by switching to the present tense ("Turns," 495) and staying there, after hundreds of lines in the past:

In courts and palaces he also reigns
And in luxurious cities, where the noise
Of riot ascends above their loftiest tow'rs,

And injury and outrage; and when night
Darkens the streets, then wander forth the sons
Of Belial, flown with insolence and wine.
(*Paradise Lost* 1.497–502)

Just as the verdurous walls of Eden and the divine enclosures of the Temple at Jerusalem fail to repel attackers, so the leafy protection of Adam and Eve immediately after the Fall proves to be inadequate against shame:

Thus fenced, and as they thought, their shame in part
Covered, but not at rest or ease of mind,
They sat them down to weep.
(*Paradise Lost* 9.1119–21)

The narrator connects Adam and Eve's imminent exile from Eden with the Jews' exile from Zion: "By the rivers of Babylon, there we sat down, yea, we wept, when we remembered Zion" (Psalm 137:1). Later, the angel Michael's account of the changes wrought by sin contains an explanation of the purpose behind the removal and ruin of paradise:

To teach thee that God attributes to place
No sanctity, if none be thither brought
By men who there frequent, or therein dwell.
(*Paradise Lost* 12.836–38)

The verbs in the excerpt's last line connect "Jerusalem laid waste" (*Paradise Regained* 3.283) and paradise lost: Adam and Eve dwelled in Eden; priests frequented the Temple in Jerusalem.

After the Fall, Milton's Hebraic sense of holy place as external, separate, and enclosed gives way, doctrinally if not poetically, to a Christian emphasis on interiority, union, and the breaking of all boundaries. All of the great travel writers that Milton read—Purchas, Sandys, Heylyn, Fuller—learn the same lesson from the total destruction of the Second Temple with all of its sacred utensils:

> Strange that no Pope hath gotten a piece of *Aarons* Mitre, or *breast-plate,* to grace his wardrobe, or a parcell of the *manuscript-commandements* written by Gods finger, to adorn his *Vatican.* But divine providence hath utterly razed all foundation for superstition to build upon, in the totall abolition of these holy ornaments. . . . Nor have I ought else to observe of those holy Utensils, save that all were made of pure gold, and yet the Apostle is bold to term them, and all other legall ceremonies *beggarly*

> *elements* [Galatians 4:9], so debasing them in comparison of Christ, the author of grace, and giver of eternall life.
>
> (*Pisgah-sight* 438)[14]

Now all external holy places are gone. Like the golden utensils of the Temple, the once-golden worlds of Paradise and Jerusalem are devalued and superseded by Christ. The narrator of *Paradise Lost* has only scorn for palmers in the Holy Land, seeking the living among the dead:

> Here Pilgrims roam, that strayed so far to seek
> In Golgotha him dead, who lives in heav'n.
> (*Paradise Lost* 3.476–77)

Peter Heylyn hints at the doctrine of *felix culpa* in his description of the walls and courts that enforced hierarchical separation in the Second Temple: the *atrium gentium, atrium foeminarum, atrium populi*, and, finally, *atrium sacerdotum*. Titus and his forces destroyed these boundaries:

> The last *Court* [that of the Gentiles] [was] separate from the other by a wall of three Cubits height, adorned with certain pillars of equal distance, bearing this Inscription . . . *Let no alien* (or one that is no Jew) *enter into the holy place:* And to this wall it is that the Apostle alludeth, saying, *He hath broken down the middle wall of partition between us* (i.e. between the *Jews* and *Gentiles*) *making one of twain,* Eph. 2.14, 15. inferring hereupon, that the *Gentiles* are no more *strangers and forreiners, but fellow-Citizens with the Saints, and of the houshold of God.* v.19.[15]

Of course, the antecedent of "he" in the verse from Ephesians is not Titus, who is merely an instrument, but Christ, who performs his sacerdotal office as sacrifice and intercessor in a temple not made of stone. Milton is clear on this point: "the law of *Moses* . . . was not fully abrogated till the destruction of the temple."[16] From now on, the spiritual associations of Eden and Jerusalem afford consolation to the believing Christian: the paradise within is at hand in the kingdom of Grace; the heavenly Jerusalem of Saint John's vision (Revelation 21:2) is prepared for those who will participate in the Kingdom of Glory.[17]

By extending his reach from Eden to Jerusalem, Milton enlarges the scope of his great theme: the joy of Paradise and its felt loss, "More woe, the more your taste is now of joy" (4.369). All of the sacred travel writers touring the ruins of Jerusalem emphasize dynastic degeneration and decay, which might well be on the mind of a man whose surviving children gave him no hope of continued Miltonic greatness. His epic's opening invocation announces the supersession of the physical ("all temples") by the spiritual ("th'upright heart and pure"). Milton's poems, his spiritual progeny, have given him immortality. And yet, of course, despite the doctrinal rejection of the physical, we sense in *Paradise Lost* the pure longing for the Eden, Jerusalem, and England of his dreams. Leszek Kolakowski, in a recent essay, has written of our age of refugees, "warming their souls with the memory of their . . . home. A total homelessness is unbearable."[18] Milton, writing in Restoration London, is just such an exile, and the power of his longing has created a home in the souls of his readers for well over three centuries.

# NOTES

Quotations referenced in the text to *Prose Works* are taken from *Complete Prose Works of John Milton,* ed. Don M. Wolfe et al. (New Haven: 1953–82). Quotations referenced in the text to *Works* are taken from *The Works of John Milton,* ed. Frank Allen Patterson et al. (New York: 1931–38). Other quotations are from *Milton: Poetical Works,* ed. Douglas Bush (London: 1966); Thomas Fuller, *A Pisgah-sight of Palestine* (London: 1650); Josiah Nichols, *Abraham's Faith* (London: 1602).

1. James Holly Hanford, "Milton in Italy", *Annuale Mediaevale* 5 (1964): 49–63. See also John Arthos, *Milton and the Italian Cities* (New York: 1968).
2. Robert R. Cawley, *Milton and the Literature of Travel* (Princeton: 1951) 84.
3. The fullest analysis of these passages in a geographic context appears in Cawley 9–36.
4. Frances A. Yates, *The Art of Memory* (Chicago: 1966).
5. *An Elegie upon the Death of . . . Our Late Soveraigne Elizabeth* (London: 1603).
6. On this tripartite movement in the twenty-third sonnet, see Leo Spitzer, "Understanding Milton", *Hopkins Review* 4 (1950–51): 16–27.
7. Christopher Hill, "Milton and Marvell", in *Approaches to Marvell: The York Tercentenary Lectures,* ed. C. A. Patrides (London: 1978) 22.
8. Peter Heylyn, *Cosmography in Four Books, Containing the Chorographie and Historie of the Whole World*, 3rd ed. (London: 1667). This description comes verbatim from George Sandys' *A Relation of a Journey Begun An. Dom. 1610* (1621; 3rd ed. London: 1627) 155.
9. Michael Lieb, *Poetics of the Holy: A Reading of Paradise Lost* (Chapel Hill: 1981) 120. Professor Lieb's chapter on "Place" (119–39) examines thoroughly the relation of enclosure to the idea of the sacred.
10. The next three paragraphs are excerpted from my essay "'Audacious Neighborhood': Idolatry in *Paradise Lost*, Book 1", *Philological Quarterly* 54 (1975): 553–68.
11. Sandys 145.
12. *The Famous Workes of Josephus,* tr. Thomas Lodge (London: 1602) 6.i.127.

13. B. Rajan, ed. *Paradise Lost, Books 1 and 2* (1964); cited in *The Poems of John Milton*, ed. John Carey and Alastair Fowler (London: 1968) 491n.
14. On the destruction of the Second Temple, see also Samuel Purchas, *Purchas His Pilgrimage* (London: 1625) 5. 89–90, 94ff.; Heylyn 3. 79ff.; Sandys 192.
15. Heylyn 3. 80.
16. *The Likeliest Means to Remove Hirelings, Prose Works* 7.289.
17. For Milton on the new Jerusalem, see *Animadversions, Prose Works* 1.703.
18. Leszek Kolakowski, "In Praise of Exile", *Times Literary Supplement* October 11, 1985, 1133–34; cited in the introduction to Louis L. Martz, *Milton: Poet of Exile*, 2nd ed. (New Haven: 1986). Martz's brilliant survey of Milton's entire poetic career examines especially well the generative power of exile.

# "ENGLISH ALL THE WORLD": MARVELL IN EUROPE AND BEYOND

Margarita Stocker, University of Buckingham

More than many authors, Andrew Marvell lived not only in the private world of imagination but also in the most public world, where England was beginning to transform herself into an imperial power. The poems we read today were largely unpublished in his lifetime: he was better known as a writer of political polemic and satire.[1] While he traveled in Europe, it was usually on other people's business, his employers' or even the nation's. For this very reason, though, he was peculiarly well placed to view foreign nations through the telescope of England's interests. Strangely, he did not write very much about the countries he had actually visited. More strangely still, what he wrote tended to predate the visit. He also wrote with great feeling of places he had never seen at all. Perhaps these oddities are the explanation for a general lack of interest, in the past, in Marvell's attitudes to abroad. Yet those attitudes are central to his work. The actualities of Marvell's life matter more than most readers have been led to believe. As a writer, his concern with the world outside England reflects his experience as a courageous reformer, a civil servant, a diplomat, and, finally, a spy. Marvell was a nationalist and an internationalist; a traveler who mentally stayed at home; a poet whose imagination distilled the globe into a dewdrop, while dilating his own country into a whole universe. Those contradictions are, however, only apparent. Marvell's worldview was at once passionate and logical.

His poems voyage far and wide, from the West Indies to the Ganges, the Canaries to Lapland. For his time and his class, Marvell himself was well traveled. And although the received image of Marvell is of a somewhat passive and reclusive character—much given to reveries in gardens and the pleasures of retirement—his life was, in fact, active and colorful. Beneath what appear to be the still small pools of his lyrics, strong currents flow. Marvell rejected the "dead and standing pool of air" in an ornamental garden, but he wrote with fervor of the "waters of Time" and history, and the oceans on which European nations were establishing modern empires.

That fascination with the sea began during Marvell's childhood in the busy and growing port of Hull. His father, a clergyman, was Master of Charterhouse Hospital, an almshouse for those impoverished by "infortune of the sea", on the bank of the river Hull. Years later, one of Marvell's political opponents ascribed his rudeness to "your first unhappy education among boatswains and cabin-boys". Social snobbery apart, Marvell was certainly familiar with the everyday workings of England's maritime trade, not least because his family connections were merchants and local dignitaries. As the major northeastern avenue for England's European trade and a strategic harbor, Hull was necessarily crucially affected by both civil and foreign wars.[2] Britain's modern empire grew out of a struggle for hegemony that involved trade, religion, and war. Shipping, both merchant and military, was the critical factor. (Not surprisingly, ships are always sailing into Marvell's poems: "The ocean is the fountain of command" [*The First Anniversary of the Government* 369].) By such means Hull was closely concerned with the great events of the seventeenth century.

Throughout his life Marvell maintained his connection with the town. It is impossible to understand either his life or his works without recognizing that in his attitudes he remained at all times, and despite his varied experience, a Puritan Yorkshireman. His understanding of the wider world was determined by that background in Hull, a town in which such nonconformists flourished and where Parliament naturally found strong support during the Civil War. Marvell himself saw very little of the war, for between 1642/43 and 1647 he was traveling in Holland, France, Italy, and Spain. Where he acquired the resources for his version of the educational grand tour we do not know. (It is possible that his merchant relatives financed it in return for his meeting their foreign contacts: personal representation was vital to successful trading.) Apparently Marvell could afford the services of a fencing master in Spain, from whom he acquired the wisdom that attack is the best form of defense (*Letters* 324). No doubt this was useful advice for a future politician and satirist. After Hull grammar school and Cambridge University, the tour rounded off his own education and completed his qualifications for educating others. His obvious career options were as either tutor or clergyman, and like Milton he returned from Europe having (if he had ever considered it) rejected his father's vocation. In 1653 he became tutor to Cromwell's de facto ward, William Dutton.

Also like Milton, he returned with broader cultural experience but narrower resolutions. From a strong nonconformist background, he had now visited the major "popish" countries. What he saw in France, Italy, and Spain seems to have confirmed an anti-Catholic prejudice. Although his poetry has a cultured elegance, its most extensive references to other countries tend to reflect a peculiarly English hostility to the Catholic Counter-Reformation. The English felt keenly the current Protestant sense of isolation in Europe, fearing invasion by Catholic powers and infiltration by Jesuits and spies. Marvell himself had been approached by Jesuits while he was at Cambridge, and at his death it would be rumored that he had been poisoned by them.

While in Italy, Marvell met someone whom he regarded as one of his country's religious traitors, the poet Richard Flecknoe, who was attached to the English College in Rome. *Flecknoe, an English Priest at Rome* is the only poem that can be certainly dated to his tour in the 1640s, and it is a virulent satiric expression of reformist Puritanism. The very title is meant to strike with the force of an oxymoron: an *English* priest in *Rome*, of all places? Marvell's meeting with Flecknoe in 1646 is portrayed as the clash of true with false religion, of Protestant poet with Romish poetaster, of the plain layman with the hypocrite priest. Flecknoe is less a person than a congeries of masks, falsities, icons, and tags, a man made of paper.

Behind this vilification lies something more than mere personal malice. Flecknoe emblematizes the falsity in all things that popery represents for Protestant Englishmen. Many believed that they were living in the Latter Days, when Antichrist (the pope and his servitors) warred with true religion. Until Christ quelled Antichrist at the Second Coming, Protestantism was fighting for its life.[3] Such apocalyptic expectation may sound to us like a mad obsession, and may be of no great interest until we remember that our own century seems more and more to be characterized by apocalyptic scenarios of ultimate nuclear destruction, by fundamentalist and survivalist movements in both East and West, by religious conflicts and slogans of Holy War. Current strife in the Middle East had its equivalent in seventeenth-century Europe. The countries through which Marvell traveled were all involved in one way or another in the Thirty Years' War, which raged in northern Europe from 1618 to 1648. In that light, meeting Flecknoe is a personal skirmish symbolizing the great continental clash between Protestant and Catholic nations.

The poem is constructed as a mock Inquisition. A Protestant poet is lured to the Catholic's lair, tortured and brainwashed by a recital of his dreadful verses, and subjected to comic trials for "heresy", and (finally worn down) temporarily "converts" to Catholicism (167–70). The Protestant Marvell is really unscathed, however. Even under "torture" he preens himself upon his fortitude as a willing martyr:

> In hideous verse, he, in a dismal tone,
> Begins to exorcise, as if I were

Possessed; and sure the Devil brought me there.
But I, who now imagined myself brought
To my last trial, in a serious thought
Calmed the disorders of my youthful breast,
And to my martyrdom prepared rest.

. . . how I, silent, turned my burning ear
Towards the verse; and when that could not hear,
Held him the other; and unchanged yet,
Asked still for more, and prayed him to repeat:
Till the tyrant, weary to persecute,
Left off . . . (20–36)

For the sake of true poetry and the true faith he can withstand anything (although he would have liked an audience, to *appreciate* his fortitude). The whole comic narrative is characteristic of Marvell's capacity to play with the terms of his own Protestant commitment. The commitment itself is absolute and, like most strong religious convictions, invades every aspect of its adherent's life and thought. For reformers like Marvell and Milton, apocalyptic Protestantism was not a separable "religious" concern, for in such minds nothing can qualify as "secular". For Marvell the fact that Flecknoe is a bad poet is inextricably related to his popery. A Catholic priest is a fake Christian and a false minister, so if he claims to be a poet he must be a poetaster. The encounter of these two poets is a miniature mock battle in the only war that matters.

For this reason, in Marvell's description of his route to Flecknoe's apartment, there is little to distinguish Rome from London:

Obliged by frequent visits of this man,
Whom as priest, poet, and musician,
I for some branch of Melchizedek took

. . .
I sought his lodging, which is at the sign
Of The Sad Pelican—subject divine
For poetry. There, three staircases high—
Which signifies his triple property—
I found at last a chamber, as 'twas said,
But seemed a coffin set on the stairs' head. (1–10)

What we witness here is a parodic pilgrimage. In Puritan thought the metaphor of life as a journey was particularly potent. As in Bunyan's

*Pilgrim's Progress*, a believer might attempt to travel the right road to salvation yet be constantly deflected into the way of destruction. Popery was regarded as a false trail that misled Christians to damnation. Such "wayfaring" images were often treated in a remarkably literal fashion: in Marvell's poem they become a comic fantasy of his misguided route to a Catholic's lodging. He is fooled by the "divine" sign of "The Sad Pelican", which was a common image of Christ's power to save. The fact that this is merely an inn sign is a comic emblem of its falsity: of, in fact, popish idolatry. Flecknoe is a parodic version of the model for priests, Melchizedek. So is the pope, and like him, Flecknoe has a "triple property". He lives on the third story, the 'three staircases" a parody of the pope's three-tiered crown. In this way Flecknoe's triple power as a divine is bathetically reduced, to the fact that his residential "property" is a miserable room in the cheapest part of the building. Marvell must climb three staircases because Flecknoe cannot afford anything on a lower floor. This comment on his poverty undercuts the stairs' parodic image of a spiritual ascent. Far from finding a priest who can guide him to salvation, Marvell will find a hypocritical adherent of the false version of Christianity. This man can only lead a soul to destruction: his room is like a coffin. That, too, is a comment on Flecknoe's straitened circumstances. Marvell harps on this theme because it reflects Flecknoe's spiritual poverty as a priest, as well as his imaginative poverty as a poet. The Pelican Christ feeds the souls in his care, but Flecknoe is a papist, and so literally starving. When Marvell jokes about having to buy Flecknoe's dinner—"he had not eat this Lent"—he is not being unpleasantly superior, at least not in materialist terms. Because he is a Protestant he has access to real sustenance! Flecknoe, like all antichristians, eats God at Mass, and souls for breakfast. When Marvell asks him "if he eat meat" the sly joke is that Flecknoe is a spiritual cannibal. The poem's satire depends upon such religious tropes. In Marvell's "journey" through life, a visit to Rome leads with comic inevitability to popish "persecution". In other respects, the poem's Italian background fades behind a skit on popish folly. Marvell is convinced that "The world in all doth but two Nations bear, / The good [and] bad" (*The Loyal Scot* 236–37). Rome, of course, is the symbolic home of the bad.

Since Marvell is more interested in the universal destiny of man than in the countries man inhabits, exactly the same narrative pattern shapes an English scene, in *Tom May's Death* (1650). Although May was not a Catholic, he was another "false poet", misrepresenting England's true destiny. He was "Malignant poet and historian both" (42). May's mistake, from Marvell's point of view, was to portray republican England as if it were ancient Rome. "Transferring old Rome hither in your talk, / As Bethlem's House did to Loreto walk" (49–50): his Roman delusions were comparable to fake

Romish miracles. This symbolic exchange of places is reversed by Marvell in a comic fantasy about May's ghost. He had died of suffocation while in a drunken stupor. Farcical enough, but in Marvell's poem May is so inebriated that his ghost does not even notice the trifling fact that he is dead. By mistake he stumbles into the Romans' Elysium, where the ghosts of true poets reside. They, of course, will not allow a "poetaster" to stay, and throw him out. It is the poem's running gag that May is always being ejected from somewhere. Even his corpse is thrown out of Poets' Corner, by the disgusted ghosts of Spenser and Chaucer. His spirit can find a home only in hell, where Rome's political "cheats" will be his companions. Because he wandered, in life, from the true path in politics and poetry, May has deserved physical, literary, national, and spiritual deportation.

The poem began with May's dying, which was pretty much the same as being thrown out at closing time:

> As one put drunk into the packet-boat,
> Tom May was hurried hence and did not know't.
> But was amazed on the Elysian side,
> And with an eye uncertain, gazing wide,
> Could not determine in what place he was,
> (For whence, in Stephen's Alley, trees or grass?)
> Nor where The Pope's Head, nor The Mitre lay,
> Signs by which still he found and lost his way. (1–8)

In life, taverns like The Pope's Head were May's landmarks. No wonder (the poem implies) that in a permanent alcoholic haze May should mistake London for ancient Rome, or Elysium for his local haunts. So much for all that high-sounding talk of his. Once again, though, these taverns represent the false ideals that mislead such men. In comically reductive fashion the taverns recall the Roman Catholic hierarchy of popes and mitered bishops; similarly, the "Roman" republican government celebrated by May is a perversion of the truth.

If May had misrepresented England's destiny, what did Marvell consider it to be? In *Upon Appleton House* (c. 1652), he wrote of the doom and glorious renewal awaiting the world, which teetered on the brink of its final ruin. In the latter days the English were God's chosen people. "The Garden of the World" (322), it was England's duty to keep herself pure, to become a New Jerusalem on earth. Only then could she perform her mission in the world outside, which was to make it Protestant (and preferably English too). Her destiny was to transform the whole earth into that "Garden" of the New Jerusalem. It is to maintain England's purity that (for instance) Marvell "deports" May. Her "Garden" must "exclude the world". So he is often suspicious of influence from abroad. Even the hiring of a "foreign architect" and the cultivation of tropical flowers are treated as positively sinful (*Appleton House* 325, 2; *The Mower against Gardens* 18). On the other hand, England must export her own spirit whenever possible. To put it more brutally, if England won the current imperialist competition, the world would be hers *and* God's. This was a vision of progress: English domination would, paradoxically, free the world. Unlike the notoriously cruel Spanish, Marvell thought, the English would rather "convert" than "subdue" the American Indians. Within Europe, England might even free the Catholic states themselves (*First Anniversary* 115; *Horatian Ode* 101–4). Resolved to participate in this mission, Marvell was now writing poems directly concerned with Cromwell's policies. It was in the 1650s, before and after his more extensive travels, that Marvell wrote most about other lands. What he was interested in, though, was England. In the apocalyptic perspective of nationalist reformers like Marvell and his friend Milton, England and the world were essentially the same.

Among these was one that no longer looks political to modern readers, the haunting lyric *Bermudas.* Although England's colonial rival in the west was Spain, God had evidently reserved the Bermudas for the Protestant power. According to English writers, He had in fact deliberately hidden them from everyone else: "the remote Bermudas ride / In the ocean's bosom unespied", says Marvell. The islands are a modern version of the fabled Fortunate Isles, the land of happiness and plenty. Another "Garden of the World", "far kinder than our own" (8), they are a vision of the effortless New Jerusalem that England herself may become. God

gave us this eternal spring,
Which here enamels everything,
And sends the fowls to us in care,
On daily visits through the air.
He hangs in shades the orange bright,
Like golden lamps in a green night,
And does in the pom'granates close
Jewels more rich than Ormus shows.

. . . . . . . . . . . . . . . . . . . . . . . . . . . . . . .

He cast (of which we rather boast)
The gospel's pearl upon our coast,
And in these rocks for us did frame
A temple, where to sound his name. (13–32)

This is a painted, "enamelled" paradise. That visionary element dominates, although most of the poem's details are also accurate to the real Bermudas. Marvell's paradise remembers the islands' flatness, their flocks of birds, their rocky coasts and the pineapples planted by settlers. Persecuted Puritans had indeed fled there in the past, "Safe from . . . prelate's rage" (12): like John Oxenbridge, Marvell's friend, who probably supplied details of a place that the poet had never seen. To summon up the New Jerusalem, though, he had no need to see the islands. His vision calls upon classical and biblical images, like the cedars of Lebanon. The place name "Ormus", which contributes to the poem's exotic atmosphere, has a similar function. Made famous in England by Hakluyt, Hormuz was an island in the Persian Gulf, fabulously wealthy and particularly celebrated for its gems.[4] It was a gateway to Far Eastern trade, and Marvell corresponded with a merchant of the East India Company there, Thomas Rolt (*Letters* 323). Like the poem's other allusions, the jewels of Hormuz represent both a reality and a vision.

In the islands of the present, Marvell sees the future. The Fortunate Isles represented, for him as for other writers, the ideal image of what England could become. Such colonies as the Bermudas were "Englands out of England". Their western location was significant, for there the sun set, measuring the days that brought the promised end closer. In both space and time, the west was the destiny of humankind. In Marvell's poem "the English boat" is the English ship of state, sailing to the end of time. If she is truly fortunate, the voyage will take her to the New Jerusalem emblematized by the New World in the west. As the New World is at once itself and the future world, so the Bermudas are at once themselves and England transformed.[5] In Marvell's vision the point is precisely that they are not foreign at all.

For the New World England must fight the antichristian empire of Spain. As her saints sing their hymn, Marvell suggests the possibility that their voices may symbolically overcome the Spanish presence in "the Mexique Bay" (36). This is a reference to the fleet that, in 1654, Cromwell was dispatching to the West Indies, with orders to wrest what it could from the Spanish possessions there. That venture was judged unsuccessful, but Cromwell's "Western Design" was better served by Admiral Robert Blake. The English navy had already been set to harry Spanish fleets carrying silverplate from the New World. In the spring of 1657 Blake intercepted a major treasure fleet, which had anchored in the naturally strong and heavily fortified harbor of Santa Cruz, in the Canaries. Its reputation for impregnability did not deter Blake. His ships ran the gamut of gunfire from the shore forts to take the galleons. At this point the English were now sitting targets for Spanish gunners, and as he could not get the galleons out of the harbor, Blake fired them. Under cover of the smoke the English were able to make good their escape, aided by a sudden favoring wind, which seemed providential. Blake's remarkable feat was the most celebrated naval action of its day: even the royalist historian Clarendon thought it "miraculous". When the news reached England there was wide rejoicing, at a moment when the government badly needed a major foreign success.[6]

Meanwhile, Marvell had himself embarked for France, chaperoning William Dutton. They stayed from January to August 1656 at Saumur on the Loire, where the college had acquired a reputation for learned Protestantism that attracted to the town those of a similar bent. Marvell had been imbibing and disseminating Protestant culture, at home and abroad, while Blake was implementing Protestant triumph by force. Back in England in 1657, Marvell continued his own literary efforts by celebrating England's hero in *On the Victory Obtained by Blake*. Characteristically, Marvell makes it his business to be accurate to the details of the action, something not common in poetic eulogies of the day. This has the effect of conveying precisely the magnitude of Blake's task, and thus manifesting the remarkable nature of his success. The very strength of the fortification ennobles English daring: "Fond [Spaniards] who know not whilst such works they raise, / They only labour to exalt your praise." (93–94).

The accuracy of Marvell's account is, though, achieved within a framework of visionary celebration for England's mission in an antichristian world. Cromwell's letter of congratulation to Blake had described this "very wonderful" victory as "according to the wonted goodness and loving-kindness of the Lord, wherewith His people have been followed in all these late revolutions". In Marvell's poem Blake becomes an avatar of Cromwell himself (the "you" of the poem), who is inspired by the "higher force" of providence to godly war "in the latter days" (*The First Anniversary* 239, 109–110). As God's emissary, the English navy punishes the Spanish, in a Protestant victory like that over the Armada in 1588. The Catholic power has rifled the New World's treasure; it has brought the iron world of war to the golden, unfallen Canaries. Like the Bermudas, the Canaries are Fortunate Isles that by right belong to England's empire. In this sense the battle is symbolic of the whole earth's fate, Old and New World both. "Fate these two fleets between both worlds had brought, / Who fight, as if for both those worlds they fought" (125–26). As the "best of lands", the Canaries should belong to Cromwell, should become another limb of England (40). They symbolize the last paradise, which the English will win for all humankind:

> For they behold the sweet Canary Isles;
> One of which doubtless is by Nature blessed
> Above both Worlds, since 'tis above the rest.

. . .
O noble trust which heav'n on this isle pours,
Fertile to be, yet never need her showers.
A happy people . . .
There the indulgent soil that rich grape breeds,
Which of the gods the fancied drink exceeds;
They still do yield, such is their precious mould,
All that is good . . . (24–31, 53–56)

Marvell had not seen the Canaries either, but in mythologizing them he imparts the fervor of an otherworldly vision. In this context Blake's victory is an international sign of Cromwell's sanctification: "fame in every place her trumpet blows, / And tells the world how much to you it owes" (167–68).

Marvell had been telling a possibly skeptical world about England's mission for some time. When the distinguished lawyer Oliver St. John was sent as a legate to the Netherlands in 1651, Marvell's poem on the occasion meditated that "St. John" had been the author of the Apocalypse. The Dutch are warned to expect similarly apocalyptic results if they prove unreceptive to England's demands. When, in 1653, the Anglo-Dutch war was in full spate, Marvell's *The Character of Holland* viciously castigated the Dutch and celebrated English admirals like Monck and Blake. The poem is certainly a "character" in genre, for it uses the methods usually applied by satirists to personal slander, transferring them to a whole nation. The "personality" of Holland is brutish, gross, and anarchic. Rude things are said about Dutch fishwives (85–92). Their men are characterized, ad nauseam, as "heeren", or herrings. Nationalism and war account for the tone here, but Marvell also had personal fish to fry. Hull was one of the ports affected by the Anglo-Dutch rivalry in fishing, a long-standing quarrel not dissimilar to the Anglo-Icelandic "Cod War" of the early 1970s. Like English traders generally, Hull merchants and shippers faced severe competition from Dutch carriers. The Navigation Act of 1651 had been intended to prevent Dutch carriers from dealing with English colonies, and the war of 1652–54 was popular with English merchants. Since active hostilities profited Hull's shipbuilding yards while damaging its Dutch rivals, war was positively advantageous to Hull. One can see why Marvell's poem was so aggressive, and in this so representative of English feeling.

The Dutch were, in fact, England's major rivals in this period. This was awkward, given that the Dutch were fellow Protestants. It was to Dutch cities that radical English sectaries fled when their own country proved too hot for them. This religious asylum Marvell interprets as one of Holland's anarchic monstrosities: "Faith . . . / Never so fertile, spawned upon this shore" (63–64). Amsterdam, Europe's premier financial center, is a "mint of schism", "That bank of conscience, where not one so strange / Opinion but finds credit, and exchange" (72–74). Marvell's harping on the unnaturalness of the famously sober and prosperous Dutch seems to fly in the face of fact. This apparent perversity is because he is interested not in the real Netherlands—even though he had been there—but, as usual, in England. *The Character* is, in fact, an obverse image of the character of England. Once again we are being shown the false image of the true. He tells us that the Dutch republic is a disorganized counterpart of the English republic (77–80). Unlike the English, Dutch reformed religion is a mass of mutually incompatible splinter groups, a brood of miscegenated bastards (63–71, 75–76). The Netherlands are even a fake country, since their land is really a seabed (27–30). "Holland, that scarce deserves the name of land, / As but the off-scouring of the British sand" (1–2): the whole mess is just an inept parody of the model nation, England. They owe their very existence to the English, for "We buoyed so often up their sinking state" (112). Marvell's expression of English jealousy is an ironically apt rendering of Anglo-Dutch likenesses, the source of envy itself. Rather cleverly, his poem exploits that very problem, by making England the paradigm and Holland merely a parody.

Anglo-Dutch rivalry was especially acute in the Baltic, a political flash-point. Its profitable trade routes to Poland and Russia were controlled by Denmark and Sweden; Cromwell was also interested in forming a political alliance with Sweden, then a great power, which would form the basis of a broad Protestant front in Europe.[7] His ambassador to Queen Christina, Bulstrode Whitelocke, was successful only in gaining a trade agreement; but this was not for lack of help from Marvell. In three poems he pressed the idea of holy alliance upon Christina, with due flattery and much learned allusion, designed to appeal to the scholarly queen. In *A Letter to Dr Ingelo* (1653) he mythologizes her as a Protestant version of Astraea, goddess of justice. Together, her virgin power and Cromwell's military zeal can defeat the popish "Scarlet Whore", her antichristian counterpart. This religious juxtaposition is part of Marvell's general comparison of Christina to Elizabeth I of England. Spenser's *Faerie Queene* had portrayed Elizabeth as Una, the princess of true religion, contrasting Duessa as the Catholic Mary, Queen of Scots, a scarlet whore. As another Una, another Elizabeth, a friend to England and a Protestant "saint" (22–25, 119–20), Christina is fashioned by Marvell into another avatar of English right.[8] As godly power, the identities of Cromwell and Christina are syntactically conflated (91–97). Marvell effectively appropriates the Swedish monarch to England's current self-image. This symbolic transfer is effected by means of classical myth, which also transforms Sweden into a modern version of ancient Rome.

Marvell had not visited Sweden, and he begins the poem by asking his friend Ingelo what it is like. The Far North is popularly supposed to be frozen, infertile, and barbaric. Not for nothing was Satan himself known as the "Prince of the North": the Laplanders, also Christina's subjects, were renowned for witchcraft. Swedish copper mining prompted visions of hellish underground toil. Such a cold climate was supposed to retard the mind and ossify the imagination (for this reason Milton was anxious that it might be impossible for England to grow poets!). These superstitions lie behind Marvell's interrogation about Sweden, but he soon sets about dismissing such "deceptive rumour".[9] (Christina would hardly be charmed if he did otherwise.) Of course Sweden cannot be like that, Marvell muses, for this iron land is ruled by a golden-age queen (11–18). Her learning has made her country another center for civilization, such as was Rome in its ancient glory. Her Protestantism purifies the land, and its snowy expanse is like the whiteness of her soul. Even the Lapps are transformed by her into God's warriors (107). Minds, hearts, and words are all released from a prison of ice by the warmth of her zeal and eloquence (107–112, 115–18). These latent imagistic patterns serve to transform one myth—that the north is malign—into another: that in the Protestant mission to conquer the world Sweden and England must make a common identity. Like the English, Christina believes in a domination that is freedom (124). The poem's universal vision, one world united in Protestantism, actually has the paradoxical effect of appropriating Sweden to England. *Ingelo* is a striking instance of the way in which Marvell's universalism is simultaneously a profound nationalism. The phrase "English all the world" (*Last Instructions to a Painter* 204) is an accidental concatenation of words in one of his poems, but nevertheless it happens to express his view very accurately. *Ingelo* is in Latin, the language of European diplomacy, but its spirit is unrepentantly English.

In order to construct a myth, Marvell's ignorance of Sweden was positively useful: no facts get in the way. He was not to know that, rather inconveniently, Christina was about to convert to Catholicism. Yet his poem has that brand of realism that comes from urgent political objectives. Nor was he unfamiliar with the basic needs represented by Baltic trade, from which Hull acquired vital supplies of iron, hemp, pitch, and tar. More exotically, from Hull intrepid sailors regularly set out for northern Norway, in search of whales. In Marvell's imagination these become "huge sea-monsters . . . / That lift the deep upon their backs". To the visionary *Bermudas* they bring, even as they die, the treasure of their ambergris (9–10, 28). They too become ornaments of England's myth, for her navy appears as "An hideous shoal of wood-leviathans", terrifying her enemies (*First Anniversary* 361).

Such devotion to the cause of Cromwellian England did not go unrewarded. In 1657 Marvell's skill in languages earned him an appointment as secretary to John Thurloe in the protectorate's equivalent of the Foreign Office. Here he translated official communications and composed letters to such elevated persons as the king of Portugal. Somewhat embarrassingly, on 2 August, 1658 Marvell was required to entertain the Dutch ambassador, Nieuport. Marvell seems to have managed to be sufficiently ingratiating nevertheless. Nieuport was supposed to be welcomed with ceremonies that would confirm England's "good intention" and "great esteem" for his country, but he and Marvell amicably agreed to take all this as read and dispense with the tiring formalities.[10] Marvell's official involvement in England's international relations was matched by a new role in her internal affairs, for in 1658 he was elected as an M. P. for Hull. In 1660 Charles II was restored to the English throne, and Marvell was reelected to the new Parliament.

While he had, like many Cromwellians, lost his post in the state service, in 1663 he accompanied the Earl of Carlisle on a diplomatic mission to northern Europe, acting as a secretary and interpreter. Marvell told the Hull Corporation that he would be gone for about a year (*Letters* 39), but in fact he would not return until almost three had passed. At last he was to see Sweden, as well as Denmark and Russia. On 15 July Marvell sailed with the earl from Gravesend. Following the customary route, they landed at Archangel, taking barges up the Duina and Sucagna rivers to Vologda, and traveling by sledge toward Moscow. The complicated logistics of this journey—the management of which sometimes fell to Marvell—are easily reckoned from the fact that the party needed no fewer than two hundred sledges. Whenever formal colloquies were in order, Marvell would launch into French or Latin. In person, though, he was a rather less-successful interpreter for England than he had been as a poet. During an audience he addressed the czar as "most illustrious" rather than "most serene". Far from being serene, the Russians were mightily offended. By now, however, Carlisle's party were accustomed to all sorts of Russian stonewalling and bloodymindedness. They had come on a long, uncomfortable, and frustrating journey only to be mistreated by Russians of all classes. Carlisle would later complain that this was all one could expect from such a barbarous and irreligious lot. In Guy de Miège's account of their journey it is made clear that in the case of Russia the north's bad reputation was amply justified after all. On 18 August, 1664 they departed thankfully from Riga for Stockholm, and then on to Copenhagen by 27 October. In Sweden Marvell had committed another faux pas, translating one of Carlisle's compliments to the queen regent so literally that it became embarrassing. On the return journey the party was further plagued, by nature and man alike. The second Anglo-Dutch war was already affecting sea routes: when Carlisle's vessel ran into bad weather he had an excellent excuse to abandon it and travel by land. Yet their problems were not over yet. Near Hamburg Marvell's wagoner refused to move unless his friend was also hired. Evidently for the unhappy secretary this was the last straw, for he abandoned negotiation, "and by clapping a pistol to his head would have forced him along with him. But immediately his pistol was wrested from him", and Marvell's companions had to rescue him from a melee of angry "peasants and Mechanicks".[11] Perhaps understandably, Marvell never ventured abroad again.

It is often said that travel shows us in our true colors. Certainly this incident reveals Marvell's mettlesome character. He was a man of strong convictions and equally strong temper. He had demonstrated as much in 1662, when in a scandalous breach of decorum he had struck Thomas Clifford, another M. P., and was reprimanded by the Speaker of the House. The same strength of feeling infuses Marvell's satires on the Restoration government. As an opposition M. P. and anonymous pamphleteer, he set himself to resist tyranny. He recognized that the second Dutch war was a political error, since it weakened both countries at a time when they had a common enemy, the "most catholic king", Louis XIV of France. In *Last Instructions to a Painter* (1667) "the English boat" is now symbolized in another guise, as the ship *Royal Charles* (755–57). The Dutch had captured her in their raid on the English fleet moored at Chatham. She represents England's greater losses: Charles II has effectively sold England to the French (913–14). No longer a great and elect nation, she has become vulnerable to foreign invasion. The "Garden of the World" is now a holiday resort for Dutch admirals (523–32). In the course of the poem the Fortunate Isles of Britain imagistically metamorphose into the fortunate "floating islands" of the Dutch vessels (533–60). Now, in England's corruption by the Stuarts, the Dutch have finally stolen the "character" of the elect nation.

Marvell acted upon that conviction. From the early 1670s he was a secret agent for William, Prince of Orange and Stadtholder of Holland, who was fast becoming Europe's new Protestant hero.[12] Although Marvell died in 1678, ten years before the "glorious revolution" placed William on the English throne, Marvell and his parliamentary colleagues—now the "Whigs" —had facilitated that event. If Marvell helped to import William, this was his last and most successful attempt to import the world into the narrow compass of his native land.

In his poems Marvell is always cramming the world into spots of time. When he sets about seducing a *Coy Mistress* in the approved poetic fashion, he draws into his fantasy the farthest reaches of space and history. To love without limit, he says, they would need the vast expanses that lie between the Humber and the Ganges. They would need the eons of time that separate Noah's flood from the conversion of the Jews at the apocalypse (1–10). His love, or rather (let us not be as coy as the mistress), his *thing* would "grow /

Vaster than empires" (11–12). Yet this is, yes, fantasy, because there are limits: like all mortals, they live briefly and must die (21–32). In that sense they have not "world enough, and time" (1). Neither has the world itself, which will soon be consumed by the fires of the apocalypse. Time and the world will die together at that moment. Living in the "last age" (18), the lovers are short of both. Yet, in this witty and fantastical vision, Marvell has compressed a panorama of history and geography. According to *The Garden,* the inner landscape of the mind is limitless. Within it lies an "ocean" of creatures. The poet's imagination can, like God's, create "other worlds": better worlds, like the New Jerusalem. At the same time, it has God's ability to demolish the imperfect ones, "Annihilating all that's made, / To a green thought in a green shade" (43–48). When the world ends, God will do both at once, destroying the imperfect earth for a new creation. Equally, Marvell himself constantly obliterates foreign variety in order to remake it in England's image. The world shrinks into the poet's brain. The great Garden of creation reveals itself in an English country garden. The world's empire has a homing instinct for England. In Marvell's mental journey introversion and expansion are indistinguishable.

For him the world was always really the greater England, one Protestant isle that could grow to fill the earth. Ultimately the "Garden of the World" would *be* the world. Time and place would cease to exist. In that magical merging, all things would fall into place: into simultaneity, harmony, and unity. That ordering will be freedom, progress without movement. Traveling, whether actual or in the mind, would no longer be necessary, for everything would have arrived at its destination. In Marvell's view, we are all in the same boat.

# NOTES

Quotations from Marvell's poems are taken from Andrew Marvell, *Complete Poems*, ed. Elizabeth Story Donno (Harmondsworth: 1972). Quotations from his letters are taken from Andrew Marvell, *The Poems and Letters*, ed. H. M. Margoliouth, Pierre Legouis, and E. E. Duncan-Jones, 3rd ed., 2 vols. (Oxford: 1971).

1. The best biography is by Pierre Legouis, *Andrew Marvell: Poet, Puritan, Patriot*, 2nd ed. (Oxford: 1968). Some useful additional detail is provided by Hilton Kelliher, *Andrew Marvell: Poet and Politician 1621–78* (London: 1978). For another view, see Michael McKeon, "Pastoralism, Puritanism, Imperialism, Scientism: Andrew Marvell and the Problem of Mediation", *Yearbook of English Studies* 13 (1983): 47–65.
2. Samuel Parker, A *Reproof to the Rehearsal Transpros'd* (London: 1673) 227;

Edward Gillett and Kenneth A. MacMahon, *A History of Hull* (Hull: 1980); Pauline Burdon, "The Second Mrs. Marvell", *Notes and Queries* new series 227 (1982): 33–44; Pauline Burdon, "Marvell and His Kindred", *Notes and Queries* new series 229 (1984): 172–80, 379–85.

3. Margarita Stocker, *Apocalyptic Marvell: The Second Coming in Seventeenth-Century Poetry* (Sussex: 1986).
4. For the reputation of Hormuz, see R. R. Cawley, *Milton and the Literature of Travel* (Princeton: 1951) 78–79.
5. *Purchas His Pilgrimes* 20 vols. (Glasgow: 1905–7) dedication; Stocker 165–201; Louis B. Wright, *Religion and Empire* (Chapel Hill: 1943).
6. J. G. Stevenson, *Admiral Robert Blake* (London: 1910); G. M. D. Howat, *Stuart and Cromwellian Foreign Policy* (London: 1974) 69–94. The background to the poem is discussed in detail by Margarita Stocker and Timothy Raylor, "A New Marvell Manuscript", *English Literary Renaissance* (forthcoming).
7. D. H. Pennington, *Seventeenth Century Europe* (London: 1970) 339–61; Michael Howard, ed., *Sweden as a Great Power, 1611–1697* (London: 1968); Georgina Masson, *Queen Christina* (London: 1974).
8. Margarita Stocker, "Remodelling Virgil: Marvell's New Astraea", *Studies in Philology* 84 (1987): 159–79.
9. The opening lines are misunderstood by W. Hilton Kelliher, "Marvell's 'A Letter to Dr. Ingelo'", *Review of English Studies* new series 20 (1969): 50–57. For the north's unsavory reputation, see E. S. Bates, *Touring in 1600* (1911; repr. London: 1987) 154–62; Cawley, 50, 80–81.
10. Thomas Birch, ed., *State Papers of John Thurloe*, 7 vols. (London: 1742) 7.298.
11. See Guy de Miège, *A Relation of Three Embassies* (London: 1669) 318–19, 373–74, 430–31.
12. K. H. D. Haley, *William of Orange and the English Opposition, 1672–4* (Oxford: 1953) 57–59; Keith Feiling, *English Foreign Policy, 1660–1672* (London: 1930).

# THE EXOTIC IN RESTORATION DRAMA

## George Parfitt, Nottingham University

When the monarchy was restored in 1660 Charles II licensed Thomas Killigrew and William Davenant to run theaters in London. Both men were genteel and both, less surprisingly, royalists. Both men had experience of foreign countries, and there are good reasons to expect plays performed in England between 1660 and 1700 to show an interest in such countries.

First, there was by 1660 a long history of diplomatic and cultural contact between England and other countries, notably France, Spain, and Italy. Foreign relations had for a long time meant a steady pulse of diplomatic journeys and postings that gave extended foreign experience both to the socially prominent persons who fronted such missions and to their staffs, which included both the genteel and the less socially eminent. Moreover, J. W. Stoye has documented the growth of the Continental tour in the late sixteenth and seventeenth centuries as an important part of a genteel education,[1] while English experience of other countries was also enriched by the diplomatic and cultural visits made by foreigners to England.[2]

Second, by 1660 the English had been participating for decades in European voyages of travel and exploration throughout the world, this providing firsthand knowledge of non-European lands. English involvement is particularly evident in searches for the Northwest and Northeast passages, in exploration and settlement along the North American Atlantic seaboard, and in probings around the coasts of Africa and into the Pacific. Nontravelers could read the published accounts of voyages made by English and other explorers, and by 1660 it is possible to see the seeds of empire in English settlements abroad.[3]

Third, there is a history of exile. This includes men and women leaving England for religious or political reasons: fugitives from the Catholic restoration of Mary I, Catholic refugees from Protestant Tudor monarchs, and Puritan exiles from Tudor and Stuart Anglicanism. Most immediately relevant to the Restoration, however, is the flight of royalists during the commonwealth and protectorate. Then there is the history of foreigners coming to England as exiles of various kinds, examples being the exodus of Scots to England with James I and the influx of Huguenots from the French religious wars. This pattern of exile is often one of departure and return, the pattern sometimes being repeated. Royalist refugees often returned to England during the commonwealth for visits connected with politics or property, while religious exiles often crossed the Channel or the Atlantic for personal reasons or as domestc policies changed.

There were also other types of contact between the English and other nations. Trade is an obvious example, and there were frequent opportunities that arose from fighting, either in English forces or as a mercenary. These various kinds of association with foreign lands, when taken with the vicarious experience through print, suggest that the England of 1660 was far from isolated and that knowledge of other countries need not be confined to the genteel. But although we should expect such knowledge to be represented in Restoration drama, we should also expect this to be defined by specific circumstances.

Since the commonwealth had closed the theaters, and since licit drama after 1660 was patronized, restricted, and controlled by the monarchy, we should expect Restoration theater to be royalist, although it is a mistake to believe that a royalist stance is necessarily a simple one. Royalism does not preclude debates about succession and monarchic power, and, at least from the time of the Exclusion crisis (1678–85), royalists had problems of loyalty to solve.[4] Nevertheless, a royalist position would be likely to produce a drama that takes a negative view of aspects of the exotic that might suggest a favorable response to the interregnum. We should hardly expect a sympathetic account of Puritan exiles from the regime of Charles I or of Cromwellian successes in foreign affairs. Positively, we might expect Restoration drama to reflect aspects of royalist exile, to show interest in the cultures of countries where such exiles congregated (especially France and the Low Countries). Such interest would not necessarily be favorable, for royalists did not always have a comfortable time in exile: the experiences of Charles II himself show how desolating such exile could be. But however the exile experience might be shaped, it could be expected to include interest shown in ideas relating to politics in England. The theory and practice of absolutism in France is an obvious example, as are theories of nonresistance, discussions of state religion and religious tolerance, and the nature of Catholicism in Europe.

Such factors might be expected to define which aspects of the foreign would be emphasized in Restoration drama, but different emphases are clearly possible. Knowledge derived from exploration provides the possibility of stage presentation of exotic locations, strange customs, and costumes. Familiarity with foreign countries allows for the staging of exotic history, staging that might be instructive, exemplary, or hortatory. There is the possibility of the stage's showing something of the cultures of foreign countries, and experience of such countries could influence native theatrical techniques. The materials for presentation of all these aspects of the exotic were at hand, both through direct experience of foreign countries and in the knowledge to be gleaned from travel books, collections of voyages, guide books, even etiquette manuals. Moreover, the material conditions of Restoration drama seem to allow of such representation.

It is only after 1660 that conditions in the English public theaters allow for mimetic representation of the exotic, and here the main development concerns scenery, as the experiments of Inigo Jones in the court masque are carried over into the Restoration theater, where backdrops and sliding flats allow the possibility of exact reproduction of foreign scenes. Since Restoration theaters were covered, mimetic lighting effects could be attempted, and exploration increases the possibility of accurate costuming. But such mimetic possibilities were limited by technical inexperience and economic factors. Few people in 1660 had much experience in preparing, mounting, and operating scenery and lighting. Sets of costumes mean expense, and Restoration theater was scarcely popular drama. Government control severely restricted the number of theaters, and the evidence is that the two (sometimes one) that functioned struggled to fill seats. Yet the potential clearly existed for detailed representation of foreign settings and cultures, and the biographies of the dramatists suggest that, in many cases, they were equipped to dramatize such presentation through direct experience.

John Crowne, for example, was born in Nova Scotia and was about twenty when he first came to England. Aston Cockayne, born in 1608, was in France in 1632 and traveled also in Italy. Thomas Otway (born 1651/52) was in Holland in 1678–79, and William Wycherley (born 1640) went to France when he was about fifteen. There are several more extreme cases. Although the biography of Aphra Behn is riddled with myth, it is known that she lived in Surinam as a child and, around 1666, spent some time in Holland, apparently as a spy. George Etherege served Charles II and James II as a diplomat, coming to know Constantinople, The Hague, Ratisbon, and Paris (where he died in 1691). His last years are a form of exile, since he resisted the accession of William and Mary. Sir John Vanbrugh, born in London of Flemish descent, studied architecture in France between 1683 and 1685, being imprisoned at Vincennes and in the Bastille in 1686. Thomas Killigrew was forty-eight years old in 1660, by which time he had traveled extensively in France, Switzerland, Italy, and Spain. Roger Boyle, first earl of Orrery (born 1621, in Ireland) has a life patterned by travel, much of this between Ireland and England, but taking in France, Italy, and Germany. Against such examples there are dramatists who seem not to have traveled abroad: William Congreve (but he lived in Ireland as a child), John Dryden, Nathaniel Lee, Elkanah Settle. But these had access to books.

The plays that such dramatists wrote show clear evidence of interest in foreign settings. Aphra Behn's *The Amorous Prince* is set in "The Court of Florence", her *The Widow Ranter* in Virginia, and *The Dutch Lover* in Madrid. Cockayne's *The Tragedy of Ovid* is set in "Tomas, a city in Pontus", and his *Trappolin* in "part of Italy". Congreve's only tragedy, *The Mourning Bride*, is set in Granada; Crowne's *Juliana* in "Warsaw in Poland"; Dryden's *Secret Love* in Sicily and *Tyrannick Love* "under the Walls of Aquileia".[5]

Such listing could be extended ad nauseam and would cover a wide variety of locations. Of a sample of some seventy Restoration plays set abroad, almost a third are set in Italy, while another quarter involve Spain and another quarter settings that may broadly be called "Eastern" (ranging from Jerusalem to India). A comparable list for between 1580 and 1640 shows the same tendency to use foreign locations and a similar proportion of Italian settings. It also indicates far less interest in Spain and in "Eastern" settings. Neither before nor after the Restoration is there any sign of much concern with locations in the Low Countries, the states of Germany, the Scandinavian countries, Ireland, or eastern Europe. The "New World" of the Americas also makes little impact, although Behn and Dryden show some interest. For present purposes, the main development after 1660 lies in the opening up of the East and in the increased concern with Spain. In passing, it might be noticed how surprising some of the neglected areas are, at least on the surface, bearing in mind how important the Low Countries, Ireland, and the career of Gustavus Adolphus of Sweden are in English history of the seventeenth century.

The evidence of Restoration play texts suggests, moreover, increased interest in precise locations. Marlowe's *The Jew of Malta* and Shakespeare's *Hamlet* are formally set in Malta and Denmark, respectively, but the 1633 quarto of the former and the 1605 quarto of the latter are typical of pre-Restoration play texts in leaving location to be deduced. By contrast, Restoration texts seem concerned with greater specificity. The text may indicate a particular location within a country or city. So Dryden's *Don Sebastian* is set in the castle of Alcazor and Boyle's *The Tragedy of Mustapha* in Solyman's camp and pavilion, while Behn's *The Young King* stipulates "the Court of Dacia, between the two Armies just before the Town".[6] But it is also noticeable that a number of play texts are concerned to indicate several different locations within a city or country. In *The Young King* the second act alone moves from "A Castle or Prison on the sea" to

"Another Room in the Prison", to "A Grove", to "A Chamber". Lee's *Sophonisba* is more static, but specifies, within "Zena", "a pleasant Grove", the Carthaginian camp, the Roman camp, and Bellona's temple. For *The Indian Emperour* Dryden indicates a "pleasant Indian country", a temple, "The Magitians Cave", terrain "Betwixt the two Armies", a "Chamber Royal", "A pleasant Grotto" and "A Prison". But, of course, Tudor and Stuart plays often also contain indications of a variety of locations, and it might be objected that Restoration play texts prove little about performance, offering merely literary elaboration. But Tudor and Stuart texts rarely provide indications of location in stage directions, and the lack of scenery meant that locations could hardly be said to be represented anyway, whereas the Restoration theater used both scenery and scene changes. Moreover, instructions relating to set in Restoration texts are often theatrical rather than literary. Lee's *Lucius Junius Brutus* has "The scene draws, showing the sacrifice: one burning and another crucified . . .", while Settle's *The Empress of Morocco* refers to a "Prospect of a Clouded Sky" and Dryden's *The Rival Ladies* has "Through a Rock is discover'd. . . .". The play texts strongly suggest an interest in defining locations, these being at times both particular and exotic: Lee's temple of Bellona, Dryden's "under the walls of the Albayzin" (*Conquest of Granada* 1), Behn's "Sevana" (*The Widow Ranter*).[7]

Yet even on the evidence of the play texts, such seeming particularity is deceptive. Stage directions appear to indicate particular locations to be represented in detail on the stage—but only until we realize how often certain types of scene occur. "Camps" are indicated in, among others, *Mustapha, Sophonisba,* the second part of *The Conquest of Granada,* and *The Widow Ranter*. "Groves" are ubiquitous (Behn's *Abdelazar,* Crowne's *Charles VIII, The Rival Ladies,* etc.), as are gardens, prisons, and temples. Such repetition does not, of course, prove that each garden or prison was the same on stage, but there is evidence that stock scenes were common, while the economic realities of the Restoration stage further suggest that highly particularized scenery was generally improbable. The evidence of Restoration costuming also tells against particularization.[8]

If, as Nichol suggests, the same palace was used for more than one play (or the same cave or temple), it follows that where the set type refers to a foreign country it was likely to indicate "foreign", perhaps of some broad kind (like "Eastern") rather than any particular exotic location. "The exotic" is then little more than that which is not home. Dryden's *The Indian Emperour,* with its "pleasant Indian country", a temple, a magician's cave, Mexico, and an "Indian Hamock", clearly suggests exotic sets conveying a strong sense of otherness.

We should also bear in mind that Restoration stage sets appear, as it were, in a deep oblong box, open at one end and with a considerable area between the open end and the audience. This is the area of the proscenium, on which much of the acting took place. It would seem that, given such staging, the set of *The Indian Emperour* would read very differently from those for Lawrence's mining plays, written early in our century. Lawrence has an obvious naturalistic concern, encouraging an audience to become absorbed in the set and to believe in its authenticity. Dryden's stage seems designed so that sets are to be gazed on as distant and exotic. This "otherness" is important, but not particular. The sets for *The Indian Emperour* suggest a vague and general "Indies" rather than any specific part of Mexico. The effect was perhaps analogous to that of film Westerns, where saloons, mountains, and arid landscapes create a broad sense of frontier or Indian country, rather than a particular topography. Also, Restoration sets are located within a range from the totally familiar (the settings of London-based comedies) to that which, for most spectators, would be wholly unknown at firsthand (Mexico, Morocco). The mean point would be settings within such countries as Italy or Spain, which are European but culturally distinct from England. Locations in such countries might be familiar, because of broad resemblances between European countries and the frequency of contact between them, while remaining exotic because of cultural differences. An audience seeing Etherege's *The Man of Mode* is encouraged to regard the sets as depicting familiar territory. At the other extreme, the Morocco represented in Settle's *The Emperor of Morocco* and the Mexico of *The Indian Emperour,* while not identical, would both be striking mainly for their un-Englishness. The evidence of stage directions does not allow us to conclude that there was any consistent and detailed concern with topographical accuracy. "The exotic" would seem to be a general concept.

It would, however, be possible for the sets to provide a general sense of the exotic that was made particular by what was spoken. The verbal text, in other words, might ensure that generalized scenes were read as specific to a particular time or place. Jacobean dramatists, working without scenery, were quite capable of using texts to create such an effect, as Jonson did for *Sejanus* and Middleton for *A Chaste Maid in Cheapside.* It is therefore necessary to look at texts to see what kind of representation of the exotic they provide.

Prefacing the 1667 text of *The Indian Emperour,* Dryden provides a note on the "connexion of the Indian Emperour, to the Indian Queen", and this note suggests that Dryden had done some reading. We have seen that he is concerned to convey a sense of the exotic, but it is also evident that he wants to establish some striking contrasts between the Indians and the Spanish. One of his most impressive pictures is that for the opening of 4.3, where the set calls for "A pleasant Grotto . . . in it a fountain spouting". Here the Spanish are "lying carelessly un-armed", with Indian women, one of whom sings a Restoration love lyric, after which two of the Spaniards "Dance a Saraband with Castanietas", upon which Goyomar's Indians surprise the unarmed invaders. Dryden has created a thematically rich episode and seems concerned to shade the Mexican setting into the familiar ambience of pastoral. But he shows little interest, here or elsewhere, in using the verbal text to make the texture specific. The scene's dialogue contains almost nothing to pin the episode to the particular location in Mexico. Instead it concentrates on theme and moral statement that would, with minimal alteration, fit into a play set almost anywhere.

Boyle's *The Tragedy of Mustapha* was played at Lincoln's Inn in 1665. It concerns Solyman's invasion of Hungary and is set in "Solyman's Camp, and his Pavilion". The opening lines, by Rustan, offer a basic reading of the set:

> What influence, mighty Sultan, rules the Day,
> And stops your Course, where Glory rules the Way?
> Th' Hungarian Armies hasten from the Field,
> And Buda waits for your Approach to yield . . .

Here, elementary information is given, which can be read onto the set, elucidating what that set presumably only indicates at a general level. The set, of the type camp, is defined further by the reference to "mighty Sultan" in the very first line, but, more helpfully, the location of the camp is given as on the edge of Europe by the allusions to Hungarian armies and the city of Buda. Boyle, throughout his play, uses a limited number of exotic terms (personal names, titles of officials, a few place names) to create and maintain a sense of otherness; and he supplements this with some quite powerfully exotic stage pictures:

> Enter six Mutes. One of them advances before the rest, and kneels down, delivers Mustapha a black box with a Parchment, the Sultan's Great Seal hanging at it in a black Ribband. Then he holds up a Bow-string, and makes Signs that he should kneel, and submit to the Sultan's Sentence.[9]

But Boyle goes no further. He makes no attempt to provide a verbal texture to indicate a sense of being Hungarian or Turk, nor does he seek to develop the few particulars he does use. If his Hungary is compared with the Venice of Jonson's *Volpone,* it seems both thin and anonymous, but it is typical of Restoration plays set abroad.

Another interesting example is Behn's *Abdelazar,* set in "Spain, and in the

Camp". Spain had a long history of occupation by the Moors, and this provides the possibility of sustained comparison between two cultures that were profoundly different but that cohabited for a long time. Yet the dramatist makes little effort to develop such a possibility. In the first scene, Abdelazar reflects upon the suggestion that the Spanish queen has been in his chamber with him (she has, but Abdelazar is dissimulating):

> The Queen with me! with me! a Moor! a Devil!
> A Slave of Barbary! for so
> Your gay young Courtiers christen me—But, Don,
> Although my Skin be black, within my Veins
> Runs Blood as red, and royal as the best.—
> My Father, great Abdela, with his Life
> Lost too his Crown; both most unjustly ravish'd
> By Tyrant Philip . . .[10]

Here Abdelazar offers a Shylock-like claim to human identity and alleges a royalty parallel to that of the Spanish king. But he also registers, with reminders of *The Merchant of Venice* and *Othello*, his sense of difference. His lines quite powerfully represent the play's basic theme, the racial and cultural conflict between Abdelazar and the Spaniards, and they allow Behn to draw on associations that involve stereotyped links between darkness and evil, blackness and potency. But the dramatist is content to stay within the cliché, which is used adroitly, but without any cultural, historical, or topographical detail. Dryden's *Don Sebastian* has a similar setting, but no more concern to explore racial difference. In 4.3 the "Noble Portuguese", Dorax, removes his "Turbant" and puts on "a Peruque, Hat and Crevat". The surface difference adequately represents the level of Dryden's interest in the specifics of being Moor.

The representation of the exotic is not, however, just a matter of plays set abroad; and it is worth asking what ideas of the exotic there are in plays set in England. A majority of Restoration comedies are set here—more exactly, in London, and most exactly in the homes and pleasure haunts of the gentry.

Congreve's *The Way of the World* is, of course, a highly sophisticated play, and it concerns itself with gentry who aim to be seen as witty, poised, and expert at disguising emotions. Gentry (here and elsewhere) are not workers and have ample time for leisure. So Congreve's play opens in "A Chocolate House", moves to Saint James's Park and then to various rooms in Lady Wishfort's house. One of its characters is the country-based, would-be traveler Sir Wilfull Witwoud, whose travel plans are mocked by Mirabel and Fainall:

*Mir.* For travel! Why, the man that I mean is above forty.
*Fain.* No matter for that; 'tis for the honour of England, that all Europe should know we have blockheads of all ages . . .(2.2)

Witwoud is the play's only traveler and his plans are hardly central, but they are derided whenever mentioned. For Lady Wishfort the only appropriate traveling for Sir Wilfull would be to pagan parts:

> . . . get thee but far enough, to the Saracens, or the Tartars, or the Turks!—for thou art not fit to live in a Christian commonwealth, thou beastly Pagan! (4.2)

Lady Wishfort implicitly locates her "Christian commonwealth" in London. Her "Pagan" is up from the country and should, when abroad, show decorum by seeking an appropriate location—among Saracen, Tartar, or Turk. Lady Wishfort is hardly an idealized character, but her complacent English urbanism is not seriously challenged and the superficial nature of her allusions to the exotic is not undercut by anything from other characters. She herself knows about Spanish cosmetics and alludes to "Maritornes the Asturian in Don Quixote" (3.1). There is scattered use of French terms throughout. Mirabel has "beau-monde" (which the O.E.D. dates to 1714) in 2.2, while Millamant uses "drap de Berri things" (3.3) and the exclamatory "Ah L'etourdi!" (4.1). But such allusions are rare and only marginally inform the play's texture. No character shows much interest in non-English societies: culturally the play is turned inward.

Etherege's *She Would If She Could* (1668) is similar in containing only a smatter of foreign allusions. Courtall uses "fatigue" as a French word (1.1) and "pique" (3.1), but the latter is marginal, since the word came into English in the sixteenth century. Rake-hell boosts a sword's value by claiming that "The hilt is true French-wrought, and *doree* by the best workman in France" (3.3).[11] There is little else; little sign of anything foreign to mock or emulate. The same intimation of an insular society is found again in *The Country Gentleman,* by Robert Howard and the duke of Buckingham. It is unusual for the period in presenting the country and its values as superior to the city and its values. Among the antagonists of the "exemplary country gentleman" Sir Richard Plainbred, who "believes in old-fashioned country virtues", is Mistress Finical Fart, a middle-aged pretender to gentility who affects French words and fashions. She is type-fixed in the opening scene, with her references to fashionable French restaurants and her list of French dishes, the latter set against Sir Richard's sturdy "beef and mutton".[12]

Howard and Buckingham are obviously using a version of abroad for social comedy (and it is a significant cliché that Fart is a pretender to gentility) and in support of their rural chauvinism. True Englishness is bucolic. This is a good example of a general tendency in Restoration comedy, whereby allusion to the exotic concentrates on France and uses such allusion less to belittle French society than to assert the superior Englishness of those who avoid aping foreigners. The classic example, Etherege's Flutter (*The Man of Mode*) is absurd not so much because he pretends Frenchness as because he reneges on his natural Englishness. When aped by the English, French culture becomes absurd. Basically, the thinness of allusion to the exotic in Restoration comedy helps create the sense of the gentry turned in upon itself, complacently aloof from the foreign. For such an introverted social fragment the foreign is of little interest, but it does not follow that foreign is in itself funny. Famously, Restoration comedy is concerned with true wit. Its awareness of French sophistication in dancing, cooking, and dress is recognized in the allusions, but these are used to satirize those English who ape foreigners. Fart and Flutter are attacked for the false wit of racial treachery. Similarly, the rural Englishness of Plainbred is not so much antiforeign as pro-English. It is reminiscent of those analyses before the Civil War that had it that all would be well if the clock were turned back, and it sees the aping of foreigners as dangerous because innovatory. Allusion to the exotic can be quite neutral in Restoration comedy: it becomes pointed when used to indicate pretension to true wit. This suggests that serious exploration of otherness is rare in such comedy—but the same is true, as suggested above, with plays set abroad. Glib chauvinism can, of course, be found and used to support this point, as with the coarse and cliché-ridden racism of Dryden's *Amboyna* (which is the only Restoration play I have come across that deals with Holland, although by distancing the Anglo-Dutch theme to the East Indies).

We are, it seems, left with something of a paradox, a drama where many plays are set abroad, but where little interest is shown in the possibilities of detailed presentation of the exotic, even though the materials for such presentation were available. Is this use of foreign settings merely a convention, and the scattering of allusions to the exotic just a textural dusting?

It remains clear, despite some revisionism, that the dominant element in Restoration audiences was genteel, and that the dramatists saw themselves as addressing the gentry. But it is also clear that to describe Restoration society as a whole in terms of the gentry is ridiculous. There was no mass conversion of "puritans" to hedonism (as witness Behn's *The City-Heiress* of 1682), and the rise of Quakerism is as important a social fact as the life of Rochester. There is also no lack of serious political life in the Restoration, even if such life is (wrongly) defined in narrowly parliamentary terms. Yet there can be little doubt that Restoration comedy, together with such material as Rochester's letters and the *Memoirs of the Count Grammont*, describes a limited truth—the existence of a strongly hedonistic and cynical gentry stratum in Restoration society. This may be linked with the Caroline Cavalier ideal and with a sense of release after the period of the interregnum. But royalists who imagined that the Restoration would be of a Golden Age were often disappointed. Even while the fact of the republic almost necessitated a kingship cult with the return of monarchy, the personality of Charles II encouraged a cynical view of royal propaganda. In *Absalom and Achitophel* Dryden caught the tension perfectly: Charles/David is both a monarch of near-absolute power and a libertine. The point here is simply that the Restoration encouraged both hedonism among the victors and spiritualism among the defeated. One level of interest, then, in the exotic among theatergoers may simply have been in the exotic as locus for escapism and sensation.

Such a view used to be heavily emphasized, but Restoration drama is inevitably political in an inevitably political age. Charles II, deftly playing the merry monarch, survived Dutch wars and internal unrest throughout a long reign, but in 1688 the execution of the father (Charles I) was echoed in the flight of the younger son (James II). The Cavalier Parliament of 1661 rapidly became critical of Charles I, and it was Parliament that brought down James. Religious fears mar the period, as do failures of foreign policy. Governments survive by keeping alive memories of monarchless England and by controlling freedom of expression as far as possible. Being small and economically vulnerable, the London theater was fairly easy to control—and such themes as rebellion, democracy, the right to resist tyrants, could not be discussed in a native and contemporary setting. Such restriction may also suggest why the locations of plays set abroad show the emphases indicated earlier in this essay. Relations with France and the Low Countries were too sensitive and unstable for dramatists to feel that such locations could readily be used without drawing in banned English themes. But setting plays in relatively safe exotic locations could give some freedom, although even this degree of license was uncertain—as Lee found out with his Roman tragedy of *Lucius Junius Brutus*. Behn's *Abdelazar* illustrates what could be tried.

We saw earlier how limited the presentation of the exotic is here, but that it was enough to create the sense of not-England. Yet the themes of the play include a number that could hardly be closer to recent English history. Florella, the Spanish wife of the Moor Abdelazar, is courted by the king, Ferdinand. Abdelazar suggests that Florella kill the king, ostensibly because of his advances. Left alone she reflects:

> Murder my King! the Man that loves me too—

What Fiend, what Fury such an act wou'd do?
My trembling Hand wou'd not the Weapon bear,
And I should sooner strike it here—than there.
(pointing to her breast)
. . .
To save my King's, my Life I will expose,
No Martyr dies in a more glorious Cause. (3.1)

This is impeccably orthodox. Any Cavalier would agree, and the situation is made the more poignant in that Florella seems to have a choice of moral imperatives—refraining from regicide or losing her honor. Bearing in mind the sexual exploits of Charles II, this has an additional resonance.

In the following scene Alonzo underlines the impossibility of regicide. He is led to believe that Florella (his sister) has been bewhored by Ferdinand, but is clear that revenge is impossible for him: "Heaven can only punish a king". The queen, involved with Abdelazar, calls this view "religious Patience", but points out that if Alonzo sustains it, "All Spain must suffer" and that "Ages shall ensue/Shall curse thy Name". Alonzo's answer suggests that the way out is not regicide but sororicide:

My Sister's in my power, her Honour's mine;
I can command her Life, though not my King's.
(3.2)

Such a position would satisfy the most rigorous absolutist in the years after 1660.

Ferdinand's death raises the question of the succession. Alonzo simply asserts that Philip, Ferdinand's brother, is now "our King", but Abdelazar opposes such orthodoxy. The trickery that this clash brings needs not be detailed here, but it is important to notice how the clash is articulated in language that must have been resonant to a Restoration audience. Abdelazar speaks of "Fears of Usurpation and of Tyranny", and the cardinal speaks of proceeding to the election of a successor. In the play's last moments, Osmin, a Moor and officer to Abdelazar, unbinds the captured Philip. When asked what he is up to, he replies "To set you free, my Prince". Philip's response is figuratively interesting:

Thou are some Angel sure, in that dark Cloud.

Abdelazar's blackness had earlier been associated with the devil; Osmin's loyalty to his monarch transforms the diabolic to the angelic.

Behn's play figures Abdelazar's overthrow and the triumph of right (Philip). Florella, Alonzo, and Osmin give eloquent voice to attitudes that could only please Restoration royalists. But what is interesting is how an exotic setting has been used to allow discussion of issues that could not be given a native context. In any full discussion of such issues as regicide and succession there is always the theoretical possibility of a resolution other than that actually achieved. If there were not, there would be no tension, nothing to resolve, and Abdelazar, villain though he is, is allowed to make his case with considerable power. The obvious relevance of Behn's themes to contemporary English issues is strengthened by the stressing of such loaded words as "tyrant" and "interest". *Abdelazar* is not at all unusual in using the exotic in this way. How intricate the politics of Restoration tragedy could be is evident to anyone who reads Otway's *Venice Preserv'd,* particularly in the light of its prologue and variant epilogues.

Another way in which exotic sets work in this drama is more elusive. We saw earlier that sets that depict foreign locations tend to present the general rather than the particular. It is perhaps obvious that such generalization, supported by the heavy use of moral commonplaces, will facilitate comparisons between home and abroad, past and present. But it also contributes to a drama of universals. If one castle or grove looked much like another on the Restoration stage, if texture tends to emphasize moral absolutes rather than specifics of character or location, and if acting style tends to the formal rather than the naturalistic, it becomes easy for the plays to operate as general accounts of aspects of human experience. As such, they enunciate general propositions about values and behavior in a manner reminiscent of other aspects of seventeenth-century thought: the emphasis on legal maxims[13] and Locke's argument that moral language should be capable of fixed definition.[14] Such a use of the exotic works against that awareness of difference that is offered by exploration and cultural exchange. Such evidence will seem secondary to that which can be used to argue essential similarities. Thus the conflicts between duty and love experienced by the Indians in *The Indian Emperour* are to be seen as interesting not because they come from particular Indian experience, but because they show that such conflicts are ubiquitous. They are, in fact, much the same as the conflicts in Dryden's *Aureng-Zebe,* which is formally set on the other side of the world. In *Venice Preserv'd,* the conflict between love and friendship has nothing that could be called a Venetian anchorage in any specific sense.

So it would seem that the failure of Restoration plays set abroad to make detailed use of available knowledge of the exotic is less a matter of ignorance or stupidity than of choice, and of choice at a finally philosophical level: the specifics are simply not what is most important. In fact, it might be wise to avoid settings where connections with contemporary England's politics could be made. At a more mundane level, a generalized use of the exotic allowed the chance of some consideration of themes that could not be given a local habitation, for even impeccably royalist presentation of such themes as rebellion or absolutism in a native context could scarcely avoid giving weight to alternative viewpoints. Drama is an awkward medium in its physicality, and if this suggests why even loyalist presentations of tricky themes were prohibited in native contexts, it also suggests how problematic such themes could be even in foreign guise. Even generalized sets are palpable, while bodies, sets, and costumes are inevitably allusive in their resemblances to other bodies, sets, and costumes. Connections get made, as with *Lucius Junius Brutus,* while Restoration prologues and epilogues often go out of their way to hint how such connections might be made. This allows the suggestion that the use of the exotic in this drama is seldom historical or geographic as we normally understand these terms. The dramatists avoid the specificity that we usually regard as the essence of historical or geographic discussion and instead, by representing general otherness, suggest the ubiquity of problems, personalities, and possibilities, thus creating shapings that are formally about an exotic setting and that may yet comment upon the Restoration experience in England.

A final point returns us to Restoration comedy set in England. We saw that such comedy seldom shows much interest in the exotic and that what detail is found is often linked with ideas of racial treachery. It seems that it is un-English to show much interest in the foreign: a modest familiarity is acceptable for the gentry, but anything more is a kind of treason. The un-Englishness of the exotic is what matters here, and this helps to define true Englishness. The chauvinism that results may, as with Plainbred, be backward-looking to the point of reactionary myth making, or it may be part of that inward-looking aspect noticed in Congreve and Etherege. The richness of other lands and cultures, made available in ways touched on at the start of this essay, is largely ignored, in the interest of boosting a sense of Englishness. This had, perhaps, been badly damaged in the years of no monarch. It might also be suggested that such turning inward is what marks and makes possible the coming of British imperialism.

## NOTES

Quotations are from *The Works of Aphra Behn,* ed. M. Summers, 6 vols. (London: 1915); Aston Cockayne, *Dramatic Works,* ed. J. Maidment and W. H. Logan (Edinburgh: 1874); William Congreve, *Plays,* ed. A. C. Ewald (London: n.d.); John

Crowne, *Dramatic Works,* ed. J. Maidment and W. H. Logan (Edinburgh: 1873); John Dryden, *Works,* ed. E. N. Hooker and H. T. Swedenberg (Berkeley: 1956–); *Five Heroic Plays,* ed. B. Dobree (London: 1960).

1. J. W. Stoye, *English Travellers Abroad 1604–1667* (New York: 1968), esp. pp. 58ff.
2. Caroline Hibbard remarks that "London and the court were . . . alive with foreign agents and foreign visitors . . ." (*Charles I and the Popish Plot* [Chapel Hill: 1983] 11).
3. See, for example, R. C. Simmons, *The American Colonies* (London: 1981), especially the opening chapters.
4. See the discussion in J. C. D. Clark, *English Society 1688–1832* (Cambridge, Eng.: 1985).
5. Aphra Behn, ed. M. Summers, *Works* (London: 1915); Aston Cockayne, ed. J. Maidment and W. H. Logan, *Dramatic Works* (Edinburgh: 1874); William Congreve, ed. A. C. Ewald, *Plays* (London: n.d.); John Crowne, ed. J. Maidment and W. H. Logan, *Dramatic Works* (Edinburgh: 1873); John Dryden, ed. E. N. Hooker and H. T. Swedenberg *Works* (Berkeley: 1956– ).
6. Dryden; Orrery, *Five Heroic Plays,* ed. B. Dobree (London: 1960); Behn.
7. Behn; Nathaniel Lee, in Dobree; Dryden; Lee, *Lucius Junius Brutus,* ed. J. Loftis (London: 1968); Elkanah Settle, in Dobree.
8. Behn; Crowne. On Restoration stock scenes see A. Nicoll, *A History of English Drama 1660–1900* (Cambridge, Eng.: 1952), 1.35ff.; J. L. Styan, *Restoration Comedy in Performance* (Cambridge, Eng.: 1986) 27ff. On costume see Nicoll 49ff. and Styan 45ff.
9. Act 5 (Dobree 76)
10. Behn.
11. Congreve, *The Way of the World,* ed. K. M. Lynch (London: 1965); George Etherege, *She Would If She Could,* ed. M. Taylor (London: 1973).
12. Howard and Buckingham, *The Country Gentleman,* ed. A. H. Scouten and R. D. Hume (London: 1976). The quotations are from the prefatory "Persons in the Play", except the last, which is from I.i.
13. See J. P. Sommerville, *Politics and Ideology in England 1603–1640* (London: 1986) part 1.
14. In his *Of Human Understanding.*

# "THE VARIOUS OFF'RINGS OF THE WORLD": ABROAD AS PERCEIVED BY DRYDEN AND POPE

Timothy Cook, Kingston Polytechnic

In considering how the two major Augustan satirists saw the world outside Britain, one is faced with the difficulty that neither of them even ventured outside England. Indeed, Dryden seems never to have felt inclined to travel at all, although his long career as dramatist and translator took him mentally to several exotic places. A clue to his views on actual travel may perhaps be found in his opinion that "a Poet, in the description of a beautiful Garden or Meadow, will please our imagination more than the place itself can our sight" (*Works* 17.40). Of his anti-Dutch play *Amboyna* he writes, "No map shows Holland truer than our play" (*Prologue* 26), and perhaps for him the essence of a country and its people was best received distilled through the writer's art rather than as an ingredient of the confusing medley of experiences lived through by the traveler. In any case, his busy, highly public career probably gave him no time for expeditions overseas.

Pope's case is different. In 1714 George Berkeley, writing from Leghorn, refers to his friend's "half-formed desire of coming to Italy" (*Correspondence* 1.221), while two years later Pope himself playfully suggests an amorous rendezvous there to Lady Mary Wortley Montagu (*Correspondence* 1.370). However, nothing came of this idea or of later projects for traveling abroad with Swift and Gay. A latish letter to the former provides an explanation:

> Why cannot I cross the Sea? The unhappiest Malady I have to complain of, the unhappiest Accident of my whole Life, is that Weakness of the Breast which makes the Physicians of opinion that a strong Vomit would kill me: I have never taken one, nor had a natural Motion that way, in fifteen years. (*Correspondence* 4.179)

Since both Dryden and Pope lacked any direct visual experiences of the wider world to draw on, their awareness of abroad was bound to be shaped by whatever literary, political, and anthropological material, including received national stereotypes and imported commodities and artifacts, came their way. Their ideas of the topography of foreign countries had to be gleaned from acquaintances, from established classics, and from the various travel books available. In fact, even though both men were capable of making vigorously effective use of the London scenes they knew well in their satirical descriptions, they rarely attempt more than a few lines of foreign scene painting. Perhaps Dryden's most striking evocation of a distant place is in the opening lines of his *Prologue to His Royal Highness,* where the duke's return is compared to the end of the long Arctic winter:

> In those cold Regions which no Summers chear,
> When brooding darkness covers half the year,
> To hollow Caves the shivering natives go;
> Bears range abroad, and hunt in tracks of Snow:
> But when the tedious Twilight wears away,
> And Stars grow paler at th'approach of Day,
> The longing Crowds to frozen Mountains run,
> Happy who first can see the glimmering Sun!
> Yet though rough Bears in Covert seek defence,
> White Foxes stay, with seeming Innocence:
> That crafty kind with day-light can dispense. (1–13)

Quite apart from the satirical point, the picture is full of life and drama and feeling, probably inspired by mariners' accounts of northern voyages such as will have been on Pope's desk when he wrote to Caryll that

> the severity of the cold has turned my studies to those books which treat of the descriptions of the Arctic regions, Lapland, Nova Zembla and Spitzbergen; deserts of snow, seas of ice, frozen skies might administer some kind of shivering satisfaction (or, as the vulgar have it, cold comfort) in the comparison with my own case.
>
> (*Correspondence* 1.166)

What he then does, characteristically, is "put together several beautiful winter pieces of the poets", including some Homer, Virgil, and Milton. His researches probably inspired this fine but relatively lifeless passage in *The Temple of Fame*, describing the time-defying rock on which the temple stands:

> So Zembla's Rocks (the beauteous Work of Frost)
> Rise white in Air, and glitter o'er the Coast;
> Pale Suns, unfelt, at distance roll away,
> And on th'impassive Ice the Lightnings play:
> Eternal Snows the growing Mass supply,
> Till the bright Mountains prop th'inconstant Sky:
> As Atlas fix'd, each hoary Pile appears,
> The gather'd Winter of a thousand Years. (53–60)

The contexts are, of course, very different, but it is interesting and probably significant that Pope's Arctic comes to us in a very visual form, a beautiful, rather painterly object, whereas Dryden's is much more dramatic and dynamic, conceived imaginatively in terms of human responses and feelings. Many of Pope's descriptions seem to be assembled in a collagelike way, drawing, in this case, on the "Accounts of our Modern Travellers", at other times taking elements from admired poets and, probably, painters. Both he and Dryden were deeply influenced by the classically derived doctrine *ut pictura poesis*, and Jean Hagstrum, studying this influence, has concluded that Dryden is "not primarily a descriptive poet" but aims simply, in the Muratori manner, to bring "fresh, natural, lifelike details" into his poems, whereas Pope, whose work has frequently reminded critics of specific artists, is "more elaborately pictorial".[1] Hagstrum's distinction seems to be well illustrated in these Arctic scenes.

Although in his dedication written for Purcell's *The Prophetess* Dryden does equate "barbarity" with distance from the sun (17.325), there is no parallel in his work to Pope's use of images of the cold and barren north. The expansion of England's influence to the Arctic is foreseen in *Windsor Forest*, while the *Essay on Man* compares people hardened to vice with the cold-tolerant inhabitants of that frozen region. Pope was particularly proud of two lines in *The Dunciad:*

> Lo where Maeotis sleeps, and hardly flows
> The freezing Tanais through a waste of snows.
> (3.87–88)

Here the icy regions of Settle's triumphant vision represent a world in the grip of congealed dullness that, as it thaws, will shortly engulf civilization in its floods. It is typical of Pope's approach that the passage is a blend of borrowings from Seneca and James Thomson, just as his famous description of traveling through the Alps in *An Essay on Criticism* (225–32, and note), which might convince the unwary reader that Pope had actually been there, owes a good deal to Silius Italicus. Since Arctic and high alpine landscapes remain unchanged through many centuries, he would doubtless have seen little reason to accept Berkeley's later advice that "to enable a man to describe rocks and precipices, it is absolutely necessary that he cross the Alps" (*Correspondence* 1.222).

As nontravelers, Dryden and Pope naturally have a centripetal sense of their country's position in the world, especially as their careers as poets coincide with a period of growing national self-confidence. Indeed, one can see two successive stages of England's advance to its eighteenth-century prominence as a trading and colonizing power reflected in the major celebratory poems that they published, nearly half a century apart: Dryden's *Annus Mirabilis* and Pope's *Windsor Forest* (especially in its concluding lines, added between 1710 and 1713).

Dryden's poem shows us an embattled Caroline London, rising from the ashes of the Great Fire, and preparing for its Augustan greatness. He ends with a vision of the city as a "famed emporium" transformed from rude shepherdess by the riverside to rebuilt "maiden queen" receiving suitors from all over the world, with the Thames surpassing all Continental rivers in nautical importance. England's chief enemy at that time was, of course, Holland, "crouching at home and cruel when abroad", compared significantly with the Carthage that had to be overthrown before Rome achieved her imperial destiny. Resentment at Dutch control of the Eastern trade routes and the prosperity of their "base coast" permeates the first four stanzas. In lines that Pope was to recall, Dryden describes how

> For them alone the Heavens had kindly heat
> In Eastern Quarries ripening precious Dew,
> For them the Idumaean Balm did sweat,
> And in hot Ceilon Spicy Forrests grew. (9–12)

Indeed Anglo-Dutch competition and the general dislike of Calvinism and the House of Orange felt in Dryden's circle color his attitudes to the Netherlands throughout his working life.

These are most powerfully expressed in his propaganda play *Amboyna,* where the cruelty of the Dutch overseas is his central subject. These lines from the epilogue convey its general tone:

> With an ill grace the Dutch their mischiefs do.

They've both ill nature and ill manners too.
Well may they boast themselves an Antient nation,
For they were bred e'er Manners were in fashion:
And their new Commonwealth has set them free
Only from Honour and Civility.
Venetians do not more uncouthly ride,
Than did their Lubber-State Mankind bestride.
Their sway becomes them with as ill a Mien
As their own Paunches swell above their Chin. (7–16)

In the prologue to *The Spanish Fryar* he refers to the inbred cheating and drinking of the "Heavy Hollanders", and in the epilogue to *The Silent Woman* to Dutch peasant cowardice in the face of the French armies. However, even the generally pro-Dutch Sir William Temple, the leading authority on the Netherlands, saw them as uncourageous and "naturally cold and heavy", ascribing this to "the natural dulness of the air".[2]

When Pope came to write his conclusion to *Windsor Forest* the situation prophesied by Dryden had, after Marlborough's victories, largely become reality. Triumphant England is presented as the fountainhead of peace in a world still bristling with armies from Russia in the east to Spain in the west. She is about to extend her commercial influence, backed by the potential thunder of her military power, so as to bring about a constant inflow of goods to her shores:

Thy trees, fair Windsor! now shall leave their Woods
And half thy Forest rush into my Floods,
Bear *Britain's* Thunder, and her Cross display,
To the bright regions of the rising day . . .
For me the Balm shall bleed and Amber flow,
The Coral redden, and the Ruby glow,
The Pearly Shell its lucid Globe unfold,
And Phoebus warm the ripening Ore to Gold.
(385–88; 393–96)

The echo of *Annus Mirabilis* signals the replacement of the Dutch by the English as recipients of the world's, especially the East's, riches. A representative of this new imperial race is Belinda in *The Rape of the Lock*, her dressing table loaded with "the various offerings of the World": Indian jewels, Arabian scents, African ivory and tortoiseshell. In the quality of her contact with the wider world she is not so very different from the rather less glamorous Martinus Scriblerus, who

> had a French hat with an African feather, Holland shirts and Flanders Lace, English cloth line'd with Indian silk, his gloves were Italian and his shoes were Spanish. He was made to observe this and daily catechis'd thereupon, which his Father was wont to call "Traveling at home." He never gave him a Fig or an Orange but oblig'd him to give an account from what Country it came. (*Memoirs* 107)

Carried away by his youthfully fervent patriotism, Pope sees English supremacy as benefiting the whole world, and in particular its less-advanced peoples:

> Earth's distant Ends our Glory shall behold
> And the new World launch forth to seek the Old.
> Then Ships of uncouth Form shall stem the Tyde,
> And Feather'd People crown my wealthy Side,
> And naked Youths and painted Chiefs admire
> Our Speech, our Colour, and our Strange Attire!
> Oh stretch thy Reign, fair *Peace*! from Shore to Shore,
> Till Conquest cease, and Slavery be no more:
> Till the free'd Indians in their native Groves
> Reap their own Fruits and woo their Sable Loves . . .
> (397–410)

Dryden had foreshadowed this passage in *Annus Mirabilis,* when he had envisaged suitors coming "from the West with Gold", and Pope may have had the prelapsarian quality of the lovers in the prologue to his predecessor's *Indian Queen* in mind in these last two lines, but for the most part their ideas of the American Indians differ. Dryden's are those affected by the great pre-Columbian civilizations of Central and South America, and play heroic parts in his drama, whereas Pope's are the unsophisticated ones of the north, marking a shift in interest from Spain and its empire to England's own sphere of influence in the Americas. To its native inhabitants, Pope's attitude is paternalistic and protective. In the *Essay on Man* we meet them hoping for

> Some safer world in depths of woods embrac'd
> Some happier island in the wat'ry waste,
> Where slaves once more their native land behold,
> No fiends torment, no Christians thirst for Gold.
> (1.105–8)

For these unsophisticated souls the afterlife will simply prolong the ordinary delights of the present, in faithful dog, bottle, and wife. Elsewhere Pope wonders if Europeans assuming that friendships will be continued in Heaven are any less naive (*Anecdotes* 1.240). Years later he compares himself, in his grotto building, to one of the "true species of Indians . . . in his throwing away of Gold and Silver for Shells and glittering Stones" (*Correspondence* 4.359). Such feelings consort oddly with his own commercial interests in the slave trade, but in an earlier letter to Caryll he acknowledges the brutal realities of English involvement in America when he writes that "A plain man encounters flattery and lying at a great disadvantage, as the poor naked Indians did our guns and firearms" (*Correspondence* 1.162). In this context the contrast between the vision of Indians visiting London in *Windsor Forest* and that of their fleeing deeper into the woods in *The Essay on Man* twenty years later is significant.

Dryden, earlier, had had no illusions about the English ships that transported convicts to the American plantations; they are "common shoars", or sewers which

> through our distant Colonies diffuse
> The draughts of Dungeons and the stench of stews,
> Whom when their home-bred honesty is lost
> We disembogue on some far Indian Coast.
> Thieves, Pandars, Palliards, sins of ev'ry sort,
> These are the manufactures we export . . .
> (*The Hind and the Panther* 2.558–64)

How very different from the beneficent commerce envisaged in *Annus Mirabilis*! As for Britain's established colonists, their lack of civilized graces is the subject of the prologue to *The History of Bacon in Virginia:*

> Expect no polish'd Scenes of Love should rise
> From the rude Growth of Indian Colonies.
> Instead of Courtship and a tedious pother,
> They only tip the Wink at one another:
> Nay often the whole Nation, pig together. (13–18)[3]

It may have been visions of uncouthness such as this that later inspired Pope with the idea, sadly never followed up, of a set of "American Pastorals, or rather pastorals adapted to the manners of several of the ruder nations as well as the Americans". Whether the flattering letters and samples of verse sent him by Mather Byles of Boston caused him to revise his opinion of American culture, his correspondence does not reveal (*Anecdotes* 1.150; *Correspondence* 2.450–51; 479; 528).

By Pope's day Holland had long ceased to be England's major adversary.

As a Catholic with Jacobite friends, he would have cared little for the Dutch, but they feature in his work merely as one of the peoples governed by dullness, linked in the *Dunciad Variorum* with the Swiss and the classical Boeotians (*Dunciad* A 1.157; 3.42–43). The most memorable image associated with them in the poetry is the scatological simile comparing the spreading influence of dullness with the rings widening out from "what a Dutchman plumps into the Lakes", which a critic has linked with William III's coronation diarrhea.[4] Elsewhere Pope compares the effect of seemingly harmless dunces to a breach made in the Dutch dikes by a water rat (*Dunciad* A 337, note), but neither he nor Dryden conveys any more than a general sense of Holland's flatness and wateriness.

The Hanoverian accession gave Pope a new target in the Germans, for whom his contempt is perhaps most clear in his comparison of court wits to Westphalian hogs ingesting each other's excrement (*Epilogue to the Satires* 171–80): an image born of years of despair at the philistinism of the regime. Before George I's arrival he had warned Teresa Blount to dress in buckram to prepare herself for the stiffness of the Hanoverians and the "brush of a German beard and whiskers" on her chin, and years later he feels that, as a German, their friend Augustus Schutz may be "dull enough not to care" for Martha (*Correspondence* 1.257; 4.288). Germans and Dutchmen are more than once associated in his work with boring pedantry (*Dunciad* B 4.198; 237).

Pope seems to have had little more knowledge of Germany as a place than Dryden, for whom it was a region untouched by the muses and ruled over by drunkards (*To Sir George Etherege* 30–54). It is clear though that his reading included accounts of German country superstitions, for we find him, in the winter of 1729–30, whimsically imagining that he has died, and describing how he has been haunting mines and caverns and

> if ever he has walked above ground he has been (like the Vampires in Germany) such a terror to all sober and innocent people that many wish a stake were drove through him to keep him quiet in his grave. (*Correspondence* 4.227)

While it is the Dutch, as we have seen, who represent European civilization's low point for Dryden, his touchstone in cultural matters is France, though his admiration, as every reader of *On Dramatick Poesie* knows, was qualified. In the epilogue to *Aurungzebe* he contrasts French and English tastes in entertainment.The "true" English, who "love all naked Beauties but a Play",

> hate your Monsieur's paltry Arts;
> For you are all Silk-weavers in your hearts.

Bold Brittons, at a brave Bear-garden Fray,
Are rouz'd: and, clatt'ring Sticks, cry *Play, play, play.*
Mean time, your filthy Foreigner will stare,
And mutter to himself, *Ha gens Barbare!*
And, Gad, 'tis well he mutters; well for him;
Our Butchers else would tear him limb from limb. (14–27)

In matters of clothing and statecraft alike, he regards the English as "not generally commended for invention" compared with their neighbors:

> They must like our Taylors have all their Fashions from the French and study the French league for every Alteration; as our Snippers go over once a year into France to bring back the newest Mode, and to learn to cut and shape it.
>
> (*Works* 18.409)

Less complimentary to French taste, morals, and political savoir faire is this vignette of Frenchmen at the opera:

Each sings his part, echoing from Pit and Box,
With his hoarse Voice, half Harmony, half Pox;
*Le plus grand Roy du Monde* is always ringing;
They show themselves good subjects by their singing.
(Prologue, *Albion and Albanius* 34–40)

The French preference for tragedy over comedy is explained in terms of a difference in national temperaments:

> as we, who are a sullen people, come to be diverted at our Playes; so they, who are of an ayery and gay temper, come thither to be more serious. (*Works* 17.48)

Dryden's sense of the natural high spirits of the French is further illustrated at the end of *On Dramatick Poesie*, when the disputants go up "through a crowd of French people who were merrily dancing in the open air, and nothing concerned for the noise of Guns which had allarm'd the Town that afternoon." (*Works* 17.80–81).

In matters of religion, however, he found them much more serious. His own conversion to Catholicism could indeed have been partly motivated by the Duchess of York's account of how her

> First Emotions were from her observing the Devotions of the Catholics in

> France and Flanders, and this is no news to any Traveller; ask even our Protestant Gentlemen at their return from Catholic Countries, and they cannot but confess that the Exercises of their Devotion, their Mortifications, their Austerities, their Humility, their Charity, and in short all ways of good living are practised there in a far greater measure than they are in England.
>
> (*Works* 17.301)

It is interesting to contrast Dryden's views here with those of Pope, who deplored the "superstition" of the Barcelonians expecting the miraculous relief of a siege (*Correspondence* 1.246–47), and wrote to Lady Mary Wortley Montagu about Italy, when he feared exile from England on religious grounds, that he "should be as uneasy in a country where I saw others persecuted by the rogues of my own religion as I was so myself by those of yours" (*Correspondence* 1.385). Normally, for him, the activities and beliefs of European Catholics were to be judged by the rational standards of an enlightened Augustan Englishman. Only once do we catch him, off guard, as devoted believer in Spence's company:

> When I was looking over some things I had brought from Italy, to pick out what might be of use to his Grotto, and came, among the rest, to some beads and medals that had been blessed at Loreto, he laid them gently aside and said "These would be good presents for a Papist!"
>
> (*Anecdotes* 1.383)

Dryden's Francophile tendencies did not conceal from him the threat posed to England by Louis XIV's expansionist policies:

> The French and we still change, but here's the curse:
> They change for better; and we change for worse.
> They take up our old trade of Conquering,
> And we are taking theirs, to dance and sing.
> Our Fathers did for change to France repair,
> And they for change will try our English air.
>
> (Prologue, *The Spanish Fryar* 29–34)

By Pope's twenties that threat had temporarily diminished, thanks to Marlborough, but despite his probably Jacobite sympathies,[5] he was too patriotic not to recognize it. Later we find him fearing that a lost opportunity to destroy the French fleet at Cartagena may make England "a province to France within ten years," and toward the end of his life he rejoices over the defeat of "the Ambition and Perfidy of France" (*Anecdotes* 1.600; *Correspondence* 4.249, 460).

While he valued French writers such as Boileau, Voltaire, and Racine (with whom he had a somewhat strained correspondence), he had less respect for their countrymen, and for French taste in cultural matters, than Dryden. He strongly resented an edict reducing the interest on his father's French investments, deciding to "revenge myself on the mighty monarch by giving the more spirit to what Homer says of the injustice of kings" (*Correspondence* 1.208). Ten years after Louis XIV himself was dead he criticizes Dr. Arbuthnot for running about at the French court "with a king of sixteen, and (what makes him more a child) a king of Frenchmen" (*Correspondence* 2.318). Later he affirms, somewhat inconsistently with his own collector's enthusiasm, that "to hunt for pretty things belongs to fops and Frenchmen" (*Correspondence* 4.193). Not that there was much difference: as he wrote to the translator of *An Essay on Criticism*,

> In putting me into a French dress, you have not only adorned my outside but mended my shape; and if I am now a good figure, I must consider you have naturaliz'd me into a country which is famous for making every fine man a gentleman. (*Correspondence* 1.192)

From Lady Mary, among others, he could have derived the unfavorable impression of Versailles' vast scale and lack of "Sense" that is reflected in *The Epistle to Burlington*,[6] while more positive descriptions of France could have come from Bolingbroke. Pope writes enthusiastically to Swift about their friend's agreeable existence in "the finest country" there, with the use of the king's stable and the whole forest of Fontainebleau at his command (*Correspondence* 4.176–77). Paris seems not to be mentioned in Pope's writings, but his correspondent David Mallet characterized it as "that metropolis of dress and debauchery", and while describing the wives of Swiss burghers tells him that

> the women do not paint, as the French do, to a degree that at first very much shocks an English eye. In Paris a lady's quality may be guessed at by the quantity of red she lays on. (*Correspondence* 3.457–58)

Sadly, Pope did not rise to this. Would he have regarded Mallet's Parisiennes as vainer than his own Belinda, whose "purer blush" develops by degrees at her dressing table, or Sappho, with her "greazy" preparations for "the ev'ning Mask"?

The country that had largely replaced France as the center of cultural interest by Pope's time was, of course, Italy. Dryden was very knowledgeable about Italian painting, but references to things Italian are rare in his poems apart from a complaint or two about visiting commedia dell'arte actors, and a mention of Italian expertise in poisoning.[7] He gives us no sense of Italy as a country. Pope, on the other hand, had been told by Berkeley that

> Green fields and groves, flowery meadows and purling streams are no where in such perfection as in England: but if you would know lightsome days, warm suns and blue skys, you must come to Italy. (*Correspondence* 1.222)

Although Pope was never able to take that advice, he twice made the journey in his imagination, with friends. In *The Epistle to Mr Jervas,* sent with Dryden's translation of du Fresnoy's *Art of Painting,* he writes

> Together o'er the Alps methinks we fly,
> Fir'd with Ideas of fair Italy.
> With thee, on Raphael's Monument I mourn,
> Or wait inspiring dreams at Maro's Urn:
> With thee repose, where Tully once was laid,
> Or seek some ruin's formidable shade;
> While fancy brings the vanish'd piles to view,
> And builds imaginary Rome a-new.
> Here thy well-study'd Marbles fix our eye,
> A fading Fresco here demands a sigh:
> Each heav'nly piece unweary'd we compare,
> Match Raphael's grace, with thy soft Guido's air,
> Caracci's strength, Correggio's softer line,
> Paulo's free stroke, and Titian's warmth divine. (23–38)

If Italy is seen here mainly in terms of Renaissance painters and Roman writers, it is Italy as the scene of past imperial glory and as treasure house of classical artifacts that he envisages when flattering Lady Mary:

> I would fain see how you look on the very spot where Curtius sacrificed himself for his Country? and observe what difference there would be in your eyes when you ogled the Statue of a Julius Caesar, and a Marcus Aurelius? Allow me but to sneak after you in your train, to fill my pockets with Coins or lug an old Busto behind you, and I shall be proud beyond expression. Let people think, if they will, that I did all this for the pleasure of treading on Classic ground. I would whisper other reasons in your ear.
>
> (*Correspondence* 1.440)

Richard Wilson, *Lake Avernus and the Island of Ischia* (1752–57)

The phrase "treading on Classic ground" echoes a phrase in Addison's *Letter from Italy,*[8] a poem that responds ecstatically to the natural beauties of the country, while lamenting the degenerately subservient state of its present inhabitants. Pope's own similar views on modern Italy are most fully expressed in a passage linking French and Italian decadence, which describes how dullness sends young aristocrats

> To where the Seine, obsequious as she runs
> Pours at great Bourbon's feet her silken sons;
> Or Tyber, now no longer Roman, rolls,
> Vain of Italian Arts, Italian Souls:
> To happy Convents, bosom'd deep in vines,
> Where slumber Abbots, purple as their wines . . .
> (*Dunciad* 4.297–302)

The Italian city-states are "lands of singing or of dancing slaves"; Venice, once the Lion of the Adriatic, is "ridden by Cupid"; and the sea she dominated now "wafts the smooth Eunuch and enamour'd swain." He saw the grand tour to Italy as a positively antieducational exercise in gluttony and debauchery, during which the young traveler forgot his classical training and became instead a devotee of that most decadent of artistic exports the opera, which he had already presented in the poem as an Italian harlot triumphing over the downcast muses (*Dunciad* B 45–62). There had clearly been a sad decline since Burlington had toured Italy with two painters in his train, returning to improve English taste with a substantial collection of old masters and classical sculptures.

Of the world beyond Italy to the south and east there is relatively little trace in the original poetry and prose of Dryden or Pope. Neither poet seems much interested in Africa, which was still largely unexplored, though Pope associates Nubia at least with Scriblerian dullness. Peter the Great's victory over Charles XII of Sweden at Poltava had brought Russia forcibly to people's attention by Pope's day; he uses both men as moral examples in his poetry and records Swift's prediction of Russia's future status as an imperial power (*Correspondence* 1.234). For Dryden Muscovites had simply been exotic rarities. Pope also seems to have been more aware of China, possibly through Le Comte's *Memoirs,*[9] than Dryden: he mentions mandarins' fans in a letter to Gay and honors Confucius with a place in *The Temple of Fame* (*Correspondence* 1.188; *The Temple of Fame* 107–8).

Both men knew a certain amount about Turkey. Dryden ascribes Luther's abandonment of priestly celibacy to the influence of the Koran and describes the attractions of the Muslim heaven in an epilogue that is strongly reminiscent of a chapter in Sir Paul Rycaut's *History of the Present State of the Ottoman Empire* of 1686 (p. 197):

> . . . Mahomet laid up for ever
> Kind black-eyed Rogues for every True Believer
> And which was more than mortal Man e'er tasted,
> One Pleasure that for 'threescore Twelvemonths lasted.
> (*Constantine the Great* 40–45)

He also alludes to Turkish cookery and hypocrisy about alcohol (*The Wild Gallant* 11–12; *Astraea Redux* 187–88). For Pope, as for Shakespeare, Turkey was the archetypal tyranny, the sultan of literary London being, of course, Joseph Addison, who had "his Mutes too, a sett of Nodders, Winkers and Whisperers, whose business it is to strangle all the offspring of wit in their birth" (*Correspondence* 1.306) —a view most famously developed in *The Epistle to Arbuthnot.*

When Lady Mary Wortley Montagu accompanied her husband to Constantinople, Pope wrote to her "I attend you in spirit thro' all your ways. . . . I follow you in Books of Travells thro' every State" (*Correspondence* 1.356). En route she had intrigued him by her "edifying account of the court of Vienna, where the Ladies seem to understand that Text very literally that commands us to bear one another's burdens". He wonders how her morals will survive the journey:

> you have already (without passing the bounds of Christendom) out-travelled the sin of Fornication, and are happily arrived at the free Region of Adultery: in a little time you'll look upon some other sins with more impartiality than the ladies here are capable of.
> (*Correspondence* 1.368)

He goes on to amuse himself with thoughts of her imminent conversion to Islam and her husband's circumcision.

The other oriental country of which both poets knew something was India. Dryden, of course, set a play there and translated a life of Saint Francis Xavier, though in his nondramatic poetry all we have is a single mention of suttee (*The Hind and the Panther* 1.442). Pope had clearly also read about Hindu religious practices; he refers to the monkey god Hanuman in the Scriblerus papers and to Brahmans in his poetry (*Prose Works* 2.292; *Epistle to Bathurst* 186). Of his own paintings he writes that "nobody will . . . worship them except the Indians . . . who, they tell us, worship certain Pagods or Idols purely for their ugliness" (*Correspondence* 1.421–22). Pope makes no distinction, it seems, between the extravagantly decorated Hindu temples, with their (in Hakluyt's words) "black and evil-favoured idols",[10] and the much chaster temples of Buddhism.

His main interest in India, however, was as a source of gems, such as that stolen by a John Company factor (*Epistle to Bathurst* 361–64) to enrich a city knight (a telling symbol of the exploitation of the natives by the new economic order), and of exotic furniture, represented by the "charming Indian Screen" admired in *The Rape of the Lock,* or the decorated chest studied by Chloe as she indulges her panting lover. Pope's real view of such artifacts was probably, like Atterbury's, that they were "so extravagant, disproportion'd and monsterous that they give a judicious seer pain" (*Correspondence* 2.56).

Increasingly, indeed, Pope and his friends had come to see themselves as the arbiters of taste in a world that was supplying more and more of its commodities and ideas to enhance their environment. Dryden, living at a time when the position of England in relation to other leading powers was less established, felt that "while Poetry and Painting are arrived to their perfection in our country . . . we are of later growth than our neighbours and must be content to shake off our barbarity by degrees" (*Works* 17.325). Perhaps because of this greater uncertainty about his country's superiority, and also because he was dramatist as well as poet, he seems more prepared to involve himself, imaginatively and emotionally, with people living elsewhere. Pope's central concern is with his and his circle's mission to bring together, in their most civilized of modern nations, whatever was admirable in other cultures.

Bolingbroke had assured him that while the French and Italians might have "more lessons of Luxury to give" (one thinks of the *Dunciad* passage on the excesses of French cuisine), the English "have been these several years their masters in learning" (*Correspondence* 2.219–20). Later the much traveled Bethel told him that Burlington's Egyptian hall at York was "the finest thing he had ever beheld, in spite of Italy" (*Correspondence* 3.313). What then, he must have felt, was the point of visiting other countries when the best of the "various Off'rings of the World", in ideas as well as concrete objects, could be imported without the hazards of a voyage? He devoted himself to making his villa and grotto at Twickenham contain as many of those offerings as they could: Palladian architectural features, classical statuary, Italian paintings, exotic shells, as well as pineapples, melons, and French varieties of pear (*Correspondence* 3.451–52). Though he had once written that "to be a lover of Mankind is a more glorious Elogy than to be a lover of one's own country" (*Correspondence* 1.324), he eventually became, like his friend Bolingbroke, "a creature of this world, which is a name we give to Europe, to England, to Ireland, to the Court, to the Castle, and so diminishing till it comes to our own affairs and our own persons" (*Correspondence* 3.445).

# NOTES

Quotations are from *The Works of John Dryden*, ed. E. Hooker, H. J. Swedenborg et al., 19 vols. (Los Angeles: 1956–79); *The Letters of John Dryden*, ed. C. E. Ward (Durham, NC: 1942); *The Correspondence of Alexander Pope*, ed. G. Sherburn, 5 vols. (London: 1956); *The Twickenham Edition of the Poems of Alexander Pope*, ed. J. Butt et al., 6 vols. (London: 1939–61); *The Prose Works of Alexander Pope*, ed. N. Ault and R. Cowler (Oxford: 1936–86); J. Spence, *Observations, Anecdotes and Characters, etc.*, ed. J. M. Osborn, 2 vols. (Oxford: 1966); William Shakespeare, *The Complete Works*, ed. P. Alexander (London: 1951); R. Hakluyt, *The Principall Navigations of the English Nation*, 8 vols. (London: 1907); *The Memoirs of Martinus Scriblerus*, ed. C. Kerby Millar (New Haven: 1950).

1. See J. Hagstrum, *The Sister Arts* (Chicago: 1958) 178–79; 160–61; 235–41; 272. See also J. Warton, *An Essay on the Genius and Writings of Pope* (London: 1806) 1.325–26; and H. Erskine-Hill, *The Social Milieu of Alexander Pope* (New Haven: 1975) 276.
2. Sir W. Temple, *Observations upon the United Provinces of the Netherlands* (Cambridge, England: 1932) 105.
3. Dryden also refers to the American colonies as a refuge for dangerous nonconformists in his *Prologue and Epilogue to the King and Queen* 1–6.
4. D. Brooks-Davies, *Pope's Dunciad and the Queen of the Night: A Study in Emotional Jacobitism* (Manchester: 1985) 34; 44n.
5. See Brooks-Davies, passim.
6. *The Complete Letters of Lady Mary Wortley Montagu*, ed. R. Halsband (Oxford: 1965) 1.441.
7. See *Epilogue to the University of Oxon* (1684) 11–16; prologue to Lee's *Caesar Borgia* 34–42.
8. Text used from *The New Oxford Book of Eighteenth Century Verse*, ed. R. Lonsdale (Oxford: 1985).
9. Pope knew Louis Le Comte's *Memoirs and Observations Made in a Late Journey through the Empire of China* (London: 1697) (*Prose Works* 2.286ff. and notes).
10. R. Hakluyt, *The Principall Navigations of the English Nation*, 8 vols. (London: 1907), 2.291. Note reference to suttee (2.293). Hakluyt's material could have come to Dryden and Pope through *Purchas His Pilgrimes*, probably the fourth edition (London: 1625–26).

# DEFOE AND FAR TRAVEL

John McVeagh, University of Ulster

Daniel Defoe traveled all over England and Scotland (for half his lifetime a foreign country) and left copious records of his journeyings in the *Review* (1704–13), *A Tour thro' the Whole Island* (1724–27), and other works. This interesting domestic travel material is not the present essay's concern, except as it reminds us that, where Great Britain is concerned, Defoe was probably more expert than other writers on her geography and society. Furthermore, he drew his knowledge not just from books but from personal involvement in the life of the island as he traveled her roads and visited her towns and city centers, markets and meeting places, and took sides in their politics.

Information about his overseas travel is scantier, partly because he undertook less of it and partly because he wrote no travel journals of abroad. Consequently, his writing about the world overseas draws more on imagination than on experience. He is described by J. R. Moore (not always a reliable biographer) as knowing Holland, France, Spain, Germany, Italy, and other areas on the Continent.[1] This is too specific yet undocumented to be convincing, but generally Defoe's biographers agree that he probably gained a certain amount of knowledge of some western European countries from personal experience. However, we do not really know which countries these were and we do not know when he saw them. In addition, F. Bastian suggests a trip to Ireland.[2] But this attractive idea remains speculation.

A reason why commentators have so canvased the unresolvable question of where Defoe might have gone and what he could have seen is that Defoe himself is less than forthcoming on his European travels. We think he visited and worked on the Continent but look in vain for any details on the subject. Additionally, he can be very good at seeming to know places he never visited, which—notoriously—makes it hard in his writing to distinguish fact from fiction. His apparent authority on Africa in *Captain Singleton* (1720) or China in *The Farther Adventures of Robinson Crusoe* (1719) or Amsterdam and Paris in *Roxana* (1724) should not deceive readers into thinking that he knew those places, though some of them he may have visited. So it is with his descriptions of other parts of the world. Despite what Defoe biographers seem to have assumed, and still assume, perhaps because biography in Defoe's case calls for it, these authentic-sounding passages cannot be taken to demonstrate that he had personal experience of the regions described, and more likely they are splicings of some other writer's work with his own ideas. We may indeed be reading a convincing text that looks documented but is imagined and has little reference to the biography of its author. Of travel beyond Europe one can say that for Defoe, whatever impression his fiction might create in the reader, there seems to have been none at all.

But it is a notable fact that Defoe seems to demand attention among the writers of the period as an internationalist. He forces the reader to think beyond England and Europe. Customarily, he writes with a sense of the whole world near the forefront of his mind. His awareness of geography, the movement of history, and the interconnectedness of nations brings to bear a sense of the world context in the way he handles a particular issue, however limited the issue might be in itself. Peter Earle puts the point succinctly when he writes that Defoe evidently "had some sort of three-dimensional matrix in his head whose axes were time, space and ideas. From this matrix he could draw at random, immediately relating the effects in Virginia of something happening in the empire of the Grand Mogul".[3] This is well said, and can be illustrated from one of his ephemeral pamphlets as easily as from his well-known novels, for in spite of its occasional nature, Defoe's journalistic writing is also shaped by the global reference and the outward imagination to which Earle draws attention.

Consider for example the way in which, in his four-part *General History of Trade* of 1713, Defoe handles the problem of "owling", or smuggling in English seaport towns. The subject one might think reasonably limited. But as Defoe treats it, the whole world gets involved. *A General History of Trade* came out at the close of the War of the Spanish Succession as a fierce pamphlet controversy developed over the issue of free trade to France. Always specific as a writer, Defoe contributes to this debate but ranges beyond it. Smuggling he places at the end of the fourth section of the work so that everything leads up to it, or perhaps it is better to say, Defoe's mind works in such a way that, for him, a consideration of the ebb and flow of European and world trade focuses down on to a specific local problem.

*A General History* describes in its opening section the aptness of trade to a world rich and needy in different ways and different regions, and in subsequent sections Defoe surveys the variety of the globe's produce, the emergence of English trade and the decline of Scottish fishing. After this, in Part 4, he moves on to the French and Portuguese trade to England, which leads to the discussion of English smugglers making illicit fortunes out of the produce of the two countries. The summary may sound as if the pamphlet is miscellaneous, but rather it is ranging yet controlled. Defoe writes first to contribute his views to a controversy—French trade versus Portuguese trade, both bedevilled by smuggling—but refuses to limit himself to the solitary issue divorced from its wider context because, for him, the subject was intricately linked with the world's economic processes. He moves from the local issue to its wider implications, then back from intercontinental discussion to the midnight comings and goings on English beaches: from London or Bristol to Benin, and from Benin back to London. *A General History of Trade* is specific, occasional writing, but it expresses a worldview.

This swing of the imagination between England and remote countries, typical of Defoe's understanding of the life of his times, informs his writings on war and politics and his imaginative fiction no less than his essays on trade. We see it in his miscellaneous writings from the *Review* onward, and the novels and seminovels that follow in the 1720s are, of course, obsessed with the issue of the links existing or to be created between the British people and the population and produce of other lands. Extensive parts of *Robinson Crusoe, Moll Flanders,* and *Colonel Jack* are set in the southern Caribbean, the Far East, and the North American plantations. *Captain Singleton* imagines Africa, as *A New Voyage round the World* imagines South America. Much of *Roxana* takes place in France and the Low Countries.

But Defoe's endeavor is less to transport the reader abroad than to connect abroad with home; his purpose, to enhance English life. If his novels all take us out of London, they also return to it, so that one could say of Defoe's writing (as of Pope's) that in his vision London remains the center of the universe. He differs in this from Conrad or Kipling, later novelists who also celebrate the strangeness of the earth but do so without the Enlightenment's Eurocentric assurance, and it is this that, for all his sense of other lives, Defoe believes in and accepts. In another essay in the present volume, Tim Cook terms Pope's imaginative engagement with abroad centripetal; the poet does not go abroad, but draws the world to himself—to Belinda's dressing table or to his Twickenham grotto. Defoe's creative mind, by contrast, one might call centrifugal. But though his writing shows an outward drive, its reference is always to England, to the question of what England should make of the overseas territories described.

Although Defoe's answer to the question is utilitarian—go and exploit the world, his stories urge—his appreciation of plenitude is always there, with an extra touch of relish for and a particular interest in the barbarous or strange. Writing of Tartary and Russia in *Mercurius Politicus* (1716–20)—a work possibly his, but not proven to be so—he piles up a descriptive paragraph resonant with negatives and exotic place names until the weight of the terminology almost makes the syntax creak under the strain. Perhaps testing the language structure in such a way on such a subject appealed to Defoe; it conveyed an impression of irregularity and wildness—the message he was urging upon his reader. The Russians, he writes, had burst their barriers of

> Deserts uninhabited, Mountains unpassable, Seas unnavigable, and Mahometan Nations Innumberable. There were their Ancient Limits, when no Christian Nation but the *Poles* had any Neighbourhood with them; when they had no access to the *Baltick* Sea; had no Port but *Arch-Angel* wall'd about with the *Riphean* Mountains, or the Frozen Hills of *Laponia* and *Nova Zembla* on the *North*, and the unpassable Mountains of *Taurus* and *Caucasus*, on the *South* of *Siberia* the Tartars of *Mongul* and *Karakathay*, and were left to Struggle with Infinite Hoords of Nations, Savage and Barbarous like themselves.
>
> (*Mercurius Politicus*, August 1719: 531)

Premodern Russia is the country described here—Russia before Peter the Great. Defoe admired Peter's modernizing efforts; but aboriginal savagery, and the wild terrain that seemed to be its natural habitat, as the passage shows, appealed to his imagination also. Looking at the passage again, we sense, perhaps, a tremor in the syntax. Should the comma after "Caucasus" really follow "South", and highlight a contrast between the hills of Nova Zembla and the mountains of Taurus, with Arch-Angel lying between them? But no; such a rearrangement may be tidier, but it is not Defoe, and in any case it is not after all particularly tidy, for it leaves "of Siberia the Tartars of Mongul and Karakathay" hanging disconsolately in the air—a phrase with nothing to belong to. The style remains knotty as Defoe tries to express vast regions and realize Asia in a paragraph, and perhaps his message of natural barriers finally broken by the savage hordes affects the rhythms. Not infelicity but new perceptions testing the sentence structure are what we see in such descriptions.[4] Defoe's writings are filled with examples of this apprehension of the undiscovered world beyond European limits, and his emphatic nouns and verbs, proper names and exotic terminology, and general stylistic energy reflect his sense of its richness. Distinctions arise when we come to ask what Defoe wants to do with this knowledge, but acknowledgment must be made of his interest in far lands and seas, and of his brimming awareness of the complex movements of humanity over the globe.

Defoe is intensely concerned with England, of course. But his concern is with England in relation to other coutries, and their difference from and connections with England are what interest him. *The True-Born English-*

*man* (1701), his first literary success, punctures racial exclusivity, for example, by underlining the great mixture of nations who, over the years, have combined into the English people. The idea is not startling, but Defoe's poem works by being well informed about history and geography. Consequently, he attacks Little Englandism by enforcing the historical facts about racial mixing, wars, and colonization in Europe that have made England a part of the Continent and bound the inhabitants of the entire region together. In showing this, Defoe brings in ancient and modern politics going back to Roman times and advances his conviction—and William III's conviction, for whom he wrote—that English policy could no longer be insular, but must take on a European and international dimension.

Defoe's handling recommends this as a decision made by the historical process itself. Like Matthew Arnold a century later, he sought to awaken his sleepy readers to the significance of France, not so much culturally as politically. Launching his 1704 *Review* as a review of France, and opening it with an account of the rise of Louis XIV, baffled his readers, but Defoe was trying to make them think. He insists that anyone seeking to understand England must first understand France, now dangerously on the move. He extends the point in *The Danger of the Protestant Religion Consider'd* (1701) to cover German Protestants after the Treaty of Westphalia, French Huguenots and the Dutch after the Treaty of Munster—all Protestant Europe, in short, now seen by him as once more at risk as popery spearheaded by France grew strong throughout the Continent and further afield. France, finally, did not establish universal Catholic monarchy. But Defoe draws on the Cromwellian-Miltonic idea of God's Englishmen resisting the ungodly; during his lifetime God's Englishmen swept into world supremacy. Defoe's interpretation of the English mission is more secular than Milton's, and his special contributions are an acute sense of the politics of the moment backed up by deep geographic and historical information.

His expertise in international relations appears repeatedly in Defoe's other pamphlets and miscellaneous writings of the period. In *The Succession of Spain Considered* (1711) he probes the interests of the different powers of Europe in relation to the Spanish crisis, a subject on which, in fact, he wrote exhaustively. On trade he is copious, well informed, and, although a conventional enough mercantilist in his economic thinking, sensitive to the global as well as local implications of a trading argument. The range and detail of these writings cannot be followed through here; nor do they need to be.[5] To his information about France and near Europe, Defoe adds an awareness of the issues dividing the northern and Russian powers, the India trade and Africa trade controversies, the power politics of the Far Eastern trade, and the continuing crisis in the Caribbean.

Not every region appealed to him with equal force. Europe, of course, he wrote about most, because in politics Europe was primary, and Europe was where he lived; but Europe was never the continent he found most attractive as an imaginative writer. In his great creative decade after *Robinson Crusoe* (1719), the American seaboard colonies, Africa, and the vaguely known lands of the western Pacific—or, in short, one might say, the Southern Hemisphere in its full extent—displace France and Holland, Germany and the Baltic states, and vie with the subject of Great Britain (though not perhaps displacing Britain) as the region of primary appeal to Defoe's mind. The source of this appeal lies in the unknown or imperfectly known nature of those lands and seas. After his English, Mediterranean, and African opening experiences, Robinson Crusoe passes a lifetime on a tiny island set in the unexplored waters off the trade routes between the Caribbean and northeast Brazil, a setting in which the mind can wander and invent. In *The Farther Adventures,* the sequel, he returns to the island, now civilized and less interesting, and then leaves it behind for the Far East, returning home through China, Russia, and eastern Europe. *Moll Flanders* and *Colonel Jacque* move from a London opening to the North American plantations, then further afield. *Captain Singleton* includes a zigzagging trek across Africa from present-day Mozambique to the West African gold coast; in this imaginative journey Defoe places multitudes of elephants' teeth for want of towns, and has his adventurers meet the devil and discover the apparent source of the Nile. Rather unusually in *Roxana* (1724) Defoe chooses fashionable London and the upper-class areas in Paris and Amsterdam as his setting; on the whole his imagination does not rise to near European travel. During his last decade, in short, Defoe turned outward from Europe to the wider world. Does failure at home drive people abroad? Perhaps a reason for Defoe's greater interest in far places in his later career was his damaged political credibility after 1715, when the Whigs came in with the Hanoverians. He was driven to strange exigencies after this event, including (it has been suggested) writing in support of the Whigs by posing as a Tory journalist and hence secretly trying to tone down antigovernment attacks in opposition journals. True or not, one cannot be sure: but Defoe was in some ways constrained in his utterance after 1715, the period of his greatest imaginative works. Roaming the world in his novels must have felt liberating.

*A New Voyage round the World* (1724), though less well known than some of Defoe's other works, shows better than most the strength of his interest in remote places. What is new about the voyage is its direction: toward South America, then to South Africa and Madagascar, then further eastward beyond India and across the Pacific. This is the new element; normally in that age, ships would have returned home again at this point, their holds filled with East India produce. But Defoe's voyager makes across the Pacific for westward America, then coasts around modern Chile and Argentina to meet up with a splinter group at a prearranged spot on the Atlantic seaboard. This second group has walked across the subcontinent to test the land and its inhabitants: a vestigial Royal Society curiosity drives them, heavily colored by up-to-date colonizing instincts. The message behind the trek and voyage is utilitarian and annexationist. Defoe turns imperial the Baconian dream.

*The Four Years' Voyage of Capt. George Roberts* (1726) may be by Defoe, or it may not, and therefore not much emphasis can be laid upon it. An attraction, though, is its suggestive symbolism, typical of Defoe's fiction, which flits in and out of the narrative and gives to a far travel adventure the interest that attaches to a study of human experience. This is the sort of depth Defoe can give to adventure narratives. Roberts visits the Canary and Cape Verde islands, Barbados, and Guinea before landing destitute on the island of Saint John. Here, abandoned for years, in a mysterious and intriguing passage, he strives to climb unclimbable rocks to a town in the sky (242). He may be going mad or he may be turning into a saint; as with Crusoe, as with Gulliver, we are not sure.

Such imaginary encounters are typical of Defoe, and the roamable strange parts of the earth and the ocean are what his imagination prefers as places to inhabit, so that he can expand in them and define his proper subject. At this point a generalization seems called for. Remote journeyings of this sort appeal to the writer (and to his age in general) because they expose the theme of breaking out, transgression or energy released; hence their exotic settings. The idea of breakout perhaps seems hardly typical of the Augustan age, with its famous concern for restraint and order; but a period that invokes restraint has some perception of why restraint is needed, and yearns to be released from it, and the Augustans are no exception. The age of reason and of moderation was powerfully interested in expansion, in breaking barriers. *A New Voyage* appeals because it is a counter journey: it breaks the rules. Defoe is a writer attracted to risk and risk takers. The starting point for Crusoe and Moll Flanders is disobedience and the desire to rise into a higher station in life; they are a fictional echo of Milton's Satan—but in secular terms, and viewed affirmatively. In Defoe's fiction the risky or unknown road is always likely to be the one taken. Thus Singleton walks across Africa knowing it to be, as he says, "one of the rashest and wildest, and most desperate Resolutions that ever was taken by Man, or any Number of Men, in the World" (47)—a journey involving "excessive Heats . . . unpassable Desarts . . . no Carriages . . . wild and ravenous Beasts . . . Nations of Savages to encounter . . . Hunger and Thirst" (47–48). Crusoe's journey through China is even more foolhardy; he goes along smashing up Chinese religious statues whenever he can. There seems a correlation between exotic settings and rebellious conduct—not that the setting makes the conduct safe. Rather, it makes new enterprise possible. Defoe's trader-rovers with their shady deals breaking trade agreements and bypassing the rules of international commerce choose for their marketplace the periphery of the known world. They choose the place where—as Kipling would phrase it—there ain't no ten commandments and the best is like the worst.

But if Kipling or Conrad among modern writers seem most inward with Defoe's appreciation of the feedom to flex their muscles that English men and women could find in the far parts of the globe, the difference is that for later writers such freedom is terrible; for Defoe it is invigorating. He is untouched by the twentieth century's awareness of deterioration. Empire is young for him, and lies mostly in the future and has not yet turned sour. And, to suggest connections in the opposite direction, Defoe, as has been hinted, takes on board the improvement ethic of Bacon's *The New Atlantis*—I do not know of any evidence that he had read it—and popularizes and applies it in his dozen or so novels and seminovels. Like the traveler-scientists of Solomon's House, like Satan beating out his path toward a new-made world, Crusoe and his kind venture into all lands driven by a desire to know and test everything that they can find, and also, if it is worth having, to appropriate and possess it. Such a notion of empire is not stressed by Bacon, but it is stressed by Defoe. His heroes' and heroines' adventure stories make up his case for turning the remote parts of the earth to European advantage.

Defoe states succinctly enough his sense of unknown landscapes awaiting discovery, but, if a recent attribution is correct, it is nowhere better expressed than in his ambitious *Atlas Maritimus* & *Commercialis* (1728). The suggestion that Defoe might have written this comes from J. R. Moore, and Moore has been increasingly criticized for undocumented attributions, but a reason for considering *Atlas Maritimus* here is that important parts of it seem to be drawn from Defoe's writings anyway. Thus, whether Defoe or some other compiler put it together in 1728, the work expresses ideas that he had advocated for a lifetime. And if Defoe did write it, the *Atlas* offers a summary drawn up near the end of his writing life of all he knew and thought about the earth on which England now enjoyed the prestige of being a great power.

But the *Atlas* does not just describe; it interprets. Half the volume is given over to Europe, then follow sections on Asia, Africa, and America. The writer acknowledges Misson and other sources, but conveys its individual emphasis on further discovery, exploitation, and use. This imperialism is explicit in Defoe, whose lifetime's writings on the wider world press the argument for European and British expansion but go with an artist's perception of how complex human life is and what ironies and counterpressures inform the relationships between modern and underdeveloped, rich and poor, old and new. Crusoe subjugates the indigenous peoples around his island but recognizes a better son in Friday than he had been himself; European pride is checked. Yet Defoe also rejects the simple idea of the noble savage. Coursing through the Eastern and Pacific seas, his rover-explorers come upon tribes innocent or naturally mean, or sharpened by European contact, or familiar with Europeans but not corrupted, so that characterizations continually differ and no one stereotype is repeated. One is convinced by this representation, which accepts human variety. Defoe criticizes inhuman Christians who are slave traders, but he is not against slavery, which he recommends in a humanized form on the grounds that kind treatment will improve productivity on the plantation. Crusoe, having been a slave himself, sells Xury into slavery with Xury's permission, and on the buyer's promising to free him on certain conditions. Especially in fiction, Defoe concedes that human affairs are complex and not black and white, and the perception does much to humanize his rather assertive claims. For example, he judged invalid the Spanish title to South America because Spaniards failed to make use of the land—Dampier may be his source here—but when the argument is advanced in *A New Voyage round the World,* it is a Spanish South American who speaks. Stereotyped national rivalries are not on offer. Defoe is strongly patriotic but can usually accept other races, other creeds, though not always—the Chinese did not impress him favorably—with an imaginative warmth. We may compare Swift: in spite of his rejection of colonialism, nowhere in Swift do we sense a willing sympathy with the victims of European expansion. Anger against the colonist, yes; human solidarity, no. This, however, is a quality that we can point to in Defoe's writings. He may be dismissive or hostile, but he shows a capacity to imagine the life and feelings of those who belong to a different culture.

From the 1690s to the 1720s Defoe's attention shifted from analyzing European politics to imagining the lives of adventurous pioneers on the other side of the earth. In his closing decade his imagination gets deeply drawn to the tropical and subtropical and away from the temperate zones. He seems never to have been excited by the cold regions, presumably because of their uselessness: to an Augustan thinker, the Arctic and the Antarctic, Canada and Siberia, and northern Russia might well seem relatively unimportant because they were unexploitable. Politics too influenced Defoe's shift of interest after 1715 toward the warm south, since from then onward the South Seas and the Spanish Caribbean were displacing the Europe of the Williamite wars as centers of political struggle and of controversy. Defoe's stories reflect the fact that only an outline knowledge of the South Seas existed at that time. They appeared before the scientific delineation of the other side of the globe arising from the journeys of Anson,

Wallis, and Cook started to replace the informed geographic guesswork on which he based his fiction, and perhaps they could have appeared only at that particular juncture in the history of creative literature.

When Defoe describes exotic territories he appears precise, but is in fact inventive, and he is so because he wants to make the novels not just novels but argumentative fiction designed to serve an imperial idea. To compare him with Dampier is illuminating. Dampier is not lacking in ideas, being a confessed Royal Society scientist-observer, but he describes and measures what he sees and is content with that, and on the whole he leaves political propaganda aside. For example, Dampier's *A New Voyage round the World* (1697) hints that the gold mines on Guiaquil could be safely worked if protected from a West Indian base, but drops the subject as a golden dream. Defoe dreams out these dreams of improvement and exploitation—in Africa, in South America, and elsewhere; he turns them into practical-sounding propositions. Dampier dismisses the Mexican Spanish as mere dogs in the manger because they fail to exploit the resources of their country yet prevent others from doing so. Replacing Mexico with Chile and Argentina, Defoe fills out this idea in *A New Voyage round the World* until it forms the subject of a substantial narrative. Dampier tells of a Moskito Indian abandoned for three years on Juan Fernandez, throwing in plenty of detail to bring the story to life: gun barrel hacked into harpoons, clothes wearing out, tame goats multiplying, house building. Surely Defoe built on this in *Robinson Crusoe*? Dampier says that his company thought of colonizing Mindanao, sharing as they did every skill required for a civilized life. The idea receives deeper treatment in Crusoe's *Farther Adventures*.

Defoe may have picked up such hints from Dampier and other travel writers and reworked them, but the reworking shows a determined set of ideas at work. He changes location and emphasis, ignores distracting facts (like the lists of turtles and mangroves, seals, hatchets, and catfish that clog Dampier's narrative) and deepens a chronology into an imaginative fiction. His free handling and rejection of masses of detail mark the difference between a travel book and a novel. The fact that the idea both writers share—explore the globe, know it, and use it—is much stronger in Defoe than in Dampier shows the advantage a writer may derive from a due negligence of facts when they get in the way of ideas. This is not to underrate Dampier, one of the best travel writers of the age.

"Defoe's characters roam Europe just as they roam the rest of the world," writes Peter Earle.[6] But really, as we have seen, they do not. Apart from Roxana in France and Holland and Crusoe's return journeys through Spain and Portugal, and leaving aside the special case of England, not one of the major novels takes as its setting a country placed on the continent of Europe. Instead they concentrate on far travel in unfamiliar regions, where, presumably, Defoe could speculate on life's possibilities in a freer way than in the Old World with its heavy weight of familiarity, tradition, and the pressure of past time. Of the controversial Baltic region, where the doings of Gustavus Adolphus and Peter the Great kept Europe talking for decades, Defoe wrote exhaustively. But he never set a novel there; it seemed not to release his imagination. France, Italy, and Portugal, and a number of other countries that he may have traveled through, figure very often in the essays, commentaries, and histories that he wrote from the 1690s to the 1730s. But he wrote no imaginative fiction of the first order about Italy, nor about Germany and the Alps, nor about the Iberian peninsula, nor about the Mediterranean area, and he produced no journal of the grand tour. Several minor works that Defoe may have written or touched up include material set in the European heartlands—Germany and eastern France and their contiguous areas; *Memoirs of a Cavalier* is one such fiction. Still, some element is missing that gives the major writings creative depth. That element is remote geography.

Defoe's creative energies needed room to expand in, and imaginary far travel to the all but unknown regions of the globe was the idea that supplied it. A striking feature is that his fiction stays within the tropical belt. Furthermore, he concentrates on land life, not on sea life, for while sea travel features importantly in his narratives it is there as passage rather than primary subject. (Compare Conrad again.) This becomes even more noticeable if we remove from consideration the pirate lives once ascribed to Defoe but now judged doubtful attributions. The other point is that Defoe is no escapist romancer. Far countries attract him because they release his imagination, but his essential subject remains human interaction and not flight from human contact, and the controlling interest of his major fictions is their delineation of the emergence of a polity out of the collisions of travel, rough living, and dangerous adventure. Journeys and far journeys are involved all the time, but their goal is settlement and construction.

Drawing together the points suggested in this essay, we might say that Defoe's interest in remote countries was stimulated by what was known about them, but even more by what was unknown, and that it was in the opportunity to mix fact and fancy creatively given to him by the imperfectly known geography of the far parts of the world that he found the best way of delineating his social and political views. Hence we are not offered by Defoe exotic escapism but the analysis of real issues such as the reactions of the personality to stress, the formation of social groups, and their fracture, and the evolution and structure of political authority. All this grounds his fiction in solid experience. The advantage of exotic settings is that they enable experiments to be imagined in society and politics that might seem less credible if located in overpoliticized Europe. Besides, self-understanding may be easier abroad; Crusoe in York might never have realized his potential. Such questions could be posed in the Old World but might seem more easily treated in narratives removed from familiar surroundings in a Europe shackled by tradition and the inheritance of centuries. The entrepreneurial Caribbean and risky North Africa, the unpoliced Far Eastern waters, the global underworld of Madagascar, and the vague western coasts of Central and Southern America—these supplied the appropriate conditions for the analysis of civilization that Defoe was interested in. We might feel that he was lucky to live in a geographically in-between age—a period of semidiscovered lands as yet unclaimed, or unheld, by Spain, and seas crisscrossed by ambiguous rovers. But the material did not make him a great writer; rather, he gave the raw material significance.

## NOTES

Quotations from *Captain Singleton* are from the Oxford English Novels edition (London, New York, Toronto: 1969), ed. Shiv K. Kumar.

1. J. R. Moore, *Daniel Defoe, Citizen of the Modern World* (Chicago and London: 1968) 275, 278.
2. F. Bastian, *Defoe's Early Life* (London: 1981) 68–80, 326.
3. Peter Earle, *Defoe* (London: 1976) 45.
4. See P. N. Furbank and W. R. Owens, *The Canonisation of Daniel Defoe* (forthcoming) ch. 10.
5. See John McVeagh, "Defoe and the Romance of Trade", *Durham University Journal* 70 (1978): 141–47.
6. Earle 75.

# SWIFT AND MANKIND

## Alan Downie, Goldsmiths' College

At the beginning of Part 3 of *Gulliver's Travels* we are told how, after leaving Madras and sailing for the East Indies, Gulliver's ship is "driven five days to the north-north-east, and then to the east" by "a great storm". It is then boarded by pirates. "I observed among them a Dutchman, who seemed to be of some authority, though he were not commander of either ship", Gulliver explains:

> He knew us by our countenances to be Englishmen, and jabbering to us in his own language, swore we should be tied back to back, and thrown into the sea. I spoke Dutch tolerably well; I told him who we were, and begged him in consideration of our being Christians and Protestants, of neighbouring countries, in strict alliance, that he would move the captains to take some pity on us. This inflamed his rage; he repeated his threatenings, and turning to his companions, spoke with great vehemence, in the Japanese language, as I suppose, often using the word *Christianos.* (196; pt.3.ch.1)

Although *Gulliver's Travels* was first published in 1726, the episode in question is set in 1707, when England and Holland were indeed "in strict alliance" in the War of the Spanish Succession. The importance of the connection between the Dutch and the Japanese is twofold: First, after their earlier brief flirtation with Christianity, the Japanese, by the early eighteenth century, were notoriously anti-Christian; hence the significance of the Dutchman's betrayal of Gulliver and his companions to the Japanese pirates. Second, the Dutch, despite being Christian, were the only Europeans tolerated by the Japanese.

Among the restrictions imposed by the Japanese upon the Dutch was the condition that they were not to advertise their Christian faith. Swift drew the obvious conclusion: in some way, the Christianity of the Dutch had been compromised. In the episode that we have been considering, the simple comparison between Dutch behavior and Japanese behavior is made, and the Dutch are found wanting. The Japanese captain "said we should not die". "I made the captain a very low bow", Gulliver continues, "and then turning to the Dutchman, said, I was sorry to find more mercy in a heathen, than in a brother Christian" (197; pt.3.ch.1). Once Swift fastens on a point, he is reluctant to let go. He returns to the issue at the end of Part 3 of *Gulliver's Travels.* Given a letter from the king of (imaginary) Luggnagg to the emperor of Japan, and passing himself off as a shipwrecked Dutch merchant, Gulliver seeks safe passage. He virtually gives himself away, however, when, as a final favor, he asks to be excused "the ceremony imposed on my countrymen of *trampling upon the Crucifix*".

Swift at once seeks to explain the reason for Japanese tolerance of the Dutch, and to satirize their lack of Christianity:

> When this latter petition was interpreted to the Emperor, he seemed a little surprised, and said, he believed I was the first of my countrymen who ever made any scruple in this point, and that he began to doubt whether I were a real Hollander or no; but rather suspected I must be a CHRISTIAN. (262; pt.3.ch.11)

The emperor duly complies with the "singularity" of Gulliver's "humour", but the latter's troubles are not quite over. On boarding a Dutch ship bound for Europe, he is asked "whether [he] had performed the ceremony abovementioned". When Gulliver tries to avoid a straight answer, "a malicious rogue of a skipper went to an officer, and pointing to me, told him, I had not yet *trampled on the Crucifix;* but the other, who had received instructions to let me pass, gave the rascal twenty strokes on the shoulders with a bamboo, after which I was no more troubled with such questions" (263; pt.3.ch.11).

Quite deliberately, Swift has repeated the same points at the opening and the ending of Part 3 of *Gulliver's Travels.* First, the Dutch are not Christians in any meaningful sense; indeed, far from simply avoiding the advertisement of their faith, they seem to go out of their way to repudiate Christianity, even so far as to trample on the crucifix. Second, the Japanese, despite their notorious reputation for cruelty, particularly toward Christians, are in practice more humane than Dutchmen. It was not the first time Swift had made use of a reference to a Far Eastern nation to provide a perspective on Dutch behavior. The opening of *Some Remarks on the Barrier Treaty, between Her Majesty and the States-General* (1712) is quite distinctive:

> Imagine a reasonable Person in *China,* were reading the following Treaty, and one who was ignorant of our Affairs, or our Geography; He would conceive their High-Mightinesses the States-General [of Holland], to be

> some vast powerful Commonwealth, like that of Rome, and Her Majesty to be a Petty Prince, like one of those to whom that Republick would sometimes send a *Diadem* for a Present, when they behaved themselves well; otherwise could depose at pleasure, and place whom they thought fit in their stead. Such a Man would think, that the States had taken our Prince and Us into their *Protection.* (6.87)

Once again we see Swift, this time in a polemical rather than a satirical work, making use of faraway lands to score rhetorical points. It was a favorite ploy. By insisting that the observer is a foreigner "ignorant of our Affairs, or our Geography", Swift reverses the strategy he had adopted in *Gulliver's Travels.*

Clearly the special relationship between the Dutch and the Japanese is crucial to the point Swift is trying to make in *Gulliver's Travels.* From the accession of William and Mary in 1689 onward, the English and the Dutch had been firm allies in the wars with the France of Louis XIV. However, Swift was one who believed that the Dutch had taken advantage of the alliance, and had used English money to fight a long and expensive Continental war that was not really in English interests. The definitive statement of this thesis was made in 1711 in what was (as far as his contemporaries were concerned) Swift's most famous political pamphlet, *The Conduct of the Allies, and of the Late Ministry, in Beginning and Carrying on the Present War,* which argued that "no nation was ever . . . treated with so much Insolence, Injustice and Ingratitude by its foreign Friends" (6.15). Swift did not have much time for the Dutch. But his satire is not aimed simply at Dutchmen, even in the instances with which we have been dealing. He has a much more general target: mankind. The conduct of the Dutch was, in a real sense, just a type of human misbehavior.

Given Swift's reputation for misanthropy, it might be reasonable to suppose that he would have subscribed wholeheartedly to the view that "abroad is unutterably bloody and foreigners are fiends".[1] "I have ever hated all Nations", he wrote to Alexander Pope, "but principally I hate and detest that animal called man" (*Correspondence* 3.103). Swift had an immense capacity for hatred: the words "hate", "hated", "hateful", "hater", "hates", and "hatred" occur over fifty times in his verse alone.[2] However, despite his expression of hatred for "all Nations", and his undeniable animosity toward the Scots, let alone the Dutch, it is doubtful whether Swift was actually surveying mankind from China to Peru when he made this observation. We must remember that he apparently changed his mind, correcting himself in his next letter to Pope. "I tell you after all that I do not hate Mankind", he explained, "it is vous autres who hate them because you would have them reasonable Animals, and are Angry for being disappointed" (*Correspondence* 3.118).

Nevertheless, Swift's response to mankind was the basis of his most famous work, "Travels into several Remote Nations of the World"—the original title of *Gulliver's Travels*—which, by offering several changes of perspective, questioned commonly held assumptions about human nature. "I have got Materials Towards a Treatis[e] proving the falsity of that Definition *animal rationale*; and to show it should be only *rationis capax*", he told Pope. "Upon this great foundation of Misanthropy (though not Timon[']s manner) The whole building of my Travells is erected". As a satirist, Swift did not hate mankind in Timon's manner: he was simply distressed at human behavior in the raw, and expected "never . . . [to] have peace of mind till all honest men" were of the opinion that man was not necessarily a rational being, but simply an animal capable of reason (*Correspondence* 3.103).

*Gulliver's Travels* was conceived as a travel book, albeit of an unusual kind. Swift was inordinately fond of "diverting" travel books. As Arthur Sherbo observes, "he everywhere uses the language, conventions, and the very details of travel literature as the vehicle for his satire of man and his institutions".[3] So aware was he of the potential of travel literature as a vehicle, in fact, that in the end, he decided to write a "History" of his own travels, which, as he told his friend Charles Ford, "will be a large Volume, and gives Account of Countryes hitherto unknown" (*Correspondence* 2.381). This turned out to be a perfectly accurate description of *Gulliver's Travels*, which informed the world about the islands of Lilliput and Blefuscu to the southwest of Sumatra, as well as the peninsula of Brobdingnag on the West Coast of North America; Balnibarbi, Luggnagg, and Glubbdubdrib to the east of Japan; and, finally, Houyhnhnmland, located somewhere to the south of Australia. Undoubtedly, these were all "Countryes hitherto unknown", and in conclusion Gulliver pondered whether or not Britain should take the trouble to conquer them "because, whatever lands are discovered by a subject belong to the Crown" (*Gulliver's Travels* 342; pt.4.ch.12).

Yet Swift never left the British Isles to research his book. As far as his creation, Lemuel Gulliver, was concerned, these wanderings were the natural consequences of an "insatiable desire of seeing foreign countries" (117; pt.1.ch.8). For Gulliver's creator, however, these were travels of the mind. To what extent did such imagined voyages indicate a desire in Swift, who was a great rambler, to travel abroad? Late in life, he joked with Pope about going to China, insisting that he would not set out until he had had a debt repaid (*Correspondence* 3.395). A decade or so earlier we find him claiming, curiously enough, to be "personally concerned" at the death of Charles XII of Sweden in 1718. "I intended to have begg[e]d my Bread at His Court", he explained, "whenever our good Friends in Power thought fit to put me . . . under necessity of begging" (*Correspondence* 2.311).[4] Yet nothing is known about Swift's connections with the court of Charles XII, nor why he should wish or expect to have found favor there.

But he did express more serious intentions to travel outside the British Isles. From time to time, he threatened, for reasons of health, to journey to Aix-la-Chappelle. In 1727, on his last visit to London, he made definite plans to undertake the trip. The young Voltaire was in England, moving within the circle of Swift's friends. Voltaire provided Swift with letters of introduction to his French acquaintances. Just as Swift was about to set out, however, news arrived that George I had died en route to Hanover (*Correspondence* 3.214–15). Advised to delay his departure, Swift hung on in anticipation of political changes that did not take place. As a result, he never did get to France. In the end, the only large body of water he ever crossed was that between England and Ireland. Indeed, such was the significance to Swift of his Irish "exile" that, as the "gateway" to the life in England from which he felt himself to be excluded, Holyhead became a symbol of his frustrated desires, and for a time he expressed a wish to be buried there (*Correspondence* 5.35).

The uneasy relationship between England and Ireland provided the motivation for many of Swift's best-known writings, and I shall refer to these in due course. First I want to consider other aspects of *Gulliver's Travels,* which, in accordance with Swift's conception of satire, was designed to "mend the World" (*Correspondence* 3.87).[5] This is an interesting phrase. In practice (in accordance with the contemporary idiom), "the World" was usually limited merely to the *polite* world of English, if not London society. ("*To know the world,*" Swift explained in his poem *Cadenus and Vanessa,* was "a modern phrase, / For visits, ombre, balls and plays".) Deane Swift, Swift's nephew, regarded *Gulliver's Travels* as simply "a direct, plain and bitter satire against the innumerable follies and corruptions in law, politicks, learning, morals and religion",[6] presumably addressed first and foremost at an English audience. But Swift's horizons were far too broad to be circumscribed by a consideration of England alone.

As we have seen, one of his favorite devices was to use foreign observers to supply unexpected perspectives on familiar English habits and institutions. Goldsmith, of course, was later to develop the concept in the letters of the Chinese philosopher Lien Chi Altangi, freely adapting material invented by others. But Swift had first seen the possibilities inherent in a work like *The Citizen of the World* at the end of the seventeenth century. Included in the list prefixed to *A Tale of a Tub* (published in 1704 but conceived in the previous decade) of "Treatises wrote by the same Author, most of them mentioned in the following Discourses; which will be speedily published" were not only "A Description of the Kingdom of Absurdities", but, more significantly, "A Voyage into England, by a Person of Quality in Terra Australis incognita, translated from the Original" (1.x1). Later Swift gave Richard Steele "a noble hint" for *The Tatler* "about an Indian supposed to write his travels into England". "I repent he ever had it", Swift wrote when the suggestion was finally taken up, not in *The Tatler*, but in *The Spectator* (No. 50—by Addison, in fact). "I intended to have written a book on that subject", he explained. "I believe he has spent it all in one paper".[7]

Is it possible that *Gulliver's Travels* was a modification of Swift's original idea? Rather than introducing a foreign visitor to England, Swift uses the Englishman Gulliver as a naive observer in his "Travels into several Remote Nations of the World". Yet the satiric strategy remains basically the same, as it often operates through a comparison between English manners and customs and those of the fictitious societies visited by Gulliver. Chapter 6 of Part 1 is "*Of the inhabitants of Lilliput: their learning, laws, and customs; the manner of educating their children. The Author's way of living in that country. His vindication of a great lady*". Quite clearly, Swift is making use of the conventions of travel literature. But he deftly turns the table on the reader. "There are some laws and customs in this empire very peculiar", Gulliver innocently remarks, "and if they were not so directly contrary to those of my own dear country, I should be tempted to say a little in their justification". They are "very peculiar", however, precisely because, in the most part, they coincide with what should be the English ideal. The Lilliputians, for instance, originally "suppose[d] truth, justice, temperance, and the like, to be in every man's power; the practice of which virtues, assisted by experience and a good intention, would qualify any man for the service of his country" (93, 94; pt.1.ch.6).

This comparison of actual and ideal is made possible by an awareness of the existence of different moral codes in other countries. It is, in fact, the essence of Swift's satiric method in *Gulliver's Travels*, which, in conclusion, draws attention to the Brobdingnagians, "whose wise maxims in morality and government it would be our happiness to observe" (341; pt.4.ch.12). In addition to regular explicit or implicit comparisons with English customs, there are regular references to *European* practices and institutions. The king of Brobdingnag, for instance, refuses to be given the secret of making gunpowder, with which, as Gulliver is quick to point out, he would have been "absolute master of the lives, the liberties, and the fortunes of his people", because of "a *nice unnecessary scruple*, whereof in Europe we can have no conception" (175; pt.2.ch.7). Or again, Gulliver confesses that he "should be prouder to listen" to the discourses of his Houyhnhnm master and his friends, "than to dictate to the greatest and wisest assembly in Europe" (326; pt.4.ch.10).

Perhaps this occasional broadening of the scope of the satire was one of the reasons that *Gulliver's Travels* was speedily translated into French and Dutch, even though (as his French translator, L'Abbé Desfontaines, remarked) "le goût des deux Nations n'est pas le même . . . tout ce qui plaît en Angleterre n'a pas ici le même agrément" (*Correspondence* 3.217). Swift himself was inconsistent on this score. When defending himself against charges of plagiarism in the "Apology" that prefaced *A Tale of a Tub* from the fifth edition of 1710 onward, he argued that "it is impossible for two Writers, of different Times and Countries to agree in their Thoughts after such a Manner, that two continued Discourses shall be the same, only *mutatis mutandis*" (*Prose Writings* 1.8). Yet when the controversy demanded a different view, as it did in *A Discourse of the Contests and Dissensions between the Nobles and the Commons in Athens and Rome with the Consequences They Had upon Both Those States* in 1701, Swift claimed that "I cannot possibly see in the common course of things, how the same Causes can produce different Effects and Consequences among us, than they did in *Greece* and *Rome*".[8] By 1727 he seems to have reverted to this earlier position. "Nous convenons icy que le goût des Nations n'est pas toujours le même", he observed in response to Desfontaines, "mais nous sommes portes à croire que le bon goût est le même par tout ou il y a des gens d'esprit, de judgement et de Scavoir". Further, "les mêmes vices, et les mêmes follies regnent par tout, du moins, dans tous les pays civilisés de l'Europe" (*Correspondence* 3.226).

It appears, then, that *Gulliver's Travels* was not only inspired by a vision of abroad, exploiting for satiric effect the differences between English customs and those of the nations visited by Gulliver; it was in fact addressed to all men of wit, judgment, and knowledge, regardless of nationality, in the belief that the same vices and follies reigned in all the countries of Europe. Well, *almost* all the countries of Europe. All but one. Ireland was unique, as far as Swift was concerned. *A Modest Proposal for Preventing the Children of Poor People in Ireland, from being a Burden to their Parents or Country; and for Making them Beneficial to the Publick* outlined an outrageous scheme for introducing a system of state-run cannibalism that, Swift explained, was calculated "*for this one individual Kingdom of* IRELAND, *and for no other that ever was, is or I think ever can be upon Earth*" (*Prose Writings* 12.116).

Despite being born in Ireland, Swift did not regard himself as an Irishman. Instead, he was "an *English* Gentleman born" in Ireland.[9] This confusion over identity massively informs his Irish writings. Swift's scorn for the Irish knew no bounds. "Remove me from this land of slaves", he cried, "Where all are fools, and all are knaves" (*Poems* 330). He felt that, as a nation, the Irish were guilty of absurdities that even "a wild *Indian* would be ashamed of" (*Prose Writings* 12.18). Swift admired the topography of Ireland, and "often spoke with pleasure of its excellent soil, fine climate[,] Harbours & many other natural advantages".[10] Ireland, he thought, should have been in a good position "to produce the Necessaries and Conveniences of Life" (*Prose Writings* 12.5). As a consequence, he was all the more bitter when he looked around him, filled with "perfect rage and resentment" at "the mortifying sight of slavery, folly, and baseness about me, among which I am forced to live" (*Correspondence* 3.289). To a great extent, the Irish were responsible for their own wretchedness, he felt, because they did not love their country, a failing that (as he put it in *A Modest Proposal*) made them "differ even from *Laplanders*, and the inhabitants of *Topinamboo*" (*Prose Writings* 12.116).

Here we find the reason for Swift's perception of being an exile in the country of his birth, and his anger at the Irish and their predicament. It made him painfully aware of the colonial nature of the relationship between England and Ireland. He explained that the solution to the problem of poverty in Ireland outlined in *A Modest Proposal*

> as it is wholly new, so it hath something *solid* and *real*, of no Expence, and little Trouble, full in our own Power; and whereby we can incur no Danger in *disobliging* ENGLAND: For, this Kind of Commodity will not bear Exportation; the Flesh being of too tender a Consistence, to admit a long Continuance in Salt: although, perhaps, I could name a Country, which would be glad to eat up our whole nation without it.
> (*Prose Writings* 12.117).

At such times, for polemical if for no other reasons, Swift chooses to identify himself with the land of his birth, earning himself the epithet with which he was subsequently lauded—"Hibernian Patriot." At other times, he found the idea difficult to accept. "I do profess without affectation", he assured Pope, "that your opinion of me as a Patriot (since you call it so) is what I do not deserve" (*Correspondence* 3.289). In his heart of hearts, Swift knew that the reasons for his championing of Ireland in the face of English oppression were more selfish.

Swift based his defense of Ireland not on a love of the country or its inhabitants, but upon a more abstract concept of personal liberty. Prior to his self-imposed exile in Ireland after the death of Queen Anne in 1714, he had spent much of his adult life in England. During his twenties, he had lived at Moor Park in Surrey, the country house of the distinguished retired diplomat and belletrist Sir William Temple. In this environment, it was natural for him to become "a lover of liberty" (*Prose Writings* 8.120), and subsequently personally acquainted with the highest politicians in the land, both Whig and Tory. "Upon my Return and Settlement here [in Ireland]", he explained in *The Drapier's Letters* in a passage that is clearly autobiographical throughout, "I thought I had only *changed one Country of Freedom for another*" (*Prose Writings* 10.86–87). He was quickly disabused. Soon he realized that gentlemen in Ireland, even English gentlemen in Ireland, did not automatically have the same rights and privileges that gentlemen enjoyed in England.

As far as Swift was concerned, the fundamental issue about the relationship of England and Ireland was simple enough: it was "whether People ought to be Slaves or no" (*Correspondence* 2.342). He drew attention to the uneasy situation in the third *Drapier's Letter,* which listed a number of key questions:

> WERE not the People of *Ireland* born as *free* as those of England? How have they forfeited their Freedom? Is not their *Parliament* as fair a *Representative* of the *People,* as that of *England*? And hath not their Privy Council as great, or a greater Share in the Administration of publick Affairs? Are they not Subjects of the same King? Does not the same *Sun* shine over them? And have they not the same *God* for their Protector? Am I a *Free-man* in *England,* and do I become a *Slave* in six Hours, by crossing the Channel?
>
> (*Prose Writings* 10.31)

It would be difficult to find a clearer expression of Swift's awareness of the differences between countries. Not only did crossing St. George's Channel (note the significance of the name) from east to west lead to the surrender of individual liberty, it involved a change of nationality regardless of one's ancestry, because (as he was at pains to point out) "all persons born in *Ireland* are called and treated as *Irishmen,* although their fathers and grandfathers were born in *England*" (*Correspondence* 3.132).

Was this why Swift claimed to "hate all Nations"? He regarded himself as English, yet seemed to be deliberately excluded from the benefits accorded other English nationals simply because he had been born in Ireland. Until late in his life, he had no desire to be thought of as Irish. "Sometimes he would declare that he was not born in Ireland at all, and seem to lament his condition, that he should be looked upon as a native of that country", Deane Swift, who knew Swift in his later years, remarked, "and would insist, that he was stolen from England when a child, and brought over to Ireland in a band-box".[11] He bitterly resented the irony that after every visit to England, he was fated to wait on some "bleaky shore" for "A passage to the land I hate" (*Poems* 330). Only when it was too late to contemplate a new life in England did Swift resign himself to living out his days in Dublin. "I chuse to be a freeman among slaves", he told Pope, "rather than a slave among

THE ENGLISH IRISH SOVLDIER

*With his new Diſcipline, new Armes, Old Stomacke, and new taken pillage: who had rather Eate than Fight.*

IF any Souldate
think I do appeare,
In this ſtrange Armes
and poſture,as a jeere,
Let him advance up to me
he ſhall ſee,
Ile ſtop his mouth,
and we wil both agree.

Our Skirmiſh ended,
our Enemies fled or ſlain
Pillage wee cry then,
for the Souldiers gaine,
And this compleat Artillery
I have got,
The beſt of Souldiers,
I think, hateth not.

My Martiall Armes
dealt I amongſt my foes,
With this I charged ſtand
'gainſt hungers blowes;
This is Munition
if a Souldier lacke,
He fights like *Iohn a dreams*,
or Lents thin *Jacke*.

All ſafe and cleare,
my true Arms reſt a while,
And welcome pillage,
you have foes to foile;
This Pot, my Helmet,
muſt not be forſaken,
For loe I ſeiz'd it
full of Hens and Bacon.

Rebels for Rebels dreſt it,
but our hot roſt,
Made them to flye,
and now they kiſſe the poſt
And better that to kiſſe,
then ſtay for Pullits,
And have their bellies
cram'd with leaden bullets.

This fowle my Feather is,
who wins moſt fame,
To weare a pretty Duck,
he need not ſhame:
This Spit my well charg'd
Musket, with a Gooſe,
Now cryes come eate me,
let your ſtomacks looſe.

This Dripping pan's my
target,and this Hartichoke
My Basket-hilted blade,
can make 'em ſmoake,
And make them ſlaſh & cut,
who moſt Home puts,
Ile moſt my fury
ſheath into his guts.

This Forke my Reſt is,
and my Bandaleers
Canary Bottles,
that can quell baſe feares,
And make us quaffe downe
danger, if this not doe,
What is it then can raiſe
a ſpirit into fearfull men.

This Match are linkes
to light down to my belly
Wherin are darkſom chinks
as I may tell yee,
Or Saſſages, or Puddings,
chooſe you which,
An excellent Needle,
Hungers wounds to ſtitch.

Theſe my Supporters,
garter'd with black pots,
Can ſteele the noſe,
& purg the brain of plots;
Theſe toſts my ſhooeſtrings,
ſteept in this ſtrong fog,
Is abl of themſelves
to foxe a Dog.

Theſe Armes being vaniſht,
once againe appeare
A true and faithful Souldier
*As you were*;
But if this wants,
and that we have no biting
In our beſt Armours
we make ſorry fighting.

*FINIS.*

Printed at *London* for *R. Wood*, and *A. Coe*. 1642.

*The English Irish Soldier* (broadside of 1642)

freemen"; therefore he "hate[d] the thought of London, where I am not rich enough to live otherwise than by shifting" (*Correspondence* 4.171).

Time and time again, Swift finds things to hate. Like a modern tourist when the exchange rate suddenly drops, Swift could not be happy in London, where things were too expensive. So he hated the very thought of it. Although he professed to hate Ireland, when he came to list the nations he hated, he began with the English. "I have ever hated all nations . . . English, Scotch, French; and the rest". Even his peculiar hatred of the Scots can be put down partly to Scotland's differing relationship with England. No doubt it was also prompted by the fact that the Presbyterians he habitually encountered in Ireland, particularly during his time as vicar of Kilroot (near Belfast), originated from Scotland.[12] But there were other painful reasons that brought home the unhappy nature of the relations between England and Ireland. Although Scotland, like Ireland, was a poor country, its inhabitants had not been denied the economic benefits of a union with England. To Swift, this seemed particularly perverse. It drove home English oppression of Ireland.

Just as Swift claimed to hate all nations including the Scots, he also claimed to "hate and detest that animal called man". However, as he explained to Pope, although he hated mankind in general, "I h[e]artily love John, Peter, Thomas and so forth" (*Correspondence* 3.103). Is it just coincidence that, in the same way that he begins his list of hated nations with the English, when he lists the names of those he loves, the first Christian name he mentions is that of John? *Gulliver's Travels* is an indictment of mankind, one that Swift promised to give to the world "when the world shall deserve" it (*Correspondence* 3.102). He finally decided the time was ripe when he visited England in 1726. Yet, earlier, he had confessed: "If the World had but a dozen Arbuthnetts in it I would burn my Travells" (*Correspondence* 3.104). As it happens, John was the Christian name of his good friend, the physician Dr. Arbuthnot. What was more, Arbuthnot was a Scotsman!

As we have seen, Swift's awareness of abroad makes itself felt in the most unexpected places. His insistence on comparing and contrasting the characteristics of various nations provided not only the basis of the satire in *Gulliver's Travels*, but, in a way, of his satire *tout court*. At the heart of Swift's satire is the urge to *discriminate*, not simply between nations or races, but between individuals. When William Congreve ended his "Letter to Viscount Cobham" with a couplet

> Believe it, Men have ever been the same,
> And all the Golden Age, is but a Dream.

Swift, characteristically, could not let it pass without comment. "I have read my friend Congreve's verses to Lord Cobham, which end with a vile and false moral", he wrote to Bolingbroke and Pope. "I remember [it] is not in Horace to Tibullus, which he imitates", he continued, "'that all times are equally virtuous and vicious'". Once again, Swift had to differ from the rest of mankind. "It is more probable that there may be an equal quantity of virtues always in the world", he explained, "but sometimes there may be a peck of it in Asia, and hardly a thimble-full in Europe" (*Correspondence* 3.329).

Once more Swift insists on reference not just to England, but to Europe as a whole. James Joyce referred to Ireland as "an afterthought of Europe".[13] As we have seen, Swift, too, had misgivings about Ireland's situation, in both a literal and a figurative sense. Like Joyce, Swift was fated always to regard himself as an outsider, even in the land of his birth. His personal awareness of the significance of place in the life of the individual doubtless influenced the techniques he made use of in his satires on mankind. But Joyce, unlike Swift, chose to leave Ireland and live on the Continent. It is a paradox that a writer who never left the British Isles has, nonetheless, left an enduring impression of the differences between nations as one of his principal artistic legacies. *Gulliver's Travels* is the work of a man who had had the time and the inclination to observe mankind at length, and who had finally decided to bequeath his reflections to "the world", not to entertain it, but to "vex" it. Swift, in one important sense at least, *is* Gulliver: not with respect to his character's naivete, but because, like Gulliver, Swift was a man who felt himself to be generally out of step with the societies in which he lived, whether in England or in Ireland. It was for this simple reason that he continually forced his readers to compare societies: "For who can read of the virtues I have mentioned in the glorious Houyhnhnms, without being ashamed of his own vices, when he considers himself as the reasoning, governing animal of his country?" Who indeed!

# NOTES

Quotations are from *Gulliver's Travels,* ed. Peter Dixon and John Chalker (Harmondsworth: 1967); *The Prose Writings of Jonathan Swift,* ed. Herbert Davis et al., 10 vols. (Oxford: 1939–62); *The Complete Poems of Jonathan Swift,* ed. Pat Rogers (Harmondsworth: 1983); *The Correspondence of Jonathan Swift,* ed. Harold Williams, 2 vols. (Oxford: 1965–72).

1. Nancy Mitford, *The Pursuit of Love* (1946; Harmondsworth: 1985) 113.
2. Michael Shinagel, ed., *A Concordance to the Poems of Jonathan Swift* (Ithaca and London: 1972) 370–71.

3. Arthur Sherbo, "Swift and Travel Literature", *Modern Language Studies* 9 (1979): 114–27.
4. See also *Prose Writings* 5.11.
5. On Swift's view of satire, see also *Prose Writings* 12.32–37.
6. Deane Swift, *An Essay upon the Life, Writings, and Character of Dr. Jonathan Swift* (London: 1755) 206.
7. Harold Williams, ed., *Journal to Stella* (Oxford: 1948) 1.254–55.
8. Jonathan Swift, *A Discourse of the Contests and Dissensions between the Nobles and the Commons in Athens and Rome. With the Consequences They Had upon Both Those States,* ed. Frank H. Ellis (Oxford: 1967) 125.
9. See *Prose Writings* 10.62, where Swift describes William Molyneaux in this way. Swift felt the same about himself.
10. As reported by John Lyon in his annotations to his copy of John Hawkesworth, *The Life of the Revd. Jonathan Swift, D. D.* (London: 1755), preserved in the Forster Collection (No. 579) in the Victoria and Albert Museum Library, London (fol. 8 of the preliminaries).
11. Deane Swift, p. 26.
12. See Louis A. Landa, *Swift and the Church of Ireland* (Oxford: 1954, repr. corr. 1965) 19–21.
13. Herbert Gorman, *James Joyce* (New York: 1939) 135.

# THOMSON ABROAD: TRAVERSING REALMS UNKNOWN

James Sambrook, University of Southampton

In a sense Thomson went abroad to become a man of letters when in 1725 at the age of twenty-four he left his native Scotland never to return; but the future author of "Rule, Britannia!" was a zealous supporter of the Union and did not regard England as a foreign country. The first work he wrote there was *Winter* (published April 1726), a new kind of devotional, descriptive, reflective poem. Though its descriptions are mostly of landscapes that Thomson could have seen near his boyhood home, there is a twenty-line passage near the end of the poem describing a thaw in the Arctic Ocean, when ice fields break up with an awesome noise, bringing danger and fear to the weary, hungry crew of a ship, "lost amid the floating Fragments",

> While Night o'erwhelms the Sea, and Horror looks
> More horrible. (340–41)

Details of this episode of mental travel are drawn from accounts by Frobisher, Barents, and other northern explorers,[1] though the unwieldy Leviathan at line 349 splashes in from the Book of Job; the overall tone and intention of the entire passage also owe more to Job than to Frobisher, for Thomson's chief concern is to assert that providence watches over men even where nature wears her cruelest aspect:

> Yet, *Providence,* that ever-waking *Eye*
> Looks down, with Pity, on the fruitless Toil

Of Mortals, lost to Hope, and *lights* them safe,
Thro' all this dreary Labyrinth of Fate. (355–58)

These lines on providence are retained as the conclusion of the expanded Arctic excursions in all later versions of *Winter*, all of which include more detail concerning nature's cruelty, beginning with additions in the second edition (July 1726) introducing a forlorn and hungry bear in the snowy wastes of Russia and packs of luridly savage wolves tearing the infant from the breast and digging up graveyard corpses in the Alps and Apennines (388ff; 389–413).

Cruelty and fear are leading motifs of foreign excursions in the next instalment of the *Seasons, Summer* (1727), where 120 lines are devoted to "various Summer-Horrors", mostly culled from popular travel accounts of North Africa. Thomson retells an old travelers' tale about a rich merchant and a poor carrier who both died of thirst in the Sahara Desert, the merchant having given the carrier ten thousand ducats for one cruse of water (657–62 and note).[2] He draws upon Defoe and Lucretius for his description of the plague (706–31), and upon Virgil's *Georgics* for his forest fire (632–42), but where Virgil tells of an Italian olive grove set alight by a careless shepherd, Thomson has Africa's "aromatic Groves" rather less probably and more exotically being fired by the noonday sun. Various travel books contribute to the savage beasts whose roars resound through the wilderness "From *Atlas* eastward to the frighted *Nile*" and terrify a mysterious unhappy solitary, perhaps a shipwrecked sailor or escaped slave (669–97). Lucan's *Pharsalia* provides a sandstorm and the fearsome serpent that forbids access to a spring; Lucan also supplies the heroic Cato, who withstands the monstrous terrors of the desert in his struggle to preserve Roman liberty against Caesarism (651–56; 663–69; 698–705). Here for the first time political history shapes Thomson's handling of foreign scenes.

Thomson ventures only briefly south of the Sahara, to sketch a region of great wealth and romantic beauty, rich in gold and gems, where cooling fruits grow on the "balmy Banks" of the River Niger, or in "Spicy *Abyssinian* Vales", where a multitude of beauteous creatures play in the shade of the peaceful elephant, "And Birds, of bolder Note, rejoice around". By contrast, its human denizens, of "gloomy Hue / And Features gross", are given "to ruthless Deeds, / Wan Jealousy, red Rage, and fell Revenge" (616–31). Thomson takes the widely held view that a black skin and a savage nature are both the effects of a tropical climate. His entire African excursion emphasizes the bizarre and repellent aspects of that continent, in striking and deliberate contrast to the immediately preceding lines of *Summer*, which constitute a panegyric on his homeland: "Happy Britannia . . . Island of Bliss", home of liberty, temperance, and industry.

There is no foreign excursion in the next of the *Seasons, Spring* (1728), but some of the savage North African beasts of *Summer* reappear to "growl their horrid Loves" in a somewhat parodic account of animal mating (830). The political allegory *Britannia* (1729) has little exotic material, but at one point Thomson elaborates the conventional "river of trade" metaphor and, drawing on Pliny and modern travelers' accounts, graphically portrays the annual onrush of the Nile flood:

When o'er his rocks,
And roaring cataracts, beyond the reach
Of dizzy vision pil'd, in one wide flash
An *Ethiopian* deluge foams amain. (229–32)

Thomson's first heroic tragedy, *Sophonisba* (1730), is set at the time of the Punic Wars in a North Africa that is conceived as a place where sandstorms, earthquakes, and monsters have their counterpart in the fierce unbridled passions of men, and where the ultimate horror is to be alone in the desert. Evidently the scenes of *Summer* continue to dwell in Thomson's imaginative eye.

It comes therefore as no surprise that the African desert episode is expanded when Thomson revises *Summer* for the first complete edition of *The Seasons*, published in 1730. The added passage is extravagant and exotic, for it describes a petrified city where the "nitrous penetrating salts" deposited in a sudden sandstorm have turned every inhabitant to stone,

in various attitudes surprized
By sudden fate, and live on every face
The passions caught, beyond the sculptor's art.
(728–30)

The Saharan petrified city was first mentioned in the seventeenth century, but Thomson heard of it in the winter of 1728–29, when an envoy from Tripoli was living in London and the story was revived, discussed, and elaborated in newspapers and journals. The petrified city readily appealed to an imagination already fascinated by the idea of people struck to statues by natural calamity. In the first edition of *Summer* (1727) lightning strikes a shepherd, who remains "like a Statue grim'd with Age" (781); a little later lightning strikes again to reduce an unlucky woman to a heap of pallid ashes beside her lover, who stands like a sculpted mourner on a tomb, "For ever silent, and for ever sad" (876).

Revisions to *Winter* in the 1730 edition introduce an Arctic counterpart to the petrified city. Returning to *Hakluyt* and other travel compilations in order to elaborate his description of explorers' sufferings, Thomson tells of the deaths of Sir Hugh Willoughby and all his crew in 1553–54, when they were forced to overwinter during a voyage in search of the Northeast Passage; but, prompted perhaps by sailors' references to frozen rigging, he adds fictitiously that the crew,

> Each full-exerted at his several Task,
> Froze into Statues; to the Cordage glued
> The Sailor, and the Pilot to the Helm. (933–35)

Other additions to the Arctic excursion in *Winter* follow their sources in travel literature less freely and fancifully: for instance, a description of the subterranean lodgings that enable miserably barbarous Samoyeds and Ostyaks to survive the Russian Arctic winter, or an account of the strange shapes assumed by ice when it is worked upon by the sea (936–46; 659–64). In this second passage Thomson stresses beauty, rather than the horror that hitherto had dominated his descriptions of the Arctic.

The 1730 edition of *The Seasons* includes the earliest texts of *Autumn* and *A Hymn*. In *Autumn* there is a sublimely romantic vision:

> where the *Northern* Ocean in vast Whirls
> Boils round the naked melancholy Isles
> Of farthest *Thule*, and th'*Atlantic* Surge
> Pours in among the stormy *Hebrides*. (862–65)

There are also scattered references to places in Europe, but no sustained foreign excursion. The *Hymn,* though, reaches its climax in a mental voyage

> to hostile barbarous Climes,
> Rivers unknown to Song; where first the Sun
> Gilds *Indian* Mountains, or his setting Beam
> Flames on th'*Atlantic* Isles.

In all these places "God is ever present, ever felt":

> He sustains, and animates the whole;
> From *seeming Evil* still educes *Good*
> And *Better* thence again, and *Better* still,
> In infinite Progression. (101–16)

Even the African and Arctic horrors are parts of the ultimately harmonious and beneficent creation of God, whose ways we may not understand but whose goodness we cannot doubt. All is beneath the ever-waking eye of providence.

As the first complete edition of *The Seasons* went on sale, in June 1730, Thomson was brushing up his French and Italian in readiness for his departure on the grand tour as paid traveling companion of Charles Richard Talbot, son of the solicitor general. Thomson and Talbot left England in November 1730 and returned late in 1732 or early in 1733; at various times they were in Paris, Lyons, Avignon, Venice, Florence, and Rome, but records are so scanty that we can infer only the broad outlines of their itinerary; it is not known whether they visited any countries other than France and Italy. Two months before setting out Thomson declared that he wished to travel in order to store his imagination "with Ideas of all-beautiful, all-great, and all-perfect Nature. These are the true materia poetica". By December 1730, when he and Talbot had settled in Paris for the winter, the poet was beginning to see his materia poetica in a political light, for he notes that "a *poetical* landscape of countries, mixed with moral observations on their governments and people, would not be an ill-judged undertaking". At the same time he reveals some of the political coloring that such a poetical landscape might receive under his hand. He writes: "amidst all that external and showy magnificence which the French affect, one misses that solid magnificence of trade and sincere plenty" of England, "where industry and liberty mutually support and inspirit one another". He adds, "I shall return no worse Englishman than I came away".[3]

Writing from Rome in November 1731, Thomson has lost his enthusiasm for traveling: "One may imagine fine things in reading of antient authors, but to travel is to dissipate that vision.". By the time he is back in Paris on the homeward journey in October 1732, his disillusionment is complete. In his eyes the fine natural scenes "are saddened by the misery of their Inhabitants": bad government, particularly in priest-ridden Italy, "has not only extirpated almost human Arts and Industry, but even disfigured Nature herself"; the country described by ancient poets and historians could hardly be recognized by a modern traveler.[4]

Out of this experience Thomson wrote *Liberty*, published in five parts, 1735–36, a history in the form of a vision that begins and ends with the author musing among the ruins of Rome. In the first part of the poem, entitled "Antient and Modern Italy Compared", once-fertile Campania, now undrained and depopulated, witnesses to the ill effects of tyranny; so, more eloquently, does Rome itself, "the Tomb of Empire"; Cicero's Tusculum has degenerated into a convent, "where Superstition dreams"; the coast of Baia, once graced with villas and temples, is now an earthquake-torn desolation. Such descriptions of the abject state of modern Italy are drawn

George Lambert, *Classical Landscape* (1745)

from the life but owe something also to travel books.[5]

There is less description in the remaining four parts of the poem, which recount the progress of liberty from its first great flowering in Greece to its establishment in Britain. Generally the visual images of the poet are swamped by the political ideas of the historian; but from time to time in his narrative Thomson paints a scene. In Switzerland, for instance, he sees:

> The hollow-winding Stream: the Vale, fair-spread
> Amid an Amphitheatre of Hills;
> Whence, vapour-wing'd, the sudden Tempest springs:
> From Steep to Steep ascending, the gay Train
> Of Fogs, thick-roll'd into romantic Shapes:
> The flitting Cloud, against the Summit dash'd;
> And, by the Sun illumin'd, pouring bright
> A gemmy Shower: hung o'er amazing Rocks,
> The Mountain-Ash, and solemn-sounding Pine:
> The snow-fed Torrent, in white Mazes tost,
> Down to the clear Aetherial Lake below:
> And, high o'er-topping all the broken Scene,
> The Mountain fading into Sky (4.348–60)

Also he allows his imaginative eye to make grand geographic surveys. Thus he roams along the boundaries of the Roman Empire, from "*Caledonia's* dim *Caerulean* Coast" to Mount Atlas "Amid the restless Clouds and leaning Heaven", from the Caspian Sea to "blest Arabia", from the Rhine to the Volga, and from Mauritania

> To where the *Nile* from *Ethiopian* Clouds
> His never-drain'd ethereal Urn, descends.
> (3.229–53)

To the north of the empire's frontiers Thomson finds

> A sullen Land of Lakes, and Fens immense,
> Of Rocks, resounding Torrents, gloomy Heaths,
> And cruel Desarts black with sounding Pine;
> Where Nature frowns;

and where

> a Race of Men prolific swarms,
> To Various Pain, to little Pleasure us'd;

On whom, keen-parching, beat *Riphean* Winds;
Hard like their Soil, and like their Climate fierce;
The Nursery of Nations. (3.516–33)

These northern tribes, hardened by their climate, were able to overrun the Roman Empire when its republican virtues had been lost under the Augustan tyranny; ancestors of the English, they fabricated the "Gothic" form of government upon which English constitutional liberties are founded. What is implicit here is made explicit at the opening of the fifth and last part of the poem, "The Prospect", where Thomson contrasts the real blessings of British liberty and industry with the insubstantial splendors of the tropics and the Orient. He argues that the bracing climate of the temperate north (not the far north) has a beneficial effect on human nature: it activates men to the pursuit of wealth and preservation of freedom.

*Liberty* glorifies the Protestant north, particularly Britain. The remains of ancient architecture and statuary and the artistic achievements of Renaissance Italy and modern France (4.131–264; 5.471–518) can yield worthy cultural models for Britons to emulate, but, for the most part, foreign lands provide awful examples of the sloth, frivolity, tyranny, and corruption that Britons must beware of. Thomson here foreshadows at great length the theme of his national ode "Rule, Britannia!", first sung during a performance of the masque *Alfred* on August 1, 1740. *Liberty* certainly shows that Thomson returned from his mental travels no worse an Englishman than when he set out.

Between *Liberty* and *Alfred* Thomson wrote *Poem to the Memory of Lord Talbot* (an elegy on the father of his grand tour companion) and two plays, *Agamemnon* and *Edward and Eleonora.* None of these works has significant descriptions of abroad, but two of them feature abandoned solitary figures upon foreign seashores, like the one in *Summer.* In the *Poem to Talbot* the castaway is one of Thomson's patrons exiled to an Irish bishopric; in *Agamemnon* he is the not dissimilar figure of a faithful counselor kidnaped by his enemies and marooned upon the "wildest of the Cyclade Isles". There is no significant use of foreign settings either in the new works of Thomson's last years, his plays *Tancred and Sigismunda* (1745), and *Coriolanus* (1749), and his Spenserian allegory *The Castle of Indolence* (1748)

The case is different with Thomson's revisions of *The Seasons* for the edition published in 1744. As in its earlier versions, the revised *Spring* has no significant foreign material, but *Autumn* receives a notable addition when, in the light of new reading, Thomson revises his earlier scientific explanation of the origin of springs and rivers. He now calls up man's enlightened scientific intelligence, that "pervading Genius, given to Man / To trace the Secrets of the dark Abyss", to

> Strip from the branching *Alps* their piny Load,
> The huge Incumbrance of horrific Woods
> From *Asian Taurus*, from *Imaus* stretch'd
> Athwart the roving *Tartar*'s sullen Bounds,

and open the subterranean strata of the world's mountains: those whence "wide *Siberia* draws her lonely Floods", "*Abyssinia*'s Cloud-compelling Cliffs", and "the dire *Andes*", at that time thought to be the highest on earth. The armchair traveler looks upon the mountains and sees beneath them a divinely ordered system of natural reservoirs and siphons that regulates the watercourses and supports "The full-adjusted Harmony of Things" (2.777–835). Footnotes to this passage reveal Thomson's dependence upon the latest edition of an old standard scientific work, the *General Geography* (1733) of Bernhard Varenius, and a contribution by Edmund Halley to the *Philosophical Transactions* of the Royal Society; but the sublime tone of the entire episode, not to mention the conspicuous and challenging allusion to *Paradise Lost* at lines 783–84, implies that the scientific intelligence that moves mountains has a heroic quality. Geographic excursion helps to make *The Seasons* a new kind of heroic poem.

The most considerable additions to the 1744 edition are in *Summer*, which is nearly half as long again as in 1730, most of this increase being accounted for by a great enlargement of the tropical excursion to more than three times its 1730 length. In *Summer* 1727 and 1730 Thomson's mental travel is mostly restricted to the North African desert, but in 1744 he ranges from Siam to South America. In 1727 and 1730 the exotic material is introduced as a recital of "various Summer-Horrors". Thomson's manuscript corrections, made in 1743, show him toying with the phrases "Prospects now, appalling", "fierce *torrid Summer*", and "dire to view the *torrid Summer*" before settling on the significantly different form of introduction printed in 1744:

> Now come, bold *Fancy*, spread a daring Flight,
> And view the Wonders of the *torrid* Zone.
> (2.631–32; 613–14)

In this excursion pleasures and pains are to be equally balanced.

So the tropical sun is said to be "gayly fierce", and we are immediately told that its fierceness is mitigated by "the general breeze"; here Thomson adds a scientific note garbled from Varenius's *General Geography* (1733), which was evidently a major source for the new science in the 1744 *Seasons*. Another scientific footnote links precious stones, luxuriant vegetation, and exotic fruits (referred to in *Summer* 1727) with the "double seasons" of the tropics (638–45). In 1727 Thomson drew attention to the fortunate paradox that tropical fruits contain cooling juices: in 1744 and again in 1746 he enlarges that earlier brief reference into an ecstasy of innocent sensuous delight.[6] "Bear me *Pomona*", he exclaims, as in imagination he enjoys the lemon, lime, orange, coconut, or pomegranate, or reclines beneath "the spreading Tamarind that shakes / Fann'd by the Breeze, its Fever-cooling Fruit", or seizes a pineapple:

> Quick let me strip thee of thy tufty Coat,
> Spread thy ambrosial Stores, and feast with *Jove*.

There is a feast too that delights and satiates the wandering eye in "Plains immense . . . interminable Meads . . . vast Savannahs . . . Prodigious Rivers", and all the scenes "where retir'd, / From little Scenes of Art, great *Nature* dwells" (663–702). Among the gaily painted birds and the hippopotamus (both the subject of footnotes), the crocodile, and other exotic creatures, the only perversion of nature comes from men, who turn the naturally wise and gentle elephant into a fearsome war machine. This account of tropical animals is a blend of the Book of Job, *Purchas*, and modern accounts, including Jerome Lobo's *Voyage to Abyssinia,* translated by Samuel Johnson in 1735.

Father Lobo and other Jesuit missionary descriptions are major sources for the next imaginative flight by which Thomson contrives to "burst" the "Desart-barrier", "Shoot o'er the Vale of *Sennar*", and "ardent climb the *Nubian* Mountains" to Abyssinia; but he goes to Milton and *Purchas* for the paradisal qualities of

> A Land of Wonders! which the Sun still eyes
> With Ray direct, as of the lovely Realm
> Inamour'd, and delighting there to dwell.
> (747–83)

In earlier days this paradise was marred by civil wars fomented by Portuguese commercial greed and religious bigotry, but now the only terror is an equatorial thunderstorm, which is introduced with a dramatic darkening of tone and is described with due attention to meteorological detail, drawing on Lucretius and the latest edition of the *Spectacle de la Nature* (1737) by Antoine Pluche. This dreadful natural phenomenon, though, is a wonderful part of providential harmony, because such storms fill the Nile "With all the mellow'd Treasures of the Sky", so that "*Egypt* joys beneath the spreading Wave" (784–821). In earlier poems (*Britannia*, 228–33; *Liberty*, 2.48–50; 3.252–53; 4.605) Thomson referred several times to the mystery of the course of the Nile, the strange fact that it was the only river to flood in summer, and the ancient fable that traced its source to the sky; but in *The Seasons* (1744) he offers the best available factual account, based upon Jesuit missionaries' exploration of the Blue Nile, believed in his day to be the main branch of the river.

Having traced the course of the Nile, Thomson's imaginative eye darts over the world's great rivers from Siam to South America, in each case picking out some small, strange picturesque or societal detail:

> From *Menam*'s orient Stream, that nightly shines
> With Insect-Lamps, to where Aurora sheds
> On *Indus*' smiling Banks the rosy Shower . . .
> Wide o'er his Isles, the branching *Oroonoque*
> Rolls a brown Deluge; and the Native drives
> To dwell aloft on Life-sufficing Trees,
> At once his Dome, his Robe, his Food, and Arms.

A footnote, based on Guy Tachard's *Voyage to Siam* in John Harris's *Compleat Collection of Voyages and Travels* (1705), explains that the "Insect-Lamps" are fireflies; the tree houses on the Orinoco come from Raleigh's *Description of Guiana*, probably by way of *Purchas*. As in the earlier flight over "vast Savannahs", the eye of fancy tires as it takes in the immensity of rivers such as the Amazon or "Sea-like *Plata*":

> In silent Dignity they sweep along,
> And traverse Realms unknown, and blooming Wilds,
> And fruitful Desarts, Worlds of Solitude,
> Where the Sun smiles and Seasons teem in vain.
> (827–49)

The endless pouring of mighty rivers is in *Autumn* evidence of the providential "full-adjusted harmony of Things", but in *Summer* it is regarded in a more limited, political aspect as a "wondrous Waste of Wealth". Like the prolific vegetation and precious minerals of the tropics it cannot benefit the natives, whose political institutions are as tyrannical as the sun itself (860–97).

The rest of the tropical excursion (898–1102) in 1744 is mostly a catalog of horrors, beginning with the serpent and other dreadful desert beasts and the fearful solitary, all carried over from *Summer* (1727) with some additional lurid circumstances. Two of the most extravagant desert horrors of earlier versions, the stories of the two tombs (1727) and the petrified city (1730), are now omitted, possibly because Thomson now thought they were fabulous. In their place is a sandstorm, based in part upon Lucan's *Pharsalia* and

Addison's *Cato,* with meteorological detail from Varenius. This is followed immediately by a typhoon at sea (again with meteorological particulars from Varenius), the description of which ends with a tribute to the courage of Vasco de Gama, who fought with stormy seas, "By bold Ambition led, and bolder Thirst / Of Gold." Thomson was aware that the activities of Henry the Navigator and his admirals heralded the arrival of Europe's cruel sons in both Indies; a constant theme of geographic excursions in *The Seasons* is that progress entails loss as well as gain. From the general celebration of commerce and navigation Thomson turns without irony to "that cruel Trade, / Which spoils unhappy *Guinea* of her Sons", as he graphically describes sharks devouring the human cargo of a slave ship overwhelmed by the typhoon; this passage inspired a famous painting by Turner. The last of the summer horrors here, as in 1727, is plague, the description of which is now greatly elaborated in order to incorporate a scientific explanation, drawn, as Thomson's footnote acknowledges, from a treatise by Richard Mead.

The tropical excursion of *Summer* 1727 contained only one footnote (referring to the travelers' tale about the two tombs): *Summer* 1744 has eleven, most of them "scientific". A stronger emphasis on scientific fact also characterizes the 1744 additions to *Winter,* where there are now seven footnotes, compared with one in 1730. As in the additions to *Summer,* there is now a more even balance between the attractive and the repulsive aspects of remote nature and primitive society. Thomson now moves in easy stages toward the Arctic: first evoking the delights of skating in Holland and sled racing in Scandinavia and Russia, before presenting the forbidding aspect of winter viewed by a state felon exiled to Siberia, which is paradoxically a "Prison of unbounded Wilds". The exile's prospect is a waste of snow, with frozen rivers

> That stretch athwart the solitary Vast
> Their icy Horrors to the frozen Main:

his only relief is when the annual caravan

> Bends to the golden Coast of rich *Cathay*
> With News of Human-kind. (799–809)

These regions harbor ermine, sable, and deer, whose life and beauty are evoked before we are told in brutal detail (from Virgil) the method by which they are hunted. This northern excursion is a series of contrasts between delight and horror.

Next Thomson refers briefly to the nomads of Tartary, whose restless, warlike ancestors migrated to Europe and overthrew the Roman Empire, as he narrated in *Liberty*.[7] In *The Seasons*, however, he devotes far more space to the peaceable Lapps, who "ask no more than simple Nature gives" and follow a frugal, contented existence in a landscape that seems enchanted. In the polar night of winter a blue crust of ice reflects the waving blaze of the aurora borealis, and vivid moons "light the Chace, / Or guide their daring Steps to *Finland*-Fairs", Summer reveals

Lakes and Floods,
Where pure *Niemi*'s fairy Mountains rise,
And fring'd with Roses *Tenglio* rolls his Stream.
(845; 874–76).

Thomson's long, highly idealized description of Lapland remains close to his sources, which are principally Olaf Rudbeck's *Lapland Illustrated*, appended to the 1704 edition of Johannes Scheffer's *Lapponia*, and Olaus Magnus's *History of the Goths, Swedes, and Vandals* (1658): the account of a recent scientific expedition, *The Figure of the Earth* (1738)[8] by Pierre Maupertuis, provides the roses and even the fairies, for in a footnote Thomson quotes Maupertuis as saying that the lake and mountain of Niemi "seem'd rather a Place of Resort for *Fairies* and *Genii* than Bears". Abruptly turning from the beautiful to the sublime:

Still pressing on, beyond *Tornea*'s Lake,
And Hecla flaming thro' a Waste of Snow,
And farthest *Greenland*, to the Pole itself,
Where failing gradual Life at length goes out,
The Muse expands her solitary Flight.
(887–91)

The ranging, untiring imaginative eye sweeps along the northern coasts of Asia, at which point Thomson incorporates from the 1730 edition his story of Willoughby's frozen crew and his description of the miserably barbarous Samoyeds. The apathy of these gross savages has been implicitly contrasted with the enterprise of the Elizabethan explorers; it is now contrasted with the rapid progress of Russia under the vigorous leadership of Peter the Great. "What cannot active Government perform, / New-Moulding Man" (950–51), exclaims the poet as he reviews the achievements of a much celebrated modern hero. Though elsewhere in *The Seasons* it is sometimes suggested that climate and natural resources condition men's lives, here we are shown how a great man can transform society and redirect history.

The civilized order that Peter imposes is, however, not our last view of the far north, for Thomson continues his long Arctic excursion with a version of the first-edition lines about the terrors of sailors caught in breaking ice fields; in 1744, as in 1726, he concludes that man is helpless without the protection and guidance of providence. Finally, the conscious intention of *The Seasons* is to praise God's power. The "varied God" is immanent in the whole variety of the natural world, as much in the inexplicable dreadfulness of the tropics and Arctic as in the harmonious revolution of the English seasons. For the larger purposes of his poem, Thomson's geographic excursions, like those in Shaftesbury's *The Moralists, a Rhapsody* (1709), serve to put man in mind of the author of the incomprehensibly fearful and wondrous works of nature. Shaftesbury's imaginary flight "from the Frigid to the Torrid Zone", through "the darkest and most imperfect parts of our Map", provided Thomson with a sea "immur'd in Walls of Crystal", freezing winds that never weary, and an Arctic thaw that brings out "vast Sea-Monsters", as "great as Islands"; it gave him peaceful elephants on the banks of a great river and the desert with all its monsters, including "scaly Serpents", which with other horrors were "fit to raise our thoughts in Admiration of that *Divine Wisdom*, so far superiour to our short Views".[9] Thomson's far more extensive journeying from the pole to the equator, over the great rivers, deserts, forests, and mountains of four continents presents the imagination with objects almost too great for comprehension. The intention of such writing is made clear by Addison in *Spectator* 489: "The Imagination prompts the Understanding, and by the Greatness of the sensible Object, produces in it the Idea of a Being who is neither circumscribed by Time nor Space". Foreign excursions constitute one special class of the numerous progresses from natural object to the idea of God that recur throughout *The Seasons* in all its versions, early and late.

Between the earlier and later versions of *The Seasons* comes *Liberty*, which, despite its quasi-religious message that Britannia rules by heaven's command, is concerned largely with secular political themes. To some degree those themes are foreshadowed in the allusion to Cato and liberty in *Summer* (1727) and in catalogs of Greek, Roman, and British worthies in the early editions of *Winter* and *Summer*, but their full development occurs only in revisions made to *The Seasons* after publication of *Liberty*. Geographic excursions in 1744 often turn into little cyclical histories of human societies, showing perhaps a fall from Golden Age innocence into Iron Age experience (850–55), or a growth from sullen barbarism into animated civilization (936–87), or even a regeneration of corrupt civilization by vigorous barbarism (834–42): some primitive societies are happy virtuous (843–86), some are not (860–97; 936–46); progress entails gain and loss. However, despite his awareness of all these possibilities, Thomson in *The Seasons* generally inclines to the opinion he holds in *Liberty*, that arts, trade, and manufacture flourish best in free societies in the temperate zone; so does the spirit of enterprise that underlay the widening global influence of western Europe and growing importance of Britain in the world during the eighteenth century.

Thomson draws upon his firsthand experience of Italy in *Liberty*, but most of his knowledge of foreign parts in both *Liberty* and *The Seasons* comes from books: even his most vivid and haunting descriptions of Scottish scenes are the work of an armchair traveler equipped with a lively imagination and Martin Martin's *Late Voyage to St. Kilda* and *Description of the Western Isles*. His early friend and biographer Patrick Murdoch tells us that the amusements of the poet's "leisure hours were civil and natural history, voyages, and the relation of travellers, the most authentic he could procure".[10] The sale catalog of Thomson's library at his death in 1748 has survived:[11] it includes an impressive array of travel books in English and French, mostly quite modern, about half of them published between 1730 and 1744.

Thomson's reading also gave him the history and science that are as prominent as geography in the later versions of *The Seasons* and as devotion in the earlier versions. Though he is commonly praised for his close observation and particularized description of natural objects, he frequently calls upon his reader to see what is invisible to the corporeal eye: for instance, osmosis, the smiling God, the North Pole (495–96; 859–62; 889–93). In *Autumn* the "vast eternal Springs" that "lie conceal'd / From mortal Eye" are laid bare by the "pervading *Genius*" of scientific intelligence (773–76). "Thomson abroad" is usually a mental traveler. He absorbs a great variety of travelers' tales, and in "Imagination's vivid Eye" and "the Mind's creative Eye" (459; 1016), he sees "*Abyssinia's* Cloud-compelling Cliffs", the "golden Coast of rich Cathay", "*Hecla* flaming thro' a Waste of Snow", and countless other visionary wonders.

Wordsworth quotes the following lines from *Summer* as a "beautiful instance of the modifying and *investive* power of the imagination":

> in *Cairo*'s crouded Streets,
> Th'impatient Merchant, wondering, waits in vain,
> And *Mecca* saddens at the long Delay (977–79).

He adds: "much of" *The Seasons* "is written from himself, and nobly from himself".[12] Johnson observes that "The great defect of *The Seasons* is want of method. . . . Of many appearances subsisting all at once, no rule can be given why one should be mentioned before another",[13] but the very looseness of the work's structure makes us aware that the associative mental processes of the poet have to stand in place of narrative continuity or logical argument; the principle of organization is a fluid movement of mind. Thomson's mental travel, which annihilates time and space, is in keeping with the general subjective cast of *The Seasons.* He is concerned less with "abroad" itself than with the emotional, intellectual, and devotional experience of an imaginative consciousness responding to exotic nature. The poet's armchair traveling is an exploration of his own powers of imagination.

# NOTES

References to the poetical works of Thomson are to the following editions: *The Seasons,* ed. James Sambrook (Oxford: 1981); *Liberty, the Castle of Indolence, and Other Poems,* ed. James Sambrook (Oxford: 1986).

1. Frobisher's voyage is in Hakluyt; those of Barents and others are in John Harris's *Compleat Collection of Voyages and Travels* (1705), which Thomson used often in *The Seasons.*
2. The story is at least as old as the sixteenth century; it is retold in *Purchas* and Harris's *Travels*; Thomson's immediate source was probably Patrick Gordon's *Geography Anatomiz'd* (4th ed., 1704).
3. *James Thomson (1700–1748), Letters and Documents,* ed. A. D. McKillop (Lawrence, KS: 1958) 73, 78.
4. Ibid., 79, 81.
5. The sources are detailed in A. D. McKillop, *The Background of Thomson's "Liberty",* Rice Institute Pamphlet 38 (July 1951): 26–40.
6. This feature of the tropics colors a letter of 1748 by Thomson to his friend William Paterson in Barbados: "I image you reclining under Cedars, and Palmettoes; and there enjoying more magnificent Slumbers than are known to the pale Climates of the North; Slumbers rendered awful, and divine, by the solemn Stillness, and deep Fervors, of the Torrid Noon! At other Times, I image you drinking Punch in Groves of Lime of Orange Trees, gathering Pine-Apples from Hedges as commonly as we may Blackberries, Poetizing under lofty Laurels, or making Love under full-spread Myrtles." (*Letters and Documents* 195).
7. In *The Seasons* Thomson virtually repeats some lines of *Liberty*:

   A boisterous Race . . .
   Who little Pleasure know and fear no Pain,
   Prolific swarm. (242.836–38)

   Cf. pages 147–48 above.
8. Dates of publication are of the English translations.
9. *Characteristicks of Men, Manners, Opinions, Times* (1714) 2.382, 384, 388.
10. *Works of James Thomson* (1762) 1.xviii.

11. *Sale Catalogues of the Libraries of Eminent Persons*, A. N. L. Munby, ed., (1971) 1.47–66.
12. *Prose Works*, ed. W. J. B. Owen and J. W. Smyser (Oxford: 1974) 3.72, 74.
13. *Lives of the English Poets*, G. B. Hill, ed., (Oxford, 1905) 3.299–300.

# "A SAFE BRIDGE OVER THE NARROW SEAS": CROSSING THE CHANNEL WITH SAMUEL RICHARDSON

**Peter Sabor, Queen's University, Ontario**

Coleridge's declaration that reading Fielding after Richardson "is like emerging from a sick room heated by stoves, into an open lawn, on a breezy day in May"[1] has been remarkably influential. With few exceptions, critics still regard Richardson as the master of domesticity, exploring man's heart while neglecting his social life. Mark Kinkead-Weekes, one of the best commentators on Richardson, asserts that his main characters "have to stay put in order to write and receive the letters", producing "a curious effect of stasis, which Tennyson probably had in mind in telling Fitzgerald of his love of 'those large, still books'".[2] Even Percy Adams, whose *Travel Literature and the Evolution of the Novel* discusses the heavy debt owed by fiction to travel books, describes *Clarissa* as "domestic" and one of the "great exceptions" to the mass of fiction set "along the highways and over the oceans".[3]

The circumstances of Richardson's life seem to lend weight to the prevailing view of his fiction. Almost alone among major authors, he neither spoke nor read any language other than English; nor did he leave England in his life, even for trips to Scotland or Wales. The longest journey he is known to have made was with his parents as a child of ten, when the Richardson family removed from Mackworth, Derbyshire, to London (Eaves and Kimpel 5–6): a distance of some 130 miles. He had not, he told his correspondent Lady Echlin, "had the Opportunity of seeing Sea Prospects, and hardly any Rocks but the inland ones at Tunbridge"; and to Thomas Edwards he wrote, "I know nothing of Situations of Places, Distances, Contiguities" (Eaves and Kimpel 73). In the 1740s Richardson took occasional journeys to such unexotic parts of southern England as Bath, Tunbridge, and Hampshire; in the 1750s he remained still closer to London; and toward the end of his life he went almost nowhere at all. In 1759, after a journey of twenty-five miles, he declared himself "so shatter'd, that I find I must give up all Excursions above 10 Miles out and in" (Eaves and Kimpel 516).

While Richardson the man remained planted in London for most of his life, however, Richardson the reader traveled widely in Europe and beyond through the means of travel literature. Although no record of his library survives, thanks to William Sale's investigations we do know of over five hundred works that Richardson printed, many of which were travel books, containing detailed accounts of foreign lands.[4] Shortly before *Pamela* was published in 1740, for example, Richardson printed John Breval's *Remarks on Several Parts of Europe* (1738) in two massive folio volumes, a scholarly work with copious illustrations and a useful index, and while writing *Clarissa* in 1744, he was also printing Volume 1 of John Harris's *Navigantium atque Itinerantium Bibliotheca. Or, a Complete Collection of Voyages and Travels*, another huge folio "illustrated by proper charts, maps, and cuts", in which several hundred travel writings are translated into English from various languages. The extent to which Richardson's reading of travel books such as these permeated his own fiction has been largely overlooked. In this essay, instead of following Richardson the psychological novelist to the back of the cave, as have so many critics of his novels since Diderot published his "Eloge de Richardson" in 1761, I shall follow the trail of his fiction across Europe, with occasional excursions into America and the West Indies.

*Pamela*, the first of the three novels, seems an unpromising starting point for such an exploration; the fifteen-year-old servant girl who becomes the wife of a country squire is hardly known for her travels abroad. As the novel unfolds, however, it transpires that Mr. B. has taken the grand tour, attended by his Swiss servant Colbrand, and as his sister Lady Davers reminds him maliciously, his stay in Italy involved him in some difficulties:

> We all know, said she, that since your *Italian* Duel, you have commenc'd a Bravo; and all your Airs breathe as strongly of the Manslayer as of the Libertine. (*Pamela* 347)

Incensed by this account of his past, Mr. B. provides his own version of the episode. Far from being a "Bravo" himself, he first defended a friend from an attempted murder, than challenged the assassins' employer to a duel, which took place at Siena. Subsequently, B. traveled to Innsbruck and Munich, at least in the first edition of the novel; in Richardson's final, heavily revised version of the text, intriguingly, we hear nothing of Austria or Germany.[5]

Another character in *Pamela* has traveled farther afield than Mr. B.: his former mistress and mother of his child, Sally Godfrey. As B. tells Pamela, she left their child—named Goodwin, "that her Shame might be the less known"—in his care, set sail for Jamaica, and settled there (396). His guilt did not last long: "I was full of Spirits and Inconsideration. I went soon after to travel; a hundred new Objects danced before my Eyes, and kept Reflection from me" (399). The juxtaposition of the two sets of travels here is telling. For Sally Godfrey, leaving England is a means of restoring her tarnished reputation; far removed from her former environment, she can begin life anew as a marriageable widow of good character.[6] Her husband is a flourishing entrepreneur, who even sends his stepdaughter "a little Negro Boy, of about ten years old, as a Present, to wait upon her" (399). For Mr. B., in contrast, leaving England is purely a means of enhancing the pleasures of his hedonistic life. In the final revision of *Pamela*, in which B. becomes a more elevated and decorous character, Richardson makes a significant alteration here; B. still finds "new objects of pleasure" dancing before his eyes, but no longer specifies that they are seen abroad (Penguin ed. 505). In *Clarissa* and *Sir Charles Grandison*, both published before his final revision of *Pamela* was completed, Richardson depicted numerous rakes debauched by foreign travels; in recasting his first novel, he ensured that B. should not placed in this category.

The part played by foreign travel in the original, two-volume *Pamela* is, admittedly, slight, taking place entirely in the form of Mr. B.'s recollections. These reminiscences continue in Richardson's little-read sequel to *Pamela* (1741), but here, in addition, we find Pamela and her husband traveling to Europe together. B., it now emerges, has been to Europe twice since his grand tour. After narrowly escaping an ambush by the family of a girl he attempted to seduce, he "thought it was better remove the Seat of [his] Warfare into another Kingdom", and spent a further twelve months in France "in the best of Company".[7] Subsequently he toured Scotland and Ireland for six to eight months with a few friends, and made a third, brief trip to France to see his friends safely landed there. To balance these references to his rakish past, B. also alludes airily to his knowledge of papal affairs, declaring, as a seasoned traveler: "I well remember the Argument, when I was at *Rome*, used to the Pope, on such an Occasion" (3.280).

As well as recounting his European travels to his wife, Mr. B. prepares her for some extensive traveling of her own. In the first part of *Pamela* the heroine regrets her linguistic limitations, asking B. for words to express her gratitude in another tongue: "learn me some other Language, if there be any, that abounds with more grateful Terms" (305). In the sequel, B. belatedly carries out this request. Pamela informs Lady Davers that she is reading Fénelon's *Telemachus* (a work printed by Richardson) in the French, under the tutorship of her husband, "who teaches me on his Knee, and rewards me with a Kiss whenever I do well, and says, I have already nearly master'd the Accent and Pronunciation" (3.95). Later, we hear that Pamela is learning Italian, as well as French, from her devoted and talented husband, who "reads me Pieces of manuscript Poetry, in several of the modern Tongues (for he speaks them all)" (4.7). Oddly, however, Pamela's progress in these languages seems uncertain. In Volume 4, announcing for the first time his intention of taking Pamela on a tour of France and Italy, B. declares: "I propose to give you a Smattering of the French and *Italian* " (4.43), as though she were still ignorant of both. Later Pamela herself, in her strictures on Italian opera, admits to knowing "nothing of the *Italian* Language" (4.110), and at the masquerade where B. first encounters her rival, the countess, Pamela is unable to understand either the countess's Italian or another masquerader's French. Shortly afterward, however, her close friend Polly Darnford declares that Pamela "makes a great Proficiency in the *French* and *Italian* Languages," thanks to the "best Schoolmaster in the World" (4.146).

Pamela, then, embarks on her tour with an uncertain knowledge of languages, in contrast to her multilingual husband, but she travels with an open mind. B. has already warned her that many English travelers acquire little more than depravity abroad, "yet every one", she reflects, "does not return with so little Improvement, it is to be hop'd" (4.11). She sets off in resolute fashion. Having already made a sea crossing to the Isle of Wight, she is not alarmed by the straits of Dover, and feels above her nephew Jackey's "Fear of crossing the salt Water" (4.389). She resolves to write to her parents not of the "Manners, Customs, Curiosities, *&c* of the places we see" (4.389), since capable writers have done so already, but rather of her own family. She will be absent for two years, and is "under some Concern" at spending so long a period in Roman Catholic countries, but she will seek out Protestant chapels and is aware that "when we are at *Rome,* we must do as they do at *Rome*" (4.396).

Regrettably, Richardson gives us none of Pamela's letters during her two-year absence. Instead, she writes a retrospective résumé of her travels to Polly Darnford, now Lady G., outlining her progress through Holland, the Netherlands, France, Italy, and Germany. Traveling has affected her party in various ways. Lord Davers, like many English travelers in Europe, finds his health has improved, presumably through the warmer climate of southern

Europe. Miss Goodwin has become "a perfect Mistress of the *French* language, and speaks *Italian* very prettily" (4.399), while Pamela's children are adept in French and are required to speak only French to one another in the nursery. Pamela's rival the countess, whose earlier stay in France and Italy at the tender age of twelve or thirteen had made her "a little too gay and unsettled" (4.312), now profits from her journey. She accompanies Pamela's party from Florence to Innsbruck, "assiduously attended" by Lord C—(4.398), and to Pamela's relief accepts this suitor's hand in marriage. Traveling, which had overexcited the young girl, has matured the young woman. The weak-headed Jackey has, predictably, been wholly corrupted by his travels; slavishly imitating French fashions, he is "more an Ape than ever" (4.402). Worse still, he has barely escaped conversion to Roman Catholicism, "having got into Company with a *Dominican* at *Padua*, a *Frenchman* at *Milan*, and a *Jesuit* at *Paris*" (4.402–3).

Traveling, like alcohol, elicits but does not furnish the traveler's characteristics. Pamela, despite acquiring a command of "two or three Languages"—French, Italian, and presumably German or Dutch—returns with "an Heart as intirely *English* as ever", combining, according to Miss Towers, "the *French* Politeness, and the *English* Frankness and Plainness of Heart" (4.400, 402). Reflecting on the English "travelling Gentry", she complains of the early age at which they make their grand tours. Sent abroad as "unlick'd Cubs", they are too callow to benefit from European culture and customs, and only too ready to abandon themselves to vice (4.404). She seconds Locke's objections, in his *Thoughts on Education*, to early travel in Europe, but disagrees with his proposal that the tour should take place between the ages of seven and fourteen; instead, she proposes a tour of Great Britain at the age of fourteen or fifteen as a preparation for the responsibilities of foreign travel. Pamela's characteristic sharpness is provoked by her thoughts on the immature traveler, "running thro' a Kingdom, and knowing nothing of it, but the Inns and Stages, at which he stopp'd to eat and drink" (4.416), a description remarkably apposite to some package-tourists of today.

Pamela's strictures are also applicable to the youthful Mr. B., but not, of course, to the magisterial paterfamilias of the end of *Pamela 2*. B.'s family travels are followed by a final European tour, this time "in the Service of the State" (4.469), which he carries out for three years while Pamela raises their six children at home. B., declares Richardson, distinguished himself "in such a manner, as might be expected from his Qualifications, and Knowledge of the World"; the apparent irony here is surely unintended. No longer the blundering booby grappling persistently with the fifteen-year-old Pamela's décolletage, this is B. the seasoned statesman, a much-traveled man of affairs, who writes memoranda for his wife's benefit on the virtues of Italian opera, with a learned note on recitativos, and on the advantages of an experienced Scottish tutor, who will combine "the natural Boisterousness of a *North Briton*" with the "fantastic politeness of a *Frenchman*" (4.341).

Lovelace, hero of Richardson's second novel, *Clarissa* (1747–48), has traveled still more widely than B., but with largely pernicious results. In the early stages of this immensely long novel, his travel stories, like Othello's, play a crucial part. Letters that Lovelace writes to Clarissa describing foreign countries and customs, although at first condoned by the Harlowe family, lead gradually to the clandestine correspondence that enables Lovelace to abduct her from Harlowe Place. And Mr. Harlowe's implacable enmity to Lovelace begins with his hearing rumors of gambling debts that Lovelace has contracted on his travels. Unlike Sir Charles Grandison, a still greater traveler but one whose first love is always England, Lovelace has no ties to his mother country. Before abducting Clarissa, he boasts to Anna Howe that "all the countries in the world were alike to him" (*Clarissa* 216); his disdain for England matches his contempt for its laws. At the French court he has learned how to corrupt servants; in Florence and Rome his libertinism "endangered his person and his liberty", making his stay there "shorter than he designed" (563). In a passage that parallels Pamela's earlier strictures, Clarissa's cousin Morden describes the excesses of Englishmen such as Lovelace on the supposedly enriching grand tour. On their return, "foreign fashions, foreign vices, and foreign diseases too, often complete the man", who comes to "despise his own country and countrymen, himself still more despicable than the *most* despicable of those he despises" (563). For Lovelace, traveling, which "gives the sexes charming opportunities of being familiar with one another",[8] is primarily a path to sexual gratification, with France and Italy representing havens of eroticism. In a notorious passage added to the heavily revised edition of 1751, Lovelace outlines his fantasy of kidnapping and raping both Anna Howe and her mother on board ship, while sailing along the French coast, and shortly after he boasts off some successful philandering in Paris, concluding, triumphantly, "The English, Jack, do not often outwit the French" (675). Should Clarissa refuse the offers of marriage he makes after raping her, he will, he declares, reestablish his libertine's reputation with "one tour to France and Italy" (1085). Mocking Anna Howe's suitor Hickman, who has traveled only in Holland, Lovelace exclaims, "Never in France or Italy? . . . That's a wonder, sir, when on the continent!" (1092). Roman Catholicism is also a spur to his lust. In seducing a nun at Paris, a passage added in the third edition, he feigns conversion at the hands of a priest, priding himself on the strategy by which "she not only *brought* me a father, but *made* me one" (Everyman 3.509).

At the end of *Clarissa*, as Lovelace's compulsive lust is displaced by obsession with death, his vision of France and Italy darkens, becoming less erotic than funereal. In asking Belford for news of Clarissa's impending death, he insists that Paris be used metonymically: "say not in so many dreadful words what the event is—only that you advise me to take a trip to Paris: and that will stab me to the heart" (1303). A few days later, Clarissa uses the same metonymy in a letter to her friend Judith Norton: "I am entering upon a better tour than to France or Italy either!" (1338). But if taking a trip to Paris is equated with Clarissa's death, it is also, for Lovelace, the start of a final, large-scale tour of Europe, ostensibly to resume his rakish ways. On two occasions he announces his proposed route in minute detail, while anticipating a reunion in Paris "with my friend Belford, who by that time I doubt not will be all crusted and bearded over with penitence, self-denial and mortification" (1432). His insistence on just which cities and sites he will visit—Bavaria, Dresden, Berlin, Vienna, the Tyrol, Florence, and Turin, among others—sounds disconcertingly prosaic, until we realize he is thus ensuring that his route will become known to Colonel Morden, his eventual slayer: traveling and seeking death become one. For the last hundred pages of *Clarissa,* Lovelace and Morden crisscross Europe, their routes leading inexorably to an encounter that finally takes place at Trent. As Lovelace succumbs to a sword thrust from his adversary, his protracted analogy between death and foreign travels has been literally enacted.

Although Clarissa, in many ways Lovelace's antithesis, has never been abroad, both Europe and America are frequently present in her mind. For much of the novel she dwells on the possibility of removing to Florence, to seek the protection of her cousin Morden. Two considerations discourage her: the possibility that Morden is already en route to England, and the dangers of the journey, with its arduous Alpine crossing or hazardous sea voyage, for an unprotected woman. When Lovelace himself offers to escort Clarissa to Florence, his suggestion, like his proposals of marriage, is deftly couched in a way that will ensure her refusal. Instead, Clarissa rests her hopes on Morden's arrival in England, an event delayed for four months. As Robert Schmitz observes, "Clarissa and the reader are left in suspense while he makes the slowest progress ever recorded for a trip from Florence to England":[9] Morden finally meets Clarissa only hours before her death. Fleetingly, Clarissa considers the possibility of escaping to "one of our American colonies—never to be heard of more by my relations, whom I have so grievously offended" (754). The idea is swiftly abandoned as, after the rape, her desire for death becomes paramount, but it is oddly echoed in a later, independent proposal by the Harlowe family that she "go to one of the plantations" (1197). Arabella, Clarissa's sister and her most vindictive persecutor, outlines the project in some detail. Clarissa would reside in Pennsylvania until the age of twenty-one, boarding with a respectable widow, and thus ridding her parents "of a world of cares, and fears, and scandal" (1256). Clarissa's reply reveals that America, as well as Europe, has faded from her mind. She will go to Pennsylvania willingly "if nothing happen within a month" (1257); her death takes place sixteen days later, well within the appointed time. It is notable that although, like Richardson, Clarissa never leaves English soil, unlike him she is made fluent in Italian and French. Intriguingly too, this fluency is increased in the revised third edition. In the original text Clarissa, according to Anna Howe's eulogy, "was not fond of" conversing in Italian and French, and was only beginning to study Latin (1468). In the recension she has no such hesitations about conversing, and although still a beginner in Latin "would soon have made herself an adept in it" (Everyman 4.496).

At the beginning of *Sir Charles Grandison* (1753–54), Richardson's final novel, the heroine Harriet Byron is also described as an "adept" in languages, but only in Italian and French. Unlike Clarissa, she knows nothing of Latin, or Greek, and—with a glance at Richardson's friend Elizabeth Carter—declares that the only woman who is mistress of both "wants of all things to be thought to have unlearned them" (*Sir Charles Grandison* 1.49). Like Clarissa, Harriet Byron never leaves her native land, and like Pamela she is mordantly critical of the many ill-behaved English travelers abroad. Paradoxically, the woman who marries the greatest traveler in Richardson's fiction, and surely one of the greatest in any English novel, is also Richardson's most powerful critic of that hallowed eighteenth-century institution, the grand tour. Sir Charles, she concedes, has traveled "to some purpose" (1.182), but in the same letter she insists that "human nature [is] the same in every country, allowing only for different customs" (1.184–85). Harriet's early strictures on travel are muted, but later in the novel, when she is forced to share Sir Charles's affections with her Italian rival Clementina della Porretta, her complaints are redoubled:

> Travelling! Young men travelling! I cannot, my dear, but think it a very nonsensical thing! What can they see, but the ruins of the gay, once busy world, of which they have read? . . . And when this *grand tour* is completed, the travell'd youth returns: And, what is his boast? Why to be able to tell, perhaps his *better*-taught friend, who has never been out of his native country, that he has seen in ruins, what the other has a juster idea of, from reading. (2.291)

No one in Richardson's novels makes the case against foreign travel more powerfully. Even after her marriage to Sir Charles, their mutual reconciliation with the affronted della Porrettas, and their declaration that a reunion in Italy will soon take place, Harriet remains firmly on English soil:

Richardson's appendix explains why childbirth and nursing prevent her from making the anticipated journey abroad. Only once does Harriet find herself in Italy, "a dreary wild, covered with snow, and pinched with frost," but this is a landscape of her dreams, in which she travels between countries at will, the scene changing "from England to Italy, from Italy to England" (3.149).

Effortless travel, the subject of Harriet's dream, is the stuff of Sir Charles's life.[10] For eight years, from the age of seventeen to twenty-five, he had undertaken a remarkably protracted grand tour, having previously visited all the British dominions in Europe except Gibraltar and Minorca. Unlike the great majority of eighteenth-century travelers, confined to a well-trodden route, he has visited virtually every part of Europe and gone on to "parts of Asia, and even of Africa, Egypt particularly" (1.181). An exceptionally accomplished linguist, only his grasp of Slavonian, refreshingly, seems uncertain. Although confined abroad on his father's capricious behest, he sends him valuable presents while requesting that his already modest allowance be halved. He is constantly engaged in benevolent actions for his compatriots abroad, putting his knowledge of European customs to good use, and even saves their lives on several occasions. He travels at astonishing speed, once completing the journey from Calais to London in a single day, and is utterly indifferent to the many hazards he must confront. All but airborne, he is the prototype of today's jet-setter, a term that could have been coined for him:

> Seas are nothing to him. . . . he considers all nations as joined on the same continent; and . . . if he had a call, he would undertake a journey to Constantinople or Pekin, with as little difficulty as some others would . . . to the Lands-end. (2.30)

The passage is echoed in Sir Charles's own valediction at the end of the novel, in the presence of Harriet, to the assembled della Porretta family:

> Friendship, dearest creatures, will make at pleasure a safe bridge over the narrow seas; it will cut an easy passage thro' rocks and mountains, and make England and Italy one country. Kindred souls are always near. (3.454)

When, for once, in less than perfect health, he ascribes his indisposition to a recent lack of traveling; to restore his vigor he will undertake a month's tour of Italy, described as "my little route" (2.602).

Despite his thoroughly cosmopolitan experiences, however, Sir Charles remains at heart a proud English nationalist. Early in the novel a debate takes place between two of Harriet's admirers, Sir Hargrave Pollexfen and John Greville, in which Sir Hargrave belittles Greville's enthusiasm for all things European: "He has got such a taste for foreign diversions, that he cannot think tolerably of those of his own country, be they ever so excellent" (1.106). Other characters are similarly besotted with Europe: the foppish Mr. Barnet, who "humm'd an Italian air; of which however he knew nothing" (1.20); the grotesque Captain Salmonet, who "spoke English as a Frenchman . . . but pronounced the word character as an Irishman", appearing "in a middle way between a French beau and a Dutch boor" (2.20–21);[11] and the illiterate Sir Walter Watkyns, who cannot spell in English yet supposedly "has both French and Italian at his fingers ends" (2.85). Sir Charles, in contrast, however adept at traveling, regards all countries as barbarous next to his own. Would his father, he states plaintively, but recall him to England, he would say "Adieu to travelling! Adieu to Italy, for ever!" (2.220). And in an astute analysis of his character, Harriet's Aunt Selby inquires, "How could Sir Charles, so thorough an Englishman, have been happy with an Italian wife", when "his long residence abroad, has only the more endeared to him the Religion, the Government, the Manners of England" (3.263).

Paradoxically, it is *Sir Charles Grandison,* ostensibly the most international of Richardson's novels, that most firmly delineates the boundary between England and abroad. Sir Charles, with his strictures on "those whose National Religion and Interest are directly opposite to ours" (3.264), passes as citizen of the world but is at heart John Bull. Among his most memorable pronouncements is one made to the furious Lady Olivia, whose overtures of love he has rejected. Seizing her poniard with characteristic dexterity, he declares: "Unhappy, violent woman, I return not this instrument of mischief! You will have no use for it in England." (2.380). His is the novel in which Richardson's list of characters divides the world into men, women, and Italians, and the extravagant comportment of the operatic della Porrettas, not to mention an assortment of Italian spies, sadists, bravos, and assassins, makes the distinction more than a faux pas. Lady Mary Wortley Montagu's expostulation that when Richardson "talks of Italy, it is plain he is no better acquainted with it than he is with the kingdom of Mancomugi"[12] is clearly exaggerated, yet it is true that Richardson's knowledge of Italy is literary rather than firsthand, and that none of his Italians has the verisimilitude of his English characters. It is also notable that the detailed account of an Alpine crossing from France to Italy, much admired in the eighteenth century, seems to derive from a specific literary source, William Windham and Pierre Martel's *An Account of the Glacieres or Ice Alps in Savoy.*[13]

While the prevailing view that Richardson's fiction is largely bound to English house interiors is quite untrue, it would be equally misleading to depict the novelist as an advocate of unfettered cosmopolitanism. The striking lack of interest displayed by his characters in the monuments of European culture is also disconcerting; the Casino at Bologna, to which Richardson devotes a clearly extraneous footnote (2.472), receives more attention in *Sir Charles Grandison* than all the glories of Florence or Rome. Clarissa and Harriet Byron never leave England; Pamela and, eventually, Mr. B. settle into snug domesticity after their voyages; and even Sir Charles, "to whom seas and mountains are nothing" (3.458), at last puts an end to his travels. The "safe bridge over the narrow seas" of which he speaks with such ceremony (3.454) must be set against Richardson's insistence, in his appendix, on the perils of Alpine crossings and the Bay of Biscay. To Sir Charles's fantasy of an England united with Europe, Richardson might answer with E. M. Forster, "'No, not yet' . . . 'No, not there'."[14]

# NOTES

Quotations are from T. C. Duncan Eaves and Ben D. Kimpel, *Samuel Richardson: A Biography* (Oxford: 1971); *Pamela: or, Virtue Rewarded*, ed. T. C. Duncan Eaves and Ben D. Kimpel (Boston: 1971); *Clarissa or, the History of a Young Lady*, ed. Angus Ross (Harmondsworth: 1985); *Clarissa*, Everyman edition (London: 1932); *Sir Charles Grandison*, ed. Jocelyn Harris (Oxford: 1972).

1. *Table Talk*, July 5, 1834; Thomas M. Raysor, ed., *Coleridge's Miscellaneous Criticism* (London: 1936) 437.
2. *Samuel Richardson: Dramatic Novelist* (London: 1973) 421.
3. *Travel Literature and the Evolution of the Novel* (Lexington, KY: 1983) 147. Remarkably, Adams does not consider *Sir Charles Grandison* at all.
4. *Samuel Richardson: Master Printer* (Ithaca: 1950). Jocelyn Harris, who suggests that Richardson "gave more than a cursory glance" to books "which to some extent he must have chosen to print", also notes that Keith Maslen has found two hundred further works printed by Richardson; see her "Learning and Genius in *Sir Charles Grandison*", *Studies in the Eighteenth Century* 4, ed. R. F. Brissenden and J. C. Eade (Canberra: 1979) 169.
5. See *Pamela: or, Virtue Rewarded*, ed. Peter Sabor with an introduction by Margaret Anne Doody (Harmondsworth: 1980) 451. This edition is based on Richardson's final revision, first published in 1801.
6. Madeleine Blondel, who points out that exile in Jamaica is often a means for women in the eighteenth-century novel to restore their tarnished reputations, compares the case of Sally Godfrey with that of Lady Mellasin in Eliza Haywood's *The History of Miss Betsy Thoughtless* (1751); *Images de la femme dans le roman anglais de 1740 à 1771* (Paris: 1976) 1.165 note 240.
7. *Pamela: or, Virtue Rewarded* (1741) 3.191. Quotations from the continuation of

*Pamela* are from the first edition; no satisfactory modern edition exists.

8. *Clarissa* (London: 1932) 2.419. This text is based on the third edition of 1751.
9. "Death and Colonel Morden in *Clarissa*", *South Atlantic Quarterly* 69 (1970): 346–47.
10. See my "*Amelia* and *Sir Charles Grandison*: The Convergence of Fielding and Richardson", *Wascana Review* 17 (1982): 6.
11. Margaret Anne Doody compares Captain Salmonet's "mixture of pronunciation, part French, part Irish" to that of Foigard in Farquhar's *The Beaux' Stratagem* (1707); *A Natural Passion: A Study of the Novels of Samuel Richardson* (Oxford: 1974) 284.
12. Letter to Lady Bute, October 20, 1755; *The Complete Letters of Lady Mary Wortley Montagu*, ed. Robert Halsband (Oxford: 1967) 3: 91.
13. J. C. Hilson and Rosalind Nicol, "Two Notes on *Sir Charles Grandison*", *Notes and Queries* new series 22 (1975): 492–93.
14. *A Passage to India* (Harmondsworth: 1979) 316.

# SMOLLETT'S NOVELS AND THE WIDER WORLD

Jerry C. Beasley, University of Delaware

Tobias George Smollett, born a Scotsman, departed his native Dumbartonshire in 1739 and traveled to London with high hopes that his tragedy, *The Regicide*, would make him an instantaneous success in the world of English letters. Failure greeted him abruptly, and roughly too; he was unable to persuade anyone who mattered that his play was worthy of production. Friendless, demoralized, he then failed also in his initial attempts to establish himself in London medical circles, though he had received excellent professional training during an apprenticeship with the distinguished Glasgow surgeons William Stirling and John Gordon. From his youth (he was only eighteen when he left home) Smollett considered himself an alien in his adopted land of England. Despite later literary successes and eventual prominence, he never got over his early disappointments or feelings of dislocation. His situation was not unique, of course; many transplanted Scots and Irishmen met with equal discouragement and had to endure at least equally painful denial of access to the centers of eighteenth-century English life as they saw them. But Smollett's sense of himself as alien seems to have been especially acute, and it made him forever a traveler—in mind, if not perpetually in body. He rarely if ever felt at home.

For the young Smollett, it appears, London was the great world and he a stranger who had ventured into it—not by accident, to be sure, but not altogether happily either. For the mature Smollett, the Smollett we know best from several very fine and very important novels, the great world was larger than London or even England, but it was on the whole no better a place. Life itself was a hard adventure and it was always a matter of being in motion, of passing through time and space from one moment to the next and from this place to that. Travel is a presiding metaphor in almost all of Smollett's imaginative writing; and it provides the structural framework for the plots of all his novels. Going abroad, as Smollett often did and as many of his characters do, extended the range of one's knowledge (he thought) and deepened one's understanding both of the world and of the self. To know the people and customs of a foreign land was to know better the people and customs of one's own native land—or, in Smollett's case, one's adopted land. To confront the great world beyond through the characters of its men and women and through the institutions they had created was to confront the self, to be forced into existential experience of the troublesome meaning of individualism and into awareness of the elemental human need for a stable, harmonious, loving community that one might call home.

Smollett's first novel, *The Adventures of Roderick Random* (1748), takes its hero to the Caribbean aboard a British man-of-war (the episode is revealingly autobiographical) and then subsequently sends him across much of Europe.[1] His second and third novels, *The Adventures of Peregrine Pickle* (1751) and *The Adventures of Ferdinand Count Fathom* (1753), contain lengthy European episodes. The eponymous hero-villain of the latter work is, in fact, quite literally born a traveler; he enters the world roughly aboard a wagon as it crosses the boundary between Holland and Flanders and then spends most of his early childhood strapped to his camp-following mother's back as she moves about the European landscape with the allied army during the closing years of the War of the Spanish Succession (1702–13). *The Adventures of Sir Launcelot Greaves* (1760–61) and *The Expedition of Humphry Clinker* (1771), Smollett's last two novels, restrict their focus to the scenery of the British Isles, though the characters are constantly in motion. By a seemingly odd contradiction, Smollett traveled abroad more extensively during the decade framed by these two works than at any other period of his life. It is no doubt significant that he was very ill for most of this time and that he traveled as much for his health as for the satisfaction of his curiosity. Illness made him reflective; as he looked upon the wider world from the perspective of one seeking not only amusement and edification but (futilely) relief from the suffering that racked his tubercular body, he looked more closely than ever at the land he knew best.

*Sir Launcelot Greaves* came at a critical point during a long period of debilitatingly frenzied work that finally left Smollett exhausted, frail, extremely irascible, and nearly desperate for change and rest. He wrote the novel for serialization in his *British Magazine* (it was the first novel by a major British writer to be published in this manner), and his intent no doubt was to improve monthly sales for this new periodical venture. Composition began while Smollett was in the King's Bench prison serving out his punishment for a viciously libelous attack on Admiral Charles Knowles published in another magazine he edited, the *Critical Review*. *Sir Launcelot Greaves* is, however, a mellow tale—or at least it is more mellow than the three novels that had preceded it. Its titular hero is a quintessentially English gentleman, a comic figure modeled on Don Quixote who roams the countryside confronting and righting wrongs (some of them quite horrendous) by the force of his worthy example until the progress of his career in loving righteousness and Cervantean idealism leads him to rest in rural serenity at Greavesbury Hall. The novel projects a fantasy of wish fulfillment deriving from its author's obvious need for detachment from the very real hardships and very real pain of his daily experience.

During the years that followed, Smollett achieved that detachment—or at least he diverted himself from the continued frenzy of his work, from the increasingly torturous effects of his illness, and from the inexpressible sorrow brought on by the death of his only child, Elizabeth, at the age of fifteen. Within months of her loss he departed with his wife for the Continent, and from November 1763 to April 1765 the family lived in Nice. Their return to England was temporary. Smollett's last novel, *Humphry Clinker*, was written from first page to last after he had removed permanently in 1768 to the warmer climate of Italy. The move did not restore his health; he died at Leghorn, three months after the publication of his novel in London in June 1771. It apparently did, however, restore his happiness through memories of his beloved Scotland, a place he had visited rarely following his departure in 1739 but to which he returned imaginatively in a long and loving section of *Humphry Clinker* set in the region of Loch Lomond and Leven-Water—Smollett's boyhood home, the "Arcadia of Scotland" as it is described in his novel. It is here that the valetudinarian Welshman Matthew Bramble completes his own quest for health and tranquillity, something his author was helpless to do.

It is clear that for Smollett the novelist, travel represented a way of living—or thinking about living. The same was true for Smollett the translator, the compiler, the editor, the historian. Much of his most important work outside the domain of fiction was devoted to literature and to places not English. In the very year during which *Roderick Random* appeared he published also a translation of the French writer Le Sage's celebrated picaresque romance, *Gil Blas*; no translation has since superseded Smollett's. His *Don Quixote* came out in 1755, and has been characterized by Carlos Fuentes in the foreword to a recent reprint edition (1986) as the most sensitive, if not the most lexicographically reliable, translation ever produced. During the 1760s Smollett collaborated on a major English edition of the works of Voltaire.

These distinguished translations and other, lesser efforts of the same kind were no doubt bookseller's jobs undertaken for money, but they signify the degree to which Smollett's imagination was engaged by cultures other than his own. There are further signs of such engagement in his labors as historian, most of them devoted to the English past (his four-volume

*Complete History of England* [1757–58] is a truly accomplished work of its kind), but one of them, *The Present State of All Nations*, a significant attempt to write a comprehensive account of the modern world. Published first in weekly sixpenny numbers during the early months of 1768, the *Present State* was then reissued in eight bound volumes before the end of that same year, after Smollett had left for Italy. This work, though partly by other hands, displays Smollett's astonishingly comprehensive knowledge—gained both from reading and from travel—of the geography, customs, and politics of all of the important countries of the Western world as it was known in the eighteenth century.[2]

It is in his efforts as editor, compiler, and travel writer that Smollett's interest in lands abroad emerges most conspicuously. In 1754 he prepared for the press an elegant edition of a work by Alexander Drummond, brother of the lord provost of Edinburgh, entitled *Travels through Different Cities of Germany, Italy, Greece, and Several Parts of Asia, as Far as the Banks of the Euphrates*. At this same time he was busy with a massive bookseller's project impressively called, when finally its seven volumes appeared in April 1756, *A Compendium of Authentic and Entertaining Voyages*. None of the work in this *Compendium* is Smollett's own, but to prepare it he had to read widely in the huge abundance of travel literature available at the time. The experience proved valuable when, in 1766, he completed and published his own *Travels through France and Italy*.

Because Smollett's book of *Travels* is treated at length elsewhere in this volume, little comment on it is required here. But it must be said that the work is much more than at first glance it appears to be, simply one more among many eighteenth-century narrative exercises in cultural tourism. Written as an account of its author's extended excursion to the Continent from 1763 to 1765, the *Travels* is powerfully descriptive—candid in its treatment of people and customs, vigorous and forthright in its appraisals of European art and architecture; it is even more powerfully imaginative and reflective. Smollett was no dilettante, and he despised the effusions of connoisseurs and virtuosi who, in his view, traveled and wrote only as excuses to indulge and celebrate themselves. Deeply learned in history, deeply attentive to and knowledgeable about painting, sculpture, and the other fine arts, he made his narrative a vehicle for thoughtfully sharp (and sometimes wickedly caustic) commentary on the people he encountered and the institutions and artifacts he looked at with his observant eyes. For his candor he earned the title "Dr. Smelfungus", bestowed upon him by Laurence Sterne in *A Sentimental Journey* (1768).

The epithetical joke was unkind and unfair, but it does point our attention to a quality that Smollett's *Travels* shares with Sterne's unmistakably fictionalized narrative of a similar excursion. In both works the narrative voice is a contrived persona, a deliberate projection of an authorial self—Sterne's Yorick, Smollett's unnamed letter writer. The tones of every voice and the substance of the observations each spreads across the pages of his narrative combine detachment with deep engagement, reflection upon an observed self with explicit reaction to an observed world. The balance between detachment and engagement, reflection and reaction is different in the two works. Sterne's portrait of Yorick when he is at his most effusively sentimental is all but explicitly ironic and bemused; Smollett is harder to catch in such maneuvers, though the letters that make up his narrative are frequently as indirectly self-revealing of the character of the intensely imagined author-traveler as they are shrewd in their assessments of the subjects he writes about. But the point is that both Sterne and Smollett transformed the traditions and conventions of the familiar travel narrative, reimagining them in near-novelistic terms as occasions and devices for the study of character acting in response to environment. Henry Fielding had done much the same thing some years earlier in his *Journal of a Voyage to Lisbon* (1755).

Percy G. Adams, in *Travel Literature and the Evolution of the Novel* (1983), refers to all three of these works by Sterne, Smollett, and Fielding as evidence of the degree to which the two primary modes of narrative writing in the eighteenth century blurred in the consciousness of those who employed them, reinforcing and nurturing one another. In this light it is easy to see Smollett's *Travels* as a kind of companion piece, even a prelude of sorts, to his last and finest work of unqualified fiction, *Humphry Clinker*. The one narrative is convincingly authentic but enriched by its author's impulse to fictionalize; the other is undisguisedly fictional, but grounded in the close observations of its letter-writing travelers as they respond to everything they see, meanwhile revealing themselves through their language and through the details upon which they actually fix their attention.[3] The *Travels* ranges over the culture of western Europe; *Humphry Clinker* comes home again, and it is all the wiser and finer because its author has been abroad.

In *Humphry Clinker* Smollett turns his observant eye closely upon the British landscape and the people who inhabit it, though he does register once again his interest in the wider world by introducing accounts of the eccentric Lismahago's journeyings among the North American Indians. Smollett's last novel differs from all of his earlier fiction in the manner of its narrative. An epistolary novel, it allows each letter-writing traveler—Matthew Bramble, his nephew and niece Jery and Lydia Melford, his sister Tabitha, their servant Winifred Jenkins—to describe and reflect upon their experiences in all of the places they visit together: Bristol, Bath, London, Edinburgh, and the many other stops along the path of their journey. Collectively their letters provide not only a set of incisive character studies but also an anatomy of British society and culture in the late 1760s. Long passages turn upon such subjects as class conflict, or tensions arising from England's painful political passage into the revolutionary period of the last quarter of the century, or the increasing urbanization at the dawning of an industrial age, or religious controversies as figured in the preaching of the enthusiastically Methodistic Clinker. There are scenes set in spas, theaters, court assemblies. The novel vibrates with satiric energy; Smollett delights in the exposure of pretensions and follies, including the pretensions and follies of the letter writers themselves. But the vision of *Humphry Clinker* is finally comic. Its structure, like that of a travel narrative, is deliberately fragmented and episodic, but at last the story resolves itself into wholeness as the travelers prepare to complete their circular journey from Wales, through England and Scotland, and back to Wales again.

*Humphry Clinker* restricts the geographic range of its travelers, but its record of their progress from conditions of personal discontent and interpersonal discord into happiness and harmony repeats a pattern we find in Smollett's earlier, more expansive novels of worldwide adventures. Travel always brings about collision with a reality that is harsh, corrupt, marred by human failure to conform to any meaningful idealism of moral conduct. The world as Smollett's characters meet it threatens terrifying entropy instead of comforting order; it inevitably scatters experience, since wholeness is possible only in a stable community founded upon the principles of selfless love. Such love is so rare as to seem almost illusory, and the kind of universal environment its predominance would make possible in human affairs only a fantasy. This fantasy, as old as the Christian mythology of the restored paradise promised by the redemptive suffering and death of Christ upon a cross created by a sinful world, certainly compelled Smollett's moral imagination. It raised ideas of tranquillity and rest. But his literary imagination was moved even more by the spectacle of human questing after fulfillment of the fantasy or, more often and much more troublingly, striving selfishly against everything that it represented and everything that it demanded for its fulfillment.

In all of Smollett's fiction, character matters more than place. It is people who define the world, who express its meaning, who corrupt it by their conduct and by the institutions they create. Thus, even in his early novels of adventures abroad—*Roderick Random, Peregrine Pickle, Ferdinand Count Fathom*—Smollett rarely indulges in detailed scenic description. The naval adventures recorded in chapters 24–37 of *Roderick Random* take Smollett's hero to Carthagena, but we see almost nothing of the exotic West Indian environment. Instead, Roderick's narrative turns upon an intensive account of the miseries inflicted upon him and his mates by the incompetence and cruelty of the officers under whom they serve. The ship—called *Thunder*, but modeled after the *Chichester*, Smollett's own ship during the 1741 expedition—is a miniature version of the world; it sails in foreign waters on a mission into disgrace, and the fluid medium of the sea itself suggests a continuity between Roderick's harsh experiences on shipboard and those he had endured at home, as a boy in his native Scotland and as a young man in London. The episode (in Chapter 29) of the terrifying bombardment throughout which Roderick, accused wrongly of a crime, lies chained to the poop deck—brains and bodies blown into bloody pieces all over him—demonstrates the ferocity of the world's hostility to the value of the individual life and to the idealism of community and order ultimately promoted by the novel in its resolution. In this episode we catch Smollett at one of his darkest moments. But the darkness here is only relatively greater than that found elsewhere in the novel, in the record of adventures set closer to home; the violence and cruelty of Roderick's shipboard life are consequences of human corruption that is limited neither to place nor to nationality.

In an earlier, equally grim episode during the same sequence of Roderick's naval adventures, Smollett develops a hellish picture of the human condition at its lowest and most miserable. Shortly after he has been dragooned into service aboard the *Thunder* by a London press gang, Roderick has his first sight of the ship's sick berth below deck, where "about fifty miserable distempered wretches" lay in hammocks "suspended in rows" so closely together in the darkness that, "deprived of the light of the day, as well as of fresh air", and breathing "nothing but a noisome atmosphere of the morbid steams exhaling from their own excrements and diseased bodies", they were "devoured with vermin hatched in the filth that surrounded them" and left "destitute of every convenience necessary for people in that helpless condition" (*Roderick Random* 149; ch. 25). This picture, along with the rest of Roderick's account of his life as a sailor, has been taken as authentic ever since it was first written. No doubt it is authentic, as Smollett meant it to be. But its significance resides not so much in its literal accuracy as in its evocative power as a picture of human suffering caused by inhuman cruelty.

Later, his naval experiences behind him, Roderick passes through Europe on his way back to England. In France he encounters a thieving, lusty Capuchin friar named Balthazar, a character whose hypocrisies and deceptions Smollett most definitely associates with the French people and their detested Catholicism but who is in no essential way different from other disreputable types Roderick has met before. During brief service with the French army (ch. 43–44), then engaged against England and its allies in the long War of the Austrian Succession (1740–48), he rails at the false bravado of the French soldiers and the ineptitude of their officers—the echoes of his outraged denunciations of the English naval administration and its admirals are unmistakable. What fixes Roderick's attention throughout these episodes of foreign travel, and elsewhere in his narrative, is the "villainy of mankind" (p. 242); and that villainy is universal. The restlessness that precipitated his initial departure from his Scottish homeland thrust Smollett's hero into a knowledge of the world that he could not have anticipated possessing, and it is this knowledge—demoralizing and at once thrilling to his increasing sense of just indignation—that he takes back to England with him. Such knowledge is necessary and inescapable, but it is almost disastrous to his chances of happiness. Roderick becomes a prisoner of his own rage and cynicism in response to the world at large; he winds up literally in the Marshalsea and has to be rescued providentially by his author.

The theme of imprisonment figures importantly in all of Smollett's early novels, and it is closely related to the theme of travel itself. There is a paradox here. If life is a journey into the wide world of experience and then out again, as the narrative structures of the novels suggest, then it is a dangerous journey not only because the world threatens the self but because the self, in response to the world, threatens its own integrity and safety. In both a metaphoric and a literal sense, the idea of motion is seductive—never more so than in the new age of travel during which Smollett lived and wrote. Smollett's fictional versions of the eighteenth-century traveler revised the ancient mythology of the quest and discovered firsthand that freedom of movement did not necessarily mean ease of progress toward liberation of the self. Like Ulysses and Bunyan's Christian, and like Robinson Crusoe as well, Smollett's vigorous young adventurers find their way blocked by obstacles, disastrous accidents, sloughs, monsters of temptation and despair; the greatest threat they all must face and escape is enclosure within the isolating walls of self-absorption.

*Peregrine Pickle* was written at least in part after Smollett's first tours to the Continent in 1749 and 1750. No doubt his travel experiences determined him to send the exuberantly roguish hero of his new novel off to some of the same places he had recently visited. Perry lacks Roderick Random's fundamental good nature—the "modest merit" Smollett attributes to his young Scotsman in the preface to his first novel (xxxv). The victim of some of the same cruelties in childhood as Roderick, Perry is a rebel and a prankster at home who continues the same habits when he goes abroad. Much more than Roderick, he is the initiator of his own momentum, though many of the effects of his journeying are the same. Smollett's impulse in the European portions of both *Roderick Random* and *Peregrine Pickle* is that of the satirist. In the latter work he specifically parodies the conventions of the grand tour, introduces European characters—most conspicuously the French—and holds them up to ridicule, and also brings Perry into confrontations with fellow English travelers whom he mocks and toys prankishly with, sometimes cruelly, as a means of exposing their foolishness while simultaneously affirming his own superior intelligence and wit. The resemblances to the *Satyricon* of Petronius are unmistakable, but Smollett turns those resemblances back upon his hero. Perry's scatological jokes at the expense of the guests at a great dinner held in imitation of Trimalchio's feast (ch. 48–49) are funny but unspeakably mean-spirited. Smollett and the reader, like Perry, delight in the intestinal and other miseries suffered by all but themselves; yet it is clear from this episode alone that the Englishman abroad is no finer or more admirable a figure than the inhabitants of the countries he visits.

Perry's adventures do occasion some fairly explicit references to familiar European scenery. At one point (in Chapter 43) he adopts the disguise of a Frenchman and goes touring about, visiting "the Luxembourg gallery, Palais Royal, all the remarkable hotels, churches, and celebrated places in Paris" (207)—his real motive being, as we learn later in the same chapter, his "vanity", which has suggested to him the pleasures of profiting by "his talents among the fair sex", on whom he resolves to employ "his utmost art and address" (209). Chapter 44 occasions a Smollettean tirade against the French system of justice, which, "on the maxim of Herod" (211), responds to any crime by punishing multiple suspected offenders when it cannot precisely identify a guilty party. The same chapter goes on to display Perry's own questionable ideas of justice. He is "a professed enemy to all oppression" (212), but Smollett embroils him in a duel during which he fights unfairly, is wounded, and is at last victorious—"for the glory of Old England" (216). Ironically, the dubious glory is more for Perry than for England, as the entire episode has been occasioned by resentment over his antagonist's interference in one of his many frivolous affairs of the heart.

Perry's European travels provide an analogue for his adventures at home. Whether in England or abroad, the characters he meets are types who may be found anywhere—the fop; the boor; the pretentious fool; the misanthrope; the dupe; the leering nobleman; the corrupt politician; the man of avarice, lust, or gluttony; the whore; the virginal maiden. Willful roguishness replaces Roderick Random's righteous indignation and rage, but the results are much the same. Perry's self-conscious arrogance against those he justly scorns, and his aggressive pursuit of sexual pleasure not only with loose women but at the expense of virginal innocence, leave him finally in a deplorable condition of loneliness and imprisonment. The restless wanderer becomes an exile. Only when he acknowledges that he has been little better than the selfish, cruel world he has so ruthlessly scourged can Perry gain release from the trap he has set for himself. The episode of his recognition occurs, significantly, while he is locked up in the Fleet prison following his arrest ostensibly for a real debt he had neglected to pay but actually for an attack he had published against a corrupt minister whose favor he had been courting. The paradox of Perry's situation illuminates the paradox of experience itself as it is represented in Smollett's stories of adventurous travel. Confrontation between the individual and the great world is both inevitable and necessary, but the confrontation produces destructive conflict and threatens to leave the self in a condition of miserable isolation. Cynicism has its awful price. It is not by accident that Smollett makes Peregrine Pickle say, shortly after his imprisonment in chapter 105, "a jail is the best tub to which a cynic philosopher can retire" (678).

Ferdinand Count Fathom, the titular hero of Smollett's third novel, is no rogue errant but a thoroughgoing villain. The pattern of his experience nevertheless repeats that defined in *Peregrine Pickle*. Born on the move and trained from his infancy to lie, steal, cheat, and deceive, Fathom in his youth crisscrosses the European continent first as a soldier and then as a bogus Polish nobleman. His talents enable him to dupe many of the people he meets, while his arrogance makes him an easy mark for numerous superiors in the arts of the confidence man. In all settings, from fashionable assemblies to gaming houses to private homes, his fraudulence mirrors and exposes the fraudulence on which the great world and its characters—French, Spanish, Dutch, German, English—are founded. When Fathom travels to England, the land of his ancestors, he ironically imagines himself another conquering hero like Caesar—"Ah ha, old England", he exclaims at the moment of his landing in Chapter 27, "I have thee fast" (*Ferdinand Count Fathom* 129). The irony is at Fathom's own expense, as events are to prove. The aim of all his traveling is to bring the world, its people and its riches, under his power and into his possession. This aim defines both his villainy and his folly, which will at last combine to bring him only to ruin.

George M. Kahrl has remarked of *Ferdinand Count Fathom* that, despite its interest as a novel in which Smollett gave the greatest loose to his preoccupation with the world abroad, the idea of foreign travel actually had "only a secondary and desultory influence" upon his conception as a whole; "though localities are often specified", there is almost a "total absence of distinguishing features of geography or society". In "none of his novels", Kahrl protests, did Smollett allow himself such "varied opportunities for contrasting one nationality with another, and in none did he have less to say on the subject.".[4] Kahrl is right, but his remarks are beside the point. To the jaundiced eyes of the predatory Fathom the world is everywhere very much the same; differences of place, nationality, and culture amount to little. To put this another way: in *Ferdinand Count Fathom* Smollett internalized the villainous energies of the worldwide human environment. Fathom is a representation of those energies who gives them precise definition, and his portrait is besides a thoughtful study of the aberrant criminal character. The two functions complement one another. Fathom is in some sense a reflection of every character type he meets. The reflection is dark: if Fathom is so unrelievedly evil, what must the world be?

The answer is clear. The world is criminally evil and dark—it is full of frauds and charlatans, thieves and swindlers, whores and bawds and rakes; but it is finally not so bad as Fathom is. Smollett places his hero-villain in the midst of darkness, but even more emphatically he throws him into relief against a separate reality of idealized virtue as figured in the exemplary characters of Renaldo and Monimia. Both of these paragons are Europeans transplanted to England, and so their significance, like that of the other universal character types Fathom encounters, is global. In the end their example triumphs and Fathom is undone. Brought low by his own predatory selfishness, his energy spent, he languishes in prison until at last he is released by the benevolent generosity of Renaldo and Monimia, now united in love but formerly the objects of Fathom's supreme expenditures of wicked industry and ingenuity.

*Ferdinand Count Fathom*, far from obscuring the meaning of Smollett's uses of travel in his novels (as Kahrl would seem to suggest), actually clarifies that meaning for us. Its representation of the world as dominated by what is represented in Fathom suggests a comprehensive vision of human insufficiency that occurs in every story that Smollett wrote. Motion is inevitable as a condition of living; it thrills, energizes, delights, horrifies, instructs. Motion is experience itself, and for Smollett the novelist the great object of attention is the gallery of human characters that experience places on display. Specific settings, customs, politics, institutions are decidedly less important—though it is undeniably true that, as a somewhat xenophobic Briton, Smollett missed few opportunities to disparage Europeans as living in the shadows of unenlightened law, politics, religion, and social convention.[5] Curiosity about the world is a good, for it expands the range of the individual's view. But it is also a danger, for the world has the power to corrupt—as Roderick Random and Peregrine Pickle learn to their cost, as Ferdinand Count Fathom knows almost from the instant of his birth. Sir Launcelot Greaves and Matthew Bramble know it too. Greaves finds his quixotic idealism tested every inch of the way along his road to eventual triumph and rest; Matt Bramble, a would-be misanthrope, must purge himself of a tendency to respond furiously to infuriating reality before he can settle into equilibrium and joy.

Smollett understood that the individual could survive the journey of life with integrity intact and with happiness to look forward to only through discovery of and persistence in an idealism of selfless love. He was much more reflective than any of his fictional characters; even his early novels, with their relentless patterns of progressive degradation followed by descent into a nadir of hopelessness and then by eventual release, give unequivocal signs that he was projecting interpretive fables; they are Christian fables, expressions of faith in a providential universe. The psychological and moral relevance of these fables does not rest upon what Smollett's characters think, but upon what they do in response to what they feel. Roderick Random must act upon the real meaning of his love for the beauteous and faithful Narcissa; Peregrine Pickle must give himself to the lovely Amelia, abandoning his attempts to seduce and ruin her; Fathom must accept all that Renaldo and Monimia are, and he must come to be like them; Greaves must persist, Matt Bramble must arrive at the proper sympathetic response to the idyllic Scottish countryside.

Smollett, like most of his fictional characters, was himself ambivalent about the human issues raised by their experience. Travel fascinated him precisely because it offered freedom for his restless energies, and what he observed wherever he went seems usually to have confirmed him in his own raging impatience with mankind. His mature life, no doubt including the many months and years of effort he devoted to the composition of his novels, was a long struggle to arrive at some reconciliation between the idealism he clung to and the reality that made him frequently cynical. He was an irascible as well as a restless man, and his personal struggle threatened profound alienation by dark imprisonment of the self in angry rejection of everyone and everything else. At least one biographical critic has suggested that this struggle led him near to madness.[6] Whether Smollett ever achieved personal reconciliation is impossible to know; but in the fantasies that were his novels he certainly did achieve it. Roderick Random, Peregrine Pickle, and Ferdinand Count Fathom find release from the prison cells to which their journeys through the great world have brought them; Sir Launcelot Greaves and the travelers in *Humphry Clinker* pass through and overcome a world that is geographically smaller but morally and psychologically just as expansive—Smollett knew, as a consequence of his own experience abroad, that travel was a state of mind and spirit rather than of body and place.

It was finally the self that Smollett explored in his novels, and not just the world through which his imaginary people moved. Travel provided for him a metaphor by which he could delineate the engagement between imperfect human character and an imperfect, exasperating, ridiculous, cruel, wicked, destructive reality—a reality that was, of course, largely a human creation. He represented that reality unflinchingly and relentlessly; but somehow he never stopped believing, against all the evidence he himself could amass in his busy, teeming stories of restless adventuring, that idealism, decency, goodness would give the last definition to the meaning of experience. In his novels at least, Smollett resolved the paradox with which he himself daily lived and about which he always wrote. If human life is a journey into a domain that inevitably corrupts and threatens to destroy the essential humanity of the self, it is also—it must be, or we are doomed—a journey into knowledge and, at last, redemption.

# NOTES

Quotations are from *The Adventures of Roderick Random*, ed. Paul-Gabriel Boucé (Oxford: 1979); *The Adventures of Peregrine Pickle*, ed. James L. Clifford, rev. Paul-Gabriel Boucé (Oxford: 1983); *The Adventures of Ferdinand Count Fathom*, ed. Damian Grant (Oxford: 1971).

1. Roderick's naval adventures are based on Smollett's own observations as a surgeon's mate during the disastrous British expedition to Carthagena in 1741. The engagement there was among the most important of the so-called War of Jenkins' Ear. For a very full discussion of Smollett's use of his naval experience in *Roderick Random* see George M. Kahrl, *Tobias Smollett: Traveler-Novelist* (Chicago: 1945) ch. 1.
2. In the late 1750s and early 1760s Smollett also collaborated on a large project entitled *The Modern Part of an Universal History*; this work, like the *Present State* after it, is worldwide in scope.
3. Charles L. Batten, Jr., has observed that it is actually very difficult to classify *Humphry Clinker* either as a travel book or as a novel; see his *Pleasurable Instruction: Form and Convention in Eighteenth-Century Travel Literature* (Berkeley and Los Angeles: 1978) 21–23. Batten is surely wrong to feel such confusion, but he does point to the ingenious mixing of novelistic and travel narrative Smollett achieved in his work.
4. Kahrl 54.
5. This is the case not only in his novels, but also in many of his other works, including the *Present State* and, of course, the *Travels.*
6. See G. S. Rousseau, "Towards Maturity and Mental Collapse", *Tobias Smollett: Essays of Two Decades* (Edinburgh: 1982) 1–9.

# TOURISM AND CULTURAL CHALLENGE: THE CHANGING SCENE OF THE EIGHTEENTH CENTURY

Jeremy Black, Durham University

Travel for pleasure increased in the eighteenth century. There is no relevant reliable statistical series, but all contemporary commentators were certain of a marked increase, particularly after the end of the Seven Years' War in 1763. This phenomenon was in no way restricted to the British. Across most of Europe there are indications that increasing numbers of the social elite traveled for pleasure, their tours being far from short. Their goals were similar. Swedes, Poles, Germans, and Russians wished to visit Paris and Italy as much as British tourists did. There were several reasons for this situation. One that must not be discounted was the role of fashion. The eighteenth century was at the higher social level increasingly a consumer society affected by fashions; news of the latter spread by the growing number of ephemeral publications and the literature of social manners. Travel became fashionable as a means of finishing the education of youths, as a source of social polish, and as a pleasant and desirable way in which to spend periods of leisure. A linked reason of great significance was the cosmopolitan nature of European society during the period that has been described as the Enlightenment. This contrasted with the situation in the sixteenth and seventeenth centuries, when cosmopolitan links were made in accordance with or in defiance of the strident animosities of competing religious camps.

The eighteenth century was scarcely an age free from religious intolerance, and in Britain there was a constant polemic directed against Catholic Europe. Indeed anti-Catholicism could be described as the principal ideological commitment of the period.[1] However, though animosity remained a marked feature of the period, tourism to countries following a different type of Christianity ceased to be hazardous. Furthermore, the sense of a common European cultural inheritance was no longer obscured by an awareness of hostility. To British tourists Rome was now an ancient source of cultural inspiration, Paris the present forcing-house for European culture and ideas.

The value and dangers of this cosmopolitanism were the principal items on the agenda of public debate over tourism, an agenda and a debate that changed singularly little between 1660 and 1780, even if the examples cited did alter to a certain extent. The varying fortunes of the Jacobite challenge and the changing location of the Jacobite court affected the extent to which tourism could be seen as politically dangerous. As such, tourism constituted but part of a wider debate over cosmopolitanism, English cultural integrity, and Britain's role in the wider world. There was considerable tension over cultural borrowing from Europe. While the British hated French politics, they aped French fashions, or rather a large section of the upper orders did. This provided much of the tension. Criticism of the situation arose from a sense of cultural unease. It also arose from a certain amount of—not class conflict, for a fully articulated class system did not exist—but social tension. It is not surprising that this was most marked in London, the prime cultural sounding board and market in Britain, and in the London press. It was certainly believed that, as Lord Raymond claimed in the Lords, "the people of England are by nature or habit enemies to foreigners", though Baron Pöllnitz, a widely traveled German writer, denied it. The diplomat Lord Glenorchy referred to "the difficulties strangers meet with in England",[2] but it is difficult to investigate these claims. Most foreigners visited London only, and it was there that the "foreign" court of William III and the Hanoverians was located. As the capital contained the largest population both of settled and of transient foreigners, and as many of them competed for jobs, it is unsurprising that most instances of violent xenophobia came from London. The Holstein envoy Petkum was beaten up by riotous footmen in 1718, ten years later the Tripolitanian ambassador's secretary was attacked "perhaps from a dislike of the secretary's habit, or to his being a foreigner",[3] in 1736 the Sardinian envoy's chapel was disrupted by anti-Catholic demonstrators during a service. Foreigners were jostled in the streets, foreign sailors involved in brawls.

Popular hostility had cultural consequences, as when French theatrical companies were greeted with violence in London in 1738, 1739, 1743, 1749, and 1755.[4] Xenophobia was a staple of political comment, cultural preferences serving as a supposed indicator of political tendencies. This was brilliantly expressed in the food symbolism used in so many attacks on the court and on the Walpole ministry. In place of the "roast beef of Old England", the ministry was accused of preferring Continental food, and, in particular, French cuisine with its rich sauces supposedly disguising the absence of meat and the fundamental insubstantiality of the meal. The classic instance is *The Norfolk Congress*, a prose squib that appeared in November 1728, with a ballad version the following month. This account of the autumnal gathering of Walpole's cronies at his new mansion of Houghton in Norfolk made much of food imagery. Before the guests depart for the hunt they receive a breakfast of foreign dishes and after the hunt a dinner of the same that did not agree with their "English stomachs". Walpole's policy was linked to his appetite: "But now French sauces will go down". Underlining the criticism was an element of truth. Many ministers, in particular the duke of Newcastle, were conspicuous for their love of French cuisine. Newcastle lavished attention on his French food, and pestered Earl Waldegrave, envoy in Paris, for a supply of truffles and truffled pies.

Criticism was also marked at the aping of French fashions and coiffures. The Frenchified tastes of the upper orders were blamed for the economic difficulties affecting British workmen, and clothing was a standard item of opposition propaganda. In 1732 there was a fuss over press accusations that most of the clothes worn at court on George II's birthday were French. The establishment of a rival court around Frederick, Prince of Wales, and his patronage of the opposition and willingness to make conscious "nationalistic" gestures provided a fresh opportunity for the opposition to exploit the situation. Court and ministerial patronage of opera provided opportunities for opposition publicists in plenty. Opera was held to be degenerate and morally dubious, the ambivalent sexuality of the singers—castrati and men dressed as women—supposedly symbolizing its corrupt and alien nature.

Much of the literature of xenophobia, the patriotic polemic, was clearly due to opposition propaganda, and, in particular, to opposition to the supposed consequences of the Williamite and then Hanoverian accession. This focused three distinct strands, Jacobite opposition to the usurpers, "country" hostility to the court, and Tory suspicion that Whig ministers, in order to curry favor with the crown, were betraying national interests. However, behind these clearly political assumptions can be discerned a state of cultural fear. For many, Britain was less sophisticated, urbane, attractive, and fashionable than France, the indigenous culture less rich than the Continental counterpoint of classical restraint and baroque exuberance. The attraction of the latter in particular, and it lay behind the vogue for Italian opera, was a major one, presenting as it did the manifestation in sumptuous earthly form of something mysterious, magical, and splendid. The most surprising people were affected. Samuel Davies, a nonconformist American divine touring Britain on a fund-raising mission in the 1750s, visited Glasgow University:

> saw . . . a collection of pictures lately imported from France. One was the picture of the dead body of Christ taken off the cross and carrying to the sepulchre. The prints of the nails in his hands and feet, the stab of the spear in his side, the effusion of the blood, etc were so lively, that they unavoidably excited a sort of popish devotion in me.[5]

Lockean philosophy, deistic religion, and the English cultural inheritance could not compete successfully with Continental culture. It was hardly surprising that they were to capitulate later in the century to the indigenous developments of sensibility, neo-Gothicism, Romanticism, and evangelicalism. In the meantime a large number of the social elite not only toured abroad to no apparent useful purpose, for this was to happen in the following century also, but also actively patronized alien cultural developments both abroad and at home. Enjoying Italian opera in Milan was bad enough. Patronizing it in London was both more conspicuous and worse, and led to doubts about ideas and inclinations supposedly acquired abroad.

The tension between cosmopolitanism and the patriotic response can be seen both in the response to tourism and in the writing that it inspired. From the scholarly perspective there are three categories of extant tourist writing: manuscript accounts, accounts published by contemporaries, and those published subsequently. These three categories should be grouped into the first and third, and the second, there being a clear division between material that was intended for publication and that designed for personal recollection, family or friends. It could be suggested that a lack of clarity has arisen from a habit of conflating these types of material and treating them indiscriminately as sources for the grand tour. It is rather the case that travel literature should be sharply differentiated from letters and journals never intended for publication. There is little doubt that artifice could play a role in the latter. A youth writing home to his parents might have many reasons to disguise his activities and gloss his responses. Journals were shown to others, letters handed around by friends and relations. However, even if the written record was therefore contrived, there was a major difference between writing for a small and intimate circle, and producing a work for a large anonymous market, in which the sole identifiable readers would be publishers and booksellers concerned about commercial appeal. The conventions expected by the market and the reviewers had to be respected.

Most of the well-known accounts of tourism in this period fall into the category of travel literature. They vary in their methods, tone, and areas covered—Addison's prose is not like that of Smollett—but they share a concern with impact and style. It is not surprising that scholars have concentrated on these writers. Their views were and are most accessible, through being printed. Because they wrote for publication, their writings are easier and more attractive to read than subsequently printed accounts that were never thus intended. Many of the writers were major literary figures. Furthermore, much of the work on tourism has been done by amateurs lacking the time, resources, or dedication to search for manuscript sources, and by literary scholars whose forte has generally lain elsewhere. It is not surprising that both groups of writers have concentrated on readily accessible published material by prominent figures. There is nothing necessarily wrong about this, provided both that such accounts are not taken as typical of the writings or views of tourists and that the extent to which they should be taken as works of literature is appreciated. An obvious example is Tobias Smollett's *Travels through France and Italy*. It is well established that this was a work to which plagiarism had contributed and that many of the letters it contained, supposedly written from France and Italy, were in fact written after his return to England. Percy Adams commented: "the only defense of Smollett to be offered is that his methods, both in editing the voyages of other writers and in writing his own, were not at all unusual in his day".[6]

Smollett, like Johnson and Goldsmith, had been a prominent journalist, an eager and partisan polemicist in political matters. Journalism not only provided a somewhat precarious income. It also was the only way in which men of a humble social background could play a major role in the political world. Journalism sprang from, provided, and sustained a comprehensive and partisan worldview in which everything was related, all suffused with politics, political commitment and views themselves moral statements. Thus travel literature could provide political statements or, at least, an ideological slant on what was reported and how it was discussed. Writers were not neutral figures. Their works commonly sought to make specific as well as general points for a readership that was politicized and did not recognize any barriers to partisan viewpoints and political images. There was no more reason why travel literature should be immune than history or ecclesiastical writings, both of which were heavily politicized. Thus Joseph Addison in his *Letter from Italy to the Right Hon. Charles Lord Halifax, in the Year 1701* (1703) and his *Remarks on Several Parts of Italy* (1705) argued that it was best to live under small commonwealths. The peasantry of the "savage mountain" of San Marino were presented as happy, because free, while papal government had brought the once prosperous Campagna to desolation. Addison's Whiggish *Remarks* proved very influential, going through ten editions by 1773. It was referred to by tourists, such as Andrew Mitchell in 1734.[7] However, at the same time it was criticized. Two Tory critics were the London newspaper *Mist's Weekly Journal* and the earl of Orrery. In its issue of July 8, 1727 the paper attacked two Whig writers by name: "The English prove so wretched voyage-writers, that this paper could scarce enumerate the gross blunders of a Burnet and an Addison". Orrery referred to "Mr. Addison, whose Travels are not the most shining and accurate part of his works".[8]

Partisanship varied by author and topic. It could be focused in reporting the pretender's court in Rome or the reverence shown by Catholics for relics, or made more general and diffuse in moral reflections on the supposed consequences of autocracy and Catholicism, though the former alone was also grounds for condemnation, as in *An Account of Denmark* by the Whig politician and diplomat Robert Molesworth. The kings of France and the papacy had few defenders in Britain outside the private world of English Catholicism and the marginalized world of Irish Catholicism. Rather than defending autocracy or Catholicism, as Whig polemicists claimed they did, Tory writers also attacked them. During the period of Whig one-party rule from 1714 until 1760 they argued that Britain was not distinct from the Continent, and that Whig government might produce the same pernicious circumstances as were discerned abroad.

The common theme was one of hostility to the Continent, a process eased by the fact that the vast majority of tourists spent all or most of their time in Catholic countries. These were either monarchies, particularly France,[9] Savoy-Piedmont,[10] and Naples; princely territories, such as Parma and Modena; or the republics of Genoa and Venice, which were generally seen as decadent and decayed. The areas in the empire (Germany) most visited, particularly prior to the Hanoverian accession, were the Rhenish and south German territories on the route from the Low Countries to Italy. They also were generally Catholic and princely. The only region visited extensively in which a different political culture was present was the Low Countries, where the republican Protestant United Provinces formed an obvious contrast to the monarchical Catholic Austrian Netherlands.[11]

Most writers wrote from a perspective of hostility and suspicion toward the Continent. The splenetic tone of Smollett simply made more personal the general reflections found widely in other works. The thrust of Smollett's *Travels* and his place in the diatribe against tourism were clear to an anonymous writer in the *St. James's Chronicle,* presumably the printer-conductor of the paper, Henry Baldwin. In the issue of May 10, 1766 nearly half the front page was devoted to an extract from the book preceded by a note:

> These *Travels* forming a distinct number of letters addressed to several friends, and written from different places, it is impossible to give the reader a summary of them. In general, they are entertaining, curious, and

> instructive, and will be found of singular use to such as may have occasion to go abroad. In this Paris-loving age, we will venture to say, they will not be without their merit also, in keeping others at home; as after the very contemptible, but just character given in them of the French, who is not through necessity driven there, will wish to spend his money among them? The following will furnish the English traveller with no incompetent idea of what he has to expect.

Though the value of individual travel could be accepted, the fashion for tourism was derided. The contrast is apparent in Francis Lynch's play *The Independent Patriot* (1737). Dedicated to Richard, third earl of Burlington, a Whig who had, as a result of several years in Italy, become an enthusiastic patron of Palladian architecture, thus arousing the criticism of Hogarth, it praised tourism in his person, claiming that he had traveled "to improve his mind for the embellishment of his country". However, the dedication continued:

> Happy had it been for themselves, and for their country, if all our travelling youth of condition had followed the example of Your Lordship: Had they, like you, turned their thoughts to the solid and useful, we should not have seen so many of them returning . . . only with the weaknesses and vanities of foreigners. Had they, like your Lordship, studied to improve first their own taste, and next that of their country, there would have been no foundation for satyrizing that affected, false, modern, musical taste, which partly gave rise to the following scenes.

The play presented the folly of travel and the consequent threat of cultural subordination. The taste for Italian opera was seen as arising from tourism:

> The reigning taste's all Italian. Music has engrossed the attention of the whole people: The Duchess and her woman, the Duke and his postilion, are equally infected—The contagion first took root in the shallow noodles of such of our itinerant coxcombs as were incapable of more virtuous impressions. (*The Independent Patriot* page 2)

The musical Lady Wardle instructs Dulcissa:

> Now my Dear, you are naturally well-fashioned and are blessed with a taste: Improve it—Travel, Dulcissa—Make the tour of Italy; but set your heart most on dear Rome—Oh, Dulcissa! no tongue's able to express the charms of dear Italy—The Italians pay us English women an adoration little short of that due to the Deity . . . hear the song composed for me by my dear Cardinal.

Lady Wardle presents travel as a correction for what she claims are the deficiencies due to limited education. In the London society depicted by Lynch, a private world of cultural assumptions, tourism could be seen as the key to culture, "taste" was crucial and "taste" could only be acquired abroad. Tourism thus both distanced the elite from public cultural assumptions and expressed this distance, or so it could be suggested:

> Travelling's thrown away upon the tasteless . . . Mr. Medium, a handsome figure of a man, with an uncommon share of sense and learning, they say; but for want of taste he's returned from his travels with not one qualification of the Gentleman . . . I'm indebted to travelling for all that's easy and careless in my deportment.

To Dulcissa's question the fop Addle replies: "When I have made the tour of Italy, Gad, you shall see me taste all over".[12]

It could be suggested that much travel literature can be understood only in light of the savage public attack on tourism, that the literature should generally be located between this discourse and the actual views of most tourists, difficult as those are to fathom. The discourse was not unchanging.

Two major changes can be discerned. First, much of the criticism of tourism in the first half of the century was made by commentators in Britain, such as newspaper writers. In 1725 *Mist's Weekly Journal* claimed that tourists simply wenched and drank, adding: "If you ask them questions concerning the laws and governments of the countries they have visited, you will find they know no more of those matters than they do of Terra Australis incognita". Writing of a friend who had been to Italy, the author of the *Craftsman* noted in 1728, "I was extremely pleased to find that notwithstanding his travels into countries of slavery and arbitrary power, he was still full of those noble and virtuous sentiments which are so peculiar to us Englishmen". The paper was later to proclaim France "the hot-bed to our English youth, where they are immaturely ripen'd, and therefore soon become rotten and corrupt at home", and to claim: "Some people are so Frenchify'd that nothing but what comes from that Nation will go down; and they seem to be as fond of French politics as of French fashions. This may be pardonable enough in our fine travell'd gentlemen, whom the French court hath polished from all the rust of their native country". In 1742 the *Universal Spectator* referred to "our Petit Maîtres, and their polite governors who make the tour of Europe only to glean every vice and folly they meet with".[13] This was the period when tourism was socially generally restricted to the elite and when the clear model was the grand tour to France and Italy. After 1763, as increasing numbers traveled, Continental tourism became both less socially exclusive and more varied in type. In place of

Henry William Bunbury, *Englishman at Paris* (1767)

aristocratic youths' traveling for two or three years, it became more common both for people to travel later in life and for them to go abroad for shorter periods. It was in the context of a changing tourism both that most writers of travel literature, of works intended for commercial publication, wrote and that most literary figures went abroad. It could be suggested that some of them wrote in light of the heritage of domestic criticism. This certainly appears to be the case with Smollett.

A second major change has been discerned by the German scholar H. J. Müllenbrock. He has claimed that in the opening decades of the century English travel literature was characterized by a political fervor directed against arbitrary power, and that in the second half of the century a shift occurred toward a more tolerant stance: "English writers slowly groped their way towards a more conciliatory treatment of other countries". Müllenbrock suggested that the 1760s "saw the beginning of a tentative emancipation from the conventional Whig attitude towards the outside world". English travel literature became more sympathetic to countries hitherto grossly stereotyped, and "former ideological prejudices were shed".[14]

It could be suggested that there was indeed a different flavor about British society in this second half of the century, beginning in the 1760s, and that this influenced travel literature. Though fears about the dangers of political corruption had not lessened, they were not associated to the same degree with foreign cultural and political challenges. Much of this was due to George III. He, like his grandfather, had stressed ostentatiously at his accession his intention to avoid Hanoverian influences and be a British monarch. However, the expulsion of some Hanoverian courtiers and the prominent use of English in 1727 soon waned and it was easy, and accurate, to accuse George II of favoring Hanoverian interests and policies. In contrast, George III never went to Hanover, and, although he cared greatly about the electorate and at times fostered its interests at the expense of Britain, he was much more cautious about doing so than his grandfather and great-grandfather had been. There was no Hanoverian mistress, while the Hanoverian chancery in London kept a very low profile. There was criticism of Hanoverian influences, but they were muted compared to the situation prior to 1760. Political considerations altered the focusing of xenophobia: under George III the villains were Scots, such as Bute and Mansfield. The collapse of the Jacobite challenge in 1746 was followed by a reorientation in British domestic politics in the 1750s and early 1760s. The net effect was a reduction in tension as all political groups came to support the dynasty, if not the court. This both reduced the intensity of opposition to the latter and prepared the way for George III's patriotic stance at his accession. An easing of domestic political tension was accompanied by victory abroad in the

Seven Years' War. Britain after the Peace of Paris (1763) was certainly, compared to the Walpole years, a self-confident, vigorous, dynamic society, less impressed or threatened by France. Indeed it was to be France that experienced Anglomania. The countries rising in political importance, particularly Austria, Prussia, and Russia, did not pose a cultural threat and their political challenge was indirect. Xenophobia did not disappear. It continued in all its brutal manifestations, but underlying it there was less of a feeling of fear. The balance between Britain and France was definitely tilted by the midcentury wars in more than just the political sphere. The anxiety of the Walpolean period, an age when domestic threats, whether from pro-Hanoverian ministerial corruption or Jacobitism, were linked to foreign interests and influences, was lessened, first by "the sense of miraculous liberation from an alien grasp"[15] that greeted the accession of George III, and second by the clearly domestic nature of the politics and polemics of paranoia in the Wilkite period. There were exceptions to the latter. In 1771 the opposition newspaper the *Whisperer* advanced at length its claim that the ministry had covered up a conspiracy of British traitors and Catholics with France that had led to a fire at the Portsmouth naval base.[16] However, such suggestions were not common, and, in general, between 1760 and the French Revolution British publicists discussed domestic political developments without reference to a set of values derived from and expressed in cultural xenophobia.

The 1760s did not witness only a political reorientation. There was also a definite cultural shift. A Britain "more secure in her national pride and sense of cultural achievement"[17] moved from the rococo influences of earlier decades toward a less-obviously derivative art and dependent culture, epitomized by the foundation of the Royal Academy in 1768. It was not that British culture was cut off from that of the Continent, but rather that the interchange was on a more equal footing, though there were obvious exceptions, particularly in music. Reynolds's role as "a member of a cosmopolitan community of artists of his own generation" has recently been stressed.[8]

It is against such a background that Müllenbrock's suggestions should be considered. I have argued elsewhere that his concept of a stridently Whig travel literature's becoming more conciliatory is not appropriate in the case of tourist accounts that were not designed for publication.[19] That does not mean, however, that there was not indeed a shift in travel literature. The didactic tone of much earlier writing diminished. Such a statement is not unhappily subject to statistical demonstration, but comparisons can be made. Sacheverell Stevens began his tour in 1738, and though his book did not have a publication date, the dedication to the princess dowager of Wales was dated 1756:

> The following faithful narrative will plainly show under what a dreadful yoke the wretched people of other nations groan, their more than Egyptian task-masters having impiously robbed them of the use of that glorious faculty, their reason, deprived them of their properties, and all this under the sacred sanction of religion . . . they thus miserably lie under the scourge of the tyrant's rod, and the merciless fangs of ecclesiastical power.

When such comments as these in the book were written is unclear:

> I beg leave to conclude with the following short reflection, which is, that if, from the foregoing faithful account of the wretched and miserable state of slavery and subjection, both ecclesiastical and civil, both in body and soul, other nations are reduced to by their arbitrary tyrannical governors, one single reader should be made sensible of the inestimable blessings he enjoys, be upon his guard against any attempts that may be made to deprive him of them, either by wicked ministers at home, or by enemies from abroad, and become a better subject, or a sincerer Christian and Protestant, it will afford me the highest satisfaction, and I shall flatter myself, that I have not altogether laboured or lived in vain.[20]

In contrast, the historian William Coxe, who had acted as "bearleader", or traveling tutor, to Lord Herbert, published in 1784 his *Travels into Poland, Russia, Sweden, and Denmark.* The dedication offered no reflections, while the preface was devoted to explaining Coxe's sources. Patrick Brydone, who toured Sicily and Malta in 1770, publishing an account in 1773 that was favorably received by reviewers and public, was able to write of the "Resemblance of the Catholic to the Pagan rites" without presenting the former as a threat to Britain. Though a son of the manse, Brydone was prepared to confess the appeal of Catholicism, which he presented in terms of the emotions that it could inspire:

> I have observed, with pleasure, that glow of gratitude and affection that has animated their countenances; and am persuaded that the warmth of enthusiastic devotion, they often feel before their favourite saints, particularly their female ones, must have something extremely delightful in it; resembling, perhaps, the pure and delicate sensations of the most respectful love. I own I have sometimes envied them their feelings; and in my heart cursed the pride of reason and philosophy, with all its cool and tasteless triumphs, that lulls into a kind of stoical apathy these most exquisite sensations of the soul. Who would not chuse to be deceived, when the deception raises in him these delicious passions, that are so worthy of the human heart; and for which, of all others, it seems to be the

> most fitted? But if once you have steeled it over with the hard and impenetrable temper of philosophy; these fine-spun threads of weakness and affection, that were so pliable, and so easily tied, become hard and inflexible; and for ever lose that delicate tone of sensibility that put them into a kind of unison and vibration with every object around us.[21]

Peter Beckford wrote that: "the kindness we daily receive on the continent demands every return that civility can repay". The surgeon Samuel Sharp, who toured Italy in 1765–66, publishing in the latter year his *Letters from Italy Describing the Customs and Manners of that Country*, which was praised by Johnson though criticized by Baretti, felt it necessary to apologize in his preface in case he caused offense to Catholic readers. His apology conceded the possibility of a difference between Catholicism in Britain and abroad:

> Should the more reasonable Catholics of England think I have been too particular in my Descriptions of the superstitious Practices of their Religion, I must beg leave to remind them of their own frequent Declarations, that, in this enlightened Age, those Pageantries are continued abroad, merely to comply with the Weakness of the ignorant Multitude, who would imagine the Fundamentals of their Faith shaken by any Retrenchment of those Ceremonies; and, if this be their Avowal, certainly what a Papist disapproves of, a Protestant may describe without giving Offence.[22]

If travel literature changed, it might be asked how much this literature influenced the perceptions of tourists. Clearly, much depends upon the assessment of the latter. John Stoye characterized British travelers, albeit of the previous century, as "receiving the same memories or images, learning to share the same stock of historical commonplaces".[23] This is a view that is difficult to accept after reading the accounts of many eighteenth-century tourists. It is true that there was a considerable degree of repetition in their itineraries and in their descriptions of buildings, though it is possible to suggest that many of these descriptions performed a function akin to that which is now discharged by the holiday snapshot. These repetitious descriptions could also be found in the travel literature, which was scarcely surprising as the prime function of the latter was to serve as a guide for tourists and to provide them with advice. In his book, which took an epistolary form, Sharp wrote:

> I do not mean to trouble you, or my other Friends, during my stay abroad, with descriptions of statues, churches, and pictures; for, besides,

> that I can say no more on that subject than what every account of Italy, every guide for travellers, furnishes in a most tedious abundance, I have generally found the reading of such descriptions insipid and tiresome; indeed, how can it be otherwise, since the touches of a Raphael, or Michael Angelo, must be seen to be admired, and are no more susceptible to a description in words, than is the air of a musical composition. These accounts, however, are both pleasant and useful in the hands of a traveller, who, if he compare them with the originals, will borrow a thousand hints, which would otherwise escape the most diligent observer.[24]

Travel literature appeared on a continuum stretching from works devoted solely to details for tourists, ranging from descriptions to notes on coinage, to books that were essentially reflective. There was a subjective element in both categories: it was by no means obvious what should be described or what advice should be offered to tourists. As it is by no means clear what travel literature if any tourists used or read, references generally being sparse or to "the guide", it is difficult to assess what type they preferred and what effect, if any, it had. Scholars find travel literature that was opinionated most interesting, but it is by no means clear either that tourists read any or that they did not prefer books such as *The Gentleman's Guide in His Tour through France by an Officer,* which advised on how to save money. Provided with bearleaders and couriers, wealthy tourists did not need to read guides, while all tourists could find in most major towns factual guides to the local sites. In his *Familiar Letters from Italy,* written mostly in 1787, Peter Beckford referred to his visit to Venice in 1785: "If you wish to see a more particular account of the government and curiosities contained in this city, permit me to refer you to an ingenious publication in the French language, by Jean Baptiste Albrizzi, which I have found very faithful in the account it gives".[25] William Bennett's advice to future travelers at the end of his tour was "to be provided with a good courier".[26] A good book was not mentioned.

It is thus by no means clear that the travel literature best known today was used by tourists. It is indeed possible that it was rather read generally as a form of fiction, as interesting works similar to picaresque novels. As such, travel writing seems to have become more fashionable from the 1760s. The current project for an eighteenth-century short title catalog will provide some statistical guidance, though the large number of eighteenth-century titles that were not programmatic poses problems: not all tourist books carry "travels," "France," or "Italy" in their title. One book, appropriately titled *Another Traveller! or Cursory Remarks and Critical Observations Made upon a Journey through Part of the Netherlands in the Latter End of the Year 1766,* published in 1767, noted that "travelling is the mode, and that it is no less the mode to print travels". Clearly intended as a reply to Smollett—"I set out with a disposition of being pleased (a disposition which I would gladly recommend to future travellers)"—the work also appears to have been written for armchair travelers, rather than for tourists, while it clearly sought to dispel prejudices:

> though it is become so much the fashion among my countrymen of late to decry foreign customs and manners, and to cry up whatever is of British growth, whether right or wrong; I shall nevertheless take the liberty so far to differ from them, as to commend whatever in my judgment has appeared commendable, without dread of the forfeiture of my allegiance; and even to do justice to a monk where I have found him worthy, and I hope without the imputation of being a papist. By such candid proceedings I flatter myself it is not impossible but that I may be able with reason to remove the illiberal prejudices of some of my readers and to laugh away the childish notions of others.[27]

As travel literature grew in volume it thus became more diversified in tone and content. This alone would suggest that its role in defining tourists' perceptions should not be exaggerated. The latter defy easy generalization, as is only to be expected given the variety of individuals who traveled for pleasure and their different experiences. British tourism changed in character, but at no given moment was it uniform, and to treat it thus would be inappropriate. There is no ready contrast between the imaginative writers and the mass of the remaining tourists. If some tourists dwelt largely on topics of cost and convenience, the Dutch "stum" and "stews" that were to be consumed by one or the overcharging complained of by Philip Francis, others were sensitive to the picturesque qualities of what they saw, increasingly so as the century advanced. One anonymous account of 1776, written by a tourist going down the Rhone by boat, described Viviers as "a poor little place not affording any tolerable accommodation for travellers. It affords however much amusement to the picturesk [sic] eye . . . the broad front of this range of rocks was beautifully illuminated by a purple gleam from the setting sun". Robert Arbuthnot, sailing down the Danube from Regensburg in 1785, wrote from Linz, where the ship was windbound:

> the weather has been hitherto so delightful that I have remained almost constantly upon deck admiring the prospects which are presented on each side. Nothing can be more agreeable than sailing down the Danube. The banks afford the finest variety of scenery imaginable, sometimes running through a rich well cultivated and well inhabited country, and sometimes rolling majestically in a deep valley, surrounded on each side with lofty

mountains and precipices, covered with tall trees from the summit down to the water's edge.[28]

Some tourists recorded or offered their correspondents masterpieces of religious or political prejudice, or both; others displayed a sensitive awareness of the variety of arrangements that human society could produce. If some found bigotry and despotism abroad, John Swinton exclaiming in 1730 "so superstitious and bigotted are the Portuguese",[29] it is worth pointing out that in many respects such judgments were justified: the fate of a Catholic in Britain was better than that of a Protestant in Iberia.

By 1780 British tourism had developed considerably. Geographically it had changed its nature. If the ideal tour remained the grand tour, the aspiration of most tourists Paris and Italy, a wish that was to be transmitted by Romanticism to the Alps and the Mediterranean and eventually by Victorian tastes to snow and sun, increasing numbers were either travelling to other areas as well, or occasionally, generally on a second tour, instead, or accepting a truncated tour. Comparatively speaking, relatively few tourists traveled to Iberia, the Balkans, eastern Europe, Scandinavia, or even on the outer crescent to Italy, through the United Provinces, Hanover, Berlin, Dresden, Prague, and Vienna to Venice. However, the generally peaceful nature of central Europe between 1763 and 1792, with the exception of the short War of the Bavarian Succession (1778–79), helped the growth of travel on the last route. It is unclear how far this geographic diversification altered the perceptions of travelers, the perception of travel. If by 1780 a well-traveled tourist was expected to have seen the court at Vienna, the paintings at Dresden, and Frederick the Great's military reviews, it seems that this expectation was largely one fostered within elite social circles. The vast majority of tourists neither went to these places nor expressed any wish to do so, insofar as these can be determined. However, the growing number of tourists who visited these areas, leading the British envoy in Dresden to complain in 1769 "I have within this month, had an inundation of English, who have nearly eaten me out of house and home. The nine and twentieth left me a week ago. . . . They are most of them gone on to Berlin",[30] helped to destroy the previous cultural image of tourism, as being essentially a visit to Catholic Europe, with the exception of the United Provinces, the latter never particularly popular with the aristocracy. At the same time the urban focus of tourism—long stays in major cities, where interest and facilities were both present, interspersed with swift journeys through unpromising countryside—was diffused by increasing interest in the latter, not the classical sites of Italy, but wilder scenery and sensations. It was no longer necessary for a mountain, waterfall, or lake to have been mentioned by Virgil or Livy for it to attract tourists.

While some tourists sought wilder sights and sites, Switzerland becoming a goal rather than an obstacle, others were transforming places on the Continent into towns where they could feel at home, could live for a while, rather than feeling themselves tourists or in need of broadening their mind. Both Nice and Naples attracted comparatively large numbers seeking to pass the winter in an attractive climate. Three hundred British tourists spent the winter of 1784–85 in Nice. Instead of being a town most noted for the celebrations of the miracle of St. Januarius—the liquefaction of the saint's blood—Naples was increasingly seen as the place to go in winter, particularly for those who were not well.

Thus tourism altered. As increasing numbers of less-affluent tourists traveled, a shorter and less-expensive alternative to the grand tour that excluded Italy and concentrated on Paris and the Low Countries developed. Tourism in western Europe both ceased to be mysterious and could less readily to be perceived either as an aristocratic recreation or as a cultural threat. To a certain extent it became commonplace, if not for individual tourists, then at least for travel writers. The success of travel literature as a genre and the greater appeal of accounts of travel to exotic regions posed problems for conventional travel writing. As a source for imaginative writing, travel in western Europe became interesting only if there was a very personal response to the areas traveled through and a very individual choice of those traveled to or if the tourist's experience of the commonplace could be made interesting by his descriptive powers or by the particular events that happened to him. This was the challenge that faced imaginative travel writing about western Europe by 1780.

# NOTES

1. J. M. Black, "The Challenge of Autocracy: The British Press in the 1730s", *Studi Settecenteschi* 3–4 (1982–83) 107–18; Black, "The Catholic Threat and the British Press in the 1720s and 1730s", *Journal of Religious History* 12 (1983) 364–81; Black, "Richard Rolt, 'Patriot' Historian", *Factotum* 16 (1983) 19–23.
2. W. Cobbett, *The Parliamentary History of England* 13 (1812) 574; Pollnitz, *Lettres et Mémoires* 5th ed. (Frankfurt: 1738) 3:298–300; Glenorchy to duke of Kent, January 22, 1724 (new style), Bedford, County Record Office, Lucas papers 30/8/829.
3. *Original Mercury* 24 Sept. 1728.
4. Black, *Natural and Necessary Enemies. Anglo-French Relations in the Eighteenth Century* (London: 1986) 179.
5. G. W. Pilcher, ed., *The Reverend Samuel Davies Abroad* (Urbana, IL: 1967) 102.
6. Percy G. Adams, *Travellers and Travel Liars 1660–1800* (Berkeley: 1962) 90.
7. British Library, Additional Manuscripts (hereafter BL.Add.) vol. 58319 f.7.

8. John, Earl of Orrery, *Letters from Italy* (London: 1773) 159.
9. Black, "An Englishman Abroad in the 1730s", *Postmaster* 6 (1980) 18–21; Black, "France and the Grand Tour in the Early Eighteenth Century", *Francia* 11 (1984) 407–16; J. Lough, *France Observed in the Seventeenth Century by British Travellers* (Stocksfield: 1985); Lough, *France on the Eve of Revolution. British Travellers' Observations 1763–1788* (London: 1987); Black, "On the Grand Tour in 1699–1700", *The Seventeenth Century* 2 (1987) 199–213.
10. Black, "The Grand Tour and Savoy-Piedmont in the Eighteenth Century", *Studi Piemontesi* 13 (1984) 140–64; Black, "Savoy-Piedmont in 1699", *Studi Piemontesi* 15 (1986) 189–94.
11. H. L. A. Dunthorne, "British Travellers in Eighteenth-Century Holland: Tourism and the Appreciation of Dutch Culture", *British Journal for Eighteenth-Century Studies* 5 (1982) 77–84; Black, "The Eighteenth-Century Grand Tour: A New Account", *Lamar Journal of the Humanities* 13 (1987) 7–18.
12. F. Lynch, *The Independent Patriot* (London: 1737) dedication, 2, 23, 25, 42, 50.
13. *Mist's Weekly Journal* September 18, 1725; *Craftsman* July 6, 1728, July 21, 1739, July 12, 1740; *Universal Spectator* April 3, 1742.
14. H. J. Müllenbrock, "The Political Implications of the *Grand Tour*: Aspects of a Specifically English Contribution to the European Travel Literature of the Age of Enlightenment", *Trema* 9 (1984) 7–21.
15. G. Newman, *The Rise of English Nationalism. A Cultural History 1740–1830* (London: 1987) 171.
16. *Whisperer* October 5, 1771.
17. L. J. Colley, "The English Rococo", *Rococo. Art and Design in Hogarth's England* ed. M. Snodin (London: 1984) 17.
18. R. Rosenblum, "Reynolds in an International Milieu", *Reynolds* ed. N. Penny (London: 1986) 44.
19. Black, *The British and the Grand Tour* (London: 1985) 171; Black, "Grand Tour", *Studi Piemontesi* 13 (1984) 150–51.
20. S. Stevens, *Miscellaneous Remarks Made on the Spot in a Late Seven Years Tour through France, Italy, Germany and Holland* (London: n.d.) dedication, 391.
21. P. Brydone, *A Tour through Sicily and Malta* 2nd ed. 2 vols. (London: 1774) 1:160–61.
22. P. Beckford, *Familiar Letters from Italy* 2 vols. (Salisbury: 1805) 2:323; S. Sharp, *Letters from Italy* 3rd ed. (London: n.d.) iv.
23. J. Stoye, *English Travellers Abroad, 1604–1667* (London: 1952) 18.
24. Sharp, *Letters* 1–2.
25. Beckford, *Familiar Letters* 2:156–57.
26. Bodleian Library, Oxford, MS. Eng. Misc. f. 54, fo. 203.
27. R. Coriat, *Another Traveller!* 2 vols. (London: 1767) 1:vii, 34, 32–33.
28. Anon. account, 1721, BL. Stowe Mss. 790 fo. 160; Francis, July 12, 1772, BL. Add. 40759 fo. 2; Anon., 1776, BL. Add. 12130 fos. 60–61; Arbuthnot to Sir Robert Murray Keith, May 28, 1785, BL. Add. 35534 fo. 183.
29. Black, "Portugal in 1730", *The British Historical Society of Portugal Annual Report and Review* 13 (1986) 76.
30. G. Smyth, ed., *Correspondence of Sir Robert Murray Keith* 2 vols. (London: 1849) 1:123.

# STERNE'S *A SENTIMENTAL JOURNEY* AND THE TRADITION OF TRAVEL LITERATURE

**Thomas M. Curley, Bridgewater State College**

Few writers surpassed Laurence Sterne in his literary enthusiasm for travel. He could affirm that a "curiosity of seeing new things . . . seems wove into the frame of every son and daughter of Adam" because he lived in an age of travel and discovery, distinguished by an insatiable curiosity for new and accurate data about mankind everywhere around the globe (*Sermons* 1.234). *A Sentimental Journey through France and Italy by Mr. Yorick* brilliantly mirrored the widening geographic horizons. Its publication occurred in 1768, when Captain Samuel Wallis returned from his discovery of Tahiti, Lieutenant James Cook took command of his momentous Pacific voyages, Boswell first won fame with his *Account of Corsica*, and Johnson renewed his promise of a Highland tour that would result in one of the greatest travel books of the century. Modern readers can better understand the uniqueness of Sterne's artistic achievement by placing *A Sentimental Journey* in the generally forgotten context of contemporary geographic literature. Such a perspective demonstrates that the novel adapted geographic conventions inherited from the Renaissance and the Enlightenment to become an unprecedented travelogue of subjective spiritual exploration, "altogether of a different cast from any of my forerunners" and in anticipation of some of the best Romantic narratives of travel (*A Sentimental Journey* 82).

That the author had a ready familiarity with travel literature is abundantly clear in his writings. The satiric grand tour of France in Volume 7 of

*Tristram Shandy* is the symbolic heart of his dynamic antinovel. The epigraph proclaims this fact—"Non enim excursus his ejus, sed opus ipsum est" [For this is no digression, but the work itself]—and the ensuing narrative of Tristram's flight from death is a rollicking parody of Piganiol de la Force's *Nouveau Voyage de France* (1724, 1755), interlarded with unflattering allusions to Germain Brice's *Description de la Ville de Paris*, Jacob Spon's *Recherche des Antiquités et Curiosités de la Ville de Lyon* (1675), Joseph Addison's *Remarks on Several Parts of Italy* (1705), and Bishop Joseph Hall's *Quo Vadis? A Just Censure of Travel* (1607). Moreover, Percy G. Adams supposes the ultimate inspiration for both Tristram's tour and Yorick's journey to be John Dunton's eccentric and fictional *Voyage round the World . . . of Don Kainophilus* (1691).[1] There can be little doubt that *A Sentimental Journey* echoes standard criticisms of grand touring as espoused by Bishop Hall and mocks prejudiced travel accounts like Tobias Smollett's *Travels through France and Italy* (1766) and, in all likelihood, Samuel Sharp's *Letters from Italy* (1766).

Besides this internal evidence, there are numerous possibilities of Sterne's wide reading in the genre to be found among his library holdings. *A Facsimile Reproduction of a Unique Catalogue of Laurence Sterne's Library* lists 2,505 items, of which approximately sixty-seven works—or 2.6 per cent of the entire collection—can be described as geographic literature.[2] Although, in fact, this catalog merely includes Sterne's books among others and cannot register what he actually read, the sufficiently respectable number of travel books is typical of such holdings in gentlemen's private libraries in the century. Furthermore, most of the geographic sources for his prose fiction noted above, specifically, the works by Piganiol de la Force, Brice, Addison, Smollett, and Sharp, are in the catalog, along with such comic-satiric authors influencing Sterne as Swift, Cervantes, Rabelais, Scarron, and Le Sage. The subject matter of the travel books in the catalog encompasses almost the entire known world at the time, from North America and northern Europe through Britain and the Continent to Africa, Greece, the Near East, India, China, Japan, and the South Seas. In addition to individual descriptions, atlases, and navigational aids, there are four large contemporary collections of voyages and travels (including a 1767 compilation in seven volumes) and at least eight guidebooks on France or on the grand tour. Whichever of these works Sterne personally examined, the library holdings were clearly comprehensive enough to satisfy his curiosity about the globe and to supply much of the raw material for his parodies of Continental travel by Tristram and Yorick.

Not only do his novels burlesque identifiable descriptions and guidebooks, but his sermons, like *A Sentimental Journey*, make important use of a pilgrimage metaphor to express everyman's search for spiritual fulfillment.

This venerable Christian metaphor, which blossoms into the underlying theme of Yorick's wanderings, surfaces in several *Sermons of Mr Yorick*, especially in *Sermon 4. Follow Peace:* "we are required to follow [peace], and not to cease the pursuit, till we have used all warrantable methods to regain and settle it: —because . . . without this frame of mind, no man shall see the LORD. For heaven is the region, as well as the recompense, of peace and benevolence; and such as do not desire and promote it here, are not qualified to enjoy it hereafter" (*Sermons* 2.220). The peace and benevolence recommended here describe both the psychological means and the spiritual end of Yorick's ostensibly secular pursuit of happiness. Setting himself apart from conventional and splenetic tourists, the parson is a priestly Quixote in an emotional empirical quest for the divinely ordained cosmic unity within the national diversity of the human race. Neither a Seven Years' War with France nor chauvinistic stereotypes about foreigners prevent him from making his separate peace with King Louis and plumbing the essential brotherhood of mankind.

Of all the influences shaping Yorick's travels, the most obvious are his creator's own trips to France (January 1762 to June 1764) and to Italy (October 1765 to June 1766). No doubt the memory of Sterne's first Continental excursion in search of good health for his tubercular condition filtered into the creation of *A Sentimental Journey*. On that trip he enjoyed a generally buoyant frame of mind, an enthusiastic reception at Paris because of his *Tristram Shandy*, and other pleasant experiences that inspired episodes in Yorick's expedition. Sterne's record of the French sojourn in his letters contains whole sentences, witty sentiments, and a pervasive atmosphere of high spirits and Shandean horseplay directly incorporated into the fictional journey. But biography is not art, and his correspondence differs from the novel in its lack of a cohesive theme and in its contrary conclusions about the benefits of travel. Where Yorick perpetually revels in the vitality of movement and emotion, Sterne actually tired of his trip and returned home like the novel's grumpy tourists, Smelfungus and Mundungus, critical of foreigners. If Sterne confessed in 1764 that "there is the Pour & the Contre for every place" in the humane spirit of the novel, he nevertheless considered "Old England preferable to any Kingdome in the world" (*Letters* 201). Only when a lesson of religious import occupied his mind for the later novel did he hilariously convert a tiresome journey into a cosmopolitan pilgrim's progress that integrated moral preoccupations of Renaissance tourism, scientific techniques of Enlightenment explorers, and a unique Shandean drive for intimate emotional communication.

First of all, *A Sentimental Journey* embodied an influential Renaissance ideal of grand tourism, which, even in adulterated form, survived in eighteenth-century accounts of the Continent. Yorick's aim to "learn better manners" by an "assay upon human nature" (75, 115) relates directly to the humanistic precept to study foreign culture, rather than natural history, for intellectual and ethical improvement. Commentators like Roger Ascham, Francis Bacon, and James Howell agreed in encouraging young men to cultivate right reason and serve the public good by concentrating on the distinctly human phenomena of Continental learning, politics, religion, and social mores, especially in an urban environment. Sterne's knowledge of such educational goals in grand touring is indicated by their full enumeration in *Sermon V. The Prodigal Son,* which, with its biblical theme and affirmation that "Joy, is another name for Religion", bears directly on the final spiritual discovery of *A Sentimental Journey*. According to the sermon, the chief advantages of foreign travel are "to learn the languages, the laws and customs, and understand the government and interest of other nations,—to acquire an urbanity and confidence of behaviour, and fit the mind more easily for conversation and discourse; . . . and by shewing us new objects, or old ones in new lights, to reform our judgments—by tasting perpetually the varieties of nature, to know what *is good*—and by observing the address and arts of man, to conceive what *is sincere,* —and by seeing the difference of humours and manners, —to look into ourselves and form our own" (*Sermons* 1.233; 234–35). In Shandean fashion Yorick pursues a comparable moral education in France to uncover the psychological and spiritual universals of human life for his personal growth and the reading public's good. Despite his revealing double entendres among foreign females, he is intellectually earnest to penetrate "the *nakedness* of their hearts, and through the disguises of customs, climates, and religion, find out what is good in them, to fashion my own by" (*A Sentimental Journey* 217–18). For all the sexual suggestiveness, his subjective study of the objective world yields rich spiritual rewards that ultimately constituted the supreme educational purpose of Renaissance grand touring. As James Howell wrote in his *Instructions for Forreine Travell* in 1642, any other knowledge had relatively little merit unless by "seeing and perusing the Great World, one learne to know the Little, which is himself. . . . But principally, unlesse by surveying and admiring his works abroad, one improve himself in the knowledge of his Creator, . . . and this indeed, this *Unum necessarium,* should be the center to which Travell should tend."[3] Yorick indeed achieves both self-discovery and a rhapsodic perception of God's harmonizing immanence within the complexities of His creation.

*A Sentimental Journey* capitalized on another distinctive feature of Renaissance tourism by characterizing both Yorick and his French associates according to traditional national stereotypes advertised in early guidebooks. Jean Gailhard's *The Compleat Gentleman* in 1678 briefly lists some of the European types as follows: "In *Behaviour:* French courteous. Spaniard lordly. Italian amorous. German clownish".[4] Furthermore, Gailhard and other Renaissance writers advocated a method of grand touring that reinforced these generalizations. They asked tourists to accept these stereotypes beforehand, then superficially survey aristocratic sights tending to confirm their truth, and return home convinced of England's superiority over the Continent. Cried up as an educational experience, the grand tour rested on preconceptions to be preserved abroad by a sufficiently generalized round of inquiries that would leave British prejudices untested and British patriotism intact. Thus, two influential tourists represented in the library holdings attributed to Sterne, Gilbert Burnet and Joseph Addison, went so far as to turn their travels into a tour de force attack on Continental Catholic nationalities to publicize Protestant English virtues. Not until after the mid-eighteenth century did much of a protest arise against these stale assumptions obstructing a valid picture of foreign cultures, even if British prejudices against Continental countries hardly diminished in many travel accounts. Sterne's novel promoted the burgeoning cosmopolitanism; it simultaneously exploits and undercuts popular national stereotypes implicit in Yorick's English reserve and the French hosts' vivacious graciousness in order to oppose the prejudices of cranky British tourists typified by Smelfungus and Mundungus in the tale. When the French officer in the story repeats Sterne's own epistolary pronouncement on the equality of countries penned three years before, a refreshing tolerance has happily replaced the author's earlier distaste for England's traditional enemy: "*Le* POUR *et le* CONTRE *se trouvent en chaque nation*; there is a balance, said he, of good and bad every where; and nothing but the knowing it is so can emancipate one half of the world from the prepossessions which it holds against the other—that the advantage of travel, as it regarded the *scavoir vivre,* was by seeing a great deal both of men and manners; it taught us mutual toleration; and mutual toleration, concluded he, making me a bow, taught us mutual love" (180–81).

Initially in the novel, national stereotypes act as barriers to sentimental communication. The portrayal of Yorick subsumes the reputed British traits of eccentric individualism, liberty-loving patriotism, and emotional repression, all of which hinder either social or sexual intercourse with foreigners. He is, at the outset, very much a true-blue Briton in the mold of Smelfungus and Mundungus and fully lives up to Oliver Goldsmith's poetic conception of the typically unfriendly Englishman in *The Traveller, or A Prospect of Society (1764):*

> That independence Briton prize too high,
> Keeps man from man and breaks the social tie;
> The self-dependent lordlings stand alone,

> All claims that bind and sweeten life unknown.
> (*The Traveller* 339–42)

Conversely, Frenchmen in the novel display different temperamental attributes of sociability, levity, and refined sentimentality that Yorick will come to imitate in his quest for a finer sensibility. If, according to Goldsmith, France qualified as

> Gay sprightly land of mirth and social ease,
> Pleased with thyself, whom all the world can please
> (*The Traveller* 241–42)

then Yorick arrives at the perfect place to escape the emotional deficiencies of his English personality. His sudden exclamation that inaugurates the trip, "They order, said I, this matter better in France" (*A Sentimental Journey* 65), signals the thematic importance of the French stereotype, which must be tested, partially rejected, and partially absorbed into a cosmopolitan vision of mankind during his grand tour. His choleric preface, written appropriately in the carriage seat of a desobligeant, emphasizes his insularity by discounting the value of travel, depreciating communication with foreigners, and celebrating his country's self-sufficiency. Guidebooks on grand touring often insisted on the cultural superiority of England, and Sterne mocks this parochial convention by echoing Bishop Hall's diatribe against Renaissance tourism in Yorick's misplaced preface lauding his homeland: "But there is no nation under heaven abounding with more variety of learning—where the sciences may be more fitly woo'd, or more surely won than here—where art is encouraged and will soon rise high—where Nature (take her altogether) has little to answer for—and, to close all, where there is more wit and variety of character to feed the mind with—Where then, my dear countrymen, are you going—" (84–85). Translating here the Latin title of Hall's *Quo Vadis,* Yorick ends the preface with the delicious irony of praising England and yet snubbing visiting Englishmen who dare to disturb his patriotic reveries in Calais. The contradiction makes his jingoism ridiculous; "*As an English man does not travel to see English men,* I retired to my room" in a fit of homebred solitariness, only to sally forth from Calais and learn to chasten his chauvinism by becoming a citizen of the world through travel.

Before his departure from Calais, there is a duel between his conscience and passion for the Flemish woman that comically internalizes the divergent national characters of the two people. Their conversation dramatizes the confrontation between his ingrained English self-consciousness and the instinctive sentimental urges embodied in her foreign, if attractive, pulsations at his fingertips; "This certainly, fair lady! said I, raising her hand up a little lightly as I began, must be one of Fortune's whimsical doings; to take two utter strangers by their hands—of different sexes, and perhaps from different corners of the globe, and in one moment place them together in such a cordial situation. . . . —And your reflection upon it [said she], shews how much, Monsieur, she has embarrassed you by the adventure. . . . —the heart knew it, and was satisfied; and who but an English philosopher would have sent notices of it to the brain to reverse the judgment?" (*A Sentimental Journey* 96). An assumption of a French national character influences the presentation of Yorick's subsequent contacts with gracious and warm-hearted people on the road from Calais to Paris and climaxes in the chapter appropriately entitled "Character. Versailles". In this section Count de B**** first receives a conventional compliment about French politeness from Yorick in return for the gift of a passport and then is shocked by the parson's denial of the French stereotype by the end of the interview. Whereas, according to Yorick, the English "kept more apart", the French "are a loyal, a gallant, a generous, an ingenious, and good temper'd people as is under heaven—if they have a fault—they are too *serious. Mon Dieu*! cried the Count, rising out of his chair. *Mais vous plaisantez*" (*A Sentimental Journey* 232–33). The good parson has ridiculously turned the notion of national types topsy-turvy by applying the stock English trait of seriousness to a Continental people who preferred their time-honored reputation for Gallic gaiety.

In depicting Yorick's gradual emancipation from nationalistic prejudices, Sterne had recourse to a newer Enlightenment tradition of travel that dictated a far more rigorous and comprehensive examination of the globe. Yorick eventually emerges as something of a scientific explorer of the human heart engaged in an inductive psychological fact-finding mission to discover a cosmopolitan empathy with the French national character and a heartfelt sympathy for the spiritual roots of our common humanity. The historical foundation for this empirical mode of travel can be associated with Francis Bacon's stirring appeal for the advancement of the Nova Philosophia by a worldwide collection of physical and cultural data. The Royal Society later championed this ambitious design by urging a more careful and systematic program of geographic research in travel literature. Eighteenth-century spokesmen zealously endorsed a professional and codified survey of the world, and the epoch-making voyages of Cook marked the fruition of scientific travel in England. A major consequence of the contemporary geographic revolution was a growing demand for an impartial appraisal of alien races and places, an intellectual ideal that pervades *A Sentimental Journey*. Tourists of the Age of Johnson sometimes replaced the narrow Renaissance focus on aristocratic urban sights with a greatly enlarged field of investigation embracing all levels of society and all aspects of nature. The broadened geographic perspective made a more accurate assessment of cultures possible and caused sophisticated observers to challenge national stereotypes: "It is therefore as easy to say, that the English are good-natured, the Scotch selfish, the French fickle, the Spaniards grave, the Germans heavy, and the Swiss uncouth, as that Raphael's style is grand, Michelangelo's robust, Correggio's graceful, Carracci's bold, Titian's full of truth and so forth. But what clear notions do such epitomizing epithets convey to the mind of those who wish to know something positive about the styles of painters and the character of nations?"[5]

The above questioning of national stereotypes was not by Sterne but by Samuel Johnson's fiery Italian friend, Joseph Baretti, the other notable cosmopolite in a current debate over debased tourism provoked by Smollett's *Travels through France and Italy* and Dr. Sharp's *Letters from Italy* in 1766. Published in the same year as *A Sentimental Journey*, Baretti's *Account of the Manners and Customs of Italy; with Observations on the Mistakes of Some Travellers, with regard to that Country* (1768) shared with Sterne's novel an identical aim to curtail the malignity and insularity of Englishmen abroad by arguing the case for openness to diverse human experience. "A judicious man travels", Baretti wrote, "in order to profit himself by observing the varieties that this wide world affords, and not to make himself uneasy because men are not to be found wise according to his model in every part of the globe. The variety of the world, is, on the whole, beautiful; and to a well disposed mind will be pleasing" (2.317). If Smollett (Sterne's Smelfungus) is the novel's archetype of the splenetic traveler, then Sharp (probably Sterne's Mundungus) is Baretti's exemplar of the untrustworthy tourist for reasons that similarly reflect the impact of the Enlightenment on travel. Without the language or rank or health to survey Italy comprehensively, Sharp is charged by Baretti with succumbing to Protestant prejudices and nationalistic clichés and with being a superficial observer careless about uncovering discriminating details: "a traveller ought to shun nothing, to slight nothing" (2.320). Baretti's overall critique of tourism, with its noble call for mutual respect and love among nations, is a rational equivalent of the sentimental journeying recommended by Sterne's fiction. After all, Baretti's dearest wish, like the French officer's in the novel, is "that both English and Italians, Spanish and Dutch, Parisians and Genevese, and in fine Turks, Jews, and Christians may be civil and humane to each other whenever chance shall bring them together, and whenever they shall stand in need of each other's benevolence and humanity" (2.96). Sterne wholeheartedly agreed.

In Sterne's hands enlightened procedures of exploration serve the ends of sentimental travel. Yorick undertakes an essentially empirical examination of benevolent sensations and expressly ignores the usual aristocratic sights to

Henry William Bunbury, *A Tour to Foreign Parts* (published 1778)

conduct a probing Lockean study of the meaningful minutiae of existence, disclosing the primary psychological principles behind the secondary national qualities of the human race: "The man who either disdains or fears to walk up a dark entry may be an excellent good man, . . . but he will not do to make a good sentimental traveller. . . . Nature is shy, and hates to act before spectators; but in such an unobserved corner, you sometimes see a single short scene of her's worth all the sentiments of a dozen French plays compounded together" (*A Sentimental Journey* 257). Even such a trivial detail as a French barber's views about wigs deserves reporting for a reason that scientific travelers of the day would have applauded: "I think I can see the precise and distinguishing marks of national characters more in these nonsensical *minutiae*, than in the most important matters of state; where great men of all nations talk and stalk so much alike, that I would not give ninepence to chuse amongst them" (160). Implicit in this passage is a cognitive leap from observed fact to general reflection that glimpses a scientific mode of thinking present in contemporary descriptions and underlying the novel's inductive narrative progression and cumulative emotional insights. Early encounters with a kindly monk and the Flemish woman build to general hypotheses about sentimental touring and feeling upon leaving Calais, followed by successive confrontations with an amiable cast of characters that culminate in an ecstatic recognition of God's boundless love inhering in the totality of His animate creations and merging diverse national characters in a single human race. Facilitating sentimental communication between traveler and foreigners is the faithful French guide, La Fleur, a true interpreter of the universal language of the heart who helps to teach Yorick to speak and think in French and to be one with his Gallic acquaintances. By an accumulation of empirical evidence resting in intimate psychological interaction, Yorick's experiment in human fellowship proves the possibility of mutual understanding and the reality of divine love.

Women are the prime earthly movers of love, whether it be sexual or spiritual in nature, and therefore appear at regular intervals in the novel as dominant objects of Yorick's quest for cosmopolitan communion with the human family. In the opening chapters the Flemish woman receives the kind of comprehensive inquiry that real tourists devoted to Continental cities: "Lord! said I, . . . recollecting that I had been little more than a single hour in Calais—What a large volume of adventures may be grasped within this little span of life by him who interests his heart in every thing, and who, having eyes to see, what time and chance are perpetually holding out to him as he journeyeth on his way, misses nothing he can *fairly* lay his hands on" (*A Sentimental Journey* 114). Any sexual innuendo in this episode is also integral to future meetings with the pulsating Grisset, the inviting Fille de Chambre, the distraught Maria, and the peacemaking Piedmontese woman as part of Yorick's gradual perception of the interrelatedness of sexuality, sensibility, and spiritual love: "all comes from thee, great—great SENSORIUM of the world!" (*A Sentimental Journey* 278). An ambiguous chapter like "The Conquest", which captures both Yorick's sentimental bonding with the Fille de Chambre and his self-disciplined separation from her, espouses the mysterious paradox of soul and body, reason and passion, and love and lust commingling in human nature. The divinely ordained contradiction that is a human being must be accepted, nay, even cherished in the search for the God of love who commanded men to love one another by loving themselves: "Ye whose clay-cold heads and luke-warm hearts can argue down or mask your passions—tell me, what trespass is it that men should have them? or how his spirit stands answerable, to the father of spirits, but for his conduct under them?" (*A Sentimental Journey* 237).

Whatever its debt to humanistic and scientific conventions of travel, *A Sentimental Journey* is, finally, a radically innovative travelogue, imbued with a bracing emotional and imaginative response to human life that authors of the Romantic Age would make famous. Yorick may implement current ethical and empirical standards of tourism but certainly breaks with tradition in his subjective approach and exclusive attention to unlocking the inner sanctum of the human psyche by means of his sympathetic imagination and feeling. The heart replaces the head as he iconoclastically and humorously violates the usual practice of rational and objective inquiry abroad to pursue an inward journey following the map of the mind rather than the signposts along the road. Concrete facts serve his fertile imagination as symbolic clues of Nature's unifying presence behind all the sublunary dichotomies that he perceives between spirit and matter, conscience and instinct, male and female, Briton and Frenchman, and God and man. His very description of sentimental wayfaring could, with some philosophical qualifications, apply to the Romantic explorations of a Wordsworth or a Thoreau in their poetic and prose affirmations of cosmic harmony and love: "'tis a quiet journey of the heart in pursuit of NATURE, and those affections which rise out of her, which make us love each other—and the world, better than we do" (*A Sentimental Journey* 219).

Sterne obviously intended to strike out a new path in the form and content of travel literature when he fashioned his novel. Repetitious place names substitute for progressively changing chapter headings; the preface appears within the narrative to poke fun at the habits of actual travelers; and a breathless Shandean style permeates the account to impart a vivid vicarious experience of powerful feeling recollected in the course of a peripatetic education in sensibility. On the score of novelty alone, *A Sentimental Journey* is a notable feat of genius and differs from the "laughing good temperd Satyr against Traveling" in Volume 7 of the equally original

*Tristram Shandy* (*Letters* 231). The later novel is, to be sure, a laughing good apologia for sentimental travel's transforming traditional tourist techniques into an incomparable Shandean commemoration of life's divinely directed dynamism. Countering Yorick's grumbling preface on the uselessness of travel by ailing, inquisitive, and necessitous tourists is a later chapter, "In the Street. Calais.", proclaiming the absolute worth of a compassionate exploration of this wide world: "I declare, said I, clapping my hands chearily together, that was I in a desart, I would find out wherewith in it to call forth my affections" (*A Sentimental Journey* 115). In contrast to cheerful Yorick, surly Smelfungus and Mundungus are so critical of foreign sights as to ensure their perpetual dissatisfaction even with heaven at the end of their earthly pilgrimages: "was the happiest mansion in heaven, to be allotted to Smelfungus and Mundungus, they would be so far from being happy, that the souls of Smelfungus and Mundungus would do penance there to all eternity" (p. 120). This casual evocation of the pilgrimage motif has important ramifications for the meaning of the novel.

As Sterne remarked, *A Sentimental Journey* was truly "his *Work of Redemption*", not only for being less prurient than *Tristram Shandy* but also for being fundamentally religious in purpose (*Letters* 398–99 note 3). After all, his final and best novel recounts a joyful pilgrimage to southern France echoing the inspired words of the Bible in language that Coleridge, despite reservations about the work, praised as "prose which is in fact only another kind of poetry".[6] Whereas Smelfungus and Mundungus would seem incapable of appreciating heaven itself, Yorick experiences something of a heaven on earth near the end of his French tour. The account of Moulins and the Bourbonnais rises to mystical heights of beatific revelation. The sentimental parson becomes a Christlike Good Shepherd and Good Samaritan realizing an ecstatic communion with the "great SENSORIUM of the world!" (278) and engages in a secularized Eucharistic agape with a pastoral Maria Redemptorix ("thou shouldst eat of my own bread and drink of my own cup" [273]) and with peasants at a "feast of love" (281) consisting of bread and wine. Such spiritual epiphanies are few and fleeting in life, and the novel inevitably ends as it began in the everyday world of uneasy moral compromises, unresolved psychological tensions, and unfinished travel. In the last chapter Yorick's descent from Mount Taurira (Mont Tarare) dramatizes his return to the mundane realm of human experience: a fragile peace treaty with the Piedmontese woman verges on collapse; licentious passions war with innocent prayers; and neither pious ejaculations nor final gestures of entreaty remain immune to dubious double meanings. "So that when I stretch'd out my hand, I caught hold of the Fille de Chambre's END OF VOL. II" (291). Except for momentary intimations of immortality, the novel concludes indeterminately to capture the formless vitality and ongoing flux at the heart of Sterne's literary achievement. His untimely death intercepted his plans for a sequel depicting Yorick's tour through Italy, but the reader is left with a tale that, although seemingly incomplete, is a full and faithful representation of human life as a never-ending journey.

Not surprisingly, the novel's zestful libertarian spirit and inventive affirmation of Christian values earned it the accolades of influential readers at the dawning of the revolutionary Romantic age. A few early-nineteenth-century authors and reviewers recognized their literary ties to an exuberant narrative, which, in resuscitating older conventions of travel literature, managed to shift its locus of inquiry to the ever new revelations of personal feeling and spiritual meaning that Romantic travelers thirsted to apprehend and record. "And, much as has been said against him", Thomas Carlyle observed of Sterne, "we cannot help feeling his immense love for things around him; so that we may say of him, as of Magdalen, 'much is forgiven him, because he loved much.' A good simple being after all".[7] *A Sentimental Journey* had, indeed, originated in a great age of English travel but, as Goethe enthusiastically acknowledged, looked forward to an era of profound emotional discovery throughout the Western world: "It is for this reason that I call attention to a man who initiated and fostered the great epoch of purer knowledge of human nature, of noble toleration, gentle love, in the second half of the previous century".[8]

# NOTES

Quotations are from *The Sermons of Mr Yorick*, 2 vols. (Stratford-upon-Avon: 1927); Laurence Sterne, *A Sentimental Journey through France and Italy by Mr. Yorick*, ed. Gardner D. Stout, Jr. (Berkeley and Los Angeles: 1967); *Letters of Laurence Sterne*, ed. Lewis Perry Curtis (Oxford: 1967).

1. Percy G. Adams, *Travel Literature and the Evolution of the Novel* (Lexington, KY: 1983) 171–72. See also Stout 332–36; Van R. Baker, "Sterne and Piganiol de la Force: The Making of Volume VII of *Tristram Shandy*", *Comparative Literature Studies* 13 (1976): 5–14; and Alan H. Vrooman, "The Origin and Development of the *Sentimental Journey* as a Work of Travel Literature and of Sensibility". Diss. Princeton U, 1940.
2. *A Facsimile Reproduction of a Unique Catalogue of Laurence Sterne's Library* (New York: 1930).
3. James Howell, *Instructions for Forreine Travell*, ed. Edward Arber (London: 1869) 71–72.
4. Jean Gailhard, *The Compleat Gentleman* (London: 1678) 179.
5. Joseph Baretti, *An Account of the Manners and Customs of Italy; with Obser-*

*vations on the Mistakes of Some Travellers, with regard to that Country* (London: 1768) 2.114–15.

6. Samuel Taylor Coleridge, a letter of 1828 to Alaric Watts, excerpted in *Sterne: The Critical Heritage*, ed. Alan B. Howes (Boston: 1974) 357.
7. Thomas Carlyle, *Lectures on the History of Literature* 2nd ed. (London: 1892) 171, excerpted in Howes 381.
8. Johann Wolfgang von Goethe, *Uber Kunst und Alterthum. Lorenze Sterne*, January 5, 1826, excerpted in Howes 432.

# GOLDSMITH AND NATIONALITY

John McVeagh, University of Ulster

This essay brings together Oliver Goldsmith's analysis of English culture, his Irish upbringing, and his awareness of the wider life of humanity. The elements are distinct, but they harmonize, for his Irishness and world awareness both influence the way in which he responds to England, his adopted home. One could say that for Goldsmith, an Irish expatriate, living in England meant making comparisons; and comparisons tend to spread outward. Nationality and cultural relativity form one of the main topics of his pen.

To sound the keynote we may turn to Goldsmith's poem *The Traveller*, written in 1764. Here, imagining himself on top of the Alps, he surveys mankind from "the shudd'ring tenant of the frigid zone" to "the naked negro, panting at the line"—not from China to Peru but from north to south. Nationality, not nature, is his subject, so gardeny Italy is first contrasted with its underdeveloped people; then follow the patriotic Swiss, the sprightly, dangerous French, and the phlegmatic Dutch—familiar stereotypes somewhat updated since Addison. This brings Goldsmith to the English:

> Pride in their port, defiance in their eye,
> I see the lords of human kind pass by,
> Intent on high designs, a thoughtful band
> By forms unfashioned, fresh from nature's hand;
> Fierce in their native hardiness of soul,
> True to imagined right, above control,
> While even the peasant boasts these rights to scan,
> And learns to venerate himself as man.
>
> (327–334)

A stern, thoughtful race of fighters: it seems a positive character by which the English reader might feel flattered. But Goldsmith undercuts English pride by suggesting something ridiculous in the way in which they stalk past feeling pleased while an observer views them impassively from a mountain top; there's a Lilliputian touch to it. Generally, Goldsmith's attitude to the English exhibits this sense of irony and of difference.

In Letter 91 of *The Citizen of the World* (November 17, 1769), Goldsmith's Chinese traveler Lien Chi Altangi comments on the irascible English character. Common porters, he says, meeting in a busy street will lay down their loads and fight rather than pass each other by. Again, Englishmen have boasted of this bulldog aggression, but in the philosopher's view it stems from a blindness of the mind:

> But in England the poor treat each other upon every occasion, with more than savage animosity, and as if they were in a state of open war by nature. In China, if two porters should meet in a narrow street, they would lay down their burthens, make a thousand excuses to each other for the accidental interruption, and beg pardon on their knees; if two men of the same occupation should meet here they would first begin to scold and at last to beat each other. One would think they had miseries enough resulting from penury and labour not to encrease them by ill nature among themselves, and subjection to new penalties, but such considerations never weigh with them. (2.369–370)

A state of "open war" and miseries increased "by ill nature among themselves": such is the characterization offered. Goldsmith puts his finger on a violence endemic in English life that, as we shall see, he judges to be a psychological and not just a physical problem.

On the level of sentiment, Goldsmith can sound patriotically English. For instance, in *A Comparative View of Races and Nations* (June 1760) he describes the special love all people feel for their native country—a theme that in his hands, we might think, must refer to Ireland. And possibly it does so, in a sense. But Goldsmith continues as follows:

> Hail Britain, happiest of countries! happy in thy climate, fertility, situation and commerce; but still happier in the peculiar nature of thy laws and government. Examine every state in Europe, and you will find the people either enjoying a precarious freedom under monarchical government, or what is worse, actually slaves in a republic, to laws of their own contriving. What constitutes the peculiar happiness of Britain, is, that laws may be overlooked without endangering the state. In a mere republic, which pretends to equal freedom, every infringement upon law is a dissolution of government, and must consequently be punished with the most unremitting severity; but in England, laws may be sometimes

> overlooked without danger. A King who has it in his power to pardon, gives the government at once the strength of the oak, and the flexibility of the yew. (3.67–68)

Such lines show Goldsmith, no blinded devotee, and capable of criticizing, as a writer who also sides with England, and can entertain a certain degree of sympathy. If the feeling appears surprising in an Irishman, it is perhaps, in an Anglo-Irishman, less so. Still, the English seem to Goldsmith an enigma. He discerns problems in English politics and in the wider culture, and he locates their source in the English character. Being English by adoption and by political settlement, but, as an Irishman, lacking the English temperament, this is something he might well find puzzling. Lien Chi Altangi hints a reservation of the sort when he tries to characterize the English people but is forced to decide, finally, that he cannot decide, and is not in a position to make up his mind:

> Whenever I attempt to characterize the English in general, some unforeseen difficulties constantly occur to disconcert my design; I hesitate between censure and praise: when I consider them as a reasoning philosophical people, they have my applause; but when I reverse the medal, and observe their inconstancy and irresolution, I can scarcely persuade my self that I am observing the same people. (2.468)

The philosopher's point is that English men and women are less rational than emotional in their convictions, but its wider application shows when Goldsmith discerns in *An Enquiry into the Present State of Polite Learning* (written in 1759) a cultural backwardness or lack of true civility in the English race of which the English themselves are unaware. He terms the English peripheral. They live relatively unvisited on the edge of the European landmass, hence are unrefined, and produce therefore a coarse literary culture—for instance, the bloody stage drama so disgusting to the French. Reminiscent of the judgment of Voltaire, this assessment is exactly the one that Goldsmith as expatriate might be expected to make about England, but that an English writer born and bred would not say or, if he agreed with it, might boast about. Goldsmith is not boasting. In *The Bee* he writes succinctly that

> The vulgar of England are without exception, the most barbarous and the most unknowing of any in Europe.
>
> (1.480)

What Goldsmith thought of the Irish character, by contrast, can be inferred from an interesting side comment he makes in 1760 on the fate of English people who go to Ireland to live. It also shows his thoughtful assessment of national character. Once transplanted, he says, such people

> in time lose their melancholy serious air, and become gay and thoughtless, more fond of pleasure, and less addicted to reasoning. This difference of disposition cannot properly be said to arise from climate or soil, which is in general the same as in England; but merely from the nature of their government. They live in a fruitful country, sequestered from the rest of mankind, protected by a powerful nation from foreign insult; and regardless of neighbouring greatness, they have no important national concerns to make them anxious, or cloud their tempers with the solemnity of pride. In such circumstances they are contented with indolence and pleasure, take every happiness as it presents, are easily excited to resent, and as easily induced to submission. (3.84)

The passage may be deliberately provocative. But if so, who is being provoked? Goldsmith must have known what he was writing about, but can it be true that the Irish climate and soil are the same as in England? Did the Anglo-Irish after Swift feel that England protected them from insult? Would they agree they had no important national concerns? Swift and Edgeworth on each side of Goldsmith convey a different picture of eighteenth-century Irish life. As so often, Goldsmith may be teasing.

Returning to *The Traveller*, we can see why Goldsmith strives to keep before us the puzzle of the world-dominating English. He is ambivalent about English civilization. At one moment he calls the English "Fresh from Nature's hand", that is, more natural than the other races of Europe; then he warns of the denaturing effect that too much political individualism has had on the English community.

> That independence Britons prize so high,
> Keeps man from man and breaks the social tie;
> The self-dependent lordlings stand alone,
> All claims that bind and sweeten life unknown;
> Here by the bonds of nature feebly held,
> Minds combat minds, repelling and repelled.
> Ferments arise, imprisoned factions roar,
> Repressed ambition struggles round her shore,
> Till over-wrought, the general system feels
> Its motions stopped or frenzy fire the wheels.
> (339–348)

*The Traveller* is not an early poem; it resumes a long-drawn-out concern in Goldsmith's writing with the question of England's political morality. Letter 50 of *The Citizen of the World* in June 1760 had defined English freedom as a mixture of democracy curbed by monarchy; take away kingly power, the essay warns, and you take away an element of liberty. Such an analysis runs against some stock political attitudes of the day. Goldsmith would not have agreed with Dunning's motion in the Commons of 1780, had he still been living at the time, that kingly power needed to be diminished, and he did not support Wilkesian liberty. As he handles the subject, political freedom for the English is not to be found in the people's large-scale involvement in making the laws, nor in fewer laws as such, nor in the preservation of property. Rather, it lies in an adjustment of the community's interests, and its enemy is wealthy men who have banded into a power group so as to manipulate the laws in their own favor.

The same idea is expressed in *The Vicar of Wakefield*. Donald Davie commented of this novel that in its contention between king and party, or between the king and the section of a party, the novelist wants us to believe that the right and the demands of liberty are on the king's side. And he calls it "a bad miscalculation" on Goldsmith's part to put these sentiments into Dr. Primrose's mouth, since Dr. Primrose is "a silly".[1] Davie is right, surely, about the liberty issue, but I think we might find it hard to agree with his view of Goldsmith's judgment. To see the political statement as weaker because Dr. Primrose makes it is to overlook Goldsmith's special blend of irony with rhetoric. He handles weighty issues lightly without trivializing them; not many writers can do this. If you take the irony away, you leave a starker, less-interesting literature. Dr. Primrose is not perfect, but he is "a silly" in worldly terms, and worldliness is one of the novel's targets.

Moving beyond politics into the broader field, *The Vicar of Wakefield* contrasts genteel manners and high life with sound living and unspoiled human nature, and places the latter among the unpretentious and the low. Cherished moments are the low scenes, like Michaelmas eve at farmer Flamborough's, where the Primroses burn nuts and play hunt the slipper. Goldsmith drew upon his Irish recollections as he wrote the scene, and here, we may say, Ireland steps in to modify fashionable English attitudes to leisure. Comparable scenes are Mr. Burchell's return from the fair with gingerbread boxes and a skin purse for the vicar's daughters, and the informal merrymaking that rounds off the story. On these occasions unforced feelings vigorously expressed convey a picture of true felicity. Goldsmith contrasts the town ladies who (with Squire Thornhill) interrupt the Flamborough party games, and the contrast is so sharp as to make the comedy rather stark. The ladies are called Lady Blarney (no Irish connection that I know of) and Miss Caroline Wilelmina Amelia Skeggs. They turn out to be prostitutes; they sport pretentious names, imitating the royal family; false through and through. Goldsmith obviously enjoyed writing this scene, which shows at some length and in broad comedy how the Primrose and Flamborough families' hearty vulgarity and the genteel manners of the pretenders to fashion react to one another: each first stupefies the other into silence, then the artificial dialogue of polite society takes over, freezes everyone's spirits, and kills the occasion stone dead. Goldsmith, in spite of the comedy, delivers a stinging blow against the mobility and superficial relations of the culture of the time; fashion, one might say, is here contrasted with truth.

But the novel is not just a satire on affectation—in any case, an old theme. Goldsmith exposes in modern terms the dominant ideology of Whig eighteenth-century England. This becomes clear in the prison scene, where Dr. Primrose's address to the inmates turns into a critique of the property-worshiping political establishment of the day. Particularly, Dr. Primrose attacks the legal aspect of this vested interest, and he does it by condemning the imposition of the death penalty for property crimes. Here are the closing lines of his speech:

> Our Saxon ancestors, fierce as they were in war, had but few executions in times of peace; and in all commending governments that have the print of nature still strong upon them, scarce any crime is held capital.
>
> It is among the citizens of a refined community that penal laws, which are in the hands of the rich, are laid upon the poor. Government, while it grows older, seems to acquire the moroseness of age; and as if our property were become dearer in proportion as it increased, as if the more enormous our wealth, the more extensive our fears, all our possessions are paled up with new edicts every day, and hung round with gibbets to scare every invader.
>
> (4.150; *The Vicar of Wakefield* ch. 27)

Here again is the contrast, basic in Goldsmith, between original nature and misdirected civilization. And does that paragraph close with an image from Ireland?

But, we may ask, what is the good political state? Why do certain aspects of English life strike Goldsmith as so unnatural? Here is where the influence of Ireland comes in, and, additionally, the traveler-poet's sense of the wider world. What Goldsmith noted as the egotism of English politics, the self-absorption of genteel English fashion and a pervasive contempt among English society for the lower classes and for simple habits of life—all this ties up with his recollections of another kind of civilization over the Irish Sea, and with his awareness of the diversity of lives helping to fill up the globe.

The plays also oppose upper- with lower-class culture, and of the two, as far as their capacity is concerned for satisfying human needs, lower culture is given the edge. Young Marlow in *She Stoops to Conquer* (1773) can only act naturally when slumming because polite society freezes his feelings, and Goldsmith parodies the idea in Tony Lumpkin, who cannot escape fast enough from his mother's drawing room to be free in the tavern. Even in the tavern though, a shabby drinker objects to a singsong with the expression: "O damn anything that's low, I cannot bear it" (5.117; act 1 scene 2). This parody of the parody Goldsmith throws in as a grace note or an extra joke. A variation on the theme shows Hardcastle vainly drilling his outdoor laborers as house servants (5.125–128; act 2 scene 1). The hopeless laborers fail to learn etiquette because they are not adapted to it and do not want to adapt, and although the scene is comic, real behavior is shown struggling against having artificial behavior imposed upon it, and real behavior wins. If we realize that Hardcastle is asking for the impossible when trying to turn human beings into genteel robots, and silly for wanting to try, sympathy for a moment moves away from the assumptions of the polite world and toward the values of low people.

It would not be a wild speculation to say that, in scenes like these, Goldsmith's self-distancing from the values of aspiring English men and women and his exploration of low themes and low subjects have a personal emphasis. Scenes of Irish life and of English low life are re-created in Goldsmith's writings not condescendingly but with a reminder that their natural spirit can renovate both individual and community. Essays and poems like "Revolution in Low Life" and *The Deserted Village* speak out on behalf of the low and simple both for their own sake and for the sake of the rich. Goldsmith's message in these writings is that men and women can be better off in the deeper sense when, materially, they are less well off. A combination of his early life in Ireland and his years of wandering on the Continent underlined for him the importance of this idea.

Goldsmith took Ireland with him to England and abroad. When things got tough he recalled Ireland. He talked about returning there in 1758, depressed by London neglect. Discussing a book on Samuel Butler, he drew a parallel between himself and the earlier poet, whose modesty combined with the world's indifference had led him to starve in the same streets in which Goldsmith then suffered (1.206–209). Commenting on the note of reminiscent tenderness in Goldsmith's letters back home, Katherine Balderston suggests that he never really wished to return permanently to Ireland.[2] Presumably Goldsmith could not return to Ireland if he was to be a writer, which at that time meant living in London. However, his refined idealizations could have come only from an expatriate belonging to two countries yet also belonging to neither.

Goldsmith uses the double perspective as a way of seeing things more clearly. One issue he raises is the relationship between the cultural center and the cultural periphery, and he is a true Augustan in preferring (in one mood) cosmopolitanism to regionalism; but equally he appreciated the noncosmopolitan, such as the culture of old Ireland, fast disappearing as he wrote. His *Description of the Manners and Customs of the Native Irish*, published in December 1759 (3.24), argues that not only remote civilizations but the lives of nearby peoples should be studied. Goldsmith wrote this before Cook's voyages had made a fashionable thing out of the South Seas and their alternative life-styles. How does he make his point? He relates how the traveler out of Dublin leaves fineness behind him in exchange for wretched squalor, but receives in a miserable hut dignified and unembarrassed hospitality from the poor inhabitants. The essay's implication for its first readers is: curb your English pride. Arthur Friedman, Goldsmith's editor, queries whether Goldsmith was the author of this piece, but gives it the benefit of the doubt and includes it in his edition. While hardly crucial, it would be quite nice to think Goldsmith wrote the story. An echo sounds through it of Baucis and Philemon, and so do hints of the Pocahontas story and a suggestion of the idea of the noble savage. But whatever the essay's origin in the history of ideas, it implies a critique of the English reader's preconceptions about good society. The traveler's mind is widened. He recognizes the unexpected Ireland that suffers materially but remains generous in spirit. Goldsmith's objection to England was that she was a country materially obsessed, but spiritually undernourished.

Goldsmith shows his other side—upholding the values of the center, or of London, against those of the country, or the other country—in his 1760 review of William Dunkin's letter to Lord Chesterfield. This piece of would-be wit by a provincial Irishman Goldsmith damns as excruciatingly arch, and he comments acidly on the disadvantage Dunkin labors under, bred at a distance from the center of politeness. A writer so placed, he writes,

> must have a great degree of modesty or understanding, who does not give a loose to some vanities which are apt to render him ridiculous every where but at home. Bred among men of talents inferior to himself, he is too apt to assume the lead, as well from the press as in conversation, and to over-rate his own abilities. His oddities among his friends are only regarded as the excrescencies of a superior genius; among those who live beyond the sphere of his importance, they are considered as instances of folly or ignorance. (1.231)

Goldsmith may be unimpressed by some tendencies in fashionable England. But as he implies when slapping down big fish in little pools, even among his compatriots, he feels no kinship with provincialism of mind.

His sense of Ireland and of his own past life there and the cognate subject of national and cultural variety, all with a particular bearing on England, come together throughout Goldsmith's writing. Leaving aside other, smaller pieces, we may consider *The Captivity*, an oratorio libretto he wrote in 1764 that was never performed, does not seem to have been set to music, and, though not bad, is not particularly well written. It appeals, however, as a typical expatriate's piece. In Act 1 an Israelite prophet urges the captive tribes, working and weeping in Babylon, to turn back to their God; the Babylonians, on the other hand, threaten reprisals if they refuse to praise the city. National cultures are in conflict, expressed as religion; nationhood lost or reasserted is the issue. In Act 2 a second prophet begs the repetition of a hymn that recalls his long-lost country, and in the next air all the people sing a reproachful chorus to the fond deceiving memory, turning the past to pain. Returning in Act 3, the first prophet finally urges his uprooted people not to yield to the false values of their masters (4.214–231). *The Captivity* is no great poem; nor did it have to be, for an oratorio. But, given the poet's situation, its themes are suggestive: nostalgia and loss, the expatriate experience, realistic acceptance, duty, a sort of vague hope. *The Captivity* is about otherness; it dramatizes an awareness of difference.

Similar themes, it is true, run through Handel's midcentury oratorios—*Messiah, Israel in Egypt, Judas Maccabaeus* and the rest—all of which were set to words written by English writers and carried not an Irish but an English resonance. So a hard-and-fast national point is not to be made out of Goldsmith's libretto; he may be writing to England's sense of herself as a nation embattled against the world. He may be writing as an Irishman captive in a foreign land. Actually *The Captivity* ends on a positive note: Cyrus rescues the Jews, Babylon falls. But it is rescue. In a Handel oratorio, victorious self-assertion tends to close the work resoundingly. The difference may be significant.

What comes out of all this is Goldsmith's balancing act, or ability as a writer to sway between England and Ireland as the situation demands. He can distance himself from either country. It seems to me he does do this, and perhaps he had to. But this is not to say that he sits upon the fence. He can raise firm Irish objections against English policy. In a 1757 review perhaps recalling Swift, he insists that "the properest means of increasing our own power"—which means Britain's power—is by "increasing that of a country which contributes to our wealth"—meaning Ireland. He goes on to stress "the manifest error, in politics" of "a government which endeavours to enrich one part of its dominions by impoverishing another, and of chusing to have but one flourishing kingdom when it might be possessed of two" (*Works* 1.91–92). These Irish writings show that Goldsmith kept alive his sense of otherness and used it to challenge the attitude surrounding him during his writing life: English self-sufficiency.

Another important factor was his experience of life outside Britain. We know that Goldsmith's century saw—or felt it saw—the wider world finally revealed in its true conformation, and in the process Augustan literature deepened its awareness of the diverse cultures, histories, and civilizations that inhabited the globe. All writers were touched by these new perceptions of the world accessible, the world varied, the world modifying any one life-style by showing a dozen contrasting others—but Goldsmith assimilates them more thoughtfully than most. In *The Bee* he describes himself as a permanent wanderer or a hermit without a hermit's ease. "Out of my own country", he writes, "the highest character I can ever acquire, is that of being a philosophic vagabond" (1.370).

What he does not do is worship mere journeying. He is scornful of dull travelers. He writes off Van Egmont's book of European and Asian travels in the 1750s as leisurely insipid sauntering: there is no point to it. He stressed too how illusory it could be to travel after knowledge, describing in *The Citizen of the World* how seekers of wisdom walk in a circle round and round and round. This was published in 1760, a year after Johnson's *Rasselas*, whose theme it shares, and may signify folly or that the height of wisdom is to return to your starting point. Just as enigmatic is Goldsmith's story of the cobbler-philosopher who has traveled everywhere necessary to learn about the true nature of things and now sticks contentedly to his last. Wise of him, according to the proverb; but under questioning he admits that his travels have taken him around the parish but not a step beyond its boundaries. Do we smile at his tiny mind, or do we admire his sanity? Put the two stories side by side and you have Goldsmith's skepticism about travel and his skepticism about nontravel illustrated on the same page.

Goldsmith valued travel knowledge of the right sort because he drew from it an awareness of contrasts, and therefore a sense of proportion. Many of his minor writings impress upon his readers the manners of different places and times, each illustrating an aspect of the manifold life of humanity, and in the reviews and essays he wrote in the 1750s and 1760s a picture is built up of global diversity. Not to fall into mere listing, let me still suggest his range: he covers the subjects of northern Europe (3.145), New York province (1.35), Paraguay (1.50), travels in western and eastern Europe (1.62), German literature (1.84), Ireland under several headings (1.90, 228; 3.24, 118), various aspects of Chinese life and letters in *The Citizen of the World,* travels through Asia (1.183), and travels through Italy (1.90). There is nothing on Africa. There is not much of importance on the Pacific regions. These are not significant omissions for Goldsmith's lifetime.

However, the essays also enforce an attitude. In one mood Goldsmith can harp on the superiority of Europe; in another he rebukes the vanity of such an assumption. He enforces characteristic truths: most people's limited mental horizon, the relativity of manners, the mistakes caused by regional pride, and the unbalancing effect of specialist knowledge. Reviewing a French Jesuit's history of Paraguay, he warns the reader not to be taken in by credulous religious adventurers, who, by the nature of their preconceptions, are compelled to be unreliable. He disparages James Hanway on southern England with the interesting objection that Hanway is too earnest against tea! "Why so violent an outcry", Goldsmith mildly returns, "against this devoted article of modern luxury?" (1.80). He is not being frivolous. Hanway's eccentricity indicates a defect in taste. In the same way a hundred years later Matthew Arnold strove to isolate great poetry by the touchstone of an individual line. The priority emerges again when Goldsmith compares modern and fourteenth-century accounts of Asia and describes as the worthwhile traveler one alert enough to the lives of men and nations to give fresh significance to what he sees. Here he draws the distinction between mere travel and instructive travel:

> One who sits down to read the accounts of modern travellers into Asia, will be apt to fancy that they all travelled in the same track. Their curiosity seems repressed either by fear or indolence, and all are contented, if they venture as far as others went before them. Thus the same cities, towns, ruins, and rivers, are again described, to a disgusting repetition. Thus a man shall go an hundred miles to admire a mountain, only because it was spoken of in scripture; yet what information can be received from hearing, that Aegidius van Egmont went up such an hill, only in order to come down again. Could we see a man set out upon this journey, not with an intent to consider rocks and rivers, but the manners and the mechanic inventions, and the imperfect learning of the inhabitants, resolved to penetrate into countries as yet little known, and eager to pry into all their secrets, with an heart not terrified at trifling dangers, if there could be found a man who could unite thus true courage with sound learning, from such a character we might hope much information. Even though all he should bring home was only the manner of dying red in the Turkish manner, his labours would be more beneficial to society, than if he had collected all the mutilated inscriptions, and idle shells on the coasts of the Levant. (1.184)

The doings of men and nations are of interest to Goldsmith, not the collecting of oddities and curiosities and the description of inanimate scenery. It is another Augustan preference.

His cultivation of a broad range, yet insistence on place, is evident when Goldsmith writes on topics that are not travel, but are to do with travel or are analogous to travel; all have a bearing on the way he responds to England and to English life. So he attacks James Buchanan's pronouncing dictionary for its narrow method. Buchanan was recommending Scottish modes of speech as the norm: provincialism. Reviewing German writing, Goldsmith concedes that foreign satire seems grotesque because the different manners of different countries develop peculiar types of humor impossible to translate. That is, Goldsmith acknowledges difference and national individuality, and asserts the need in art to take into account a nation's makeup or basic character. So he judges Gray's *Odes* a misdirected work because the slow, lasting, tenacious English mind is not suited to the irregular transitions—essentially Mediterranean outbursts—of the Pindaric style. Goldsmith's interesting advice to Gray is that he will be a better poet if he studies the people.

Such priorities connect many of Goldsmith's apparently loose writings. His world curiosity, his qualified English appraisal, and behind both the Irish base experience combine into a harmonious philosophy. The essays collected as *The Citizen of the World*—though it reads more like a novel than like loose essays—recommend the outlook of the expatriate who sees England unblinded by Englishness and who sees her, therefore, as she is. Through his Chinese traveler, Goldsmith brings to bear on English culture an awareness of the habits of the wider world, trying as he does so to unlock some of the rigidities of the insular English mind. Travel is recommended to wear off shortsightedness (2.22). Fashions in beauty are juxtaposed from different regions (2.25). The philosopher is set apart from the vagabond as a wanderer who thinks, and who unites the world by travel because he assimilates and compares experience, even back to his first sensations, and by this means gives his thought depth. Goldsmith in this place uses the lovely illustration of an ever-widening river to explain his meaning, and it is surely an image of his sense of the way he himself had developed as a writer.

> . . . a man who leaves home to mend himself and others is a philosopher; but he who goes from country to country, guided by the blind impulse of curiosity, is only a vagabond. From Zardusht down to him of Tyanea, I honour all those great names who endeavoured to unite the world by their travels; such men grew wiser as well as better, the farther they departed from home, and seemed like rivers whose streams are not only encreased but refined, as they travel from their source. (2.41)

Goldsmith might have found the idea of cultural relativity in books; doubtless he did. But the forcefulness of the idea surely comes from his personal experience. His travels through European countries must have impressed it

George Chinnery, *How Qua, Senior Hong Merchant at Canton, China* (date not known, artist alive 1774–1852)

on him as a fact, and one may feel, therefore, regarding those undocumented wanderings of the 1750s, that their significance for Goldsmith's development as a thinker is hard to overestimate. Not just Continental Europe is in question here, although the Low Countries, France, Switzerland, Germany, and perhaps Italy were among the countries he visited. Goldsmith earlier still—before Culloden—made a journey to Edinburgh and through the highlands of Scotland in which he saw that country still intact under the culture of the clan.

More important than where he went was the way in which he traveled: alone and on foot; not supported by money in the bank; not whisked in and out of foreign countries and away from difficulty by letters of introduction to powerful people; not, in other words, safely, but taking a risk. According to the story, Goldsmith kept himself alive by playing on the flute—tunelessly, he adds in *The Traveller*. For a firsthand account of this journey, how many conventional journals of the grand tour might we not give up? But no details have survived.

I stress Goldsmith's footloose, unprovided travel because, although Wordsworth and after Wordsworth Goethe walked around the Continent, and many others must have done, I know of no important writer before 1780 who did the same; Goldsmith is the odd one out. Of course, nearly everyone traveled, but the usual thing was to plan it out carefully beforehand. Compare Addison early in the century, financed by the Whigs; or Boswell, his pockets bulging with recommendations to Rousseau, Voltaire, Paoli, and others; or Sterne and Smollett, Gray and Beckford, comfortably upholstered mentally and physically before they set out; or Gibbon indulging his nice taste. Goldsmith in place of all this comfort experienced life abroad in a rough and needy way, and with the minimum of insulation from hardship. Here perhaps the elements of this essay may be allowed to come together; the kind of travel he undertook provided him with an important element in his cosmopolitanism: grass-roots experience of other nations and their ways of life. Of the writers mentioned, Goldsmith had the closest contact with the low.

There remains Goldsmith's curiosity about abroad in books: mental traveling, to add to the physical. Here the point to emphasize is his ability to see around the expected attitude and to reveal an original way of thinking. Discussing Mallet on Celtic remains, he comments that learned men have overconcentrated on Greece and Rome and neglected their own cultural origin, and he compares this blindness with that of "conquerors who, while they have made inroads into the territories of their neighbours, have left their own natural dominions to desolation" (1.6). We detect here, surely, an Irish resonance, and the application can hardly be missed to an England moving toward material supremacy but forgetful of her real needs.

Goldsmith in such writing ranges afield, yet always returns to base, and brings fresh thought to bear on the stock notions of the day. Hence in the fashionable Augustan age, when the newer fashion for Greece was challenging the idea of Rome, he reiterates the significance of Celtic remains. This was not Irishism; Celtic civilization includes for Goldsmith the Icelandic myths and the northern sagas, which means that even when writing about the Celts he is thinking of abroad and of home at the same time. Such a philosophy expresses the traveler's and expatriate's outlook. In one sense, everything about Goldsmith—his wanderings, his professional false starts, his miscellany of genres, his hack work—suggests that he lacked a center. But his center was the whole world.

# NOTES

Quotations are from *The Collected Works of Oliver Goldsmith*, ed. Arthur Friedman 5 vols. (Oxford: 1966).

1. See Donald Davie's essay in *The Art of Oliver Goldsmith*, ed. Andrew Swarbrick (London: 1984).
2. Katherine Balderston, *The Collected Letters of Oliver Goldsmith* (Cambridge: 1928) ix.

# "EXTENSIVE VIEW": JOHNSON AND BOSWELL AS TRAVELERS AND OBSERVERS


## Paul J. Korshin, University of Pennsylvania


Samuel Johnson and James Boswell made one famous journey together in summer and autumn 1773. They used the trip for different purposes—Johnson as the basis for his *Journey to the Western Islands of Scotland* (1775), his one travel book of enduring value, Boswell as the foundation of his biography of Johnson. Since we are accustomed to look at these two writers together, despite the tremendous differences in their personalities and relative literary merits, their three-month journey together is a good way for us to see some of the broad distinctions in the styles of eighteenth-century travel writing. Johnson's *Journey* is a social and intellectual history of a primitive part of a civilized country; one of its subjects is the sort of people who would now form the basis of the studies of ethnologists and anthropologists. In the eighteenth century, before such specialized fields had evolved, a man of letters could do a respectable job of chronicling the history of such folk as the Highlanders and the Western Islanders. Johnson did a magnificent survey, one of the best travel books of his—or any other—century. Boswell did not have Johnson's intellectual depth or—despite all his own European travels—a great historical knowledge of other cultures, but his *Journal of a Tour to the Hebrides* (1785) became the prototype for the most successful biography of all time. So Johnson focused on the land he visited, its people, and their culture. Boswell used the setting merely as a backdrop for a dramatic montage of the conversation and opinions of his century's greatest literary figure.

The differences between these two men are even more paradoxical than my comparison suggests. Johnson, after all, was not much of a traveler. Although he made journeys to Scotland, north Wales, and—briefly—northern France, we associate him mainly with his native West Midlands and with his adopted home of London. The most famous single couplet from his poetry, "Let Observation with extensive view / Survey Mankind from China to Peru", implies much travel, but *The Vanity of Human Wishes*, which this couplet introduces, is neither a poem of prospects nor a travel work. Johnson's "Observation" is a condensed version of Milton's overview of exotic lands in *Paradise Lost*, but when we look at it more closely, it is both less and more. Between China and Peru, after all, there is almost nothing of mankind to observe and a great deal of Pacific Ocean. So Johnson's prospect is a literary style rather than a gaze through an optic glass. And Johnson, we must remember, disdained Milton's powers of observation, since he noted that Milton's stay of two months in Florence in 1638 was "a time indeed sufficient if he desired only to ramble with an explainer of its antiquities or to view palaces or count pictures, but certainly too short for the contemplation of learning, policy, or manners".[1] Johnson thought that Milton "had read much and knew what books could teach", but he found his powers of observation defective because he "had mingled little in the world, and was deficient in the knowledge which experience must confer".[2] Johnson's opinion is especially interesting in view of the fact that Milton had traveled a good deal more than he had and had mingled in public life to the extent of being actively involved in the government of the protectorate. So when Johnson finds his great predecessor deficient as an observer, we are meant to understand that by the mid-eighteenth century the concept of "observation" has taken on additional meanings to the merely visual. One does not merely gaze while on one's travels; in order really to see, one must study such ancillary topics as "learning, policy, or manners". In many ways, Johnson was establishing a pattern for travel writers of future centuries.

Boswell was the European traveler that Johnson was not. From the time that he first left Scotland, he seems to have been in flight, whether from his repressive childhood and the father he detested or from the constraining mores of his native land. He is among the least idle of all travelers, for his journals are more detailed than most records that travelers have kept over the last few centuries. Indeed, the book that first gave Boswell a measure of literary fame—a fame that he eagerly courted—is a travel book, *An Account of Corsica* (1768). There can be little doubt that one of the reasons for Boswell's writing it, for his visiting the island republic, was that there had been little done before in English about Corsica. Hence his book would surely attract attention. But the attention that Boswell certainly did gain had little to do with his powers of observation: his descriptions of Corsica are shallow and derivative. He was more a collector of interesting personalities than he was a student of customs and intellectual milieux. Hence the best part of Boswell's travel book is not the account of Corsica, it is the accompanying *Journal* of the trip, with its firsthand reports of the conversations, policies, and personal style of the country's great leader, General Pascal Paoli. As I will point out below, Boswell's first travel book is a foreshadow of what he would publish in 1785 in *The Journal of a Tour to the Hebrides, with Samuel Johnson, LL.D.* While his *Account of Corsica* at least made some of the usual obeisance of the travel genre toward describing the manners and mores of the country, the part of which Boswell was proudest was his presentation of Paoli, complete with scattered specimens of Paoli's sayings (one cannot call these brief sayings "conversation"). In his *Tour,* Boswell has a more interesting subject on whose comments he could report. Paoli was an interesting apostle of liberty, but Johnson was the leading literary figure of the later eighteenth century, dead little less than one year, about whose personality and table talk a large audience was curious. So, Boswell's development as a travel writer, or perhaps as a commentator on traveling, is considerable over the two decades from the *Account* to the *Tour,* and in the same way, Johnson's thoughts about and attitudes toward travel changed, albeit over a longer period.

Johnson's first book is a travel book. This work, his translation of a French version of an unpublished and incomplete Portuguese manuscript by the Portuguese Jesuit Father Jeronimo Lobo, had very little vogue in the eighteenth century, but the mere fact that Johnson translated it, at the behest of a bookseller, shows that the contemporary book trade was willing to support travel literature of virtually every kind, no matter how obscure. Lobo's missionary zeal and his descriptions of Ethiopia in the third decade of the seventeenth century, which in Johnson's version of 1735 is entitled *A Voyage to Abyssinia,* are, like many other eighteenth-century accounts of exotic places, attractive because so much that they detail is foreign to the European experience. But Johnson does not regard Lobo's work as being valuable simply because it is arcane:

> The reader will here find no regions cursed with irremediable barrenness, or bless'd with spontaneous fecundity, no perpetual gloom or unceasing sunshine; nor are the nations here described either devoid of all sense of humanity, or consummate in all private and social virtues, here are no Hottentots without religion, polity, or articulate language, no Chinese perfectly polite, and compleatly skill'd in all sciences: he will discover, what will always be discover'd by a diligent and impartial enquirer, that wherever human nature is to be found, there is a mixture of

> vice and virtue, a contest of passion and reason, and that the Creator doth not appear partial in his distributions but has balanced in most countries their particular inconveniences by particular favours.[3]

Indeed, the attraction of Abyssinia is that the region and its people are standard rather than exotic. The land fits no extremes of description, and the people are neither unusually primitive nor fantastically civilized. Perhaps it is fair to say that Lobo's account of Abyssinia would strike the average European reader as strange; doubtless the popularity of travel books about distant lands always has been due to their unfamiliar subject matter. But Johnson tenaciously interprets Lobo's book as *non*exotic, and thus signifies to us that his principal interest in traveling is to learn how to make a more thorough assessment of human nature.

Since so much of eighteenth-century English writing deals with travel or with accounts of foreign places, it is natural that Johnson, who is a miscellaneous writer, should have touched upon travel literature either by alluding to it or by writing it. The pervasiveness of the idea of being abroad in the eighteenth century is such, however, that Johnson also refers to the motif of the voyage with astonishing frequency.[4] In his poetry, whether we think of Thales about to depart from the city in *London* or the global observations of *The Vanity of Human Wishes,* different sorts of travel metaphors abound. His periodical essays recount many voyages of various kinds, although once again Johnson prefers to treat the vicissitudes of human nature as a result of traveling rather than changes in the landscape as we move from place to place. Johnson is more the philosophical voyager than he is the naturalistic observer of scenery. His famous *Adventurer* essay, usually described in anthologies as "A journey in a stage coach", actually takes four days and involves a trip from the city "into the country", but we never hear into *what* country the journey goes nor anything that the travelers encounter on the way. Although Johnson alludes in that essay to that most whimsical of fictional travelers, Don Quixote, he gives far less detail of his voyagers' surroundings than Cervantes gives about Spain; in fact, he gives no "travel" information at all. Instead, we learn that travel is an occasion for surrealistic self-maskings and encounters with total strangers. In talking to fellow travelers, it would seem, just as in lapidary inscriptions, a person is not upon oath to tell the truth.[5]

The story of Rasselas embraces a travel book as well, but in all of the voyages from Abyssinia to Cairo (and in the internal narrations in which Imlac, Pekuah, and other characters describe their journeys) we hear practically nothing about the names of exotic places, as we do with Milton's poetical catalogs, or about the beauties of the Nile valley, the Abyssinian uplands, or the ruins of antiquity. Johnson no doubt formed his account, at least in part, on a number of travel books that deal with Africa, but his characters actually undergo an educational tour in the manner of the title character in Andrew Michael Ramsay's *The Travels of Cyrus* (1727). In that work by the Scottish expatriate, who wrote originally in French, Cyrus travels, early in the sixth century B.C., from Persia through Egypt, Greece, Crete, and Babylon with never a single account of any natural or human phenomenon except for the Hanging Gardens of Babylon, which Cyrus describes in just a word or two. Cyrus's real travels are intellectual, and the true purpose of his voyage is educational, with the education coming at the hands of the leading philosophers of the early sixth century B.C. In the same way, the people in *Rasselas* receive an education from a fictional philosopher, Imlac, through a series of lessons in the way people live either in or outside of societies, and the choices that one makes about how to live. The travel in *Rasselas,* while we know that it covers much space and time, never acts to broaden the characters by itself; human experience, as we witness it by encountering many varieties of human nature, is Johnson's major agent of change.

Johnson's casual travel is much like that of his fictional characters. He was intensely interested in his surroundings, and often surprised his companions by the intricate wealth of detail that he could command. But he found the physical action of traveling uncomfortable and preferred company in the form of other people with whom he might talk or books. The pretty woman with whom (according to Boswell, at least) he would have vastly wished to travel rapidly in a post chaise was not scenery; Johnson enjoyed the company of women more than many of his contemporaries, and clearly saw this idealized feminine companion as someone with whom he could converse. Consider the first trip that Johnson ever took with Boswell, in early August 1763. Boswell was about to set out to Holland on the first leg of his grand tour, and Johnson accompanied him in the Harwich stagecoach as far as the packet boat to Utrecht. There is much good conversation in the stagecoach, according to Boswell, although some of the exchanges sound as if Boswell were also recalling Johnson's famous *Adventurer* essay. However, when the talk slackens, Boswell notes, Johnson "had in his pocket '*Pomponius Mela de situ Orbis,*' in which he read occasionally, and seemed very intent upon ancient geography".[6] So Johnson, like many a twentieth-century traveler, has a pocket edition with him, but it is not a trashy novel, it is quite an obscure minor geographer of the second century. We may wonder, although Boswell clearly does not, why Johnson should choose to improve his mind en route with such recherché work. We may further wonder (again, Boswell does not) why Johnson closes his first letter to Boswell, who is at this time in Utrecht, with a request for information about the intellectual state of Holland: "I hope you continue your journal, and enrich it with many observations upon the country in which you reside. It will be a favour if you can get me any books in the Frisick language, and can enquire how the poor are maintained in the Seven Provinces".[7] So Johnson saw Boswell's travel much as he did his own, as an occasion for enrichment.

Johnson's emphasis on travel as an undertaking that we view in terms of literary qualities, whether by alluding to books of which a certain vista reminds us or by actually reading one book or another as he travels, is consistent with his notion of intellectual enrichment. One ought to be using one's time to learn more about oneself and the world; hence travel is an intellectual occupation, not an idle diversion. He would criticize Milton, as I noted earlier, for preferring books and "what books could teach" to mingling in the world and the knowledge that one gathers from experience. Thus Johnson is at his best as a travel writer when he blends observations from both books and empirical observation together in the same description. This talent, which he exhibits to perfection in his mature travel book, *A Journey to the Western Islands of Scotland* (1775) dominates his travel writing. So, when he and his companion reach the islet of Inch Kenneth in the Hebrides, Johnson at once tells us that "Romance does not often exhibit a scene that strikes the imagination more than this little desert in these depths of western obscurity, occupied not by a gross herdsman, or amphibious fisherman, but by a gentleman and two ladies, of high birth, polished manners, and elegant conversation".[8] In fact, Johnson is about to proceed upon as thorough and circumstantial an account of ancient ruins as we find anywhere in the *Journey*, so his framing the prolegomenon in such a way that he reminds us of the fantastic elements of romance shows his method of travel-enrichment well. Romance pleases, but we know its fantasies to be fictions; the literature of travel, in order to please us, should establish ties to the world of pleasure that we find in fiction. These ties do not make travel literature suspect as fraud; if they are well made, they enhance the aura of credibility that the book presents. In closing his description of the castles of the Hebrides, Johnson characteristically notes: "These castles afford another evidence that the fictions of romantick chivalry had for their basis the real manners of feudal times, when every lord of a seignory lived in his hold lawless and unaccountable, with all the licentiousness and insolence of uncontested superiority and unprincipled power".[9] The reflections are not particularly pleasant; Johnson is no lover of arbitrary rule. Nor is romance true. But the experience of travel illustrates that romantic fictions had a basis in real life. The books derive from reality, reality does not derive from books.

It is evident, then, that Johnson saw travel as much more than a metaphor or an emotional and artistic experience. For him, travel is a kind of didactic, or teaching, undertaking, one that allows us to check the notions we derive from the study and the library against empirical evidence itself. The romances were not true, but they had a basis in fact. When we travel, we move not just through space and time, but through an internal space of the intellect as well. There is an anecdote that Boswell assigns to 1783 in his *Life* and that, since it does not have his own authority, may be accurate; it is about an exchange between Goldsmith and Johnson about the membership of the Literary Club. Goldsmith wished to enlarge the club, "to give it an agreeable variety; for (said he,) there can now be nothing new among us: we have travelled over one another's minds. Johnson seemed a little angry, and said, 'Sir, you have not travelled over my mind, I promise you'".[10] Travel could furnish one with new information: as Johnson remarked to Boswell in 1783 about his visit to the Hebrides, "I got an acquisition of more ideas by it than by any other thing that I remember".[11] But traveling over one's intellect is an activity that Johnson found inexhaustible and unending.

Boswell did keep the journal that Johnson urged him to do in 1763, and the result is his meticulously detailed commentary on his grand tour of the Continent. The grand tour in the eighteenth century was a familiar round; virtually every man or woman who made it was following in the footsteps of previous travelers. Boswell, like other contemporary travelers, used several guidebooks, and even retraces the route of Addison exactly, right down to the tiny detail of trying the famous echo at an unfinished palace near Milan, just as Addison had done, by firing a pistol and counting the reverberations. Addison, in his *Remarks on Several Parts of Italy* (1711), noted fifty-six repetitions of the pistol shot. Boswell, ever the accurate observer, notes, "I fired a pistol from the window of an upper story opposite to a wall; the sound was repeated fifty-eight times".[12] This kind of detail is fascinating, but unfortunately rare, for Boswell was an excellent but also an uneven observer. Part of his problem was that his mental state, which he freely discusses, sometimes predisposed him to melancholy, and during such periods he abandoned his journal. Thus his brilliant passages of realistic accuracy are interspersed with memoranda, copies of ancient inscriptions that he found curious, personal letters that he sends and receives, and other materials that are of only peripheral relevance to his traveling.

The literary side of traveling, the broadening of the intellect, does not often appear in Boswell's journals. If he ever carried a copy of an ancient classical author in his pocket as he traveled about Italy and Germany, he does not tell us, although testing one's own perceptions against those of classical antiquity was a popular recreation of literate voyagers in the eighteenth century. But Boswell is not wholly uninterested in travel as an intellectual recreation; he does mention books when the illustration will prove helpful. In the Preface to *An Account of Corsica*, for instance, he alludes to Johnson's *Dictionary* as his guide in spelling: Johnson at this time in his works is still "Mr. Samuel Johnson" (Boswell will introduce the "Dr." in the *Life*).[13] Another use Boswell made of books in the *Account* is also familiar with travel writers. This is to draw the basis of his description of Corsica from various established works on the subject. He had a number of books to choose from. The anonymous *General Account and Description of the Isle of Corsica* (1739), while brief, nevertheless discusses every port, town, and element of terrain on the island; Boswell had only to follow the descriptions in order, enlarging them occasionally with his own observations or those from other books. Goury de Champgrand's *Histoire de l'Isle de Corse* (1749), also available to Boswell, is a much more comprehensive account, and Boswell uses it, too, for historical background.

However, Boswell makes no attempt to disguise his dependence upon other authors, and to be fair to him, most travel writers of the eighteenth century stress tradition instead of originality. Few travelers were in a position to do archival research or other study of primary sources, and Boswell is as good as the best of them. Of course, a great literary craftsman like Johnson could infuse his *Journey to the Western Islands* with much original observation, but again we must remember that Boswell in Corsica is a young man writing his first book. The best evidence that we can cite of this circumstance appears at the end of his preface: "Whether I may merit any portion of literary fame, the publick will judge. Whatever my ambition may be, I trust that my confidence is not too great, nor my hopes too sanguine".[14] Boswell's ambition is much greater than his originality. His three long chapters include one on the physical situation of Corsica; it consists mainly of quotations from the various geographic authorities on the island. There is another very derivative chapter on Corsican history. And, finally, Boswell's third chapter, on the present state of Corsica, is almost entirely a summary of his reading. All in all, then, the *Account* is not really a travel book, it is a self-promotion. In this context, Boswell's work starts to make more sense, and his comparisons of this relatively uncomplicated society with England become appropriate. So the following obiter dictum, of small relevance to the Corsicans, shows us how travel can lead to useful reflections:

> It will be long before the Corsicans arrive at the refinement of conducting a news-paper, of which London affords an unparalleled perfection; for, I do believe, an English newspaper is the most various and extraordinary composition that mankind every produced. An English news-paper, while it informs the judicious of what is really happening in Europe, can keep pace with the wildest fancy in feigned adventures, and amuse the most desultory taste with essays on all subjects, and in every stile.[15]

Since the dispassionate accuracy of eighteenth-century English newspapers was not widely appreciated at the time, we may speculate that Boswell was recalling his own practice of writing minor fictions for the daily press. But so far as his account of Corsica is concerned, it would be quite sufficient to say that the Corsicans had no daily newspapers in the 1760s.

Yet while the *Account* falls far short of being a distinguished travel book, the *Journal of a Tour to Corsica; and Memoirs of Pascal Paoli,* which accompanies it allows us to see Boswell at his best. That best is the role of a follower and interviewer of the illustrious and famous. Boswell saw Corsica as a place where, as he grandly put it, "nobody else has been". In fact, the usual traveler on the grand tour had not been to Corsica; nor could the usual visitor obtain a letter of introduction to the island's leader from Rousseau, as Boswell did. Paoli quickly took Boswell into his confidence, so that he is able to record many specimens of the great leader's conversation. The travel book becomes a lesson in political science as Boswell, an exotic foreigner on Corsica, just as Gulliver is a sought-after wonder on his *Travels,* is able to say that he "had every day some hours of private conversation with" Paoli. Here we see an early instance of Boswell's journalistic skills: "From my first setting out on this tour, I wrote down every night what I observed during the day, throwing together a great deal, that I might afterwards make a selection at leisure".[16] The specimens of Paoli's conversation have less to do with Boswell's trip to Corsica than they do with his desire to assemble a body of intelligent sayings; the English reading public was fascinated by the *ana* of the noted and the notorious alike. The *Account of Corsica* is undistinguished, then, as a travel book, but as a prototype for the gifted assembling of a random collection of table talk that Boswell would offer in his later, Johnsonian, writings, it is highly effective. The formality with which Boswell makes the general speak, for example, foreshadows his predilection for giving Johnson's conversational utterances sonorous periods, even when we know that Johnson was not always either sonorous or periodic.

The fame that *An Account of Corsica* brought Boswell was attenuated by the fact that about a year after his book first appeared the French conquered Corsica, and Paoli left to take up a twenty-year exile in England, where he attracted much notice. Thus a travel book that is not really a travel book at all succeeded in giving its author fame through association with his illustrious subject. Boswell would succeed at this effort even more dramatically with his second and last travel book, the *Journal of a Tour to the Hebrides.* He and Johnson had made their famous trip to Scotland thirteen years before; while Johnson published his *Journey to the Western Islands* within two years of the trip, Boswell evidently was in no hurry. But he rushed his book through the press quickly after Johnson's death, for he intended it as a foretaste of the biography that was to come. In a sense, Boswell's *Journal* is no more a travel book than his *Account of Corsica* had been. Boswell is perfectly capable of introducing intelligent commentary about the fabric of Scottish life, and he does precisely this when the travelers encounter scenes that would have been uncommon to the English reader. But his principal purpose is not that of the tourist, it is that of the observer of Samuel Johnson. Boswell's success in observing Johnson in an alien landscape adds a dimension to travel writing that we have not seen earlier in the eighteenth century. His collecting the sayings of Paoli, after all, had not been difficult, since Paoli was at home in his own court and Boswell had plenty of time to digest his materials. But Johnson in Scotland was more challenging to follow, for the companions moved swiftly from one set of friends to another; we do not see Johnson in familiar milieux, and when we do see him, he changes places rapidly. Paoli had not expressed many prejudices, whereas Boswell, perhaps to excess, pointed out the force of Johnson's prejudices against Presbyterianism, certain bodies of thought, and various people whom they met as they traveled along. Johnson was not always the best of companions, and there were days when they had virtually no conversation, either because the two men had quarreled or because one or the other felt unwell. On September 13, 1773, for example, Johnson caught cold and became slightly deaf, so Boswell and he could not conveniently converse. No matter: since Johnson had passed the night in the very bed in which the Young Pretender had slept after the battle of Culloden, Boswell seizes the occasion as the proper place for a protracted account of the escape of Prince Charles Edward (as he styles him), dressed in women's clothes, after Culloden. This digression is longer than any account of any single day on the entire tour; its relevance to travel or to Samuel Johnson is infinitesimal. But as Johnson recovers his good spirits, Boswell's depth of reporting increases, and like a dog who has seized a large piece of meat and takes it off to a corner to enjoy it alone (Boswell's metaphor), he confesses, "I was elated by the thought of having been able to entice such a man to this remote part of the world".[17]

Remote the Highlands and Hebrides certainly were in 1773, but save for the inconveniences that Johnson and Boswell had to bear from occasionally sleeping in barns and sometimes having to dine on simple food, Boswell does not give the impression of much wildness or primitiveness. When Johnson strides with rapture among the ruins of Iona, Boswell makes a particular note to avoid becoming too interested in the ancient ruins: "I resolved to stroll among [the ruins] at my ease to take no trouble to investigate minutely, and only receive the general impression of solemn antiquity, and the particular ideas of such objects as should of themselves strike my attention".[18] The experiment is a bold one, but it does not lead to anything, for evidently nothing struck Boswell enough to attract his attention. Perhaps the fact the Johnson had written at length in his *Journey* of these very ruins persuaded him that he had nothing to add. But the passage shows a tendency that appears regularly in the *Tour*, Boswell's readiness to lose interest in being a tourist and travel writer when Johnson leaves his field of vision. As a viewer of nature and of human artifacts, then, Boswell is far less successful than travelers of much more modest skills; but as a dramatic craftsman capable of exploiting the nuances of conversation, he has no peer. On many occasions in the *Tour*, he presents a confrontation between Johnson and another strong-willed, opinionated person, like Lord Monboddo, or his own father, and in these meetings the atmosphere is pregnant with the sharpness of wit. Sometimes Johnson succeeds in giving offense so completely that Boswell forbears to print even a fragment of what he said.[19] Throughout the *Tour*, Boswell also succeeds in suggesting that Johnson closely associated travel and intellectual activity, travel and books. To be sure, he does not make this connection precisely, but he records Johnson's hundreds of references to books and authors, often with a conscious knowledge of the subjects that Johnson mentions. So Boswell, too, improves as a travel writer and observer as he matures. In the *Account of Corsica*, as I noted earlier, he draws extensively on the writings of his predecessors; literature sometimes, but not often, figures in his records of Paoli's conversation. When he composed the *Tour*, nearly twenty years later, Boswell had not suddenly become better read or more scholarly. However, aided by friends who had known Johnson well and professionals like Edmond Malone who assisted him in making his account credible, he had attained a better grasp of how to present scenes with intellectual force. Boswell tells us that the *Tour* is a "journal" that he kept through the eighty-three days of the trip. Actually, it is a revised and augmented journal that he presents, just as Defoe's narrative in *Robinson Crusoe* is more full and circumstantial than what Crusoe records in the journal that he keeps in the course of the novel (until his ink runs out).

The eighteenth-century traveler, as Johnson and Boswell epitomize the figure, has developed, by the 1770s, into a blend of philosophical observer and intellectual adventurer. Johnson, early in his literary career, had doubted that voyages to foreign places produced anything remarkable, since human nature is everywhere the same. Boswell, writing his first travel book at roughly the same age that Johnson made his translation of Father Lobo, mainly copied his observations from other writers and preserved brief snippets of the table talk of one famous man. Later in his long career, Johnson had come to appreciate the travel genre more thoroughly; in his *Journey to the Western Isles* he delights in noting the singular differences among the many inhabitants that he meets. He still believes that human nature is basically alike everywhere, but he has become much more tolerant of intellectual disparities than he was as a young writer. Boswell's mature travel writing is no better at minute description than his youthful work had been, but his intimate observations of intellectual styles are far sharper than they were in his apprentice work. Although he tells us in *An Account of Corsica* that he passed several hours a day with General Paoli, he never presents a single conversational exchange between himself and the Corsican. In the *Tour,* after years of further travel and journal keeping, he readily manages dialogues that can include several speakers, complete with stage directions, humor, bathos, indignation, and other emotions. Since the *Tour* is the literary product of Boswell's longest continuous exposure to Johnson, its verbal exchanges are mainly firsthand; there are far fewer unattributed anecdotes and *collectanea* than he later presents in his *Life of Johnson.* As a travel book, the *Tour* is as good as conversational travel in eighteenth-century England can be, a three-month stagecoach journey with one excellent companion.

Travelers have always had their critics, people who suspect that they embroider the things that they say they have seen and make their exchanges of wit more witty than they were in real life. Neither Johnson nor Boswell was immune to these weaknesses of the genre. Johnson, in his fictional travel writings, sometimes studiously overlooks the greatest of wonders; the visit to the pyramids in *Rasselas* shows that he was uninterested in giving his readers a detailed account (of course, Johnson knew all the details about the pyramids, since he was well versed in contemporary Egyptology). Boswell, for all that he excels at presenting conversations, or fragments of them, was capable of augmenting the speeches of Johnson to make him sound more polysyllabic and orotund than he was. Do their travel writings suffer as a result of these shortcomings? I doubt that they do, for complete objectivity is never possible. Although the two men are strikingly different as intellects, they have come down to our own century as travelers whom we can comfortably glimpse together, observers whose most famous joint voyage still draws imitators who would follow their footsteps in the summer months. How daunting would today's tourists find making Johnson and Boswell's Highland and Hebridean journey as the originals did, in September and October! Two eighteenth-century travelers who invite imitation more than two centuries after their trip: it is hard to better the success of such travel writing.

# NOTES

1. *Lives of the English Poets,* ed. G. Birkbeck Hill, 3 vols. (Oxford: 1905) 1.95.
2. *Lives,* 1.189.
3. *A Voyage to Abyssinia,* ed. Joel J. Gold, Yale Edition of the Works of Samuel Johnson vol. 15 (New Haven: 1985) 3–4.
4. See Thomas M. Curley, *Samuel Johnson and the Age of Travel* (Athens, GA: 1976) 113–46.
5. *Adventurer* 84, in *The Idler and the Adventurer,* ed. W. J. Bate et al., Yale Edition of the Works of Samuel Johnson, vol. 2 (New Haven: 1963) 407.
6. *Life of Samuel Johnson,* ed. G. B. Hill, rev. L. F. Powell (Oxford: 1934–64) 1.465.
7. *The Letters of Samuel Johnson,* ed. R. W. Chapman, 3 vols. (Oxford: 1952) 1.163.
8. *A Journey to the Western Islands of Scotland,* ed. Mary Lascelles, Yale Edition of the Works of Samuel Johnson, vol. 9 (New Haven: 1972) 142–43.
9. *Journey,* 155.
10. *Life* 4.183.
11. *Life* 4.199
12. *Boswell on the Grand Tour: Italy, Corsica, and France, 1765–1766,* ed. Frank Brady and Frederick A. Pottle (New York: 1955) 43.
13. *An Account of Corsica* (Glasgow: 1768) xviii–xix.
14. *Account,* xxi.
15. *Account* 197–98.
16. *Account* 295.
17. *Life* 5.215.
18. *Life* 5.335.
19. *Life* 5.383: "his antagonist [i.e., Johnson] soon made a retort, which I forbear to mention"; Boswell is describing a meeting between his father, Lord Auchinleck, and Johnson, at the end of the *Tour,* in Edinburgh.

# "PATHS TO GUIDE IMAGINATION'S FLIGHT": SOME EIGHTEENTH-CENTURY POETS ABROAD

**Tony Bareham, Cyprus**

English poets in the eighteenth century were deeply interested in foreign places and in the experience of travel. If no supreme long work emerged wholly concerned with this material, in flashes we meet imaginative writing of a high order. The present essay surveys this often undervalued material, in which pure geography is often caught up with an interest in history. The impetus to visit Italy is certainly fostered as much by the ruins of antiquity as by scenery or climate. Studies contrasting the life-style and topography of places abroad with those at home also provide a mold into which observation can be poured. There is not much evidence of foreign locations serving as correlatives of inner spiritual landscapes, as they do in Wordsworth, Byron, or Coleridge; but as with many aspects of literature between 1700 and 1800, it is a sense of evolution rather than of stark revolution that careful reading elicits.

While at first Europe and the Near East command attention, the response grows to more distant voyages such as Cook's explorations in the antipodes, and the quest for the Northeast and Northwest passages. From North Pole to South Seas the poets begin to take account of these foreign wonders, as explorers bring home and publish their accounts for an ever-growing reading public. Poets felt more bound than novelists by codes of decorum, by categories of the sublime, the beautiful and the picturesque, which were prevalent by midcentury. Such prescriptions (of which Burke's *A Philosophical Enquiry into the Origin of Our Ideas of the Sublime and the Beautiful* [1756] is the most renowned) may have encouraged poets to seek out the awesome and the exotic; but in some degree they also stultified efforts to give individuality to their responses.

The influence upon literature of the work of pictorial artists like Nicholas Poussin (1594–1645), Claude Lorraine (1600–82), and Salvator Rosa (1615–73) has been demonstrated;[1] and that of the Roman engravings of Giovanni Piranesi was recognized at the time. Writing of the absence of topographical literature among the ancients, one eighteenth-century authority observed, "They have no Thomsons because they had no Claudes".

Equally, the poetic imagination was sanctioned and stimulated by a growing interest in archaeology, though there was a less-worthy side to this, manifest in Dyer's comments on the pillaging of artifacts:

> . . . the traveller
> Such antique marbles to his native land
> Oft hence conveys; and every realm and state
> With Rome's august remains, heroes and gods,
> Deck their long galleries and winding groves;
> Yet miss we not the innumerable thefts,
> Yet still profuse with graces teems the waste.
> (*The Ruins of Rome* 361–67)

An increasing number of authors now had personal experience of foreign travel. Addison and Prior visited the Continent on diplomatic business; Grainger was an army doctor who served in the War of the Austrian Succession; Dyer was a dilettante in search of material for his painting as well as his poetry; Goldsmith traveled widely as a wandering student. The grand tour encouraged many more to find their way into France, across the Alps, and into Italy. Some went even farther afield, as is witnessed by the travels of Lady Mary Wortley Montagu, for instance. Maybe the presence of a Hanoverian monarchy also helped to make Britons more aware of their European neighbors.

Yet it remains true until nearly the end of the century that the aim of the poet is to express general truths about human nature. Inevitably these can be made most readily manifest where there is most familiarity for readers with the objects displayed. Why go abroad for your illustrations when established models exist at home? But if relatively few descriptions of foreign settings exist for themselves, or act as correlatives to inner states of mind, they exist and are used as examples, sometimes of social satire, sometimes, conversely, as adumbrations of a perfection unattainable by corrupt societies at home. In the post-Cook era of the 1780s this was the treatment accorded to the newly discovered worlds of Oceania and the South Seas.

Other constraints obtain. James Grainger, for instance, was clearly moved to wonder and delight by the fecund and exotic splendor of the West Indies. But his poem *The Sugar Cane* (1764) gives expression to that delight much more in its footnotes than in its text. Within the poem enthusiasm is constricted by the neo-georgic mode in which it is cast. This is a cogent example of ebullient content being constricted and constrained by form. So too, Addison's pleasure in Italy is physical—"And trodden weeds send out a rich perfume"—but, as we shall see, this excitement is not the end product of the work. And so with Dyer's awe at the ruined splendor of Rome, and with Falconer's response to the power of the stormy Aegean. It would be easy but wrong to undervalue the force of these feelings—though standard histories of literature have tended to do so. Equally, it would be foolhardy to expect radically new methods of expressing such feelings.

An interest in landscape had been manifest in English verse for many years; when was it ever absent? But for present purposes a tradition begins with Denham's *Cooper's Hill* (1642), while Milton, first in the evocative language of *L'Allegro* and *Il Penseroso* (1631) and later in the geographic and cosmic imagery of *Paradise Lost* (1667), provided a manner and a specific vocabulary for scene painting in words. There is scarcely one eighteenth-century poem descriptive of exotic places or peoples that is not fundamentally indebted to Milton. The Warton brothers in midcentury show how that indebtedness may become stultifying. Yet this sense of conservative linguistic continuity is not all deleterious, as may be witnessed in the major "Miltonians" from Thomson, through Cowper, and on to Wordsworth himself.

In language and in form the response of poets to "abroad" is codified. The reflective poem, the eclogue, the georgic, the familiar epistle: these well-established poetic kinds provide at once the skeleton and the straitjacket of Augustan and pre-Romantic poetry of abroad.

A tendency to generalize may well influence the quality and cast of the ideas within this poetry; this manifestly happens in Goldsmith's *The Traveller* (1765), and it often leads to sweeping panoramas of rather hazy geographic accuracy. Much of the first draft of Thomson's *The Seasons* (1726–30) depends upon descriptions of locations not specific to one observed place, but extracted from avid and copious reading, and then winnowed through a vivid imagination. At the time of commencing work on his poem, Thomson had never been outside the British Isles.

The relationship between God and Nature also influences the tone and temper of the poetry. Either by temperament or by conscious effort most of the romantic poets were free from constraining thoughts about the creator of the magnificence they observed. Many of the earlier writers in verse either accepted the entire thing as God's hand, without further question, or, more interestingly, wrestled covertly to reconcile extremely warm awe with the rather tepid tenets of fashionable deism. It is not easy for these writers to avoid the cant of enthusiasm on the one side, or the sin of ingratitude on the other. Thomson finds an acceptable stance:

> Inspiring God . . .
> . . . ceaseless works alone; and yet alone
> Seems not to work; with such perfection framed
> Is this complex, stupendous scheme of things.
> (*Spring* 853–58)

But Thomson's friend, contemporary, and fellow Scot Mallet often strives vainly for such a point of accepting repose. The first part of his rhapsody *The Excursion* (1728) takes us into a quasi-Mediterranean landscape of earthquake and volcano, where we witness the destruction of a great city. But the moral conclusion—that these terrors are God's inscrutable but ultimately benevolent hand at work—carries no conviction. Mallet seems really excited by the power of destructive Nature, but only feebly capable of wrestling with the spiritual and moral problems elicited by that excitement.

Samuel Johnson observed of Grainger's *The Sugar Cane* (1764) that it would have been as appropriate (albeit as ludicrous) to have written "the Parsley-bed, a Poem", or "The Cabbage-garden, a Poem"![2] His frustration with Grainger's prolix and heavily factual work may even seem more reasonable in our age than in his own. In the mid-1760s the georgic was still a viable form, with many English examples: Philips's *Cyder* (1708), Smart's *The Hop Garden* (1762), and Cowper's disquisition on cucumber growing in *The Task* (1785), for instance.

If Virgil could write poetry about beekeeping, why should Grainger not describe cane cultivation in verse? Johnson's cavil may be misdirected. It is less the form itself or the subject matter that is at fault in Grainger's work than the inability to sustain quality of execution within that form. But for us to condemn Grainger, unread, to the poetical rubbish bin—as virtually every history of English literature does—is to miss a key example of how an eighteenth-century poet deemed it possible to combine his personal excitement at abroad with a commitment to instruction and science. In fact, Johnson's review of *The Sugar Cane* (Boswell 1.481) is much less condemnatory than the casual conversational remark cited from Boswell's *Life* above. Of course, Grainger is light-years away from recapturing the delicate limpid quality of Virgil; no English writer of georgic in the eighteenth century managed to make the strange mixture work. But Grainger's poem may stand as an example of work genuinely excited by the aural and visual stimuli of the Caribbean.

The role of painting in helping to shape the processes of selection and description in Augustan verse that treats of the world beyond Britain has already been mentioned. Landscape gardening also helped to direct the visual imagination toward informal and exotic scenery. This was the beginning of the great age of botanical collecting, with a wide range of plants and trees that are now accepted as indigenous becoming part of the landscape for the first time. And a growing sense of adventure in which Englishmen traveled at home helped to make them more sympathetic to a wider range of scenery abroad. As Snowdonia, the Peak District, and the Lakes became popular with English tourists through the century—and many travel journals illustrate this taste—so it became more natural to seek the most spectacular examples of this newly admired natural grandeur abroad.

Within the constraints and conditions outlined above there is a corpus of work, dominated by established themes and conventions, perhaps governed or subverted by specific polemical purposes, but constantly striving for means to do justice to the genuine sense of awe and wonderment presented as new vistas opened up to the observer's eye. Much English eighteenth-century poetry of abroad centers on the Mediterranean basin: the ruined glories of Rome, the unprecedented grandeur of the Alps are principal points of interest. Until the very end of this period Greece is rather less popular, perhaps because less accessible, than Rome.[3] Responses then divide into those that meditate generally upon human mutability and those that draw (often political) conclusions about the superiority of British virility and vigor. Poems of the latter kind usually also contain warnings about the danger of decadence, which is inherent even in vigorous national growth. A modern reader may, however, often feel a real tension between the fresh excitement engendered by the foreign setting and the predictable eulogy of life at home. It is the delight in Italy rather than the praise of Britain that makes Addison's *Letter from Italy* a memorable poem. The heart seems happiest abroad even when the head turns to Britain. Few authors who traveled abroad fail to express similar emotions. And outside poetry about Italy (where thoughts on mutability are most likely to be stirred, and cultural indebtedness most reverently expressed) there exists a peripheral world of writings embracing regions as diverse as the West Indies, the South Seas, and the northern polar zone. On at least one occasion we are taken out into space itself. The following survey attempts to characterize a few of these types. Diverse as may be the mise-en-scène, we shall find that the driving purpose is nearly always that of ostensible argumentation rather than spiritual self-expression. For that, we must wait until nearer the turn of the century. The eighteenth century's response to Nature and abroad is leading to Samuel Rogers, not Samuel Coleridge.

The form of Addison's *Letter from Italy* is that of the verse epistle, and this enables the poet to adopt a tone colored by personal excitement. But the addressee is Lord Halifax, patriot and statesman, and we must therefore expect a prevailing note of suavity, and some dexterous political point making. A place seeker like Addison would not, after all, be writing to his lordship unless he had something to say beyond merely reporting how pleasant he finds it in Italy! What makes the poem successful is Addison's ability to keep these social functions in tune with the positive and exciting sense of discovery that he experiences:

For wheresoe'er I turn my ravished eyes,
Gay gilded scenes and shining prospects rise,
Poetic fields encompass me around,
And still I seem to tread on classic ground.
(9–12)

Even today the traveler to Italy may share this admixture of awe at proximity to the birthplace of our cultural inheritance, pleasure at the exotic feel of the place, and excitement at its scenic variety and challenge. Addison is eager to be off exploring, reliving the past. The sophisticated Augustan is moved to the point of being comically overenthusiastic:

Sometimes, misguided by the tuneful throng,
I look for streams immortalised in song,
That lost in silence and oblivion lie,
(Dumb are their fountains and their channels dry)
Yet run forever by the Muse's skill,
And in the smooth description murmur still.
(31–36)

This nicely amalgamates the aesthete's intellectual pleasure and the first-time traveler's animal excitement. Addison is entranced by the tactile and sensory impact of Italy:

Ev'n the rough rocks with tender myrtle bloom,
And trodden weeds send out a rich perfume.
(61–62)

For a hundred and six lines this tone is sustained (marred for a modern reader, perhaps, by the fulsome cross-reference from Tiber to Boyne for his lordship's private gratification). Few Augustan poets manage better than Addison to convey pleasure in foreign scenery. Many were content to use him as a model. Forty years later, for instance, Dyer admires the same aspects of Rome, and admires them in exactly the same order as Addison. Those hundred lines of the *Letter from Italy* take in the scenery, climate, and flora of a land seen by northern visitors as wonderfully fecund. They remind us of the inestimable debt we owe our cultural progenitors in Roman antiquity. The poet's vision settles on the city's architecture, civic works, and engineering achievements, miraculous even in ruin. But they are also redolent of ominous warning of the dangers implicit in civilization's mutations from sophistication through to decay.

And then, with the snap of a trap suddenly shutting, the poem reveals itself not as chatty travelogue, but as a work of moral and political art. The whole structure hinges on one word—"but"—in line 107, and turns upon that word from descriptive to purposive; "But what avail" all the miracles so far described "While proud Oppression in her vallies reigns". We have been victims of an extended rhetorical subterfuge. The message is *not* "How wonderful it is to be abroad", but, conversely, "How much better off we are in reality at home". For sun, orange groves, and classical antiquities are no substitute for British liberty and independence. This at least is the ostensible message. In the next generation Thomson is to reintroduce this theme of freedom passing from the Mediterranean lands to Britain in *Liberty* (1735–36).

Addison's argument is that

> We envy not the warmer clime, that lies
> In ten degrees of more indulgent skies.
> (*Letter from Italy* 135–36)

"Indulgent" is subtly loaded to imply something effete and decadent in the Italian atmosphere; and is "lies" a pun, suggesting that the warmth deceives us? The moral lesson to be learned from the decline and fall of Rome was being drawn half a century before Gibbon gave it definitive expression.

Yet the real impression of *Letter from Italy* is less acutely of its chauvinistic moral drawing than of the full-blooded relish of the poet's visual and sensory experiences. He does not really sound like a man who wants to come home!

John Dyer lacks Addison's poetic accomplishment, but, derivative as it is, *The Ruins of Rome* (1740) shows us interesting deviations from Addison's stance. The worldly civility of a social epistle has yielded to a quasi-romantic meditation upon mutability. We still feel the observer's genuine emotion and excitement, but both the purpose and consequently the structure are very different in Dyer's poem. Addison gives only half his time to the delights of Italy, and then puts in an extensive caveat on behalf of Britain, but Dyer, in a poem twice as long, is into his last few lines before he arranges the turn in his argument:

Vain end of human strength, of human skill,
Conquest, and triumph, and domain, and pomp,
And ease, and luxury! O, luxury,
Bane of elated life . . .
What dreary change, what ruin is not thine?
(*The Ruins of Rome* 532–36)

This suffusion of generalized and melancholy moral stricture makes Dyer's poem very different from Addison's. By midcentury such feelings had become common in a school of poetry, receiving fullest expression in Young's *Night Thoughts* (1742–45).

For Dyer the process of decay is much more inevitable than for Addison, and the delights of Italy much more ephemeral and transient in consequence. Dyer's sense of composition is also noticeably more indebted to a sustaining background tradition that links literary with graphic art. Since he went to Italy principally to study painting, this is no surprise:

. . . the solemn scene
Elates the soul, while now the rising sun
Flames on the ruins of the purer air
Towering aloft, upon the glittering plain,
Like broken rocks, a vast circumference.
(*The Ruins of Rome* 19–23)

This has a painter's appreciation of the quality of light. Given the date of the poem, it also seems gratifyingly unstereotyped in its language.

Dyer is also capable of charming evocations of typical scenes, as thus, on a visit to the ruins of Virgil's cottage outside Rome:

. . . the gourd and olive brown
Weave the light roof: the gourd and olive fan
Their amorous foliage, mingling with the vine,
Who drops her purple clusters through the green.
Here let me lie, with pleasing fancy sooth'd
Here flowed his fountain; here his laurels grew . . .
(*The Ruins of Rome* 372–77)

Dyer is doing much more than sending home tinted poetical postcards; he is attempting an empathy with the spirit of a past master of poetry. It is possible to urge that literary histories have been very ungenerous to the integrity of this delicate period piece, which in any case provides a key example of midcentury verse treatment of Italy by a British poet.

The rather melancholy reaction to the charisma of Rome is typical, but Dyer is more circumstantial than Addison. He catalogs in turn the view from the Palatine hill, the Colosseum, the Capitol, the Pantheon, the Temple of Concord, the Temple of Vespasian, the Baths of Caracalla, Trajan's Column, and many other sights. Maybe the driving purpose of the mutability theme is swamped by the plethora of guidebook detail. Tactically the poem is far from perfect. It lacks Addison's rhetorical accomplishment. But nothing could better illustrate the change and development in the attitude to Italy that had occurred between 1700 and 1740—a change as instructive for the history of poetry itself as for the history of attitudes to abroad.

So far the poets discussed purport to record firsthand experience. But there is an alternative tradition that dispenses with this circumstantial verisimilitude. Thus, though James Thomson did visit the Continent after 1730, the nucleus of *The Seasons* was in print by then. Without polemical or political objectives, Thomson is free to range across ideal and imagined landscapes, intent on glorifying God through Nature. It is instructive to scrutinize the illustrations prepared by William Kent for the grand folio edition of *The Seasons* in 1730; they are reproduced in James Sambrook's edition of the poem. In each case, within harmonized overall design, the top half of the plate shows the schematic progress of the personified season through the relevant part of the zodiac. This then melds into a graphic evocation of quasi-realistic scenery below. Thus *Spring* has airy graces dancing in a ring around the emerging sun in its top half, while clouds and a rainbow neatly divide the "symbolic" from the "realistic" parts of the composition, and remind us of the genial uncertainty of the season. Even in the bottom half of the plate we meet a fusion of typical and ideal. In *Spring*, pastoral figures guard sheep, pipe, make love. From them the eye moves across a composite geography that is pastoral and Virgilian, yet hauntingly evocative of the reality of some Italian landscapes. These plates demonstrate most clearly the compositional method within the poem itself. Many of the descriptions of specific places were added to the poem after Thomson had been abroad. Most of these descriptions also serve to point no particular moral beyond that of God's extraordinary creative fecundity in Nature. The poet draws extensively on the method and the vocabulary established in *Paradise Lost*, but in many cases the evocations of nature do not even ask us to differentiate between "at home" and "abroad". The plowman at the beginning of *Spring* is as familiar to the plains of the Po Valley as to the valley of the Thames, and *Autumn's* pictures of nut gathering and orchard fruits draw on phenomena common to all western Europe. And though many of the later additions are more specifically exotic—*Winter*, for instance, has very evocative polar and Alpine scenes—there remains throughout *The Seasons* an ability to paint pictures that will strike the imagination of any reader regardless of the extent of his own traveling:

> . . . low the woods
> Bow their hoar head; and, ere the languid sun
> Faint from the west emits his evening ray,
> Earth's universal face, deep-hid and chill,
> Is one wide dazzling waste, that buries wide
> The works of man . . . (*Winter* 235–40)

This, again, is common to the winter of any western European country—as Milton's landscapes in *L'Allegro* and *Il Penseroso* are common. It is Thomson's closeness to this source of inspiration, together with his freshness of vision, that enables him to create his own characteristic scenery and atmosphere.

Mallet was fellow countryman, fellow student, and personal friend to Thomson. In 1728—two years before the folio edition of *The Seasons*—he published *The Excursion*. Mallet has nothing like the charismatic power of description of his more famous contemporary; most of his work is journeyman stuff, and his religious arguments are sometimes woefully thin. But *The Excursion* is a curiosity with flashes of real merit, and no account of British poetic reactions to abroad should ignore it.

Book 1 is structurally diffuse. The poet claims to be "musing in sober mood of Time and Life"; perhaps so broad and solemn a program encourages him to be too excursive. The book seems uncertain how to proceed. It sets off on a Thomsonian-Miltonic poet-in-seasonal-landscape passage, and takes us through various meteorological conditions of morning, noon, and night. Then almost as a convulsive second start we set off "next day" on a bird's-eye tour of the Northern Hemisphere, from polar regions, through Tartary and over the Caucasus; then southward to an Alpine point of vantage from which the earth at large can be surveyed. (This is precisely the structural device Goldsmith later adopted in *The Traveller*.) Mallet's vision takes in a proud Italian city smitten by earthquake, then by volcano. Since, like Thomson, Mallet did not leave Britain until after he had written his poem, this sensationalist picture comes purely from the imagination. The rhapsodical material culminates in a stunningly feeble and specious attempt to justify these malign phenomena as the workings of a just but inscrutable deity. The impression is of an author fascinated by the lurid imaginary pictures he has drawn, and drawn with crude but violent power—albeit the sort of power implicit in a child's drawing of a natural disaster—but totally incapable of explaining these things within any acceptable theology. In itself Book 1 of *The Excursion* might be peripheral even to a special study of British poets dealing with exotic settings, save for its demonstration of the midcentury tendency to deploy general landscapes. This in turn implies a readership interested in word-paintings created for their own sake.

Of this school Joseph Warton's *Enthusiast or the Lover of Nature* (1744) is typical. This poem describes unfavorably the reality of civilized and methodized nature at Versailles, where are

> a thousand fountains that can cast
> The tortured waters to the distant heavens . . .
> (*The Enthusiast,* unnumbered)

Warton prefers

> . . . some pine topt precipice
> Abrupt and shaggy, whence a foaming stream,
> Like Anio, tumbling roars; or some bleak heath,
> Where straggling stand the mournful juniper
> Or yew-tree scathed . . . (*The Enthusiast,* unnumbered)

An evocation of the Burkean sublime if ever there was one, and probably very far from what the closeted Warton would have actually liked for any sustained period in real life. This is merely aesthetic playing of games with a rich palette and heavy colors. The generalizing words—"some", "like"—telegraph for us how unspecific this landscape really is.

Book 2 of *The Excursion* sets out to explore the heavens themselves—surely one of the century's most spectacular attempts at the far reaches of abroad. Milton again may be the ultimate sanction for this flight of fancy. If, argues Mallet, earth is a series of divine wonders, how much more so are the heavens! He imagines himself traveling first across the space immediately surrounding the earth, then outward to the sun:

> A shoreless sea of fluctuating fire,
> That deluges all ether with its tide.
> What power is that, which to its circle bounds
> The violence of flame! In rapid whirls
> Conflicting, floods with floods, as if to leave
> Their place, and bursting, overwhelm the world . . .
> (*The Excursion* 2.42–47)

A powerfully written hymn to the sun follows—composed, interestingly, before the appearance of Thomson's *Summer,* with its eulogy on the same theme.

We are then moved outward through the planets, each briefly described; the poet's imagination is most stirred by the two most distant, as then thought—Jupiter with its four moons, and Saturn, "the boundary of worlds". (The discovery of Uranus, of course, was made by the astronomer royal, William Herschel, in 1781.) A touching paean of praise to the Almighty expresses the space traveler's awe at these imagined worlds, and here Mallet's reconciliation of mainstream Christianity with deism is much happier than in Book 1:

> Beauteous appearance! by th'Almighty's hand
> Peculiar fashion'd.—Thine these noble works,
> Great, universal Ruler! earth and heaven
> Are thine, spontaneous offspring of thy will,
> Seen with transcendent ravishment sublime,
> That lifts the soul to thee! A holy joy,
> By reason prompted, and by reason swelled
> Beyond all height, for thou art infinite
> Thy virtual energy the frame of things
> Pervading actuates: as at first thy hand
> Diffused through endless space this limpid sky,
> Vast ocean without storm, where these huge globes
> Sail undisturbed. (*The Excursion* 2.146–58)

Mallet also shared Thomson's admiration for Newton. The scientist died in 1727, and his apotheosis is movingly described in the ensuing passage, uniting the inscrutable creativity of God with the marvelous human wisdom of his great (and newly deceased) servant in astronomical science.

The poem then stretches out beyond the solar system, through the Milky Way, and into other galaxies to

> . . . where no landmarks are,
> No paths to guide Imagination's flight . . .
> (*The Excursion* 2.367–68)

Equally unusual, and equally neglected, are my last two examples: Grainger's *The Sugar Cane,* and Falconer's *The Shipwreck.* The former is an example of the late Augustan georgic. The latter really has no kind of formal precedent, comprising as it does an extended verse tale of personally experienced danger—albeit overlaid, to its detriment, by an encrustation of epic language and devices.

Grainger, finding himself in the West Indies after years of army medical service, and of wandering Europe subsequent to the peace of Aix-la-

Chapelle in 1748, sets out to compose a four-book georgic about cane cultivation, centerd upon the island of St. Kitts, where he settled. We have seen Johnson's unfavorable reaction, though the two men were acquainted, and elsewhere Johnson speaks quite warmly of Grainger, who, in turn, laments in his poem the separation from his English literary friends, Johnson included.

It is true that Grainger can seldom manage to be more than pedestrian, but as a scientific account in verse of the flora and fauna of the Caribbean, the poem has substantial interest. It is no more of an oddity than, say, Erasmus Darwin's *The Botanic Garden* (1789–91), which managed a brief but vigorous success at the turn of the century. English verse from 1750 to about 1790 seems not to have known quite where it was going; it is full of oddities and blind alleys. But literary histories that seek to block off both ends of these alleys are much misguided. Thus *The Sugar Cane* may indeed be a literary curiosity, but it is as valuable a supplement to knowledge of the West Indies as then available in prose, and an interesting attempt to combine science and poetry.

Grainger offers a self-conscious apologia for writing his treatise in verse:

> . . . the sacred muse
> Naught sordid deems, but what is base, naught fair
> Unless true virtue stamp it with her seal . . .
> (*The Sugar Cane* 1.219–21)

And in an age that read its classical history, its philosophy, and its natural history in verse through Statius, Lucretius, and Pliny, it needs more than merely Johnson's acerbity to deny Grainger's right to versify his agriculture.

Claiming proper sanction from Virgil—"lofty Maro, whose immortal Muse / Distant I follow, and submiss adore" (*The Sugar Cane* 2.132–33)—he explains in his preface that his ideas are "the children of truth, not genius, the result of experience, not the productions of fancy". Such an admission concedes the difference between Virgil as master and Grainger as pupil; the poem is a period oddity rather than a sustained work of art. But as its nineteenth-century editor explains,

> . . . the merit . . . is not to be estimated from its reception, nor its aptitude to catch the attention of a common European reader. The preceptive part has not merely the merit of serious utility. Grainger knew that he was writing to an age not less luxurious or refined than that of Rome in the days of Virgil . . . he has embellished his precepts with all the flowers of imagery. The attention is not long exercised by the gravity of didactic precepts, before it is relieved by some beautiful description . . .
> (Preface to *The Sugar Cane* 894)

In other words, according to well-worn post-Renaissance precepts, he evokes the useful, which he sweetens with entertainment. It remains true that, for a modern reader, the instruction is exemplary, but the entertainment is short-suited.

Book 1 deals with preparing the land and planting the cane; Book 2 describes plagues, pests, and natural disasters—including an interesting eyewitness account of hurricane devastation upon the island; Book 3 is concerned mainly with harvesting and processing the cane; the last Book describes the selection, care, and disciplining of slaves who work the plantation. Each book is carefully larded with descriptions or inset narratives. But it is really the description of cane culture itself that induces the modern reader forward, together with the enormously informative footnotes on local flora and fauna.

First reaction to the contentious Book 4 is unhistorical indignation at the author's apparent acquiescence in the slave system. At best, Grainger can only advocate self-interested paternalism in the treatment of fellow human beings torn from their homes and transported to servitude. But as a historical statement of the views of an intelligent and otherwise humane man, his position, however obnoxious, is of interest. We are offered a typically ultraconservative caveat that at least the slaves on a well-tended estate are better off than those white men who are virtually enslaved in the silver and lead mines of Europe, and who suffer far worse physical ills. At one moment Grainger does wish for a world where slavery is unnecessary—but he is too limited imaginatively to conceive of such a state, or to see how he can help bring it about:

> Oh, did the tender Muse possess the power
> Which Monarchs have, and monarchs oft abuse,
> 'Twould be the fond ambition of her soul
> To quell tyrannic sway; knock off the chains
> Of heart-debasing slavery; give to every man,
> Of every colour, and of every clime,
> Freedom, which stamps him image of his God.
> (*The Sugar Cane* 4.232–38)

But this cannot be, he implies. And in the meantime Grainger can only exercise his medical skill to alleviate the physical ills that the enslaved suffer. If you want to prevent your slaves from getting worms, Grainger is the man to read!

His interest in the Caribbean is heavily scientific. It is not a place of spiritual renewal, as it had been for Marvell's exiles, or for Shakespeare's banished duke. Grainger's passages of lyrical description usually lack the commitment with which he writes of the succulent qualities of the avocado or the medical benefits of cassia. But whatever its overall quality, *The Sugar Cane* has a place of its own in this study of the poetry of abroad.

Falconer's *The Shipwreck* may be the oddest of all of my case histories. We have moved very far from the Addisonian style of travel contrast, where the ultimate goal is to show the superiority of life at home, and from the quasi-deistic nature eulogies of Thomson and Mallet. Indeed, the only ostensible purpose of Falconer's poem is to record the real-life adventure that befell the author. Falconer was a seaman without the privileges of much formal education or family influence. He was one of only three survivors from the wreck he describes—only to be lost at sea later in another disaster. He tells how his vessel, at the end of a three-year trading expedition around the Mediterranean, is blown off course while heading from Crete to Venice.

The narrative itself is genuinely exciting as the ship is storm-driven through the Cyclades, to be wrecked off Cape Colonna, but the story is cluttered with nautical terms; often the page contains more annotation than text, particularly in Canto 2, where the battle against the storm leads to minute detail of seafaring procedures. Encompassing this in heroic couplets is a curious technical triumph in its own way:

> Shivering at first, till by the blast impelled,
> High o'er the lee yard-arm the canvas swelled:
> By spilling lines embraced, with brails confined
> It lies at length unshaken by the wind.
> The forsail then secured, with equal care
> Again to reef the mainsail they repair.—
> While some high-mounted overhaul the tye,
> Below the down-haul-tackle others ply.
> Jears, lifts and brails, a seaman each attends,
> Along the mast the willing yard descends.
> (*The Shipwreck* 2.312–21)

Presumably this plethora of detail appealed in the eighteenth century to a taste that in the next century was met by Captain Marryat, and in our own day by Dudley Pope and C. S. Forrester.

Falconer's vessel is relentlessly driven due north from Crete, rather than first westerly, then northerly into the Adriatic. She is disabled, dismasted, reduced to a sheer hulk, and finally driven ashore after two narrow escapes. But this vigorous story is not allowed to stand on its own. Falconer weaves on to it contrastive character studies of the ship's officers, which are stiffened out of real interest by the clutter of "heroic" imagery that surrounds them. And he inserts a love plot in which the owner's son has fallen in love with the captain's daughter, and been banished to sea by his father as a cure for his passion. This may even have been true, but, again, the handling of it is fearfully stilted in both language and conception.

The core of the narrative is certainly hard fact, and comprises a unique poetic account of life at sea in the midcentury. And some of the descriptions of Cretan scenery in Canto 1 have a stylized merit. Falconer remains a slave to his period, however, in deeming it necessary to elevate his simple tale of suffering by encrustations of epic machinery and periphrastic language. This leads to ludicrous overinflation, and often to weakening of tension in the narrative itself. The author, lacking the confidence of an Establishment education and background, seems afraid to let loose true originality in telling his tale simply and in natural language. To ask this of Falconer is unfair, but his subservience to established custom vitiates what might have been one of the century's most interesting poems of abroad.

The range, style, and intention of English eighteenth-century poetry describing foreign countries and foreign travel manifests tendencies and trends implicit in other kinds of eighteenth-century verse. If there is no one great poet of travel in these years, there is a significant number of attempts to encompass themes that will concur with growing public taste and interest. Material that the newly evolved novel seized upon with avid delight often defeated the poets, constrained by conservative theories of decorum in style, genre, and language. Though the theme of abroad touches upon virtually every poetic movement that characterizes the age of sensibility, nothing really warns us of the extraordinary explosion of imaginative effort that will shortly bring in the enraptured and highly individualized responses of the Romantics.

## NOTES

Quotations are from *The Miscellaneous Works of Joseph Addison*, ed. A. C. Guthkelch, 2 vols. (London: 1914); Dyer, Mallet, and Falconer in *The Works of the English Poets. With Prefaces Biographical and Critical, by Samuel Johnson* (London: 1790); Grainger in *The Works of the British Poets. With Prefaces Biographical and Critical, by Robert Anderson* (London: 1795); *The Seasons and The Castle of Indolence by James Thomson*, ed. James Sambrook (Oxford: 1972).

1. See E. W. Manwaring, *Italian Landscape in Eighteenth Century England* (New York: 1925).
2. *Life of Samuel Johnson*, ed. G. B. Hill, rev. L. F. Powell (Oxford: 1971) 2.454.
3. But see J. Buxton, *The Grecian Taste* (London: 1978), for a corrective to the view that Greece held little or no part in the eighteenth-century view of abroad.

# SHERIDAN AND THE WIDER WORLD

Jack D. Durant, North Carolina State University

In literal terms, Richard Brinsley Sheridan was really nothing of a traveler. After matriculating at Harrow in 1762, he never again returned to Ireland, the place of his birth, and he left England only once, in 1772, when he eloped to France with his future wife, Elizabeth Linley. Driven to near distraction by an overzealous suitor, one Mathews, Elizabeth had recruited the aid of young Sheridan in fleeing the country late in March, an office he had performed with scrupulous respect for her reputation, and by late April the adventure was over; her father had come to fetch her home from Lille, where she and her protector had held separate lodgings. So brief a sojourn on foreign soil, however, hardly exhausts Sheridan's intellectual and imaginative involvement in places abroad. His plays draw freely upon foreign settings, situations, and stereotypes, and his speeches and political writings, most of them devoted to foreign policy, immerse him for thirty years in the large events of three continents.

To consider his comedies in turn is to sense his maturing grasp of ethnic humor, a comic mode so immediate to him that he never attempted comedy without it. At the outset of his career it took form in the bellicose stage Irishman of *The Rivals,* Sir Lucius O'Trigger, a figure so surly and fierce as to aggravate the wrath of first-night critics and to exact from the playwright significant reconsiderations before he offered the play for its second performance on January 28, 1775, eleven days after the first performance. On this second appearance Sir Lucius was still ready enough with his whimsical Irish pugnacity, but he had lost much of his goatishness and greed and was not quite so bloodthirsty a Philistine as before. In his preface to the printed play, Sheridan apologized for any offense given, and he made yet further amends by building his second play, *St. Patrick's Day* (1775), around a clever Irish recruiting officer, O'Connor, who boasts unswerving loyalty to his homeland. Again, comedy derives from an ethnic stereotype, this time a German quack, but here the broad pig latin affected by O'Connor, in the role of the quack, draws comedy not just from the habits of mind that make nations look ridiculous to one another but also from the languages separating them. Sheridan would raise this latter ethnic reality to its highest comic level in *The Critic.*

His third play, *The Duenna* (also 1775), takes interest as ethnic comedy less in its character as a Spanish intrigue play than in its address to the abstract issue of foreignness in human perceptions. Ethnic complacencies crumble as Don Jerome, the tyrannical father of the play, a Spanish Christian, shows himself, by his own son's assessment, to be no less greedy and unconscionable than the ridiculous Portuguese Jew Isaac Mendoza, whom he despises. When placed alongside Mendoza, the hedonistic friar Father Paul adds further weight to the impression that laughter in *The Duenna* functions in significant part to explode the errors of ethnic complacency; Sheridan carries this comic impulse forward into *The School for Scandal* (1777) when he derides through Sir Oliver Surface the concept of the Christian moneylender, the Christian whose usurious greed rivals that assigned by stereotype to the Jews. The most forceful ethnic comedy in *The School for Scandal,* however, confronts the irreversible fact of ethnic identity. It occurs in the second act of the play when members of the scandal cabal construct from disparate ethnic features a grotesque portrait of Mrs. Ogle, whose "Irish front, Caledonian Locks, Dutch nose, Austrian lip, Complexion of a Spaniard, and Teeth à la Chinoise" ignite their wit (*The School for Scandal* 2.2.118–23).

It is wit that succeeds because ethnic identity cannot be eluded; and ethnic identity implies ethnic integrity, a point given comic emphasis in Sheridan's patriotic afterpiece *The Camp* (1778), in which the French turncoat Bluard earns contempt for adjusting his allegiance to the winning side, whatever its nationality. Despite the realities separating them, however, nations must communicate with one another; and, in his last comedy, *The Critic* (1779), Sheridan acknowledges this need by placing Mrs. Dangle, a committed Englishwoman, in the wild predicament of trying to understand Italian musicians through the aid of a French interpreter who speaks no English. As in *St. Patrick's Day,* the effect here turns on fractured communication, but here the social implications cut much deeper, for the languages obstructing communication among well-intentioned people are not fabricated ones but actual and living ones, and the thrust of the human effort is toward understanding, not obfuscation. The sardonic side of the scene need not be ignored; Sheridan had real misgivings about foreign entertainers' usurping British stages. Within the political atmosphere of the play, however (emboldening hearts against fears of French and Spanish invasion in 1779), the scene certainly gathers ironic, even poignant, resonances. It reflects the playwright's intricate sense of the hopes uniting the wider world and of the gulfs dividing it.

In subtle ways, then, the comedies of Sheridan offer an apt background for the convictions he took with him into Parliament in 1780. To these convictions he was faithful throughout his life, and they go far to explain his moral and intellectual involvement in the wider world. They recognize only superficial distinctions among nationalities, distinctions in social and religious customs and perhaps in physical appearances, but beneath these surfaces flourish moral and political instincts common to all people, however mean their circumstances and primitive their cultures. Of these instincts the most determined cries out for freedom—"liberty is the birthright of man" (*Speeches* 3.534)—and national character derives at a given moment in history from the quality of freedom enjoyed by the people and the length of time they have enjoyed it. If they have suffered long under oppression, they will rise up against their oppressors in as violent a way as is necessary to assert their freedom, perhaps injuring themselves at first by their own wild excesses; but once they have learned the practice of liberty, they will regulate themselves according to a natural stratification, the "higher order" possessing "all the natural advantages of their fair superiority" and the "lower orders" falling "into the rank of useful industry", which is "the nerve and sinew of a well-regulated society" (*Speeches* 2.110). By this regulation they will husband liberty in the name of the commonweal, never abandoning it to the narrow charge of one person or of a few privileged people. To them, liberty will assert more importance then ease; it will resist narrow uniformity of thought or conduct, and their presiding political purpose will be to keep their institutions under the scrutiny of a constant reforming vigilance and to lend moral and philosophic support to all people yet in the process of establishing freedom. So ran Sheridan's convictions, and with them he placed himself among the Rockinghamite and Foxite Whigs, but he declined emphatically to see himself as a mouthpiece of party. "He had as strong party feelings as any man", he admitted in 1785, "but he had those feelings, because those he was attached to, neither expected from him servility of judgment, nor pliancy of principle" (*Speeches* 1.148; see also 1.5, 10; 2.114, 157, 456–57; 3.534).

Given the force and character of his convictions, he experienced no ambivalence in confronting the first of the great foreign issues to engage him, the cause of the American colonists. Military operations in America had worn on for five years by the time Sheridan entered Parliament, but well before that time he had made clear, at least to himself, his sentiments on the parliamentary issue. In fragmentary notes for a rejoinder to Dr. Johnson's *Taxation No Tyranny* (1775), he rejected out of hand Johnson's suggestion that people must accede to the government they are born under. Were that true, he wrote, "there never would have been one alteration of the first modes of government—no Revolution in England" (Sichel 1.76). In reaction to other of Johnson's arguments, he maintained that any right of conquest earned through colonization already lay in the hands of the conquerors themselves, the colonists. An indefinite right did not accrue to the mother country; nor were the colonists bound by special debts of gratitude to her, since she had initiated colonization not for their sakes but from motives of self-gain. Moreover, their rights of self-determination—a parliament of their own or a truly fair representation at home—lay in their commercial and territorial strength (Sichel 1.474).

Since, to the mind of Sheridan, right lay from the outset with the colonists, he looked upon the coercive sanctions brought against them, first legal sanctions and then military ones, as experiments pursued by ministers simply to satiate their greed for place and pension. In one of his contributions to *The Englishman*, an opposition organ of 1779, he chided the freeholders of England for failing to perceive that their "only *natural enemies*" in "this strange war" were the ministers (*Letters* 3.310–11); and years later, in 1793, he yet maintained that in the issue of the American war "delusion was practised under the pretence of taxation" but that the country "had paid dearly for the experiment of ministers" (*Speeches* 2.232). It was a cost paid principally, he felt, in moral currency, the moral ravage of countrymen killing one another in "*a war wherein no success can furnish matter of triumph to a good mind,*" as it was put in another number of *The Englishman,* possibly his (Sichel 1.594). During the 1790s, as he argued against war with revolutionary France and against sweeping antisedition measures at home, he could cite the American war as evidence that the arrogance of ministers cannot forever damp the claims of freedom; and, in the stability and detachment of American policy, which sustained neutrality despite internal agitation in behalf of France, he could demonstrate that Jacobin hysteria need not shake the foundations of settled governments. In America he found vindication for his most treasured political principles (*Speeches* 1.20; 2.252–53).

The second of the great foreign issues to engage him, the impeachment of Warren Hastings, was virtually unique to his parliamentary experience because it did not oblige him to impugn the obduracy of incumbent ministers. Pitt himself nodded assent to the impeachment debates, and Sheridan, as advocate for an aggrieved people, cut straight to the heart of the moral issue. Like his colleague Burke, he allowed himself to see Hastings as a veritable Antichrist, and with gripping eloquence he piled offenses at his feet. On the floor of the House of Commons in February of 1787 (at the motion to impeach) and again at Westminster Hall in June of 1788 (during the trial itself), Sheridan argued the charge that in 1781, while a president of the East India Company and governor-general of Bengal, Hastings had extorted large sums of money from the vizier of Oude by insisting that he pillage the treasuries of his mother and grandmother, the begums of Oude, two princesses who, according to Hastings, had forfeited the protection of the company by inciting insurrections against it, a charge they emphatically denied. In perpetrating these outrages, said Sheridan, Hastings had violated the public trust, defamed the national integrity, invited and received bribes, defrauded his superiors, sanctioned torture, and profaned the obligations of filial piety. He had displayed a character acclimated to treachery, hypocrisy, duplicity, ingratitude, avarice, chicanery, and resourceful, complex villainy; and he had crafted the shocking handiwork of "a man born to a state at least of equality;—inured to calculation, and brought up in habits of reflection; and yet proving in the end that monster in nature, a *deliberate and reasoning tyrant*" (*Speeches* 1.423).

Sheridan felt that in impeaching Hastings, the Parliament acknowledged its duty to cleanse the nation of every hint of complicity in wanton crimes against humanity. Consequently, his case, as a vindication of all mankind, cut across ethnic lines. He snarled at Hastings's efforts to seek refuge in foreign customs and expectations, "as if he meant to insinuate that there was something in Mahomedanism which rendered it impious in a son not to plunder his mother" (*Speeches* 1.229). At the same time, however, he saw Hastings's crimes intensified by their disregard for national distinctions. Sequestered in their zenana, said Sheridan, the begums "were *enshrined* rather than *immured*. . . . Such was their sense of delicacy, that to them the sight of man was pollution; and the piety of the nation rendered their residence a *sanctuary*" (*Speeches* 1.375). To profane their pious customs and to threaten them with violent expulsion from this sanctuary was to add sacrilege to cruelty.

In thus impugning Hastings for "flagitiously levelling all the distinctions of national characteristics" (*Speeches* 1.421), Sheridan embraced Burke's view that the government of empire must honor and promote national distinctions and must legislate to preserve them.[1] From an ideological perspective, Burke could readily see in Sheridan's speech against Hastings in Westminster Hall, "such an array of talents, such an exhibition of capacity, such a display of powers, as are unparalleled in the history of oratory";[2] in the matter of Hastings's India, few disagreements divided Sheridan and Burke.

In the matter of the French Revolution, however, few agreements united them. Sheridan rejected contemptuously Burke's view that the Revolution could lead only to mob rule and military dictatorship, that it sprang from the vain dreams of philosophic rationalists whose disregard of historical precedent threatened at once the aristocratic principle on which European political order stood and the body of religion giving strength to this order. Unwilling to acknowledge presocial political rights, Burke saw the life of the individual to be rooted in that of the state, and he saw the state as a trust wherein heredity, property, and law functioned to provide order, security, justice, and labor to the several ranks of society. Since, to his mind, human rights originated in this trust, the purpose of reform was to protect the state, not to destroy it. By ripping up the fabric of established order, the French Revolution had destroyed the conditions in which liberty might flourish, and the only repair for this loss lay in restoring the former society, the society owed allegiance by all its members. Favoring the rights of the privileged classes, minimizing ideas of social progress, disregarding political grievances truly aggravated by the ancien régime, and ignoring socioeconomic changes already afoot in Europe, this austere doctrine of Burke's struck no responsive chord in Sheridan, who saw the French Revolution with the eyes of a committed radical.[3]

If atrocities accompanied revolutionary upheaval, he argued, they originated not in the thought of philosophers but in the examples of despotism taught by the old society, an "accursed system of despotic government which had so deformed and corrupted human nature, as to make its subjects capable of such acts" (*Speeches* 1.518). His conviction was that the well-regulated government then arising would eventually settle its ranks by natural ordering; and, since stability was certain to evolve with time, he set himself firmly against war with France, when this prospect gathered force in the early 1790s. While Burke and the Pitt ministry depicted Jacobinism as an armed doctrine to be felled, if necessary, in the very streets of Paris, Sheridan acknowledged no political threat from France or from Jacobin thought, and he marveled that ministers should seek to restore the Bourbons in France even though the French monarchy had always shown itself "the greatest enemy England ever had" (*Speeches* 2.109). He also decried the irony that by intriguing with supposed allies against revolutionary France, Great Britain had adopted the methods of her old monarchical enemy and had contrived thereby to cheat herself of a major consequence of the Revolution, the acknowledged benefit that France, in her revolutionary state, "could no longer go about intriguing, and setting the rest of the courts of Europe at enmity with each other" (*Speeches* 2.47; see also 2.95, 96, 110, 155).

During the conduct of the war, Sheridan complained often (against Burke and the ministry) that in seeking and maintaining alliance with foreign governments, Britain pursued a policy dangerous to her own integrity: "we took the field against the excesses and licentiousness of liberty", he insisted, "they against liberty itself" (*Speeches* 2.155). Once engaged, moreover, the alliance had proved an empty charade. Nothing had been done by any of the allies (Prussia, Austria, Sardinia, Spain, Russia) "that was to be depended upon" (*Speeches* 2.420).

A second of Sheridan's persistent themes during the war (again in response to Burke and the ministry) was that Jacobin principles abroad could not threaten political stability at home. To argue so, he said, was to bring "libel on the character of Great Britain", for "Government was the school and seminary of the soul" (*Speeches* 2.456), and "a people who have been used to rational liberty and rational rights, who have not been ground down, nor made the slaves of a corrupt government" would never resort to such desperate acts as those committed by the French, who "had been oppressed and ground down till they had lost the common feelings and the common character of humanity" (*Speeches* 2.533–34). So persuaded was Sheridan in this doctrine that he not only vehemently opposed the antisedition measures promoted by the government during the war, including the suspension of habeas corpus; he also pressed boldly for immediate parliamentary reform and participated in founding an organization for reform called the Society of the Friends of the People.

A third persistent contention held by Sheridan during the war was that Britain and her allies had stiffened the fury of France by stifling her new breath of freedom: "we drove them to the extremities that produced the evils we arraigned", he said. With arrogant gestures in behalf of the old monarchical despotism, such as the Brunswick Manifesto and the Declaration of Pillnitz, and with subsequent armed aggression in that same behalf, "we baited them like wild beasts, until at length we made them so" (*Speeches* 2.247). In 1798, five years after the opening of hostilities, the effect of this folly loomed only too darkly to Sheridan; and, while yet rejoicing in the establishment of the French republic, he gave grim warning of its increasing power, a power that "has grown gigantic from the efforts which the alien powers exerted to oppose its infant liberty" (*Speeches* 3.243). Great Britain now lay in serious peril, and the fault fell squarely upon the governing ministers, who obstinately refused to recognize the French republic and who declined opportunities for peace in the cynical hope of sustaining themselves in office while pursuing schemes to restore the Bourbons in France. To Sheridan's mind the best opportunities for peace emerged in 1800, when France under Napoleon struck at least no more menacing a posture than she had often struck before the Revolution; but when moderate peace overtures arose then, the ministers remained evasive. They professed need to know Napoleon better and to prove the stability of his government; they protested their obligations to the allies and imagined new royalist spirit in France; they persuaded themselves of disaffection and growing disarray in the French army. While Napoleon deepened his power, they defaulted on peace (*Speeches* 2.367, 415, 484, 519; 3.97, 215, 356, 379, 397).

When urging the expediency of peace in 1800, Sheridan thought well enough of Napoleon to speak of him as a "great man" who had "fully proved his title to heroic honours" (*Speeches* 3.380, 382). To be sure, he could "justly be denominated an usurper" and a "self-appointed dictator" who possessed "more power than is compatible with the liberties of France". He did not, however, possess more power than "is necessary to protect the republic, and to enable it to resist those enemies that seek to destroy it", and when his enemies had "afforded him the opportunity of turning his attention to its internal regulations", he would surely "impart to it all the blessings and happiness of a civilized peace" (*Speeches* 3.381, 383). So Sheridan argued in 1800, but by 1802 he had quite reversed his view; and, in May of that year, when a definitive treaty with France was at last presented in the House of Commons, he attacked the ministry for delaying peace too long and for deluding itself that the ambitions of Napoleon might now be assuaged. Despite the treaty of peace, he was an enemy greatly to be feared.

In revising his attitude to Napoleon, Sheridan probably responded to a set of moral principles he had enunciated in 1788 while speaking in Westminster Hall against Warren Hastings. Taking polite issue there with Burke's conviction that prudence could never be brought to the service of vice, he had insisted that as a faculty for guiding single-minded purposes it might indeed serve vicious ends. So long as the vicious mind holds itself upon a single course, it may achieve its villainies; but if, by relaxing prudence, it attempts a medley of crimes, it will surely fail, for "the Power that has not forbad the entrance of evil passions into man's mind has at least forbad their union; if they meet they defeat their object.".[4] By this reasoning Sheridan explained Hastings's wicked successes and inevitable ruinous failures in India, and by it he measured the revolutionary cycle in France: the first uprising against despotism, the civil disarray succeeding it, the emergence of Napoleon as an agent of order, and his subsequent emergence as an international menace.

Sheridan theorized that just as in private experience the overambitious villain invariably fails, so in the public realm a government "founded on, and maintained by injustice, rapine, murder, and atheism" must collapse; "there are", he said, "self-sown in its own bosom, the seeds of its inevitable dissolution" (*Speeches* 2.248–49). In acclimating itself to liberty, a recently oppressed people may proceed from revolution to violent excess, as had been the case in France; but once this excess has destroyed itself (through the destruction self-sown in it), stability emerges to complete the cycle. An anomaly of the French Revolution was that this cycle had been frustrated by the anti-Jacobin wars of the 1790s. Counterrevolutionary forces had thus prevented the Revolution from taking its normal course. Consequently, a strong central figure, a Napoleon, was needed to assist the evolution of order. In sacrificing freedom to his own immeasurable ambition, however, Napoleon had given himself up to a single-minded villainy of the sort Sheridan had described in the Hastings trial, a villainy especially dangerous to Britain because its one obsessive purpose was to destroy the British constitution. "This is the first vision that breaks upon him through the gleam of the morning", said Sheridan; "this is his last prayer at night" (*Speeches* 3.423).

The same committed devotion to human rights that brought Sheridan to the defense of America in the 1770s and to France in the late 1780s brought him no less vigorously to the defense of Ireland at the time of her "revolution" in 1782. The stage for his public declaration in behalf of Ireland was set in April of that year when William Eden, chief secretary to the lord lieutenant of Ireland, the earl of Carlisle, suddenly moved independence for Ireland in the House of Commons without first consulting with the newly seated Rockingham-Fox ministry. This precipitate conduct was intended to embarrass the ministry for its immoderate haste in replacing Carlisle at the change of government,[5] and Sheridan attacked Eden forcefully for motives "scandalously unfair to the new ministers", who had only "the fairest intentions toward Ireland"; but he went on to say that should the motion come to a vote, he would stand with Eden (*Speeches* 1.26). The motion—"to repeal so much of the Act of George I as asserted a right to the King and Parliament of Great Britain to make laws to bind the Kingdom of Ireland"—did not reach a division that day, April 8, 1782; but under the management of the new ministry and with royal assent, it was passed late in June and ratified in Ireland the following spring. It promised legislative independence to Ireland without severing her connection with Great Britain, a kingdom valuable to her security, and Sheridan approved of it warmly.

So warm was his approval, in fact, that when, in 1785, the Pitt ministry proposed a common market for the whole of the British Isles, Sheridan took up opposition not on commercial but on constitutional grounds. In its effect upon Ireland, he saw Pitt's scheme as a withdrawal of trust in the sister kingdom, a blackmail requiring Ireland to legislate against herself in order to maintain peace with England, a compromise of affection between the two countries, in short, a betrayal of the revolution of 1782. At the climax of a glowing speech, on May 30, 1785, he summarized in sardonic tones "the happy fruits of a plan whose boasted object was to cement the union of the two countries, and connect them by bonds of eternal amity and reciprocal affection". Its real effect, he maintained, would bind Ireland to British monopolies, settle British prices and duties upon Irish commerce, cripple Ireland's commercial intercourse with America, destroy her hopes of being "the depot and emporium for the foreign countries of Europe", and undermine her constitutional principles by requiring that she provide (in the form of an annual subsidy to the imperial defense) "perpetual aid to a military force at the will of the executive magistrate". In acceding to such a plan,

Irish merchants and manufacturers could not but say to the world "we have for ever surrendered our right of external legislation into the hands of the British parliament" (*Speeches* 1.146; see also 1.131–47). In truth, Pitt's plan might very well have benefited Irish commerce. Its success, however, turned on the provision that all laws made in Great Britain to regulate trade and navigation should also be in force in Ireland "*by acts to be passed in the parliament of that kingdom*" (*Speeches* 1.129). In this threat to the legislative independence of Ireland lay Sheridan's case, and largely on the strength of his case the plan suffered defeat in the Irish Parliament. As Sheridan would have it, commercial advantage gave place for once to human rights.

This is not to suggest, of course, that he was indifferent to prosperity in Ireland. When the House of Commons debated a commercial treaty with France in 1787, his closest concern was that France not receive greater advantages in the home market "than Ireland either enjoyed, or could claim" (*Speeches* 1.251). Nor did he so far delude himself as to think human rights altogether well served by the Protestant ascendancy solidified in Ireland to support Pitt's policies there. In 1795, when, to calm this ascendancy, Pitt recalled William Fitzwilliam from the viceroyalty of Ireland and punctured widespread hopes for a comprehensive Catholic emancipation bill there, Sheridan taxed him with impeachable conduct for so alienating the people of Ireland as to aggravate a virtual "separation of the empire" (*Speeches* 2.482); and when, in 1798, the political unrest in Ireland erupted into open insurrection, Sheridan held the ministries of the sister kingdoms responsible, not the Irish insurgents. In Ireland, he said, "The struggle is one, not of local discontent and political disaffection, but it is a contest between the people and the government. In such a state of things, without entering into a particular inquiry, the fair presumption is, that the government is to blame" (*Speeches* 3.269–70).

Such sentiments as these led Sheridan to see constitutional reform as the best response to insurrection in Ireland; he sought a system of representation free of religious tests and capable of addressing human needs at the level of the cottage. To Pitt, however, the best response to insurrection lay in uniting Ireland and Great Britain. Such a union, he felt, would effect the commercial goals he had fashioned in 1785. It would also secure the British Isles against the designs of Napoleonic France; and, by reducing the Irish Catholics from a majority in Ireland to a minority within the newly constituted United Kingdom, it would enforce upon them a conciliatory posture when their rights were at last settled after the union.[6] It promised many advantages while extending Pitt's own ascendancy; but, of course, it offered nothing that Sheridan would consider justice for Ireland. It did not address constitutional reform; it robbed the Irish of the legislative independence granted them in 1782; it disregarded their geographic integrity, and it questioned their capacity to govern themselves. Since Fox had seceded from the House of Commons in 1797, the burden of opposing the Irish union fell squarely upon Sheridan, and he shouldered it valiantly, offering in five speeches delivered between January 23, and February 12, 1799 arguments that might be enumerated as follows.

England was not competent to legislate for Ireland, nor could the Irish Parliament assent to union with another country, since only the abeyance of the people could alter the constitution. Nothing inherent in the union would cure the ills of Ireland or achieve advantages for her that might not as readily be achieved without it. The truth was, simply, that Pitt had found her existence to be incompatible with his ministry; she remained, in his mind, a mere "job" for English ministers. The Scottish union of 1707 provided no viable precedent for Ireland because the prosperity of Scotland did not necessarily derive from her union with England. After all, the landlords and property owners of Scotland actually lived there and took a personal interest in the nation, a case decidedly different from that in Ireland. As to the threat from France, certainly the people of Ireland were not generally subject to French ideas, nor were they by disposition opposed to England. In fact, the only enemies to England in Ireland were the ignorance and poverty there. For her own part, France placed no special hopes in keeping the governments of Britain and Ireland separated; her hopes lay rather in the confusion and discontent certain to result in Ireland from union with Britain. Where enthusiasm for the union had emerged in Ireland the people had been victims of bribery. In fact, the political climate in Ireland was in such ferment that the people could not act upon genuine sentiments, nor did their Parliament represent them. Parliamentary reform was called for, not union; and in pressing for union despite the will of the Irish people, ministers were adopting the conduct of Jacobins and United Irishmen, the republican factions they most reprobated, and were behaving toward their sister kingdom in the way that France had behaved toward Switzerland: withdrawing freedom with the promise of restoring it at a later time, when the people might merit it. If, despite all dissuasions, union must come about, let it at least accompany Catholic emancipation throughout all the British dominions (*Speeches* 3.277–325).

Of course, union did come about in 1800, without Catholic emancipation and without a strong disposition in Westminster to trust the loyalty of the Irish people. In 1807, Sheridan sought to put down rumors of sedition in Ireland by moving an examination of the state of Ireland in the House of Commons. He spoke movingly of the industry of the Irish people, of their essential loyalty, and of the poverty yet unrelieved among them. He also took occasion to appeal in their behalf for a curious moral subsidy: "Why do you not subsidize Ireland?" he asked, "and all the subsidies I ask for her is your confidence, affection, and justice to her people" (*Speeches* 3.536; see also 3.533–35). Such a dispensation of trust, he felt, belonged to the entire human community, especially to that part of it yet struggling outside the pale of freedom.

Given their force and persistence in his thinking, these kinds of broad humane sympathies came readily to the service of his last play, *Pizarro* (1799), a tragedy adapted from a literal translation of Kotzebue's *Die Spanier in Peru* (1796). Treating of the Spanish conquest of Peru in the early sixteenth century, this play so freely evoked the spirit of Sheridan's oratory that he drew upon several of his speeches in fashioning dialogue for it, and its conflicts engaged some of his most earnest political themes. In Pizarro, a tyrant dishonest to his own trust, he saw his images of both Hastings and Napoleon. In Rolla, the Inca warrior, he perceived all restive and courageous victims of oppression. In the subjugation of the Incas he discerned the onerous practice among European nations of enslaving non-European peoples (a practice he furiously decried).[7] The play worked well as theater in 1799 because it brought into a single form the theatrical and political instincts of its author, who shaped its focus to his own comprehensive view of world events. Two decades earlier, his comedies had hinted, in the detached spirit of youth, the hopes of uniting the wider world and the gulfs dividing it. His one tragedy darkened these apprehensions and deeply felt them.

This sympathetic identification with the human community best characterizes the view taken by Sheridan of the wider world. He recognized cultural distinctions; he understood and respected ethnic identities and national allegiances. His first concerns lay, however, with the aspirations for freedom common to all humankind, and to these aspirations he committed his services unstintingly. Since all but about two of his thirty-two years in the House of Commons found him on the opposition benches, he claims distinction not as an author of policy but as a spokesman for humane principle. To this principle he assigned neither national boundaries nor cultural qualifications, and through it he promoted with firm conviction the benefits of liberty at home and abroad.

# NOTES

Quotations are from *The Speeches of the Right Honourable Richard Brinsley Sheridan Edited by a Constitutional Friend* (London: 1842, repr. New York: 1969); *Sheridan's Plays*, ed. Cecil Price (Oxford: 1975); *The Letters of Richard Brinsley Sheridan*, ed. Cecil Price (Oxford: 1966); Walter Sichel, *Sheridan* (Boston: 1909).

1. Frank O'Gorman, *Edmund Burke: His Political Philosophy* (Bloomington: 1973) 103.
2. Quoted in Donald C. Bryant, "Edmund Burke's Opinion of Some Orators of His Day", *Quarterly Journal of Speech* 20 (1934): 250.
3. My summary of Burke's attitude to the French Revolution derives from O'Gorman 107–41.
4. I quote here the best-reported version of the speech, that printed in *Speeches of the Managers and Counsel in the Trial of Warren Hastings*, ed. E. A. Bond (London: 1859) 1.124. Compare with *Speeches* 1.339. My essay "Sheridan, Burke, and Revolution", *Eighteenth-Century Life* 6 (1981): 103–13, provides a fuller discussion of Sheridan's doctrine of "prudence" as it bore upon his views of the French Revolution and of Napoleon.
5. R. B. McDowell, *Ireland in the Age of Imperialism and Revolution, 1760–1801* (Oxford: 1979) 281.
6. These and other arguments for the union are discussed in McDowell 682–88.
7. My discussion of *Pizarro* draws upon John Loftis, *Sheridan and the Drama of Georgian England* (Cambridge, MA: 1977) 124–41. For Sheridan's convictions against slavery, see *Speeches* 2.8–9; 3.511–13.

# BIBLIOGRAPHY

## 1. *Travel Writing*

Adams, Percy G. *Travel Literature and the Evolution of the Novel.* Lexington, KY: 1983.

Adams, Percy G. *Travellers and Travel Liars, 1660–1800.* Berkeley and Los Angeles: 1962.

Anderson, Peter. *Over the Alps: Reflections on Travel and Travel Writing with Special Reference to the Grand Tours of Boswell, Beckford and Byron.* London: 1969.

Batten, Charles L., Jr. *Pleasurable Instruction: Form and Convention in Eighteenth-Century Travel Literature.* Berkeley and Los Angeles: 1978.

Cox, Edward G. *A Reference Guide to the Literature of Travel.* 2 vols. Seattle: 1935–48.

Curley, Thomas M. *Samuel Johnson and the Age of Travel.* Athens, GA: 1976.

Firestone, Clark B. *The Coasts of Illusion: A Study of Travel Tales.* New York and London: 1924.

Frantz, Ray W. *The English Traveller and the Movement of Ideas, 1660–1732.* Lincoln, NE: 1934.

Fussell, Paul. "Patrick Brydone: The Eighteenth Century Traveller as Representative Man". *Bulletin of the New York Public Library* 66 (1962): 349–63.

Keltie, J. Scott. "Fictitious Travel and Phantom Lands". *Harper's Monthly Magazine* 115 (1907): 186–94.

Letts, M. "Of Lying Travellers". *Contemporary Review* 118 (1920): 95–100.

Liddell, Scotland. "Travellers' Tales". *English Review* 42 (1926): 622–31.

Liljegren, S. B. *Studies on the Origin and Early History of English Utopian Fiction.* Uppsala: 1961.

Mezciems, Jenny. "'Tis not to divert the reader': Moral and Literary Determinants in Some Early Travel Narratives". *Prose Studies* 5 (1982): 1–19.

Moseley, C. W. R. D. "The Availability of Mandeville's Travels in England 1356–1760". *The Library* 5th ser. 30 (1975): 125–33.

Parks, G. B. "Travel as Education". *The Seventeenth Century.* Ed. R. F. Jones. Stanford, CA, and London: 1951. 264–90.

Parks, G. B. "The Turn to the Romantic in the Travel Literature of the Eighteenth Century". *Modern Language Quarterly* 25 (1964): 22–33.

Rice, Warner G. *Literature as a Mode of Travel.* New York: 1963.

Spraggs, G. M. "Rogues and Vagabonds in English Literature, 1552–1642". Diss. Cambridge U, 1980.

Stafford, Barbara Maria. "Toward Romantic Landscape Perception: Illustrated Travel Accounts and the Rise of 'Singularity' as an Aesthetic Category". *Art Quarterly* ns 1 (1977): 89–124.

Sutherland, J. "The Literature of Travel". *English Literature of the Late Seventeenth Century*. Oxford: 1969. 288–96.

West, Hugh Allen. "From Tahiti to Terror: Georg Forster, the Literature of Travel, and Social Thought in the Late Eighteenth Century". Diss. Stanford U, 1980.

## 2. *Travel and Tourism*

Beales, H. L. "Travel and Communications". *Johnson's England*. Ed. A. S. Turberville. 2 vols. Oxford: 1933. 1.125–59.

Black, Jeremy. *The British and the Grand Tour*. London: 1985.

Burke, J. "The Grand Tour and the Rule of Taste". *Studies in the Eighteenth Century*. Ed. R. F. Brissenden. Canberra: 1968. 231–50.

Calvert, Ian. *Travel in the Bible*. Oxford: 1974.

Cassin, Lionel. *Travel in the Ancient World*. London: 1974.

Ford, Brinsley, "The Grand Tour". *Apollo* 114 (1981): 390–400.

Fussell, Paul. *The Rhetorical World of Augustan Humanism*. Oxford: 1965.

Hibbert, Christopher. *The Grand Tour*. London: 1969.

Hindley, Geoffrey. *Tourists, Travellers, and Pilgrims*. London: 1983.

Hutton, E. M. "The Grand Tour in Italy". Diss. Cambridge U, 1937.

Jemielty, T. "Dr Johnson and the Uses of Travel". *Philological Quarterly* 51 (1972): 448–59.

Kirby, Paul F. *The Grand Tour in Italy (1700–1800)*. New York: 1952.

Lambert, R. S. *The Grand Tour: A Journey in the Tracks of the Age of Aristocracy*. New York: 1937.

Mead, William. *The Grand Tour in the Eighteenth Century*. Boston: 1914.

Plumb, J. H. "The Grand Tour". *Men and Places*. London: 1963. 67–79.

Ross, Ernest C. *The Development of the English Sea Novel from Defoe to Conrad*. Ann Arbor, MI: 1925.

Starr, Nathan C. *The Sea in the English Novel from Defoe to Melville*. Diss. Harvard U, 1928.

Stoye, J. M. *English Travellers Abroad 1640–67*. London: 1952.

Trease, Geoffrey. *The Grand Tour*. New York: 1961.

## 3. *Exploration and Discovery*

Crone, G. R., and R. A. Skelton. "English Collections of Voyages and Travels: 1625–1846". *Richard Hakluyt and His Successors*. Ed. Edward Lynam. London: 1946. 65–189.

Deisch, N. "The Navigation of Space in Early Speculation and in Modern Research". *Popular Astronomy* 38 (1930): 73–88.

De la Mare, Walter. *Desert Islands and Robinson Crusoe*. New York: 1930.

"Directions for Sea-men, Bound for Far Voyages". *The Philosophical Transactions of the Royal Society* 1 (1666): 140–43.

Gove, P. B. *The Imaginary Voyage in Prose Fiction . . . 1700–1800*. New York: 1941.

Eather, Robert H. *Majestic Lights: The Aurora in Science, History and the Arts.* Washington, DC.: 1980.
Heawood, E. *History of Geographical Discovery in the Seventeenth and Eighteenth Centuries.* Cambridge, Eng.: 1912.
Morison, S. E. *The European Discovery of America.* 2 vols. New York: 1971–74.
Nicolson, M. "Cosmic Voyages". *English Literary History* 7 (1940): 83–107.
Nicolson, M. *A World in the Moon: A Study of Changing Attitude toward the Moon in the Seventeenth and Eighteenth Centuries.* Northampton, MA: 1936.
Rose, J. "The Merchandise of Light: A Study of the Impact of the New Knowledge of the Non-European World on Some Aspects of English Thought in the Seventeenth Century". Diss. Cambridge U, 1954.
Stafford, Barbara Maria. *Voyage into Substance: Art, Science, Nature and the Illustrated Travel Account.* Cambridge, MA, and London: 1984.
Sykes, Percy. *A History of Exploration from the Earliest Times to the Present Day.* London: 1949.
Veit, Walter, ed. *Captain James Cook, Image and Impact: South Seas Discoveries and The World of Letters.* Melbourne: 1972.
Williamson, James A. "Exploration and Discovery". *Johnson's England.* Ed. A. S. Turberville. 2 vols. Oxford: 1933. 1.88–124.

### 4. *Transport and Equipment*

Bird, Anthony. *Roads and Vehicles.* London: 1969.
Galton, Francis. *The Art of Travel or Shifts and Contrivances Available in Wild Countries.* Ed. Dorothy Middleton. Newton Abbott, Eng.: 1971.
Rodger, N. A. M. *The Wooden World: Anatomy of the Georgian Navy.* Annapolis, MD: 1986.
Schreiber, H. *Merchants, Pilgrims and Highwaymen: A History of Roads through the Ages.* New York: 1962.

### 5. *The North*

Bruce, M. W. "Jacobite Relations with Peter the Great", *Slavonic and East European Review* 14 (1936): 343–62.
Murray, J. J. "Sweden and the Jacobites", *Huntington Library Quarterly* 8 (1944–45): 259–76.

### 6. *France*

Hedgcock, Frank A. *David Garrick and His French Friends.* London: 1912.
Hertz, G. B. *English Public Opinion after the Restoration.* London: 1902.
Lough, John. *France Observed in the Seventeenth Century by British Travellers.* Stocksfield, Eng.: 1985.
Maxwell, Constantia. *The English Traveller in France 1698–1815.* London: 1932.

## 7. *Alps*

De Beer, Sir Gavin. *Alps and Men: Pages from Forgotten Diaries of Travellers and Tourists in Switzerland.* London: 1932.
De Beer, Sir Gavin. *Early Travellers in the Alps.* London: 1930.
De Beer, Sir Gavin. *Travellers in Switzerland.* London: 1949.
Litz, Francis Edwards. "Richard Bentley on Beauty, Irregularity, and Mountains". *English Literary History* 12 (1945): 327–32.
Nicolson, Marjorie. *Mountain Gloom and Mountain Glory: The Development of the Aesthetics of the Infinite.* Ithaca, NY: 1959.
Schmid, Walter. *Romantic Switzerland, Mirrored in the Literature and Graphic Art of the Eighteenth and Nineteenth Centuries.* Bern: 1965.
Stephen, Leslie. *The Playground of Europe.* London: 1872.

## 8. *Italy*

Babcock, R. W. "English Interest in Italy and Italian Romantic Criticism in the Eighteenth Century". *Philological Quarterly* 26 (1947): 152–58.
Bostetter, E. E. "The Original Della Cruscans and the Florence Miscellany". *Huntington Library Quarterly* 19 (1955–56): 277–300.
Churchill, Kenneth. *Italy and English Literature 1764–1930.* Totowa, NJ: 1980.
Doran, J. *Mann & Manners at the Court of Florence, 1740–1786.* 2 vols. London: 1876.
Hamilton, Olive. *Paradise of Exiles. Tuscany and the British.* London: 1974.
Leppmann, W. *Pompeii in Fact and Fiction.* London: 1968.
Manwaring, E. W. *Italian Landscapes in Eighteenth-Century England.* New York: 1925.
Marshall, Roderick. *Italy in English Literature 1758–1815.* New York: 1934.
Maugham, H. N. *The Book of Italian Travel, 1580–1900.* London: 1903.
Mead, W. E. "Italy in English Poetry". *PMLA* 23 (1908): 421–70.
Moloney, B. *Florence and England: Essays on Cultural Relations in the Second Half of the Eighteenth Century.* Firenze: 1969.
Parks, George B. *The English Traveller to Italy: the Middle Ages.* Rome: 1954.
Parks, George B. "The Decline and Fall of the English Renaissance Admiration of Italy". *Huntington Library Quarterly* 31 (1967–68): 341–57.
Stuart, J. M. "England's Literary Debt to Italy". *Fraser's Magazine* 60 (1859): 697–708.
Von Klenze, Camillo. *The Interpretation of Italy, during the Last Two Centuries.* Chicago: 1907.
Wollaston, G. H. *The Englishman in Italy.* Oxford: 1969.

## 9. *Greece*

Bracken, C. P. *Antiquities Acquired: The Spoliation of Greece.* Newton Abbott, Eng.: 1975.

Buxton, John. *The Grecian Taste: Literature in the Age of Neo Classicism 1740–1820.* London: 1978.
Clarke, M. L. *Greek Studies in England 1700–1830.* Cambridge, Eng.: 1945.
Constantine, David. *Early Greek Travellers and the Hellenic Ideal.* Cambridge, Eng.: 1984.
Colvin, Sir Sidney, and Lionel Cust. *History of the Society of Dilettanti.* London: 1898.
Howarth, David. *The Greek Adventure.* London: 1976.
Levin, Harry. *The Broken Column: A Study in Romantic Hellenism.* Cambridge, MA: 1931.
Mango, Cyril. "Byzantium and Romantic Hellenism". *Journal of the Warburg and Courtauld Institutes* 28 (1965): 29–43.
Miller, Helen Hill. *Greece through the Ages: As Seen by Travellers from Herodotus to Byron.* New York: 1972.
Miller, William. *The English in Athens before 1821.* London: 1926.
Osborn, J. M. "Travel Literature and the Rise of Neo-Hellenism in England". *Bulletin of the New York Public Library* 67 (1963): 279–300.
Ramsey, R. W. "Sir George Wheler and His Travels in Greece, 1659–1724". *Transactions of the Royal Society of Literature* ns 19 (1942): 1–38.
Rice, Warner G. "Early English Travellers in Greece and the Levant". *Essays and Studies in English and Comparative Literature.* University of Michigan Publications 10 (Ann Arbor: 1933): 205–60.
Sayl, F., and R. Wittkower. *British Art and the Mediterranean.* Oxford; 1948.
Spencer, T. J. B. *Fair Greece Sad Relic.* London: 1954.
Stern, B. H. *The Rise of Romantic Hellenism in English Literature, 1732–1786.* NY and Menasha, WI: 1940.
Webb, Timothy. *English Romantic Hellenism 1700–1824.* New York: 1982.
Wood, A. C. *A History of the Levant Company.* London: 1935.

## *10. The Orient*

Anderson, M. S. *Britain's Discovery of Russia 1553–1815.* London: 1958.
Appleton, W. W. *A Cycle of Cathay.* New York: 1951.
Arberry, A. J. *British Orientalists.* London: 1943.
Baltrusaitis, Jurgis. "Lands of Illusion: China and the Eighteenth-Century Garden". *Landscape* 11 (1961–62): 5–11.
Bevis, Richard. *Bibliotheca Cisorientalia: An Annotated Checklist of Early English Travel Books on the Near and Middle East.* Boston: 1973.
Ch'ien Chung-shu. "China in the English Literature of the Seventeenth Century". *Quarterly Bulletin of Chinese Bibliography* 1 (1940): 351–84.
Ch'ien Chung-shu. "China in the English Literature of the Eighteenth Century". *Quarterly Bulletin of Chinese Bibliography* 11 (1941): 7–48, 113–52.
Clark, T. Blake. *Oriental England.* Shanghai: 1939.
Conant, Martha P. *The Oriental Tale in England in the Eighteenth Century.* New York: 1908.

Cross, A. G., ed. *Great Britain and Russia in the Eighteenth Century*. Newtonville, MA: 1979.
Daniel, Norman. *Islam and the West: The Making of an Image*. Edinburgh: 1960.
Edwardes, Michael. *East-West Passage: The Travel of Ideas, Arts and Inventions between Asia and the Western World*. London: 1971.
Ghassemi, A. A. Rezai. *Major Oriental Influences upon English Literature during the Late Eighteenth and Early Nineteenth Centuries, with Special Reference to Persia*. Diss. London U, 1980.
Glacken, G. *Traces on the Rhodian Shore*. Berkeley: 1967.
Holt, P. M. *A Seventeenth-Century Defender of Islam: Henry Stubbe and His Book*. London: 1972.
Holtzman, J. M. *The Nabobs in England*. New York: 1926.
Honour, H. *Chinoiserie*. London: 1961.
Hoskins, H. L. *British Routes to India*. New York: 1928.
Impey, O. B. *Chinoiserie*. London: 1977.
Khairallah, S. N. "Arabic Studies in England in the Late Seventeenth and Early Eighteenth Centuries". Diss. London U, 1966.
Kincaid, Dennis. *British Social Life in India 1608–1937*. London: 1939.
Marshall, P. J. *The British Discovery of Hinduism in the Eighteenth Century*. Cambridge, Eng.: 1970.
Marshall, P. J. "Warren Hastings as Scholar and Patron". *Statesmen, Scholars and Merchants*. Ed. A. Whiteman, J. S. Bromley, and P. Dickson. Oxford: 1973. 242–62.
Mukherjee, S. N. *Sir William Jones: A Study in Eighteenth-Century British Attitudes to India*. Cambridge: 1968.
Musa, Mohammed Ali. "The Subterranean Caverns: The East and Its Progeny in Eighteenth-Century English and French Literature". Diss. U of Arkansas, 1981.
Said, Edward. *Orientalism*. London: 1978.
Seawright, Sarah. *The British in the Middle East*. London: 1969.
Shau Yi Chan. "The Influence of China on English Culture during the Eighteenth Century". *Chicago U Abstracts of Theses* 1927–29.
Siren, Ozvald. *China and the Gardens of Europe in the Eighteenth Century*. New York: 1950.
Smith, Byron Porter. *Islam in English Literature*. Beirut: 1939.
Southern, R. W. *Western Views of Islam in the Middle Ages*. Cambridge, MA: 1962.
Spear, T. G. P. *The Nabobs: A Study of the Social Life of the English in Eighteenth Century India*. London: 1932.
Spencer, T. J. B. "Robert Wood and the Problem of Troy in the Eighteenth Century". *Journal of the Warburg and Courtauld Institute* 20 (1957): 75–105.
Tsen-Chung Fau. "Chinese Culture in England from Sir William Temple to Oliver Goldsmith". Harvard U Abstracts of Theses 1931.

## *11. Empire*

Calder, Angus. *Revolutionary Empire: The Rise of the English-Speaking Empires*

*from the Fifteenth Century to the 1780s.* London: 1981.
Flint, J. E., and G. Williams. *Perspectives of Empire.* London: 1973.
Goldstein, Laurence. *Ruins and Empire; The Evolution of a Theme in Augustan and Romantic Literature.* Pittsburgh: 1977.
Kiernan, Victor G. *The Lords of Human Kind. European Attitudes towards the Outside World in the Imperial Age.* London: 1969.

## *12. America*

Bissell, Benjamin. *The American Indian in English Literature of the Eighteenth Century.* New Haven: 1925.
Bond, R. P. *Queen Anne's American Kings.* Oxford: 1952.
Cole, Harold L. *Travels in America from the Voyages of Discovery to the Present: An Annotated Bibliography of Travel Articles in Periodicals, 1955–1980.* Norman, OK: 1985.
Cumming, W. P. "Geographical Misconceptions of the South-East". *Journal of Southern History* 4 (1938): 476–93.
Dunn, R. S. "Seventeenth-Century Historians of America". *Seventeenth-Century America: Essays in Colonial History.* Ed. J. H. Smith et al. Chapel Hill, NC: 1959. 195–225.
Durden, D. S. "Transatlantic Communication and Literature in the Religious Revivals, 1735–1745". Diss. Hull U, 1978.
Elliott, J. H. "Renaissance Europe and America: A Blunted Impact?". *First Images of America: The Impact of the New World on the Old.* Ed. F. Chiapelli. Berkeley: 1976. 11–23.
Honour, Hugh. *The New Golden Land: European Images of America from the Discoveries to the Present Time.* New York: 1975.
Jones, H. M. *O Strange New World.* London: 1965.
Keen, B. *The Aztec Image in Western Thought.* New Brunswick, NJ: 1971.
Lease, Benjamin. *Anglo-American Encounters: England and the Rise of American Literature.* Cambridge, Eng.: 1982.
Milvey, Christopher. *Anglo-American Landscapes.* Cambridge, Eng.: 1983.
Pearce, R. H. *The Savages of America: A Study of the Indian and the Idea of Civilization.* Baltimore: 1953.
Porter, H. C. *The Inconstant Savage: England and the North American Indian 1500–1660.* London: 1979.
Savage, H. *Discovering America 1700–1875.* New York: 1979.
Steele, C. *English Interpreters of the Iberian New World from Purchas to Stevens: A Bibliographical Study 1603–1726.* Oxford: 1925.
Stevens, H. N. *Lewis Evans, His Map of the Middle Colonies in America.* London: 1905.
Wagner, H. R. "Apocryphal Voyages to the Northwest Coast of America". *Proceedings of the American Antiquarian Society* ns 41 (1931): 190–96.

## *13. Africa*

Anderson, M. S. "Great Britain and the Barbary States in the Eighteenth Century". *Bulletin of the Institute of Historical Research* 29 (1956): 87–107.

Austen, R. A., and W. D. Smith. "Images of Africa and British Slave-Trade Abolition: The Transition to an Imperialist Ideology 1787–1807". *African Historical Studies* 2 (1969): 69–83.

Barker, A. J. *The African Link: British Attitudes to the Negro in the Era of the Atlantic Slave Trade, 1550–1807.* London: 1907.

Manuel, F. E. *The Eighteenth Century Confronts the Gods.* Cambridge, MA: 1959.

Perham, Margery, and Jack Simmons. *African Discovery.* London: 1942.

Rotberg, Robert I., ed. *Africa and Its Explorers.* Cambridge, MA: 1970.

## *14. The Pacific*

Alexander, Michael. *Omai: "Noble Savage".* London: 1977.

Frost, Alan. "The Pacific Ocean: The Eighteenth Century's 'New World'". *Studies on Voltaire and the Eighteenth Century* 151–53 (1976): 779–822.

Gerbi, A. *The Dispute of the New World: The History of a Polemic, 1750–1900.* Pittsburgh: 1973.

McCormick, E. H. *Omai: Pacific Envoy.* Auckland: 1977.

Megaw, J. V. S. *Employ'd as a Discoverer: Papers Presented at the Captain Cook Bi-Centenary Symposium.* Sydney: 1971.

Mitchell, T. C. *Captain Cook and the South Pacific.* London: 1979.

Parsonsons, G. S. "The Islands and Their Peoples". *La Australia del Espiritu Santo.* Ed. Celsus Kelly. Cambridge, Eng.: 1966.

Smith, Bernard. *European Vision and the South Pacific, 1763–1850: A Study in the History of Art and Ideas.* Oxford: 1960.

Veit, Walter. *Captain Cook: Image and Impact.* Melbourne: 1972.

## *15. Racial Theories*

Baudet, Henri. *Paradise on Earth: Some Thoughts on European Images of Non-European Man.* Trans. Elizabeth Wenthold. New Haven: 1965.

Berkhofer, R. F., Jr. *The White Man's Indian: Images of the American Indian from Columbus to the Present.* New York: 1978.

Buchanan, W., and H. Cantril. *How Nations See Each Other.* Westport, CT: 1953.

Burke, J. G. "The Wild Man's Pedigree". *The Wild Man Within.* Ed. E. Dudley and M. Novak. Pittsburgh: 1972.

Diamond, Stanley. *In Search of the Primitive: A Critique of Civilization.* New Brunswick, NJ: 1974.

Fairchild, H. N. *The Noble Savage: A Study in Romantic Naturalism.* New York: 1928.

Hayden, Lucy K. "The Black Pressure in Eighteenth-Century British Novels". *CLA Journal* 24 (1981) 400–15.

*BIBLIOGRAPHY*

Hayman, J. G. "Notions on National Characters in the Eighteenth Century". *Huntington Library Quarterly* 35 (1971–72): 1–17.

Hodgen, M. *Early Anthropology in the Sixteenth and Seventeenth Centuries.* Philadelphia: 1964.

Huddleston, L. E. *Origin of the American Indian: European Concepts 1492–1729.* Austin, TX: 1967.

Lovejoy, O., and F. Boas. *Documentary History of Primitivism and Related Ideas.* Oxford: 1935.

Marshall, P. J. and Glyndwr Williams. *The Great Map of Mankind.* London: 1982.

Meek, R. L. *Social Science and the Ignoble Savage.* Cambridge, Eng.: 1976.

Pagliaro, Harold E., ed. *Racism in the Eighteenth Century.* Cleveland: 1973.

White, Hayden. *Tropics of Discourse. Essays in Cultural Criticism.* Baltimore: 1985.

Whitney, L. *Primitivism and the Idea of Progress in English Popular Literature of the Eighteenth Century.* Oxford: 1934.

# A GUIDE TO AUTHORS

ADDISON, Joseph (1672–1719), visited France, Italy, Switzerland, Austria, Holland, 1699–1703 (*Letter from Italy*, 1702; *Remarks on Several Parts of Italy*, 1705); Dublin, 1709–10, 1715. See C. D. Thorpe, "Two Augustans Cross the Alps: Dennis and Addison on Mountain Scenery", *Studies in Philology* 32 (1935): 463–82.

BECKFORD, William (1759–1844), visited Geneva, 1777–78; Low Countries, 1780; Italy, 1782 (*Dreams, Waking Thoughts, and Incidents*, 1783; *Vathek*, 1787); Spain, France, 1791–92; Portugal, 1794. See J. K. Folsom, "Beckford's *Vathek* and the Tradition of Oriental Satire", *Criticism* 6 (1964): 53–69.

BEHN, Aphra (1640–89), lived in Surinam, c. 1640–58 (*Oroonoko*); visited Low Countries in 1660s. See Ernest Bernbaum, *Mrs Behn's Oroonoko* (Boston: 1913).

BOSWELL, James (1740–95), visited Low Countries, Germany, France, Switzerland, Italy, Corsica, 1763–66 (*Account of Corsica*, 1768); Hebrides, 1773 (*Tour to the Hebrides*, 1786). See D. Day, "Boswell, Corsica and Paoli", *English Studies* 45 (1964): 1–20; E. F. Stuckley, *A Hebridean Journey with Johnson and Boswell* (London: 1956).

CONGREVE, William (1660–1729), resided in Ireland c. 1670–c. 1688. See Muir, K. "The Comedies of Congreve", *Restoration Theatre*, ed. J. R. Brown and B. Harris (London: 1965): 221–37.

DEFOE, Daniel (1660–c. 1731), probably visited France, possibly Spain and other European countries before 1692. See J. Sutherland, *Defoe* (London: 1937); Ch'en Shon-yi, "Daniel Defoe, China's Severest Critic", *Nanhai Social and Economic Quarterly* 8 (1935): 511–50; J. N. L. Baker, "The Geography of Daniel Defoe", *Scottish Geographical Magazine* 47 (1931): 257–69; Arthur W. Secord, *Studies in the Narrative Method of Defoe* (Urbana, IL: 1924); M. Novak, "Imaginary Islands and Real Beasts: The Imaginative Genesis of *Robinson Crusoe*", *Tennessee Studies in Literature* 19 (1974): 57–78.

DENNIS, John (1657–1734), visited France, Italy, c. 1683.

DRYDEN, John (1631–1700), did not travel but shows anti-Dutch feeling and an interest in French and Italian culture (translation of Dufresnoy's *Art of Painting*, 1695). See J. Loftis, "The Hispanic Element in Dryden", *Emory University Quarterly* 20 (1964): 90–100; J. Loftis, "Exploration and Enlightenment: Dryden's *The Indian Emperor* and Its Background", *Philological Quarterly* 45 (1966): 71–84.

DYER, John (c. 1700–58), visited Italy c. 1730s (*The Ruins of Rome,* 1740). See A. Johnston, "Dr Johnson, John Dyer and the Ruins of Rome", *New Rambler* 14 (1964): 11–22.

ETHEREGE, George (c. 1635–91), possibly visited unspecified European countries c. 1650; Low Countries, Germany, 1685–88; France, 1688–91. See T. H. Fujimara, "Etherege at Constantinople", *PMLA* 62 (1956): 465–81; S. Rosenfeld, "Sir George Etherege in Ratisbon", *Review of English Studies* 10 (1934): 177–89.

EVELYN, John (1620–1706), historian and scientist, visited Holland 1641; France, Italy, Switzerland, 1643–46; France, 1649 (*The State of France,* 1652). See A. Ponsonby, *John Evelyn* (London: 1935); J. Bowle, *John Evelyn and His World* (London: 1983).

FIELDING, Henry (1707–54), visited Leyden 1728–29; Lisbon, 1754 (*Journal of a Voyage to Lisbon,* 1755). See *Fielding: A Collection of Critical Essays,* ed. R. Paulson (Englewood Cliffs, NJ: 1962).

GAY, John (1685–1732), visited Hanover, 1714; France, 1717. See J. R. Sutherland, "'Polly' among the Pirates", *Modern Language Review* 37 (1942): 291–303.

GIBBON, Edward (1737–94), historian, visited Switzerland, 1753–58; France, Switzerland, Italy, 1763–65; settled Switzerland, 1783. See J. J. Sanders, "Gibbon in Rome 1764", *History Today* 14 (1964): 608–15; M. Baridon, "Gibbon en Italie", *Études Anglaises* 15 (1962): 2.130–37; E. J. Oliver, *Gibbon and Rome* (London and New York: 1958).

GOLDSMITH, Oliver (c. 1728–74), brought up in Ireland, possibly visited Low Countries, 1753; France, Germany, Switzerland, Italy, 1753–56 (*The Traveller,* 1764). See Levette J. Davidson, "Forerunners of Goldsmith's Citizen of the World", *Modern Language Notes* 36 (1921): 215–20.

GRAY, Thomas (1716–71), visited France, 1739–40; Switzerland, Italy, Austria, 1739–40. See A. Macdonald, "The Poet Gray in Scotland", *Review of English Studies* ns 13 (1962): 245–56; L. Whibley, "The Foreign Tour of Gray and Walpole", *Blackwood's Magazine* 227 (1930): 813–27; F. C. Roe, "Le Voyage de Gray et de Walpole en Italie", *Revue de Litterature Comparée* 6 (1926): 189–206; M. B. Finch and E. A. Pears, "Walpole's Relations with Voltaire", *Modern Philology* 18 (1920): 13–24.

JOHNSON, Samuel (1709–84), visited Scotland, Western Isles, 1773 (*Journey to the Western Isles,* 1776); France, 1775. See T. M. Moore, "Samuel Johnson and the Literature of Travel", Diss. U of Michigan, 1966; Tsen-Chung Fau, *Dr Johnson and Chinese Culture* (London:

1945); D. J. Greene, "Samuel Johnson and the Great War for Empire", *English Writers of the Eighteenth Century,* ed. J. H. Middendorf (New York: 1971): 37-65; G. Kolb, "The 'Paradise' in Abyssinia and the 'Happy Valley' in *Rasselas*", *Modern Philology* 56 (1958): 10–16; D. Lockhart, "'The Fourth Son of the Mighty Emperor': The Ethiopian Background of Johnson's *Rasselas*", *PMLA* 78 (1963): 516–28; A. Weitzman, "More Light on *Rasselas:* The Background of the Egyptian Episodes", *Philological Quarterly* 48 (1969): 42–58; J. R. Moore, "Rasselas and the Early Travellers to Abyssinia", *Modern Language Quarterly* 15 (1954): 36–41.

MARVELL, Andrew (1621–78), visited Holland, France, Italy, Spain, 1642–46; Holland, 1663 (*The Character of Holland,* 1665); Russia, Sweden, Denmark, 1663–65 (*A Relation of the Three Embassies,* 1669). See P. H. Burdon, "Andrew Marvell and Richard Flecknoe in Rome", *Notes and Queries* 217 (1972): 16–18.

MILTON, John (1608–74), visited France, Italy, Switzerland, 1638–39. See John Arthos, *Milton and the Italian Cities* (New York: 1968); R. R. Cawley, *Milton and the Literature of Travel* (Princeton: 1951); A H. Gilbert, *A Geographical Dictionary of Milton* (New Haven and London: 1919).

MONTAGU, Lady Mary Wortley (1689–1762), letter writer, visited Vienna, Germany, Adrianople, Constantinople, Italy, 1716–18; Italy, Switzerland, 1739–41; France, 1742; Italy, 1758 (*Letters from the East,* 3 vols. 1763). See R. Halsband, "Lady Mary Wortley Montagu as a Friend of Continental Writers", *Bulletin of the John Rylands Library* 39 (1956): 57–74.

POPE, Alexander (1688–1744), unable to travel because of ill health, corresponded with travelers including George Berkeley, Lord Bolingbroke, Lady Mary Wortley Montagu. See P. Dixon, *The World of Pope's Satires* (London: 1968); A. D. McKillop, "The Geographical Chapter in Scriblerus", *Modern Language Notes* 68 (1953): 480–81; John Gay, "Mr Pope's Welcome from Greece" (London: 1776).

PRIOR, Matthew (1664–1721), visited Holland, c. 1690–c. 1697; France, Holland, 1698–99; France, 1711, 1712.

RICHARDSON, Samuel (1689–1761), did not travel but published many travel books that affected his fiction. See William M. Sale, Jr., *Samuel Richardson: Master Printer* (Ithaca, NY: 1950).

SHERIDAN, Richard Brinsley (1751–1816), visited France, 1772. See T. Moore, *Memoirs of the Life of the Right Honourable Richard Brinsley Sheridan,* 2 vols. (London: 1827).

SMOLLETT, Tobias (1721–71), traveled to London, 1739; visited West Indies, 1740–41; France, 1750; France, Italy, 1763–65 (*Travels*, 1766); Italy, 1769–71. See W. G. Waters, "Englishman in Italy: Smollett", *Anglo-Italian Review* 4 (1919): 31–45; G. M. Kahrl, *Tobias Smollett: Traveller-Novelist* (Chicago: 1945).

STERNE, Laurence (1713–68), possibly visited unspecified European countries, 1741–42; France, 1762–64; France, Italy, 1765–66 (*A Sentimental Journey*, 1768). See L. T. Milik, "Sterne and Smollett's Travels", *Notes and Queries* 201 (1956): 80–1; R. D. S. Putney, "The Evolution of *A Sentimental Journey*", *Philological Quarterly* 19 (1940): 349–69.

SWIFT, Jonathan (1667–1745), brought up in Ireland; visited England frequently between c. 1690 and 1714, 1725–26. See Max Poll, *The Sources of "Gulliver's Travels"* (Cincinnati: 1909); G. J. Pierre, "Gulliver's Voyages to China and Moor Park", *Texas Studies in Literature and Language* 17 (1975): 427–37.

TEMPLE, Sir William (1628–99), historian, visited France, Spain, Low Countries, 1648–54; Ireland, 1655–63 (*Essay on the Present State and Settlement of Ireland*, 1701); Low Countries, 1665–70 (*Observations upon the United Provinces of the Netherlands*, 1672); Low Countries again, 1674–79. See H. E. Woodbridge, *Temple: the Man and His Work* (New York: 1940).

THOMSON, James (1700–48), visited France, Italy, possibly other countries, 1730–32 (*Liberty*, 1735–36). See A. D. McKillop, *The Background of Thomson's "Seasons"* (Minneapolis: 1942); A. D. McKillop, *The Background of Thomson's "Liberty"*, Rice Institute Pamphlet 38: 2 (1951).

VANBRUGH, Sir John (1694–1726), dramatist and architect, visited France 1683–85; under French arrest, 1690–92. See L. Whistler, *Vanbrugh, Architect and Dramatist 1664–1726* (London: 1938).

WALPOLE, Horace (1717–97), visited France, Switzerland, Italy, 1739–41; France, 1765, 1767, 1775. See S. Gwynn, *The Life of Walpole* (London: 1932); see also under Gray.

WYCHERLEY, William (c. 1640–1716), visited France, c. 1655; possibly engaged in Dutch war, 1672–73; Montpelier, 1678. See R. Zimbardo, *Wycherley's Drama* (New Haven): 1965).

# INDEX

# INDEX

# INDEX

# INDEX